Histories of the Middle East

Islamic History and Civilization

Studies and Texts

VOLUME 79

Histories of the Middle East

Studies in Middle Eastern Society, Economy and Law in Honor of A.L. Udovitch

Edited by

Roxani Eleni Margariti
Adam Sabra
Petra M. Sijpesteijn

BRILL

LEIDEN • BOSTON
2011

Cover illustration: Arabic manuscript, *Les Séances. Al-Maqamat*, 5847 folio 119 verso, Bibliothèque Nationale, Paris.

This book is printed on acid-free paper.

Library of Congress Cataloging-in-Publication Data

Histories of the Middle East : studies in Middle Eastern society, economy and law in honor of A.L. Udovitch / edited by Roxani Eleni Margariti, Adam Sabra, Petra M. Sijpesteijn.
p. cm. — (Islamic history and civilization ; v. 79)
Includes bibliographical references and index.
ISBN 978-90-04-18427-5 (hardback : alk. paper)
1. Middle East—Civilization. 2. Civilization, Arab. 3. Islamic civilization. 4. Civilization, Medieval. I. Margariti, Roxani Eleni, 1969- II. Sabra, Adam Abdelhamid, 1968- III. Sijpesteijn, Petra. IV. Udovitch, Abraham L. V. Title. VI. Series.

DS57.H57 2010
956'.01—dc22

2010037331

ISSN 0929-2403
ISBN 978 90 04 18427 5

ان الله سبحانه وملائكته واهل سمواته وارضه حتى النملة في
جحرها وحتى الحوت في البحر ليصلون على معلم الناس الخير

al-Tirmidhī, *Sunan*. Cairo 1964. 4: 154 (no. 2826)

CONTENTS

NOTES ON CONTRIBUTORS

Jonathan P. Berkey is Professor of History at Davidson College. He studied at Williams College (B.A. 1981) and Princeton University (M.A. 1987, Ph.D. 1989), where Avrom Udovitch served as his dissertation adviser. He is the author of several books, including *The Transmission of Knowledge in Medieval Cairo: A Social History of Islamic Education* (Princeton University Press, 1992), *Popular Preaching and Religious Authority in the Medieval Islamic Near East* (University of Washington Press, 2001), and *The Formation of Islam: Religion and Society in the Near East, 600-1800* (Cambridge University Press, 2003), which won the Albert Hourani Book Prize from the Middle East Studies Association.

Michael Bonner is Professor of Medieval Islamic History in the Department of Near Eastern Studies, University of Michigan. He received his Ph.D. in the Department of Near Eastern Studies, Princeton University, in 1987. His recent publications include *Jihad in Islamic History: Doctrines and Practices* (Princeton University Press, 2006, 2008), and *Poverty and Charity in Middle Eastern Contexts*, co-edited with Amy Singer and Mine Ener (SUNY Press, 2003). He has been a Helmut S. Stern Fellow at the University of Michigan Institute for the Humanities, and has held the position of Professeur Invité at the Institut d'Etudes de l'Islam et des Sociétés du Monde Musulman, École des Hautes Études en Sciences Sociales, and of Chaire de l'Institut du Monde Arabe, also in Paris.

Mark R. Cohen is Professor of Near Eastern Studies at Princeton University and the current incumbent of the Khedouri A. Zilkha Professorship of Jewish Civilization in the Near East. His publications include *Jewish Self-Government in Medieval Egypt; Al-mujtamaʿ al-yahudi fi Misr al-islamiyya fi al-ʿusur al-wusta (Jewish Life in Medieval Egypt 641-1382)*, translated from the English; *The Autobiography of a Seventeenth-Century Venetian Rabbi: Leon Modena's "Life of Judah"*; *Under Crescent and Cross: The Jews in the Middle Ages*; *Poverty and Charity in the Jewish Community of Medieval Egypt*; and *The Voice of the Poor in the Middle Ages: An Anthology of Documents from the Cairo Geniza.* He is a member of the American Academy for Jewish Research.

Olivia Remie Constable is Professor of History at the University of Notre Dame. She received her B.A. in Near Eastern Languages and Literatures from Yale University in 1983 and her Ph.D. in Near Eastern Studies from Princeton University in 1989, where she worked under the guidance of Avram Udovitch. She has published *Trade and Traders in Muslim Spain: The Commercial Realignment of the Iberian Peninsula 900-1500* (Cambridge University Press, 1994), *Medieval Iberia: Readings from Christian, Muslim, and Jewish Sources* (University of Pennsylvania Press, 1997), and *Housing the Stranger in the Mediterranean World: Lodging, Trade, and Travel in Late Antiquity and the Middle Ages* (Cambridge University Press, 2003). She is currently working on a new book project which looks at Muslim communities living under Christian rule in Spain and the western Mediterranean, 1050-1300.

Hassan S. Khalilieh is a Senior Lecturer in the Departments of Maritime Civilizations and Multidisciplinary Studies and the School of History at the University of Haifa. He received his Ph.D. from the Department of Near Eastern Studies, Princeton University, in 1995, and his LL.M. in Admiralty and Maritime Law, from the School of Law, Tulane University, in 2006. He is the author of *Islamic Maritime Law: An Introduction* (E. J. Brill, 1998) and *Admiralty and Maritime Laws in the Mediterranean Sea (ca. 800-1050): the Kitab Akriyat al-Sufun vis-a-vis the Nomos Rhodion Nautikos* (E. J. Brill, 2006).

Roxani Eleni Margariti is Associate Professor of Middle Eastern and South Asian Studies at Emory University. Born and raised in Athens, Greece, she received her B.A. in Western Asiatic Archaeology from University College London, her M.A. in Nautical Archaeology from Texas A&M University, and her Ph.D. in Near Eastern Studies from Princeton University in 2002. She is the author of *Aden and the Indian Ocean Trade: 150 Years in the Life of a Medieval Arabian Port* (University of North Carolina Press, 2007). Her current research focuses on political, social, and cultural aspects of Indian Ocean merchants' networks before 1500 C.E., and on the cultural legacy and current status of Islamic monuments in Greece.

David S. Powers is Professor of Near Eastern Studies and History at Cornell University. He received his Ph.D. from Princeton in 1979.

His courses deal with Islamic civilization, Islamic history and law, and classical Arabic texts, and his research focuses on the history of Islamic law and its application in Muslim societies. He is the author of *Studies in Qur'an and Hadith: The Formation of the Islamic Law of Inheritance* (University of California Press, 1986), *Law, Society, and Culture in the Maghrib, 1300-1500* (Cambridge University Press, 2002), and *Muhammad is Not the Father of Any of Your Men: The Making of the Last Prophet* (University of Pennsylvania Press, 2009). He is founding editor of the journal *Islamic Law and Society* and sectional editor (Law) of the third edition of *The Encyclopaedia of Islam*.

Yossef Rapoport is a Lecturer in the Department of History, Queen Mary, University of London. He received his B.A. from Tel Aviv University and his Ph.D. in Near Eastern Studies from Princeton University in 2002. He has published *Marriage, Money, and Divorce in Medieval Islamic Society* (Cambridge University Press, 2005). He has worked and published on the social history of the Islamic world in the medieval period, gender, and Islamic law, and participated in the study of the *Book of Curiosities*, a Fatimid cosmological treatise, at the Bodleian Library.

Adam Sabra is Associate Professor of History at the University of Georgia. He received his Ph.D. in Near Eastern Studies from Princeton University in 1998. He is the author of *Poverty and Charity in Medieval Islam: Mamluk Egypt, 1250-1517* (Cambridge University Press, 2000), and co-editor with Richard McGregor of *The Development of Sufism in Mamluk Egypt* (IFAO, 2006). His research currently focuses on the social history of Sufism in Mamluk and Ottoman Egypt.

Boaz Shoshan received his Ph.D. from Princeton University in 1978. He is Professor in the Departments of General History and Middle East Studies at Ben Gurion University of the Negev, Israel. He is the author of *Popular Culture in Medieval Cairo* (Cambridge University Press, 1993) and *Poetics of Islamic Historiography* (E. J. Brill, 2004) and editor of *Discourse on Gender/Gendered Discourse in the Middle East* (Praeger, 2000).

Petra M. Sijpesteijn holds the Chair of Arabic Language and Culture at Leiden University and is Chargée de recherche at the Institut de Recherche et Histoire des Textes at the Centre National de la Recherche Scientifique in Paris. She obtained her Ph.D. in Near Eastern Studies from Princeton University in 2004, after which she was a junior research fellow at Christ Church, Oxford (2003-2007). Her forthcoming book is entitled *The Formation of a Muslim State in late Umayyad Egypt*. She is also the co-editor of *History and Arabic Papyrology* (with L. Sundelin, E. J. Brill, 2001), *From al-Andalus to Khurasan* (with L. Sundelin, S. Torallas-Tovar and A. Zomeno, E. J. Brill, 2006) and *Documents and Medieval Islamic History* (with A. T. Schubert, E. J. Brill, 2008). She is currently working on a history of the Egyptian countryside under the first two hundred years of Muslim rule.

ACKNOWLEDGMENTS

We would like to thank the Department of Near Eastern Studies at Princeton University for hosting a conference in May 2008, where the papers published in this volume were presented. The department's generous sponsorship made it possible for many of the former students of Avrom Udovitch to return to Princeton for an exchange of ideas in his honor. We would especially like to thank Mark Cohen and Sükrü Hanioglu for their enthusiastic support and assistance. We are also grateful to Kathy O'Neill and the entire staff of the NES department for their help with the planning and organization of the conference. Nassira Akkabi and Olly Akkerman offered invaluable help at the final stages of the publication. Their energy, enthusiasm and accuracy were very much appreciated. Finally, we would like to thank Kathy van Vliet and Birgitta Poelmans, our editors at Brill, for their encouragement and efficiency as we brought this volume to publication.

THE BIBLIOGRAPHY OF ABRAHAM L. UDOVITCH

Books

The Economic Dimensions of Middle Eastern History: Essays in Honor of Charles Issawi. Editor with Haleh Esfendiari. Princeton, NJ: Darwin Press, 1990.

Jews Among Arabs: Contacts and Boundaries. Editor with Mark R. Cohen. Princeton, NJ: Darwin Press, 1989.

The Medieval Levant: Studies in Memory of Eliahu Ashtor (1914-1984). Editor with Benjamin Z. Kedar. Vol. 22, Nos. 1-3. *Asian and African Studies 22.* Jerusalem: *Journal of the Israel Oriental Society,* 1988.

The Islamic World from Classical to Modern Times: Essays in Honor of Bernard Lewis. Editor with C.E. Bosworth, Charles Issawi, and Roger Savory. Princeton, NJ: Darwin Press, 1988.

Gli ultimi ebrei arabi: La comunità di Gerba. With Lucette Valensi. Rome: Instituto della Enciclopedia Italiana, 1987.

The Last Arab Jews: The Communities of Jerba, Tunisia. With Lucette Valensi. London and New York: Harwood Academic, 1984.

Juifs en terre d'Islam: des communautés de Djerba. With Lucette Valensi. Paris: Editions des Archives contemporaines, 1984.

The Islamic Middle East, 700-1900: Studies in Economic and Social History. Editor. Princeton, NJ: Darwin Press, 1981.

The Medieval City. Editor with Harry A. Miskimin and David Herlihy. New Haven, CT: Yale University Press, 1977.

The Middle East: Oil, Conflict, and Hope. Editor. Lexington, MA: Lexington Books, 1976.

Dictionary of the Middle Ages. 13 vols. Associate editor with Joseph Strayer (editor-in-chief) et al. New York: Scribners, 1974-80.

Partnership and Profit in Medieval Islam. Princeton, NJ: Princeton University Press, 1970.

Articles

"Alexandria in the 11th and 12th Centuries, Letters and Dcouments of the Cairo Geniza Merchants: an Interim Balance Sheet." In *Alexandrie médiévale* 2. Edited by Christian Décobert (Cairo: Institut Français d'Archéologie Orientale, 2002): 99-112.

"La fuite en Egypte: à la manière Tunisienne." In *Lucette Valensi à l'oeuvre: histoire anthropologique de l'Islam méditerranéen,* edited by François Pouillon, 37-46. Paris: Editions Bouchene, 2002.

"Juifs en terre de l'Islam." In *Etats societés et cultures du monde musulman mediéval,* edited by Jean-Claude Garcin, 125-45. Paris: Presse Universitaire de France, 2000.

"Some Mediterranean Dimensions of Islamic Sicily." In *E il buio albeggia da Oriente: Aspetti di Orientalismo in Sicilia,* edited by Antonino Pelliteri, 7-17. Palermo: Luxograph, 2000.

"Fatimid Cairo: Crossroads of World Trade—From Spain to India." In *L'Egypte Fatimide: son art et son histoire*, edited by Marianne Barrucand, 581-92. Paris: Presse Universitaire de France, 1999.

"International Commerce and Rural Society in Egypt of the 11th Century." In *Agriculture in Egypt from Pharaonic to Modern Times*, edited by A. K. Bowman and E. Rogan, 267-85. London: The British Academy, 1999.

"Juifs et musulmans en Sicile au XI-XII siècles: Espaces et communication." In *Les minorités ethniques et religieuses dans le monde Arabo-Musulman*. Rabat: Université Mohamed V, Faculté des lettres et des sciences humaines, 1999.

"New Materials for the History of Islamic Sicily." In *Del Nuovo Sulla Sicilia Musulmana*, edited by Francesco Gabrieli and Biancamaria Scarcia, 183-210. Rome: Academia nazionale dei Lincei, 1997.

"Medieval Alexandria: Some Evidence from the Cairo Genizah Documents," in *Alexandria and Alexandrianism*. Papers Delivered at a Symposium Organized by the J. Paul Getty Museum and the Getty Center for History of Art and the Humanities and Held at the Museum, April 22-25, 1993, 273-83. Malibu, CA: J. Paul Getty Museum, 1996.

"I musulmani e gli ebrei del mondo di Frederico II: linee di demarcazione e di communicazione." In *Frederico II e il mondo Mediterraneo*, edited by Pierre Toubert, 191-213. Palermo: Sellerio Editore, 1995.

"Muslims and Jews in the World of Frederic II: Boundaries and Communication." *Princeton Papers in Near Eastern Studies* 2 (1993): 83-104.

"Market and Society in the Medieval Islamic World." In *Mercati e Mercanti nell'alto Medioevo: L'Area Euroasiatica e l'Area Mediterranea*, 767-98. Spoleto: Centro Italiano di Studi sull'Alto Medioevo, 1993.

"An Eleventh-Century Islamic Treatise on the Law of the Sea," *Annales Islamologiques* 27 (1993): 37-54.

"International Commerce and Society in Mid-Eleventh-Century Egypt and North Africa." In *The Economic Dimensions of Middle Eastern History: Essays in Honor of Charles Issawi*, edited by Abraham L. Udovitch and Haleh Esfendiari, 239-53. Princeton, NJ: Darwin Press, 1990.

"Un debat satanique: defense de Rushdie ou defense de l'Islam?" *Le genre humain* 20 (1989): 63-7.

"Trade (Islamic)." *Dictionary of the Middle Ages*, 12:105-8. New York: Scribners, 1979.

"Urbanism (Islamic)." *Dictionary of the Middle Ages*, 12:307-11. New York: Scribners, 1979.

Foreword to S.D. Goitein, *A Mediterranean Society: The Jewish Communities of the Medieval Islamic World as Portrayed in the Documents of the Cairo Geniza*, 5: ix-xviii. Berkeley, CA: University of California Press, 1988.

"L'énigme d'Alexandria: sa position au Moyen Age d'après les documents de la Geniza du Caire." *Revue de l'Occident Musulman et de la Mediterranée (Alexandrie entre deux mondes)* 46 (1988): 71-80.

"Scenes from Eleventh-Century Family Life: Cousins and Partners—Nahray ben Nissim and Israel ben Natan." In *The Islamic World from Classical to Modern Times: Essays in Honor of Bernard Lewis*, edited by C.E. Bosworth, Charles Issawi, Roger Savory, and Abraham L. Udovitch, 357-68. Princeton, NJ: Darwin Press, 1988.

"Making Peace: In Stockholm with Yasir Arafat." *The Village Voice*, December 1988.

"Merchants and Amīrs: Government and Trade in Eleventh-Century Egypt," *Asian and African Studies* 22 (1988): 53-72.

"Sicily (Islamic)." *Dictionary of the Middle Ages*, 11:261-3. New York: Scribners, 1988.

"The Last Arab Jews." *United Synagogue Review* 41 (1988).

"Historia de dos ciudades: las relaciones comerciales entre el Cairo y Alejandria durante la segunda parte del siglo XI." In *El Mundo Mediterraneo de la Edad Media*, edited by Blanca Gari. Barcelona: Edicimes Argot, 1987.

"Les échanges de marché dans l'Islam medieval: théorie du droit et savoir local." *Studia Islamica* 65 (1987): 5-30.

"The Constitution of the Traditional Islamic Marketplace: Islamic Law and the Social Context of Exchange." In *Patterns of Modernity*, vol. 2, *Beyond the West*, edited by Shmuel Noah Eisenstadt, 150-71. New York: New York University Press, 1987.

"Kirāḍ." *Encyclopaedia of Islam*, New Edition, 5:129-30. Leiden: Brill, 1986.

"Islamic Law and Social Context of Exchange in the Medieval Middle East." *History and Anthropology* 1 (1985): 445-65.

"Etre Juif à Djerba." In *Communautés juives des marges sahariennes du Maghreb*, edited by Michel Abitbol, 199-225. Jerusalem: Ben-Zvi Institute, 1982.

"Bankers without Banks: Commerce, Banking, and Society in the Islamic World of the Middle Ages." *Princeton Near East paper*, no. 30. Princeton, NJ: Program in Near Eastern Studies, Princeton University, 1981.

"The Muslim Law of Partnerships in Ottoman Court Records." *Studia Islamica* 53 (1981): 109-19.

"The Jew and Islam in the High Middle Ages: A Case of the Muslim View of Differences." In *Gli Ebrei nell' alto medioevo*, 655-83. Spoleto: Centro Italiano di Studi sull' Alto Medioevo, 1980.

"Technology, Land Tenure and Rural Society: Aspects of Continuity in the Pre-Modern Middle East." In *The Islamic Middle East, 700-1900: Studies in Social and Economic History*, edited by Abraham L. Udovitch, 11-27. Princeton, NJ: Darwin Press, 1980.

"Communautés juives en pays d'Islam: Identité et communication à Djerba." *Annales E.S.C.* 3-4 (1980): 764-83. With Lucette Valensi

"Bankers without Banks: Commerce, Banking, and Society in the Islamic World of the Middle Ages." In *The Dawn of Modern Banking*, edited by Fredi Chiapelli, 255-273. New Haven, CT: Yale University Press, 1979.

"Credit and Inverstment in Medieval Islamic Trade." In *Vth International Congress of Economic History, Leningrad 1970*, edited by Herman van der Wee, Vladimir A. Vinogradov, and Gregorii G. Kotovski, 4:18-19. The Hague: Mouton, 1979.

"Time, the Sea, and Society: Duration of Commercial Voyages on the Southern Mediterranean During the High Middle Ages." In *La Navigazione Mediterranea nell'alto Medioevo*, 503-63. Settimane di studio del Centro Italiano di studi sull'alto medioevo, no. 25. Spoleto: Presso la sede del Centro, 1978.

"A Tale of Two Cities: Commercial Relations between Cairo and Alexandria During the Second Half of the Eleventh Century." In *The Medieval City*, edited by David Herlihy, Harry A. Miskimin, and A. L. Udovitch, 143-62. New Haven, CT: Yale University Press, 1977.

"Formalism and Informalism in the Social and Economic Institutions of the Medieval Islamic World." In *Individualism and Conformity in Classical Islam*, edited by Amin Banani and Spyros Vryonis Jr, 61-81. Wiesbaden: Harrassowitz, 1977.

"Reflections on the Institutions of Credits and Banking in the Medieval Islamic Near East." *Studia Islamica* 41 (1975): 5-21.

"Egypt: Crisis in a Muslim Land." In *The Black Death-a Turning Point in History*, edited by William M. Bowsky, 122-5. New York: Holt, Rinehart and Winston, 1971.

"Theory and Practice of Islamic Law: Some Evidence from the Geniza." *Studia Islamica* 32 (1970): 289-303.

"Commercial Techniques in Early Medieval Islamic Trade." In *Islam and the Trade of Asia: a Colloquium*, edited by D.S. Richards, 37-62. Philadelphia: University of Pennsylvania Press, 1970.

"The Law Merchant of Medieval Islam." In *Logic in Classical Islamic Culture*, edited by Gustave E. von Grunebaum, 113-30. Wiesbaden: Otto Harrassowitz, 1970.

"Theory and Practice of Islamic Law: Some Evidence from the Geniza." *Studia Islamica* 32 (1970): 289-303.

"Introductory Remarks." In *Studies in the Economic History of the Middle East*, edited by Michael A. Cook, 3-10. London: Oxford University Press, 1970.

"England to Egypt, 1350-1500: Long-Term Trends and Long-distance Trade." With R. S. Lopez and H.A. Miskimin. In *Studies in the Economic History of the Middle East*, edited by Michael A. Cook, 93-128. London: Oxford University Press, 1970.

"Credit as a Means of Investment in Medieval Islamic Trade." *Journal of the American Oriental Society*, 87.3 (1967): 260-4

"Labor Partnerships in Early Islamic Law." *Journal of Economic and Social History of the Orient*, 10.1 (1967): 64-80.

"Fals." *Encyclopaedia of Islam*, Second Edition, 2:768-9. Leiden: E. J. Brill, 1965.

"At the Origins of the Western Commenda: Islam, Israel, Byzantium?" *Speculum* 37 (1962): 198-207.

Book Reviews

Review of *Ru'yat al-Yaman bayna Habshush wa-Halevi (Vision du Yemen entre Habshush et Halevi)*, by Samia Nalm Sanbar. *Annales Histoire Sciences Sociales* 4 (1994): 999-1001.

Review of *Economic Concepts of Ibn Taimiyah* by Abdul Azim Islahi. *The Middle East Journal* 44 (1990): 522-3.

Review of *Jewish Marriage in Palestine: A Cairo Geniza Study* by Mordechai A. Friedman. *Journal of the Economic and Social History of the Orient*, 30. 3 (1987): 338-41

Review of *A Mediterranean Society: The Jewish Communities of the Arab World as Portrayed in the Documents of the Cairo Geniza*, vol. 4, *Daily Life*, by S. D. Goitein. *Speculum*, 61. 3 (1986): 656-9.

Review of *Levant Trade in the Later Middle Ages* by Eliyahu Ashtor. *The American Historical Review*, 91. 1 (1986): 91-2.

Review of *Marchands d'étoffes du Fayyoum au IIIe/IXe siècle d'après leurs archives, I, Les actes des Banu 'Abd al-Mu'min* by Yusuf Ragib. *Studia Islamica*, 59 (1984): 187-8.

Review of *The Jews of Arab Lands: A History and Source Book* by Norman A. Stillman. *The Journal of Economic History*, 40.3 (1980): 609-610. *Annales, E.S.C.* 35 (1980): 845-7.

Review of *Mare Luso-Indicum: Etudes et documents sur l'histoire de l'Ocean Indien et des Pays riverains a l'epoque de la domination portugaise*. *The American Historical Review*, 81. 5 (1976): 1137-8.

Review of *Espaces et reseaux du haut Moyen Age* by Maurice Lombard, *The American Historical Review* 79. 3 (1974): 770.

Review of *The Coinage of the Mamluk Sultans of Egypt and Syria* by Paul Balog. *Journal of the American Oriental Society*, 90. 2 (1970): 288-90.

Review of *A Mediterranean Society: The Jewish Communities of the Arab World as Portrayed in the Documents of the Cairo Geniza*, vol. 1, *Economic Foundations* by S.D. Goitein. *Speculum* 44 (1969): 289-94.

Review of *Contributions to Arabic Linguistics* by Charles A. Ferguson. *Journal of the American Oriental Society* 83.4 (1963): 517.

PREFACE

For four decades Abraham L. Udovitch has been a leading scholar of the medieval Islamic world, its economic institutions, social structures, and legal theory and practice. In pursuing his quest to understand and explain the complex phenomena that these broad rubrics entail, he has published widely, collaborated internationally with other leading scholars of the Middle East and medieval history, and most saliently for the purposes of this volume, taught several cohorts of students at Princeton University. His teaching has been integral to his intellectual quest. This volume is therefore dedicated to his intellectual legacy from a uniquely revealing angle: the current work of his former students.

Our purpose is not to produce a definitive assessment of any one aspect of Udovitch's multivalent and ongoing contributions to the study of Middle Eastern economy, society and law, but instead to offer a collection of case studies that mirrors the breadth of his intellectual endeavors. Udovitch instilled in all of us a sense of the multiplicity of our field: "histories" instead of History, "legal practices" and "theories" instead of Law, "societies" instead of Society. This collection of essays reflects this sensibility. The diversity of subject matter and the breadth of chronological coverage exhibited by the papers in this volume is a tribute to the multiplicity of Udovitch's own research and teaching legacy.

Textual Genres and a Diversity of Methods

The topics covered in the pages of the current collection range chronologically from the period preceding the rise of Islam in Arabia to the Mamluk era and geographically from Western Mediterranean to the Western Indian Ocean. Thematically, the papers in this volume explore pre-Islamic modes of exchange (Bonner); formative dynamics of Islamic narrative tradition (Powers); the balance of trade and war in the maritime world of the eastern Mediterranean (Rapoport); the political negotiations of Christian and Islamic Mediterranean sovereigns (Constable); the political and social capital of a prominent Sufi master (Sabra); the extent and limits of patronage for religious scholars in Mamluk society (Berkey); the treatment of slavery in the maritime legal traditions of the Mediterranean (Khalilieh); the adjudication of water rights in Mamluk Damascus (Shoshan); the development and first expressions of Muslim institutions (Sijpesteijn); and the historiography of Western Indian Ocean port cities (Margariti). One common strand that runs through all of these contributions is the methodological emphasis on close readings and re-readings of primary sources and the juxtaposition of different genres of narratives and documents, an emphasis that characterizes much of the work of Udovitch himself. They, just like Udovitch' work, also refuse to be constrained by the separation of sources according to the religious communities that produced them—using Geniza documents to study the practice of Islamic law or Islamic normative sources to understand the history of Christian communities.

Udovitch's early career coincided with a momentous period in the writing of history in general and Middle Eastern history in particular. While the excitement over the methodology of the Annales school had taken firm root by the late sixties, at the same time the fertile reaction to it was coalescing into paradigm shifting movements in historical writing, including the schools of deconstruction and microhistory. Udovitch's own work reflects his respect for interdisciplinary interrogation that embraces the methods of anthropology and the social sciences in general, and a love of narrative and of the unlocking of the capsules of history that are single or discrete groups of documents, archaeological finds, events, and persons. To better understand the reality of how people lived and interacted in the medieval period, he grounded his efforts in rigorous linguistic and philological training and turned his attention both to well-read classic texts, and to documents of everyday life, most notably the documents of the Cairo Geniza, in the reading and analysis of which he became a leading expert. As all the participants in this volume can testify, his teaching strongly reflected his enthusiasm for texts, both documents of everyday life and representatives of more formal genres. He often taught courses focused exclusively on reading documentary materials, be they Geniza documents or Arabic papyri, and also hosted workshops in Princeton devoted exclusively to that end.

The explosion of documentary studies that started in the early days of Udovitch's career and continues today means that his work constitutes a salient model for how to proceed in the writing of Middle Eastern history. Unedited texts are still being discovered and rediscovered in libraries and collections from Ṣanʿāʾ to New York and beyond—Arabic papyri, *waqfīyas*, Geniza documents—and documentary collections surface from unexpected quarters, such as the buried documents that archaeological excavations brought to light at the desert port of Quseir al-Qadīm. In addition to these, administrative and notarial compendia and chancery documents require similar analyses and inform us in comparable ways about the unfolding of past lives. The processing of such texts is still a major mandate in the collective project of writing Islamic and Middle Eastern history, and in this volume the papers by Berkey, Constable, Shoshan, and Sijpesteijn contextualize such discrete written records in a microhistorical approach that produces a richly textured portrait of daily life in the medieval period. The juxtaposition of documentary sources with normative legal and/or narrative texts and the reading against the grain of a variety of sources and across genres are related strategies, the potential of which is illustrated here by the papers by Bonner, Margariti, Powers, Rapoport, and Sabra.

Economic History

Beyond method, the volume exemplifies a web of thematic strands within which Udovitch's contribution to Islamic history is situated. Starting with the broad realm of the economic history of the Islamic Middle East, this contribution includes the investigation of economic practices and institutions, the multiple intersections of economic and social bonds, and especially the nexus between legal theory of commerce and commercial practice. In the words of one reviewer, *Partnership and Profit in Medieval Islam* "significantly broadened our knowledge of Muslim commercial arrangements, particularly for the early medieval period."[1] The work also demonstrates the kind of economic history to be written in spite of the dearth of thick quantitative documentation. Indeed, very early on Udovitch made the case for qualitative analysis of material pertaining to Middle Eastern medieval economies, especially in light of the continuing absence of significant quantitative material;[2] the fruits of this approach are

[1] J. Bacharach, Review of *Partnership and Profit in Medieval Islam*, *Middle East Journal* 24 (1971): 274.

[2] A.L. Udovitch. "Commercial Techniques in Early Medieval Islamic Trade." In *Islam and the Trade of Asia: A Colloquium*, ed. D.S. Richards (Oxford: University of

significant and consist in the elucidation of major economic and social institutions, especially capital mobilization, credit mechanisms, and monetary instruments, partnership arrangements, and government officials' involvement in trade. In the same spirit of elucidating institutions of medieval economy, Petra Sijpesteijn "excavates" the many layers of an early eighth-century papyrus to probe the workings of the allocation of government stipends in the context of the Umayyad state's taking root in newly conquered lands. The archaeology of this document indeed allows a glimpse of "army economics" that speak directly to the structures of the early Islamic state. Michael Bonner offers a reconstruction of the institution of pre-Islamic "silent trade" by reading against the grain of Muslim jurists' discussions of the practice and juxtaposing both the legal and literary understanding of the practice in the Islamic context with anthropological and stucturalist economic theory. Rather than being an unintelligible or mysterious ritual of exchange between primitive peoples, the so-called silent trade practiced in Arabia on the eve of the rise of Islam thus emerges as a fine-tuned strategy for circumventing social barriers to commerce.

Social History

A closely related set of questions central to Udovitch's work pertain to the relationship between economic and social action and ultimately point to the common denominators—thematic and methodological—of social and economic history. Udovitch famously posited the fluidity and informality of economic relationships in medieval Islamic contexts in his 1974 article entitled "Formality and Informality." While the balance between formality and informality may continue to spark new debate—debate that in itself testifies to the fruitful nature of the argument—the broader notion of embededness of social and economic practice that permeates much of Udovitch's work is well accepted and leads seamlessly into the realm of social history. Adam Sabra offers a lively portrait of Shams al-Dīn Muḥammad al-Ḥanafī, a Sufi master of 1400s Cairo, whose intel-

Pennsylvania Press, 1970): 37; idem, *Partnership and Profit in Medieval Islam* (Princeton: Princeton University Press, 1970): 3.

lectual biography is inextricably linked to his political influence and his role as a link between his devotees and the Mamluk political elite. By subjecting the hagiographical portrait of this most important Shadhili mystic to historical analysis, Sabra unearths the political and economic dimensions of the patronage system which centered around Muḥammad al-Ḥanafī and extended from the city to the countryside. In his article, Jonathan Berkey builds on his work on the social history of medieval Islamic education. He examines the wage data that can be extracted from *waqfīyas* in order to deepen our understanding of the economic underpinnings of the learned class.

The Mediterranean and Indian Ocean: Middle Eastern History in its Geographic Context

Three of the papers mentioned above—by Sijpesteijn, Sabra, and Berkey—share with much of Udovitch's work the focus on medieval Egypt. Udovitch's current work, firmly situated as it is in the investigation of the Egyptian countryside, is also inexorably tied to the history of the Mediterranean as a whole. Mediterranean history has indeed been at the heart and the forefront of much of Udovitch's work. He became involved at a time when the post-Pirennian, Braudelian framing of Mediterranean history had fully taken hold and his apprenticeship with Lopez galvanized his Mediterraneanist outlook. He was thus able to contribute to Mediterranean history as a Middle Eastern medievalist in a way that we consider routine today.

Several of his Mediterraneanist concerns are reflected in the papers in this volume. In the realm of interdenominational relations that made the Mediterranean the quintessential arena of negotiation in the Middle Ages and render it today an exciting field of study, Udovitch sought to understand the ways in which communities interacted and accommodated differences in spite of prescriptive ideologies. In the process, he focused on the legal, economic and social adaptations some on the institutional level, that allowed for bridging "the gulf between rigid principle and supple accommodation."[3] The quest for these bridges is central in Remie Constable's paper, as she

[3] A.L. Udovitch, "Muslims and Jews in the World of Frederic II: Boundaries and Communication," *Princeton Papers in Near Eastern Studies* 2 (1993): 84.

dissects the negotiations between Tunisian Ḥafṣids and the Aragonese crown concerning privileges, especially religious freedom, for Catalan merchants and by extension all Christian traders in Muslim Tunis. This is a case of "transmediterranean communication"[4] par excellence. Yossef Rapoport's extends Udovitch's outlook on the dynamics of the Mediterranean economy as viewed "from the south." He argues for the ultimately military/naval provenance of the information on the topography and human geography of the Aegean world contained in the remarkable geographical manuscript titled "The Book of Curiosities." To Udovitch's argument that the European commercial revolution is inextricably linked to the increase of industrial production of textiles in the southern Mediterranean and a period of increased trade relations across the Mediterranean, Rapoport adds the issue of the adversarial relationship between the Byzantine and Fatimid states, and concludes that the geographical information of the manuscript emerged from a historical moment when strategic competition continued even as rigorous commercial ties increased. A mediterraneanist outlook is also evident in Hassan Khalilieh's treatment of the question of treatment of slaves in maritime commercial law; his paper, along with his previous work demonstrates the interconnection of the different Mediterranean traditions of maritime law, but also notes their divergences.

Beyond the Mediterranean, the interregional perspective and the engagement with oceanic history extend to the world of the Indian Ocean. Khalilieh's article fills in the gaps of legal theory and practice with regard to the status of slaves on board ships with material from the Malay legal tradition. Margariti's article is squarely located in the field of Indian Ocean studies, and informs the rather sparsely documented early period of medieval Indian Ocean exchanges with the unique testimony of the Cairo Geniza—recently made available through corpus of S.D. Goitein's "India Book,"[5] the importance of which Udovitch undertook to impress on his peers and students through courses he taught and papers he presented on the subject of Indian Ocean trade.

[4] A.L. Udovitch, "Muslims and Jews": 85-92.

[5] S.D. Goitein and M.A. Friedman, *India Traders of the Middle Ages* (Leiden: E. J. Brill, 2008).

Urbanism

Udovitch's interest in the study of cities in the Middle East is evident in his articles about Cairo and Alexandria and in the attention he paid to urban mercantile milieus in his work as a whole, as well as in the city-oriented investigation included in the volumes he chose to edit, including *The Medieval City* and *The Islamic Middle East 700-1900: Studies in Economic and Social History*. The former is a tribute to his teacher at Yale Robert Sabatino Lopez, whose own work exhibits a strong focus on urban history. The latter is an outcome of a Princeton seminar on economic history that Udovitch organized in the the spring and summer of 1974. The essays in both volumes approach cities as sites of economic exchange and interrogate the particulars of city life through the prism of a wide range of economic interactions between individuals and groups. From that perspective, legal, political, ideological and intellectual dimensions of urban networking become grounded in the realities of everyday life.

In the present volume, two essays approach urban life through its material components and primarily economic activities, ultimately aiming to expose the articulation of city associations. Water rights were central to economic and social life in any Middle Eastern medieval city, and Shoshan's investigation of water-related disputes though the remarkable diary of a fifteenth-century Damascene judge contributes a lively sketch of urban and suburban topography and intergroup dynamics and negotiations in the Syrian city. Exploring the portrayals of Indian Ocean port cities in medieval sources, Margariti's essay attempts to assess the ways in which urban topography reflected the place of any particular city in a broader network of entrepots, the political and strategic competition between those cities, and the material reflections of social stratification within them.

In the course of Udovitch's scholarly and teaching career, the writing of history has changed dramatically. Through his own work and in his teaching Udovitch has been indefatigable in encouraging the exploration of new sources, techniques and methodologies—a commitment to which his students in this volume pay homage. The essays collected here represent our efforts to build on his contributions to Middle Eastern History while incorporating recent developments in historiography. But Udovitch's attention to and feeling for the human experience is not confined to his research—it permeates all of his scholarly activities, as those who have benefited from his extraordinary warmth, loyalty and generosity can readily attest. It is with gratitude as well as pride, therefore, that we offer this volume both as evidence of the tradition to which we belong and as a tribute to Avrom Udovitch, our teacher.

Roxani Eleni Margariti, Adam Sabra and Petra M. Sijpesteijn.
May 2009

Bibliography

Bacharach, J. Review of *Partnership and Profit in Medieval Islam*, *Middle East Journal* 24 (1971): 274.

Goitein, S.D. and M.A. Friedman, *India Traders of the Middle Ages*. Leiden: E.J. Brill, 2008.

Udovitch, A.L. "Commercial Techniques in Early Medieval Islamic Trade." In D.S. Richards, *Islam and the Trade of Asia: A Colloquium*. Oxford: University of Pennsylvania Press, 1970: 37-62.

——. *Partnership and Profit in Medieval Islam*. Princeton: Princeton University Press, 1970.

——. "Muslims and Jews in the World of Frederic II: Boundaries and Communication," *Princeton Papers in Near Eastern Studies* 2 (1993): 83-104.

INTRODUCTION[1]

Mark R. Cohen

Abraham (Avrom) Leib Udovitch, leader in the social and economic history of the medieval Middle East, guiding light in the study of the documents of the Cairo Geniza, activist in the search for peace in the Middle East, and teacher of many of the leading young scholars of the current generation, was destined early in his life for the career and research field he chose. He was born in Winnipeg, Canada, in 1933, to Russian immigrant parents. Yiddish was the primary language of his home and his parents sent him to a secular Yiddish day school. Later he attended a Lubavitcher yeshiva in Montreal for a few years but left it to continue high school in Winnipeg. He speaks proudly of his Yiddish background to friends.

While in Montreal he became involved in the socialist Zionist youth movement, Hashomer Hatzair ("Young Guard"). He spent a year in Israel on a Hashomer Hatzair kibbutz following high school, returning with solid knowledge of modern Hebrew. He planned to immigrate with Hashomer Hatzair to Israel in the mid 1950s. However, family reasons combined with the disruption of travel to the Middle East following the Suez war of 1956, prevented him from doing so. One of the planks of Hashomer Hatzair was a binational state in Palestine, in which Arabs and Jews would live side-by-side with equal rights. Early on the seeds of Avrom's later activism on behalf of peace and justice in the Middle East conflict were thus sown.

He received his undergraduate education at Columbia University and the Jewish Theological Seminary, a dual-track curriculum in both regular university and Jewish studies. At JTS he was exposed to the great scholar of medieval Hebrew poetry, Shalom Spiegel. He once told me that hearing Spiegel expound on the symbiosis of Jewish and Arabic culture and the relative harmony between Jews and Muslims in the Middle Ages had a profound effect on him. It is easy to imagine

[1] I wish to thank Avrom's daughters, Tamar Udovitch and Mim Udovitch, as well as his sister and nephew, Rochel Udovitch Berman and Josh Berman, for their assistance filling in some of the biographical material in this essay.

that Avrom, already influenced by progressive Zionism and its sympathetic approach to the Palestinian problem, became engaged by this distant mirror of a possible world of Arab-Israeli coexistence.

Graduate studies led him first to an MA in Near Eastern Languages at Columbia, then his doctorate at Yale. There, he came under the influence of the eminent Arabist Franz Rosenthal and of the great medieval historian Robert Lopez, and became their doctoral student. Lopez was interested in the economic history of medieval Europe, and Avrom wrote his dissertation on the economic history of medieval Islam. One of his acquired interests was Islamic law and he worked with Joseph Schacht after the latter came to Columbia. For his dissertation he investigated the Islamic law of commercial partnership. The book, *Partnership and Profit in Medieval Islam*, is a pathbreaking work, in which he shows that what had always been thought to be purely theoretical in classical Islamic commercial law reflected actual reality, as perceived in the documents of the Cairo Geniza. In this he followed the path of the great doyen of Geniza studies, Shelomo Dov Goitein. The Jewish merchants of the Geniza, Avrom claimed, followed practices almost identical with ones described in early books of Islamic law, particularly Hanafi law. He posited, further, that Jewish merchants and Muslim merchants followed one and the same "'Law Merchant' of the Medieval Islamic World"—the title of one of his early, seminal articles—and that these legal practices became assimilated to Islamic law. Today, with the recent publication of Arabic letters of Muslim traders from the same period as the Geniza, we have explicit confirmation of what Goitein and Udovitch sensed from the limited sources available to them when they wrote.

The seeds of contact with the Geniza blossomed in his later research. So did his relationship with Goitein, who came to Princeton and the Institute for Advanced Study three years after Avrom arrived on the faculty of Near Eastern Studies in 1967 from a position at Cornell. It was a relationship of scholarship and friendship that lasted until Goitein's death in 1985, and the lives of the two men have some striking parallels.

Goitein, too, began his career as an Islamicist, studying at Frankfurt with the great German Jewish orientalist, Joseph Horovitz, and writing a doctoral dissertation on prayer in the Qur'ān. Like Udovitch,

Goitein became a Zionist. Like Udovitch he planned at a young age to go to live in Israel; he arrived in Israel in 1923 following the completion of his doctorate in Germany. Finally, like Goitein, Udovitch became a foremost scholar of the historical documents of the Cairo Geniza.

In Princeton, the lives of these two men became intertwined. Avrom made one of his greatest (and largely unknown) contributions to Islamic and Jewish studies by making sure, through his own connections with funding sources, that Goitein and his work were supported for the fifteen productive last years of Goitein's life. Avrom's appreciation of Goitein in the introduction he wrote to the final, posthumous volume of Goiten's *Mediterranean Society* is a tribute, not only to the great man, but also to the influence he had on this younger scholar, who substantiated Goitein's conviction about the importance of the Geniza for Islamic history in new ways.

Avrom has devoted most of his professional life to the Geniza. But he would not call himself a Jewish historian. Rather, he would say he is a social and economic historian of the medieval Islamic world (a world that embraced Jews). His many articles contain nuggets of insight into this world, based largely on the Geniza. One of these insights is his description of Islamic society as being marked by a large measure of informalism, in contrast with the more tightly organized, corporate society of the medieval Christian West. In this he joins hands with medieval Islamic social and urban historians, who have pointed to the lack of formal organization in the Islamic city and to the prevalence of informal ties in social relationships in general.

One of Avrom's many seminal contributions is his work on banking. "Bankers without Banks," one of his many characteristically catchy titles, tells it all: the Geniza points to a well-established medieval banking system, marked by informal relations rather than by buildings. Here the Islamic world, as in so many other ways, pioneered economic institutions known in the Christian West only much later. Another alluring (and alluding) title, "A Tale of Two Cities," introduces a study of commercial relations between Islamic Cairo and Alexandria and shows how intimately tied they were to one another in the eleventh century. In other articles, as well, he sought to rescue sorely neglected Alexandria for history.

One of his signature studies is "Formalism and Informalism in the Social and Economic Institutions of the Medieval Islamic World," in which he introduced the subject to generalists, presenting a fascinating merchant's letter illustrating what, for European historians, would have seemed a strange way to organize commercial life. His earliest publication, written while he was a doctoral student at Yale, is a famous article that compares Islam, the Jewish world, and Byzantium in search of "The Origins of the Western *Commenda*." The comparative view also marks his "Law Merchant" article mentioned above.

The evocative (and provocative) title, *The Last Arab Jews: The Communities of Jerba, Tunisia*, written with his wife, Lucette Valensi, introduced a new aspect to his work. Lucette influenced him to adopt a social-anthropological approach (the anthropologist Clifford Geertz at the Institute for Advanced Study also had an affect on his interest in this respect). The Jerba research, which they undertook together as a team of anthropological observers among the Jewish community of that island off the Tunisian coast, touched on Avrom's main field as a medievalist. He understood new things in the Geniza world as a result of watching these traditional Jews—merchants and authentic believers—going about their daily affairs, interacting without friction with Muslims, while at the same time preserving their distinct Jewish identity. Here again, a fascinating parallel with Goitein emerges, whose study of the Geniza world had been deeply informed by his earlier field work in Israel among Yemenite immigrants, whom he called "the most Arab and the most Jewish of all Jews."

Another of Avrom's major scholarly achievements is his co-editorship of *Studia Islamica*, a major journal in the field. Similarly, he collaborated with Joseph Strayer on the thirteen-volume *Dictionary of the Middle Ages*. Unusual for such an undertaking, the Islamic world was given full representation (as was Byzantium). Even more unusual for such a project, Avrom was given the task of overseeing entries on the Jews. He farmed that responsibility out to the present writer. As a Jewish historian I embraced the task gladly, and Avrom permitted me to commission many more entries than were to be found in any comparable general work on the Middle Ages. The results are a tribute to Avrom's commitment to make Jewish studies part of the academy and a response to the justified complaint of medievalists like Gavin Langmuir about the omission of the Jews from medieval European history.

Pioneering again, Avrom was an early promoter of the field of the economic history of the Middle East. He organized a ground-breaking conference at Princeton and edited its proceedings, *The Islamic Middle East, 700-1900: Studies in Economic and Social History* (1981). Earlier he had co-edited with European historians Harry Miskimin and David Herlihy the volume *The Medieval City* (1977), and later, along with co-editor Haleh Esfandiari, he published *The Economic Dimensions of Middle Eastern History: Essays in Honor of Charles Issawi* (1990). His interest in the Jewish component in Arab society spawned another forward-looking conference, which led to the publication of *Jews among Arabs: Contacts and Boundaries* (1989), co-edited with the present writer, and focusing on the modern period. I remember our discussion of the title for the conference and its volume. We rejected the label "Jews under Arabs" in favor of "Jews among Arabs," in order to get away from the paradigm of subaltern oppression. Indeed, the articles in that volume describe Jews living a more or less integrated existence in the modern Arab world, an echo of the era of Jewish-Arab coexistence in the middle ages. The underlying theme of that conference was already in the forefront in *The Last Arab Jews*.

The Festschrift for Charles Issawi recalls another of Avrom's accomplishments. In 1973 he attained the chairmanship of the Department of Near Eastern Studies. In this capacity he lead the department for eighteen years (with a break between 1977 and 1980), "growing" it from a small and marginal entity at Princeton to a world class center. During his long "reign" he brought great scholars like Bernard Lewis, Charles Issawi, Michael Cook, Hossein Modarressi, and M. Sükrü Hanioglu to the university.

He also established Hebrew and Jewish studies in the department at a time—the early 1970s—when Princeton lagged far behind its peer institutions in giving a home to this important field of human knowledge. In this way, he helped lay the seeds, too, for the interdepartmental Princeton Program in Judaic Studies that flourishes today. Under his leadership, moreover, the first chair in Jewish studies was established in the university, the Khedouri A. Zilkha Professorship of Jewish Civilization in the Near East, which he held until his retirement. In the mid-1980s he created, along with the present writer, the Princeton Geniza Project, which supports an on-line database of thousands of documents in Hebrew, Arabic, and Judaeo-Arabic from the Cairo Geniza that illuminate the social and economic life of Jews and Muslims in the high Middle Ages. This resource is used by scholars around the world. He also arranged for the creation of the S.D. Goitein Laboratory for Geniza Research in the Department of Near Eastern Studies, which houses the personal research archive of the late Professor Goitein and, along with the Princeton Geniza Project, supports research by graduate students in the department and by visiting scholars from around the world.

Avrom's legacy includes the cadre of students he has trained, many of whom have followed his lead in using the Geniza for Islamic social and economic history. These latter make up what may be called "the Princeton School," continuing and expanding the work pioneered by Goitein and, in his wake, Udovitch. To name them would amount to listing some of the most brilliant and innovative young historians of the medieval Muslim world. Some of them are contributors to this volume. In this, too, Avrom's career follows that of his teacher Goitein, who trained most of the older generation of Geniza historians.

What of Avrom's activism in seeking peace and justice in the Israeli-Palestinian conflict? One of its defining moments came in 1988. In the winter of that year Avrom came to my house. He told me, in confidence, that he had been invited to join a small, back-channel delegation of American Jews in a secret meeting in Stockholm with Yasir Arafat. Organized, with the knowledge and support of the U.S. State Department and the Swedish government, the purpose of the get together was to discuss the Israeli-Palestinian conflict. He also told me to watch the news! A few days later he appeared on television in Stockholm at a news conference with the four other Jewish delegates and with Arafat, living one of the more historic moments in the turn toward a peaceful solution to the Israel-Palestine conflict. As a result of that meeting, lines of communication between Arafat, the PLO, and the United States government were opened, and Arafat and his colleagues began the slow march towards recognition of Israel and towards diplomatic relations with the United States. In this respect, historian Udovitch helped make history. Upon his return, he wrote about his experience in an article, "Making Peace: In Stockholm with Yasir Arafat," published in the *Village Voice*.

The experience in Stockholm opened up a new chapter in his career through his friendship with a number of Palestinian leaders, on the one hand, and academic members of the peace-seeking camp in Israel, on the other. It set in motion a new and complementary phase to his scholarship and teaching, which included service as a member of the Brookings Institution Study Panel for Peace in the

Middle East, of the Council on Foreign Relations, and as president of the American Committee for the International Center for Peace in the Middle East.

Over the years, too, Avrom was instrumental in bringing noted Israelis and Arabs to teach or lecture at the university. During his long tenure as chairman, and afterwards, Near Eastern Studies has hosted visiting professors and researchers from both Israel and the Arab world, scholars who, on the neutral ground of Princeton's Jones Hall, have met and befriended one another, minus the rancor and tension that marks the conflict in the region. He also navigated the department through the choppy waters of the Middle East conflict, keeping it as immune as possible from the internecine hostility that mark the politics of so many other Middle East departments in the US and Europe.

All this was not without its costs. Avrom incurred criticism in some quarters for his activism. Even prior to Stockholm, before he became identified with the liberal wing (Palestinian and Israeli alike) of the Middle East peace movement, he had weathered a storm of criticism at a conference on Jews and Arabs, in Spoleto, Italy, in 1978. Avrom's paper, a balanced piece entitled "The Jews and Islam in the High Middle Ages: A Case of the Muslim View of Differences," engendered fierce attacks from some Israeli and European Jewish scholars, representatives of what I have elsewhere called the "neo-lachrymose school of Jewish-Arab history." Avrom's remarkable capacity for patience and diplomatic coolness comes across clearly in the transcript of the questions and responses that were published along with his paper in the conference volume.

Throughout, Avrom has stood firm in his belief that Jews and Muslims got along in a more or less tolerable *modus vivendi* in the high Middle Ages, an outgrowth of his early study of Hebrew poetry with Spiegel and his research on the Geniza world. I would venture to say that, for him, the medieval world of Muslims and Jews living together echoes the dream that some form of rapprochement between Israelis and Palestinians living side-by-side is still possible.

Always energetic, Avrom has old and new scholarly projects on his plate, which he pursues while he and Lucette live between Paris, Princeton, and their *pied-à-terre* in New York, enjoying the cities, family, and especially their grandchildren.

"THERE ARE *'ULAMĀ'*, AND THEN THERE ARE *'ULAMĀ'*": MINOR RELIGIOUS INSTITUTIONS AND MINOR RELIGIOUS FUNCTIONARIES IN MEDIEVAL CAIRO

Jonathan P. Berkey

Four and a half decades ago, at the outset of the career of A. L. Udovitch, the field of pre-modern Islamic social history barely existed. In the intervening years, the field has flourished, in part because of the scholarship of Udovitch himself as well as that of his students and other historians associated with the Department of Near Eastern Studies at Princeton University, of which for many years he served as chair. To some degree, the accomplishments of Islamic social historians have paralleled those of their colleagues in other fields. From the 1960s until fairly recently, the domain of social history has dominated the discipline. Naturally, however, the contingencies of Islamic history and the sources from which it can be reconstructed have posed particular challenges and have shaped the specific contours of what we can tell about the social history of the pre-modern Islamic Middle East.

The most notable feature of pre-modern Islamic social history has been its focus on one particular social group, the *'ulamā'*. In most if not all societies, education and authority over the rituals and institutions of religious expression are factors helping to mark out particular social groups as distinctive. Nonetheless, the special prominence of the *'ulamā'* in Islamic societies is widely acknowledged. That prominence is reflected, perhaps, in the fact that *'ulamā'* is one of those Arabic terms that historians routinely render in transliterated, rather than translated form, as if no English approximation will adequately capture the parameters of this social group.

This emphasis on the *'ulamā'* is somewhat problematic, at least for both the most ancient and most recent periods of Islamic history. The *'ulamā'* were not there at the outset of Islamic history: they do not correspond neatly to any social stratum in pre-Islamic Mediterranean or southwest Asian societies, and there was hardly a distinctive group of scholars devoted to elaborating and transmitting the Islamic religious and legal sciences when those sciences themselves were at best in only their most rudimentary stages. The issue of their origins and early development is one of the more intriguing open questions concerning early Islamic history—how, that is, a distinctive group of *ʿulamāʾ* emerged over the period of Umayyad and early Abbasid rule? In the modern period, too, the central social position of the *ʿulamāʾ* is not a given. In part this reflects changes in the structure of economic relations and political institutions, changes associated with the rise of a modern capitalist economy, a powerful state system, and the elites who dominate them. Of late, however, anthropologists, political scientists and others have also recognized new social networks and channels of religious authority in many contemporary Muslim societies. The individuals who populate those networks cannot easily be characterized as *ʿulamāʾ*, and sometimes the authority they wield competes with that of scholars associated with more traditional religious institutions.

Nonetheless, for a period spanning the late eighth through the nineteenth centuries, the *ʿulamāʾ* certainly constituted an important social group in almost all Islamic societies, although of course the precise nature of their social identity and (in some cases) political power varied with particular historical conditions. They formed one component, perhaps the most important component, of those social groups Albert Hourani labeled the "notables" of Middle Eastern societies.[1] Even in the medieval period, when formal political power was usually held by a variety of military elites, many of them ethnically or culturally alien to the people over whom they ruled, the *ʿulamāʾ* served an important political role, as mediators between the rulers and the local populations who looked with reverence and respect upon the leading religious and legal scholars.[2]

Quite naturally, social historians have devoted considerable attention to the *ʿulamāʾ*. In part, of course, this reflects the bias of the surviving sources, particularly the biographical dictionaries which constitute an indispensable source for medieval social history. The authors of those biographical dictionaries were, for the most part, scholars of the religious and legal sciences themselves, and their efforts to record the life stories of their contemporaries focused on the *ʿulamāʾ*, who were (in their own not disinterested view) the "heirs

[1] A. Hourani, "Ottoman Reform and the Politics of Notables," in *The Emergence of the Modern Middle East* (London: Macmillan, 1981): 36-66.

[2] I.M. Lapidus, *Muslim Cities in the Later Middle Ages* (Cambridge, Mass.: Harvard University Press, 1967): 130-42.

of the Prophet." Given the nature of the sources, the study of the *'ulamā'* is, as one former colleague of Professor Udovitch famously put it, "almost all the Islamic social history we will ever have for this [pre-modern] period."[3] But even discounting that bias in the surviving sources, there is little reason to question the general social importance of the *'ulamā'*.

Who were the *'ulamā'*? Ira Lapidus, in his ground-breaking study of medieval Muslim cities, defined the *'ulamā'* as "that part of the Muslim community learned in the literature, laws, and doctrines of Islam. They were judges, jurists, prayer-leaders, scholars, teachers, readers of Koran, reciters of traditions, Sufis, functionaries of mosques, and so on."[4] And so on indeed. This catholic definition, which in Western scholarship goes back at least to Hamilton Gibb and Harold Bowen's *Islamic Society and the West*,[5] includes all those who in some way embraced the Quranic imperative to "command right and forbid wrong." The *'ulamā'*, in other words, were not a distinct class, but a broad category of individuals from overlapping social divisions who committed themselves to Islamic religious knowledge and its transmission, and also to the application of that knowledge in law. Those covered by the term included professors in the religious schools, preachers, and judges in the *sharī'a* courts as a matter of course. But merchants, bureaucrats, craftsmen, soldiers and others too, if they had sufficient exposure to and instruction in the texts and traditions of the religious sciences, might qualify in some way as *'ulamā'*.

If much pre-modern Islamic social history is perforce the history of the *'ulamā'*, then it comes as no surprise that one particularly well-developed sub-field concerns the history of religious education and the institutions that supported them. A number of studies have focused on the *madrasa*, which by the twelfth and thirteenth century was the pre-eminent institution of higher religious and legal education in the cities of the Islamic world. Other studies have investigated the Islamic concept of *'ilm*, that is, "knowledge" of religious and legal

[3] R. Mottahedeh, review of R. Bulliet, *The Patricians of Nishapur: A Study in Medieval Islamic Social History*, in the *Journal of the American Oriental Society*, 95: 3 (1975): 491-95.

[4] Lapidus, *Muslim Cities*: 107.

[5] H. Gibb and H. Bowen, *Islamic Society and the West*, vol. 1, pt. 2: *Islamic Society in the Eighteenth Century* (London: Oxford University Press, 1967-9): 70-113.

significance, or the social networks of scholars involved in the transmission of *ʿilm*.[6] These studies of education constitute in fact one of the best-developed subfields of pre-modern Islamic history. Together they have left historians with a clear understanding of the social and political significance of the activity—the transmission of religious knowledge—which made the *ʿulamāʾ* the *ʿulamāʾ*.

Among the conclusions they have drawn, three stand out as significant here. One is that education took place in a wide variety of institutions. Some were specifically called *madrasa*s, but others were known by a variety of terms associated with Sufi activities, especially *khānqāh*. Still others were simply called mosques, reminding us that, before the rise of the *madrasa*, most religious education probably took place in mosques. Secondly, while the establishment of each institution devoted to Islamic education, whether a *madrasa* or anything else, was an act of individual charity, collectively the flourishing of institutions of education had a political dimension. Most of those who founded them belonged to the political elites of their day, and while the Saljuq vizier Niẓām al-Mulk and the Mamluk Sultan al-Ghūrī may have had very different particular goals in establishing the *madrasa*s that bore their names, it is significant that both saw the patronage of the *ʿulamāʾ* as critical to establishing their legitimacy. Finally, for all the importance of the *madrasa*s and other institutions established in the medieval period to support the transmission of *ʿilm*, education itself remained fundamentally informal, particularly in the mechanisms through which the *ʿulamāʾ* measured the quality of education and regulated access to *ʿulamāʾ* status. One result was to make it possible for many Muslims, and not simply those studying full-time in one *madrasa* or another, to associate themselves with and participate in the transmission of religious knowledge, and

---

[6] F. Rosenthal, *Knowledge Triumphant: The Concept of Knowledge in Medieval Islam* (Leiden: E. J. Brill, 1970); R. Bulliet, *The Patricians of Nishapur: A Study in Medieval Islamic Social History* (Cambridge, Mass.: Harvard University Press, 1972); J. Pedersen, *The Arabic Book* (Princeton: Princeton University Press, 1984); G. Makdisi, *The Rise of Colleges: Institutions of Learning in Islam and the West* (Edinburgh: Edinburgh University Press, 1981); C.F. Petry, *The Civilian Elite of Cairo in the Later Middle Ages* (Princeton: Princeton University Press, 1981); J. Berkey, *The Transmission of Knowledge in Medieval Cairo: A Social History of Islamic Education* (Princeton: Princeton University Press, 1992); M. Chamberlain, *Knowledge and Social Practice in Medieval Damascus, 1190-1350* (Cambridge: Cambridge University Press, 1994); D. Ephrat, *A Learned Society in Transition: The Sunnī ʿulamāʾ of Eleventh-Century Baghdad* (Albany: SUNY Press, 2000).

even to claim for themselves in some respect the title of *'ālim* (sing. of *'ulamā'*). As Lapidus noted, the *'ulamā'* were a very broad and diverse group.

Nonetheless, in most studies of the *'ulamā'* , there has been a tendency, often unrecognized, to focus on the *'ulamā'* elite, on what has sometimes been called the "patriciate"—that is, on the leading jurists, *ḥadīth* scholars, and others, those who dominated intellectual life, who held professorships in the most prominent and well-endowed *madrasas*, and who went on to serve as *qāḍīs* and other important officials. The biographical dictionaries which constitute the most important source on the lives and networks of the *'ulamā'* naturally tend to focus on the leading members of the *'ulamā'*. Some of the most expansive of these sources, most notably al-Sakhāwī's enormous collection of biographical notices of those who died during the ninth Islamic century (roughly the fifteenth of the Common Era), provide at least basic information about a wide range of learned men (and women), information that can support general conclusions of a prosopographical nature.[7] But it is usually the leading scholars who claim our attention, because they claimed the attention of their contemporaries who wrote about them.[8]

Another feature of recent social histories of pre-modern Islam has been an effort to identify and exploit new sources to supplement the chronicles and biographical dictionaries that have provided the narrative framework for our understanding of pre-modern Islamic societies. In some ways, historians of pre-modern Islam are extraordinarily fortunate. Medieval European historians have nothing like the extensive literary record—histories, biographical dictionaries, normative legal literature, etc.—available to their colleagues who study the Middle East. On the other hand, in the Middle East, virtually nothing in the way of archives has survived from the pre-Ottoman period. As a result, our understanding of the pre-modern Islamic past has been broad but shallow. We know much about life in Middle Eastern cities, and in particular about the social elites, but relatively little about rural areas and those at the base of the social ladder.

There are at least two significant exceptions to the general rule—two major archival sources which have in recent years received

[7] See especially Petry, *The Civilian Elite of Cairo*.

[8] The present writer himself has contributed to this focus on the leading scholars, having on occasion rendered the term *'ulamā'* in English as "the educated elite." See for example Berkey, *Transmission of Knowledge*: 13.

considerable attention from pre-modern historians. (A third consists of the medieval documents discovered at the Ḥaram al-Sharīf in Jerusalem.) The first, of course, is the Geniza, the eclectic repository of papers from the Jewish community of Fusṭāṭ, Egypt. As S.D. Goitein, the pre-eminent historian of the Geniza argued, these documents have broad repercussions for our understanding, not simply of the Jewish experience in the medieval Middle East, but for the larger Islamic society in which the Jews of Fusṭāṭ lived.[9] Here again, Professor Udovitch and historians working in and around the Department of Near Eastern Studies at Princeton have been in the forefront of Geniza research.

A second archival source consists of the foundation deeds (*waqfīyas*), mostly from the Mamluk period, preserved in Cairo. Two major repositories of these documents survive: one at the national archives (Dār al-Wathā'iq al-Qawmīya), and another in the possession of the ministry of religious endowments (Wizārat al-Awqāf). These deeds record the establishment of foundations or trusts (*awqāf*, sing. *waqf*), in which property is set aside under the terms of Islamic law and made inalienable, while the income generated by that property is designated for the benefit of some specific purpose or purposes. Those purposes might be private: so, for example, a trust might be established specifically for the benefit of the founder's children and descendants in perpetuity. Trusts might also be established for a more public purpose: say, to benefit a mosque or *madrasa* which the founder had constructed, to pay its employees, to provide for its maintenance and upkeep, etc. Trusts of a hybrid nature were not uncommon, in which the income generated by the trust's property was committed to a public charitable purpose, while any remainder—and the remainder might by design be considerable—was set aside for the founder's family and descendants.

The surviving *waqfīyas* in Cairo are significant for two reasons. In the first place, the trusts they represent provided the material foundations for the flourishing of religious institutions—*madrasas*, *khānqāhs*, mosques, and others—in the Mamluk period. Individuals—mostly although not exclusively members of the Mamluk political and military elite—established these trusts for a variety of reasons,

[9] S.D. Goitein, *A Mediterranean Society: The Jewish Communities of the Arab World as Portrayed in the Documents of the Cairo Geniza*, volume 1: *Economic Foundations* (Berkeley: University of California Press, 1967): 70-4.

ranging from attempts to secure some portion of their private wealth and prevent its confiscation, to genuinely pious motives of encouraging the transmission of religious knowledge. Whatever their purposes, however, the sheer number of trusts established helped to cement the social status and financial well-being of the *'ulamā'* who benefited from them. By one estimate, at the end of the Mamluk period, the majority of urban property in Cairo, as well as significant agricultural tracts outside the metropolis, was devoted to such trusts.[10]

Second, these *waqfīya*s have provided historians with another archival source, supplementing the documents of the Geniza, through which to study medieval Islamic social realities. The pioneering work was done by the Egyptian historian Muḥammad Amīn; his book on *waqf*s and social life in medieval Cairo is still the essential starting point for research using the *waqfīya*s. Carl Petry has demonstrated how a careful reading of the deeds can transform our reading of the political narrative available in the standard historical and biographical sources.[11] But students from Professor Udovitch's department at Princeton, too, have employed the *waqf* documents to reconstruct the history of Mamluk society. Given that many of the endowments were established to support particular religious institutions, it is no surprise that architectural historians have found them invaluable.[12] Perhaps the most creative research centered on the endowment deeds has been that of social historians who have employed them to provide a much fuller understanding of topics, such as the role of eunuchs in Mamluk society and the responses of that society to the persistent problem of poverty, to which the narrative sources allude.[13]

These two features of recent scholarship in the pre-modern social history of Islam—that is, its focus on the *'ulamā'* and on institutions of religious education, on the one hand, and the exploitation of new sources, especially the Cairene *waqfīya*s on the other—provide the

---

[10] M.M. Amīn, *al-Awqāf wa'l-ḥayāt al-ijtimā'īya fī Miṣr, 648-923/1250-1517* (Cairo: Dār al-Nahḍa al-'Arabīya, 1980): 278, citing the Ottoman period writer Muḥammad ibn 'Abd al-Mu'tī al-Isḥāqī.

[11] See, for example, C.F. Petry, *Protectors or Praetorians? The Last Mamluk Sultans and Egypt's Waning as a Great Power* (Albany: SUNY Press, 1994).

[12] See L. Fernandes, *The Evolution of a Sufi Institution in Mamluk Egypt: The Khanqah* (Berlin: Klaus Schwarz, 1988).

[13] See for example S. Marmon, *Eunuchs and Sacred Boundaries in Islamic Society* (New York and Oxford: Oxford University Press, 1995), and A. Sabra, *Poverty and Charity in Medieval Islam: Mamluk Egypt, 1250-1517* (Cambridge: Cambridge University Press, 2000).

background to what follows. I would like, in the first place, to draw attention to a little-studied endowment deed of the Mamluk sultan al-Nāṣir Ḥasan (d. 763/1362). Secondly, a quick study of that deed will allow us to make some more general remarks about the *'ulamā'* as a social group, and in particular about the striking if sometimes overlooked diversity of those individuals who claimed *'ulamā'* status.

Sultan Ḥasan, of course, was a prominent political figure in the Mamluk state in the mid-eighth/fourteenth century, and his ventures into the establishment of charitable trusts are well known to students of Mamluk-era social, religious, and architectural history. The son of al-Nāṣir Muḥammad and grandson of al-Manṣūr Qalāwūn, two of the principal sultans of the first century of Mamluk rule, Ḥasan was one of about a dozen or so descendants of Qalāwūn who made up what historians sometimes call the "Qalāwūnid dynasty." From the death of al-Nāṣir Muḥammad in 741/1340 until the accession of al-Ẓāhir Barqūq in 784/1382, the Mamluk sultanate was mostly held, formally at least, by a series of al-Nāṣir Muḥammad's many sons, although for much of this time, real power was held by various amirs, the leading figures in the Mamluk military establishment. Naturally this created a fair degree of tension, and al-Nāṣir Ḥasan's rule serves as a case in point. He was brought to the throne in 748/1347 at the age of eleven, but was deposed by the leading amirs in 752/1351. Returned to the throne for a second time in 755/1354, Ḥasan made concerted efforts to take command of the affairs of state himself. In the end, however, he was deposed and murdered by the most powerful of his own Mamluks.

Al-Nāṣir Ḥasan is best remembered for the grand *madrasa* complex which he constructed in Rumayla, below the Citadel, in the area between the Fatimid city of Cairo and the older settlement of Fusṭāṭ. This institution, which even in the Middle Ages was known as "the greatest *madrasa*," has received considerable attention from historians, and for good reason.[14] In the first place, its endowment deed has survived, and has been published twice, once by Muḥammad Amīn, and more recently by Howayda al-Harithy.[15] One of the most

---

[14] The phrase "greatest *madrasa*" appears in A.b.'Ali. Al-Qalqashandī, *Ṣubḥ al-a'shā fī ṣinā'at al-inshā'*, 14 vols. (Cairo: al-Mu'assasa al-Miṣrīyah al-'Āmma li'l-Ta'līf wa'l-Tarjama wa'l-Ṭibā'a wa'l-Nashr, 1964), 3:363.

[15] M.M. Amīn published a portion of al-Nāṣir Ḥasan's original *waqfīya* (DW 40/6) in Ibn Ḥabīb, *Tadhkirat al-nabīh fī ayyām al-manṣūr wa-banīh* (Cairo:

imposing and best-preserved *madrasa* complexes, it looms large in the architectural history of medieval Cairo.[16] But the institution looms large in the social and cultural history of Mamluk Egypt as well. It was far and away the largest *madrasa* in medieval Cairo, both physically and in terms of the number of teachers and students it supported. The endowment provided funds for professors and students in all four of the Sunni schools of law, as well as in Quranic exegesis, *ḥadīth*, Arabic language, and several other subjects.[17]

Sultan Ḥasan, however, established other endowments than that supporting his famous *madrasa*. In particular, I wish to draw attention to a relatively small endowment the deed for which is preserved in the Dār al-Wathā'iq collection in Cairo. This deed, No. 42/6 in the archive's collection, is typical of many of the surviving *waqfīya*s, in that it takes the form of a scroll of which the beginning section is badly damaged.[18] Nonetheless, the portions of the document pertaining to the endowment's stipulated expenditures are reasonably clear, and provide important data concerning, not the sultan's own *madrasa*, but a much smaller institution dedicated to his wife.

The institution in question is a tomb (*turba*), built to house the body of the sultan's wife, whose name is given as Bustān bint 'Abd Allāh. Little is known of this woman. That her name is given as "bint 'Abd Allāh" probably indicates that she was in origin a slave. It is clear from the document that she and the sultan had children, and that he expected that she would survive him. I have not, however, found any further information concerning this woman in the standard narrative sources. The sources do refer to another of Ḥasan's wives, named Ṭūlubīya. She, too, had a tomb, one that was studied

al-Hay'a al-Miṣrīya al-'Āmma li'l-Kitāb, 1986), 3:341-449. H.N. Al-Harithy published a complete version of a copy of the original (DW 365/85) as *The Waqf Document of Sulṭān al-Nāṣir Ḥasan b. Muḥammad b. Qalāwūn for His Complex in al-Rumaila* (Beirut: Dār al-Kitāb al-'Arabī, 2001).

[16] See now A.M. Kahil, "The Sultan Ḥasan Complex in Cairo 1357-1364" (PhD dissertation, New York University, 2002).

[17] For a summary description of the school, its expenditures and curriculum, see Berkey, *Transmission of Knowledge*: 67-70 et passim.

[18] See M.M. Amīn, *Fihrist wathā'iq al-Qāhira ḥattā nihāyat 'aṣr salāṭīn al-mamālīk (239-922/853-1517)* (Cairo: Institut français d'archéologie orientale, 1981), no. 46 (hereafter DW 42/6). This *waqfīya* was studied by 'A.Ḥ. Zaghlūl in a master's thesis at Cairo University which was unavailable to me for this project. The deed is also summarized by M. Amīn in his appendix to *Tadhkirat al-nabīh*, 3:343.

by Aḥmad ʿAbd al-Rāziq.[19] Abdallah Kahil has suggested that Bustān and Ṭūlubīya were perhaps the same woman, although this is impossible to determine from the sources at hand.[20]

The endowment mixed charitable and private purposes, and so its deed made provisions for a wide range of expenditures. So, for example, it stipulates that a portion of the endowment's income be devoted to the "poor and unfortunate" (*al-fuqarā' wa'l-masākīn*) of Mecca and Medina. The remainder, however, was to go to Bustān herself—provided that she did not remarry after the death of Ḥasan. If she did remarry, the income from her share of the *waqf* was to be added to that supporting the sultan's own *madrasa*. What is of principal interest here, however, is what was to become of her share of the endowment's income were she to die without remarrying.

In such an event, the deed makes very precise stipulations concerning how that money was to be spent. Bustān's *turba* was to be the principal beneficiary. More precisely, a range of individuals serving that tomb were to receive monthly stipends to support their work. It is worth listing the various positions (*waẓā'if*, sing. *waẓīfa*), and the monthly salaries of those who held them, in some detail:[21]

(1) An *imām* (prayer leader) was to receive 40 dirhams per month "to lead the Muslims in the five prayers and as is customary during Ramadan."
(2) Two muezzins "of fine voice" were "to pronounce the call to prayer at the appointed times," for which they would receive 30 dirhams each.
(3) Twelve Quran readers, organized into six teams of two, were to read the Quran and pray for the sultan, his children and descendants, and for the Muslims generally throughout the day, for which each reader was to receive 40 dirhams.
(4) Two *bawwāb*s were to guard the *turba*'s gate and to prevent disreputable sorts (*arbāb al-tuham wa'l-fasād*) from entering it, for which they were to receive 40 dirhams each.
(5) Four men would undertake the task of lighting, extinguishing, and care of the lamps in the tomb, for 40 dirhams each.
(6) Two *farrāsh*s would sweep and clean the tomb, for 40 dirhams each.
(7) Two eunuchs, preferably chosen from among those belonging to Bustān, or to her children and descendants, were to guard the tomb itself for 60 dirhams each.

---

[19] A.ʿAbd Al-Rāziq, "Un mausolée feminine dans l'Égypte mamluke," *Journal of the Faculty of Archaeology* (Cairo University), 2 (1977): 3-9.
[20] Kahil, "The Sultan Ḥasan Complex:" 10, n. 22.
[21] These expenditures are outlined in lines 62-135 of the *waqfīya*, DW 42/6.

(8) A professor (*mudarris*) of *ḥadīth* would receive 70 dirhams, and each of five students 20 dirhams, to conduct a class in the Prophetic traditions "on every day on which it is usual to hold lessons," a class preceded by certain readings from the Quran and prayers on behalf of the sultan, his descendants, and all the Muslims.
(9) A shaykh would receive 40 dirhams per month, and a Quran reciter (*qāri'*) and a panegyrist (*mādiḥ*) 20 dirhams each, to meet every Tuesday and Friday, during which sessions the *qāri'* should read from the Quran, books of Quranic commentary (*tafsīr*) and *ḥadīth*, as well as books of edifying tales and homilies (*raqā'iq*), while the *mādiḥ* should recite panegyrics in praise of (*madā'iḥ*) the Prophet, after which the *qāri'* should pray for the sultan and his children and descendants and for all Muslims.
(10) A primary school instructor (*mu'addib*) was to receive 40 dirhams to teach the Quran and Arabic writing to twenty orphans in a *maktab* attached to the tomb. Each orphan was to receive 30 dirhams, half of which the controller (*nāẓir*) of the endowment was to retain to provide for their clothing.
(11) Ten of Bustān's female slaves were to take up residence at the tomb and receive stipends of 30 dirhams each, provided that they did not marry.

In addition, money was provided for carpets, candles, wages for water carriers, etc. Any remainder was to be distributed to the children and descendants of Bustān by her husband, and, after their demise, to the sultan's own *madrasa*.[22]

On one level, there is nothing extraordinary about these stipulations. They were typical of those outlined by the deeds of endowment establishing the many religious and educational institutions founded in Cairo during the Mamluk period. To be sure, this was a small institution. Most of the *madrasas* which historians have discussed in great detail provided for many more employees. Sultan Ḥasan's was the largest, but others too were considerably more substantial than that connected with Bustān's tomb. Among them was the *madrasa* of Ṣarghitmish, a powerful Mamluk *'amīr* whom Sultan Ḥasan, in fact, had arrested; his institution, not far from that of the sultan, supported a professor and sixty students of jurisprudence according to the Ḥanafī rite, as well as a professor and fifteen students of *ḥadīth*.[23] But the institutions in which the religious and legal sciences were taught varied widely, and quite a few matched the *turba* of

[22] DW 42/6, lines 135-67.
[23] Berkey, *Transmission of Knowledge*: 72.

Bustān in size and simplicity.[24] That this institution was called a *turba*, and not a *madrasa*, is of little consequence, since it was common for tombs to be attached to institutions of education, and there were in fact other establishments providing for instruction in one or more of the religious sciences that were routinely known as *turbas*.[25] In this respect the tomb of Sultan Ḥasan's wife was typical of many of the religious and educational institutions of the Mamluk era.

In another respect, however, the *turba* of Bustān is clearly distinguishable from the *madrasa* which her husband had founded in Rumayla just a few years earlier. There is first of all the obvious matter of size. Moreover, the salaries of the *turba*'s employees were fairly low, particularly for those among them who were presumably the most learned—that is, who were members of the *'ulamā'*. Its professor of *ḥadīth* was paid 70 dirhams per month. This contrasts sharply with the professor of *ḥadīth* at Sultan Ḥasan's *madrasa*, who received an emolument of 300 dirhams per month (although the thirty students of *ḥadīth* there received the same monthly stipend, 20 dirhams, as did the five students at Bustān's *turba*).[26] The comparative size and wealth of the institutions reflect the broader fact that the *madrasa* of sultan Ḥasan was much better known and, we might say now, more prestigious. The larger institution is mentioned frequently in the narrative sources, and we know a good deal about the scholars who taught in it. References to the *turba* of Bustān and those connected with it are largely missing from the historical record—because, presumably, no one thought it necessary to preserve their names for posterity.

What emerges most clearly from a consideration of Bustān's *turba* and the stipulations its endowment deed makes for the salaries of those who served in it, and from a comparison with the provisions made for other institutions, is the enormous range of positions that might be held by individuals who were members of the *'ulamā'*. Even leaving aside those holding what we might call menial posts—the *bawwāb*s and lamp-lighters of the *turba*—most of those receiving a stipend from the tomb's endowment fell within Lapidus's broad definition of the *'ulamā'*, which included "prayer-leaders, scholars, teachers, reciters of Koran, reciters of traditions, Sufis, functionaries of

---

[24] Ibid.: 74-5.

[25] Berkey, *Transmission of Knowledge*: 143-6.

[26] al-Harithy, *The Waqf Document of Sultan Ḥasan*: 153-4.

mosques, and so on." In Bustān's tomb, they served as professors and students, as Quran reciters, imams, muezzins. We may know little about the relatively obscure figures who held positions in such minor institutions, since the attention of the contemporary historians and biographers was focused on their more prominent peers, but they were there, and they were employed, and they therefore had a direct connection to and interest in the network of institutions and endowments that over the course of the Mamluk period were established to support the work of the *'ulamā'*.

Bustān bint 'Abd Allāh's tomb was only one of many such institutions spread across the medieval city of Cairo. We cannot be precise about the total numbers, either of comparable institutions or of those supported by them, but clearly the totals were large. And that, perhaps, is the most important point of all. The functionaries of institutions such as Bustān's were, in effect, the *hoi polloi* of the *'ulamā'*—not the most prominent or famous scholars, but individuals nonetheless personally and professionally committed to the transmission of religious knowledge that characterized the *'ulamā'*. Moreover, it must have been through them, rather than through their better-known peers, that many Muslims would have had contact with the world of religious learning. Through those contacts, the outlook and principles of the *'ulamā'* could be diffused widely among the urban population, encouraging the Muslim population generally to identify with the interests of the *'ulamā'* and to look to them for leadership. In other words, the power of the *'ulamā'* as a group rested as much on the presence of minor figures such as those who would have served in the tomb of Bustān as it did on the fame of those who held positions in wealthier and more prestigious institutions. If the *'ulamā'* as a group did indeed have a significant social role, if they served as notables within their local communities and as mediators between those communities and their political rulers, they did so in part because of institutions such as this humble tomb of an obscure wife of a failed Mamluk sultan.

Bibliography

'Abd al-Rāziq, A. "Un mausolée feminine dans l'Égypte mamluke," *Journal of the Faculty of Archaeology* (Cairo University), 2 (1977): 3-9.

Amīn, M.M. *al-Awqāf wa'l-ḥayāt al-ijtimā'īya fī Miṣr, 648-923/1250-1517*. Cairo: Dār al-Nahḍa al-'Arabīya, 1980.

———. *Fihrist wathā'iq al-Qāhira ḥattā nihāyat 'aṣr salāṭīn al-mamālīk (239-922/853-1517)*. Cairo: Institut français d'archéologie orientale, 1981.

Berkey, J. *The Transmission of Knowledge in Medieval Cairo: A Social History of Islamic Education*. Princeton: Princeton University Press, 1992.

Bulliet, R. *The Patricians of Nishapur: A Study in Medieval Islamic Social History*. Cambridge, Mass.: Harvard University Press, 1972.

Chamberlain, M. *Knowledge and Social Practice in Medieval Damascus, 1190-1350*. Cambridge: Cambridge University Press, 1994.

Ephrat, D. *A Learned Society in Transition: The Sunnī 'ulamā' of Eleventh-Century Baghdad*. Albany: SUNY Press, 2000.

Fernandes, L. *The Evolution of a Sufi Institution in Mamluk Egypt: The Khanqah*. Berlin: Klaus Schwarz, 1988.

Gibb, H. and Bowen, H. *Islamic Society and the West; a Study of the Impact of Western Civilization on Moslem Culture in the Near East*. London: Oxford University Press, 1967.

Goitein, S.D. *A Mediterranean Society: The Jewish Communities of the Arab World as Portrayed in the Documents of the Cairo Geniza*, volume 1: *Economic Foundations*. Berkeley: University of California Press, 1967.

al-Harithy, H.N. *The Waqf Document of Sulṭān al-Nāṣir Ḥasan b. Muḥammad b. Qalāwūn for His Complex in al-Rumaila*. Beirut: Dār al-Kitāb al-'Arabī, 2001.

Hourani, A. "Ottoman Reform and the Politics of Notables," in A. Hourani, *The Emergence of the Modern Middle East*. London: Macmillan, 1981: 36-66.

Ibn Ḥabīb. *Tadhkirat al-nabīh fī ayyām al-manṣūr wa-banīh*, 3 vols. Cairo: al-Hay'a al-Miṣrīya al-'Āmma li'l-Kitāb, 1986.

Ibn Ḥishām, *Sīra al-Nabawīya*, edited by al-Saqqā, M., et. al. Cario, 1955.

Kahil, A.M. "The Sultan Ḥasan Complex in Cairo 1357-1364." PhD dissertation, New York University, 2002.

Lapidus, I.M. *Muslim Cities in the Later Middle Ages*. Cambridge, Mass.: Harvard University Press, 1967.

Makdisi, G. *The Rise of Colleges: Institutions of Learning in Islam and the West*. Edinburgh: Edinburgh University Press, 1981.

Marmon, S. *Eunuchs and Sacred Boundaries in Islamic Society*. New York and Oxford: Oxford University Press, 1995.

Mottahedeh, R., Review of Richard Bulliet, *The Patricians of Nishapur: A Study in Medieval Islamic Social History*, in the *Journal of the American Oriental Society*, 95:3 (1975): 491-95.

Pedersen, J. *The Arabic Book*. Princeton: Princeton University Press, 1984.

Petry, C.F. *The Civilian Elite of Cairo in the Later Middle Ages*. Princeton: Princeton University Press, 1981.

———. *Protectors or Praetorians? The Last Mamluk Sultans and Egypt's Waning as a Great Power*. Albany: SUNY Press, 1994.

al-Qalqashandī, A.b.'Ali, *Ṣubḥ al-a'shā fī ṣinā'at al-inshā'*, 14 vols. Cairo: al-Mu'assasa al-Miṣrīyah al-'Āmma li'l-Ta'līf wa'l-Tarjama wa'l-Ṭibā'a wa'l-Nashr, 1964.

Rosenthal, F. *Knowledge Triumphant: The Concept of Knowledge in Medieval Islam*. Leiden: E. J. Brill, 1970.

Sabra, A. *Poverty and Charity in Medieval Islam: Mamluk Egypt, 1250-1517*. Cambridge: Cambridge University Press, 2000.

THE ARABIAN SILENT TRADE: PROFIT AND NOBILITY IN THE "MARKETS OF THE ARABS"

Michael Bonner

In commercial law, as in other areas, Islamic jurists sought precedent in the practices of the Prophet Muḥammad and of those around him. At times, however, when the jurists considered the ways in which commerce must *not* be conducted, they looked back to *jāhilīya*, the "age of uncouth ignorance" in Arabia before Islam. And there they identified and described a commerce conducted under restrictions that to us now may appear rather strange. One peculiarity of this *jāhilī* trade, as we find it in texts from the Islamic period, is that it is often conducted in silence or in secret. To understand this, I will look beyond pre-Islamic Arabia for parallels, especially the "silent trade" described over many centuries by historians, travelers and ethnographers throughout much of the Old World. Many of these descriptions of "silent trade" have a mythical character; at any rate, they cannot simply be accepted as literal descriptions of real-life practices. Nonetheless, there are reasons why, in certain contexts, trade may well have been conducted in silence. In the case of pre-Islamic Arabia, a key to understanding the silence and secrecy of the marketplace turns out to be the notion of "profit," which we know from Avram Udovitch's indispensable study. Here I will situate this "profit" within a broader argument regarding nobility and political networks throughout the Arabian peninsula just before the rise of Islam.[1]

Forms and Methods of Sale in Pre-Islamic Arabia

Arabic prose narratives tell us a certain amount about the markets of Yathrib (Medina) just before and after the arrival of Muḥammad

[1] I wish to thank the Institute for the Humanities at the University of Michigan, where I first encountered the "Markets of the Arabs." I also wish to thank Robert Haug for his collaboration on this project, including the accompanying map; and David Eisenberg for an illuminating critique of an earlier version.

and Islam.[2] Otherwise, however, information on the forms and methods of sale in pre-Islamic Arabia is scarce. The poets may mention markets here and there,[3] but they have little to say about the techniques of selling. The sixth-century Byzantine historians Procopius and Menander also provide bits of information.[4] The fourth/tenth-century author Abū 'l-Faraj al-Iṣfahānī mentions pre-Islamic markets fairly often in his monumental *Book of Songs* (*Kitāb al-Aghānī*), but gives few details about how business was actually conducted there. On the whole, the harvest is meager.

Most of the information we have on pre-Islamic Arabian markets comes in Islamic juridical works and *ḥadīth*, which describe old, obsolete forms of "*jāhilī* sale" and contrast them unfavorably with Islamic law in this area. However, while these recollections are interesting, it is difficult to test them against other evidence. After all, whenever this topic comes up (which is not very often), writers and speakers are likely to refer to these very same foundational texts of Islamic law. And within these juridical and *ḥadīth* texts, the information on "*jāhilī* sale" tends to be sparse and vague. What is certain is that these legal texts and *ḥadīth* condemn the commercial practices of ancient Arabia because of the *gharar*, the indeterminate or aleatory element, that used to permeate them. Indeed, from this later, Islamic perspective, those *jāhilī* forms of sale amounted to little more than games of chance or bets.[5]

The Islamic juridical sources identify either two or three forms of "*jāhilī* sale," namely sale by touching (*mulāmasa*); sale by casting (*munābadha*); and, less often, sale by hurling a stone (*al-ramy bi'l-ḥaṣāt*). All three forms are said to have been prohibited by the Prophet himself.[6]

---

[2] M.J. Kister, "The Market of the Prophet," *Journal of the Economic and Social History of the Orient* (*JESHO*) 8 (1965): 272-6, repr. in *Studies in Jahiliyya and Early Islam* (Alsdershot: Ashgate, 1980); M. Lecker, "On the Markets of Medina (Yathrib) in Pre-Islamic and Early Islamic Times," *Jerusalem Studies in Arabic and Islam* (*JSAI*) 8 (1986): 133-47.

[3] R. Blachère, *Histoire de la littérature arabe* (Paris: Maisonneuve, 1952-66), 2:385 (a poem of Huṭay'a).

[4] I. Kawar (Shahid), "The Arabs in the Peace Treaty of A.D. 561," *Arabica* 3 (1956): 181-213.

[5] D. Santillana, *Istituzioni di diritto musulmano malichita* (Rome: Istituto per l'Oriente, 1926-38), 2:120.

[6] Other condemned forms of sale include *muḥāqala* and *mukhāḍara*: see S. al-Afghānī, *Aswāq al-'Arab fī l-jāhilīya wa'l-Islām* (Damascus: Dār al-Fikr, 1960):

"Sale by touch," *mulāmasa*, is defined as what happens when someone buys an item of merchandise after simply touching it, without having looked at it, unfolded it, or otherwise examined it. Here the buyer's choice is constricted and his agreement is based on imperfect knowledge; according to Islamic law, the sale is aleatory and invalid. This understanding of *mulāmasa* is often followed by another one, namely that the act of touching the object constitutes, in and of itself, the bargain or sale. Thus one says: "Once you touch [this] item, you have bought it." A third view, which occurs less often, is that *mulāmasa* was a practice whereby a prospective buyer touched an object, and as a consequence no one else was allowed to bid for it: an early version of our "setting aside" or "putting on hold." The seventh/twelfth-century Syrian scholar al-Nawawī provides a handy summary of these three "interpretations."[7]

In the lawbooks, this pre-Islamic "sale by touching," *mulāmasa*, is always discussed together with "sale by casting," *munābadha*.[8] Here the item for sale is cast or thrown, often by the seller at the buyer, an odd procedure for which no coherent reason is ever given. Even more bizarrely, the casting is sometimes described as a reciprocal activity, with both parties hurling garments at one other. As in the case of *mulāmasa*, it is also said that the act of casting the item may constitute the sale in itself.

Some jurists and lexicographers found this *munābadha* baffling and connected it, quite sensibly, to another form of *jāhilī* sale which is mentioned occasionally in the Islamic lawbooks, namely "casting a pebble or stone." Some of these authors further maintained that these two forms were identical: in other words, that what was going

46-58. However, within the juridical literature these forms of sale are not associated consistently with pre-Islamic Arabia.

[7] al-Nawawī, *Ṣaḥīḥ Muslim bi-sharḥ al-Nawawī* (Beirut: Dar Iḥyā' al-Turāth al-'Arabī, 1984), 10:155. Ibn Qudāma, *al-Mughnī* (Cairo: Dar al-Manār, 1367/1948), 4:207-08, provides a longer summary of the *fiqh* on this question; see also al-Muṭarrizī, *al-Mughrib fi tartīb al-mu'rib* (Beirut: Maktabat Lubnān, 1999): 232. For the *ḥadīth*, with early juridical discussions, see 'Abd al-Razzāq, *al-Muṣannaf* (Beirut: al-Maktab al-Islāmī, 1983-87), 8:226-9, nos. 14987-14992; Mālik, *Muwaṭṭa'* (Beirut: Dār al-Gharb al-Islāmī, 1996), 2:196-8, Buyū' 35; al-Bukhārī, *Ṣaḥīḥ* (Leiden: E. J. Brill, 1862-1908), 2:25-6, Buyū' 62-3; Muslim, *Ṣaḥīḥ*, Buyū' 1-3, in al-Nawawī, *op. cit.*, 10:154-5; Abū Dā'ūd, *Sunan* (Cairo: Maṭba'at al-Sa'āda, 1369/1950), 3:346-7, Buyū' 25; further references at Wensinck, *Concordance et indices de la tradition musulmane* (Leiden: E. J. Brill, 1992), 6:146-7, 342.

[8] The references in the previous note therefore apply here as well.

on in *munābadha*, "casting," was really the casting of pebbles or stones. Here again, al-Nawawī identifies three "interpretations."[9]

> The first interpretation is, "I'll throw the stone and sell you whichever one of these garments it lands upon," or similarly, "I'll sell you some of this land, as far as this stone reaches [when I throw it]." The second interpretation is that one says, "I'll sell it to you on condition that you are allowed to exercise choice [in the matter only] until I throw this stone." The third interpretation is that the two parties make the very act of throwing the stone [constitutive of] the sale: thus one would say, "When I throw the rock at this garment, then it is sold to you."

These are, in brief summary, the ways in which sale by touching and casting are construed within Islamic law. It is noteworthy, however, that when the jurists set about interpreting these practices, they tend to go in quite different directions. Some of these interpretations are also difficult to square with the foundational texts of *ḥadīth* on which they are based, such as the following tradition which was transmitted in Mecca:[10]

> Muslim—Muḥammad b. Rāfiʿ—ʿAbd al-Razzāq—Ibn Jurayj—ʿAmr b. Dīnār—ʿAṭāʾ b. Mīnāʾ—Abū Hurayra, who said: "Two kinds of sale have been forbidden, namely *mulāmasa* and *munābadha*. As for *mulāmasa*, it occurs when each of the two parties touches the other's garment, without considering [or examining].[11] *Munābadha* takes place when each of them throws his garment at the other, without either of them looking at the other's garment."

It is difficult to understand why the two parties touch each other's garments or hurl them at each other. If one is a buyer and the other a seller, what is the point of these reciprocal actions? Another problem regards the merchandise: it appears here that what is for sale is the clothing—their *own* clothing that they are wearing at the moment—that the two parties touch or hurl.[12] Some legal texts

---

[9] al-Nawawī, *Sharḥ*, 10:156. For the identity of *munābadha* and *al-ramy bi'l-ḥaṣat*, see al-Muṭarrizī, *Mughrib*, 232.

[10] al-Nawawī, *Sharḥ*, 10:154-5. The *ḥadīth* occurs elsewhere, including ʿAbd al-Razzāq, *Muṣannaf*, 8:228, no. 14991, *Bāb bayʿ al-munābadha wal-mulāmasa*.

[11] Note the lack of grammatical object after "considering," *bi-ghayr taʾammul*. ʿAbd al-Razzāq's version has an implied object: "without unfolding [the garment]," *bi-ghayr nashr*.

[12] In a possible parallel in Japan, a group of Ainu trading with the Japanese in the seventh century sent old men who examined the "colored silk stuffs and other articles which had been piled up," and then "changed the single garments they had on, each taking up one piece of cloth in his hand, went on board their ship and departed. Presently the old men came back again, took off the exchanged garments, and laying

understand the situation in precisely this way, and relate it to a scenario of barter exchange, whereby both parties strip off their robes and swap them, sight unseen.[13] This, however, is a procedure of doubtful utility, especially in a large marketplace. The overall result is obscurity and confusion. For the Muslim jurists, in any case, the main lesson of all this is that any sale that takes place "without examination and mutual consent" must be condemned.[14]

The Tradition on the Markets

We have noted that information on pre-Islamic Arabian commerce is scarce, apart from these juridical and *ḥadīth* texts. However, it turns out that there is another source of information on this topic. This is a narrative tradition on "the markets of the Arabs before Islam" (*aswāq al-ʿArab qabla ʾl-Islām*) which appears in several literary sources, beginning in the third/ninth century.[15] This narrative tradition describes a sequence of markets held every year, moving in a clockwise spiral throughout the entire peninsula. According to its internal evidence, the tradition refers to the situation in Arabia around the turn of the seventh century CE.[16] Before we discuss what it says about forms and methods of trade, we may briefly outline its contents.

---

them down along with the cloth they had taken away, went on board their ship and departed...." W.G. Aston, trans., *Hinongi: Chronicles of Japan from the Earliest Times to A.D. 697* (Tokyo: Charles, E.T, 1972): 2:264, cited by S. Kurimoto, *Silent Trade in Japan*, in *Research in Economic Anthropology*, vol. 3, ed. G. Dalton (Greenwich: JAI Press, 1980), 100.

[13] Mālik, *Muwaṭṭa'*, 2:197, Buyūʿ 35, no. 1948 (on the sole authority of Mālik), "each says to the other, '[let's exchange] this for that'" (*hādhā bi-hādhā*). Cf. Santillana, *Istituzioni*, 2:121.

[14] al-Nawawī, *Sharḥ*, 10:155; Ibn Qudāma, *Mughnī*, 4:208.

[15] Ibn Ḥabīb, *Kitāb al-Muḥabbar* (Hyderabad: Dāʾirat al-Maʿārif al-ʿUthmānīya, 1941): 263-8; al-Yaʿqūbī, *Taʾrīkh* (Beirut, 1960), 1:270-1; al-Marzūqī, *Kitāb al-Azmina wa'l-amkina* (Hyderabad: Dāʾirat al-Maʿārif, 1914), 2:161-70; A.Ḥ. al-Tawḥīdī, *Kitāb al-imtāʿ wa'l-muʾānasa* (Beirut: Dār Maktabat al-Ḥāyat, 1965), 1:83-94; al-Baghdādī, *Khizānat al-adab* (Beirut: Dār al-Kutub al-ʿIlmīya, 1967), 4:431-2; al-Qalqashandī, *Ṣubḥ al-aʿshā* (Cairo: al-Muʾassasa al-Miṣrīya al-ʿĀmma li'l-Taʾlīf wa'l-Tarjama wa'l-Ṭibāʿa wa'l-Nashr, 1964), 1:410-11.

[16] I discuss the tradition more fully in two forthcoming articles, "The Tradition on the Markets of the Arabs," and "'Time Has Come Full Circle': Markets, Fairs and the Calendar in Arabia before Islam."

The yearly sequence began in Dūmat al-Jandal, in north central Arabia.[17] The Arabs came there "from all directions" and stayed for varying amounts of time, after which "they went their various ways to other markets like it." Dūmat al-Jandal had characteristics that set it apart from the other markets in the sequence. One of these was its disputed political sovereignty. Dūma lay near or along the desert frontier between the Byzantine and Sasanian empires. Arab clients of the two empires made claim to it and worked out their rivalry in rather strange ways.[18] The winning "king" had the right to take customs dues or tithes from the market, and to sell goods there before anyone else could do so. Another peculiarity was Dūma's specialization in slavery and prostitution: we are told that "most of the Arabs there were slaves" (*qinn*) and that people there "used to force their slave girls into prostitution."[19]

The next market in the sequence took place at al-Mushaqqar in the region of Hajar, not far from the coast of the Gulf.[20] This territory fell under the dominion or protectorate of the Persian Sasanian Empire. The Sasanian rulers appointed "governors" from a local Arab dynasty, the Banū ʿAbdallāh b. Zayd of the clan of al-Mundhir b. Sāwī, of Tamīm. These Arab rulers of al-Mushaqqar, like those of Dūma, had free rein in the market, taking customs dues (*mukūs*) or tithes (*ʿushūr*) for themselves. We are also told that caravans arrived at al-Mushaqqar bearing aromatics from South Arabia, and that "the Persians would come there, crossing the sea with their merchandise." Mushaqqar is described as "such a lovely land that no one who saw it could stay away," so that it "acquired [population] from every clan of the Arabs and even from non-Arabs."

Ṣuḥār and Dabā were the next stops, in ʿUmān on the Gulf coast below the Straits of Hurmuz.[21] Here we have another Arab dynastic

---

[17] On Dūma, al-Bakrī, *Muʿjam mā istaʿjam* (Beirut: Dār al-Kutub al-ʿIlmīya, 1998), 2:182; Yāqūt, *Muʿjam al-buldān* (Beirut: Dār Ṣādir, 1955-7), 2:487-9; Afghānī, *Aswāq*, 232-9; *EI*[2], s.v. "Dūmat al-Djandal" (L.V. Vaglieri), 2:624-6.

[18] Ibn Ḥabīb, *Muḥabbar*, 263-4, a riddle contest; al-Marzūqī, *Azmina*: 2:161, apparently has them playing hide-and-seek.

[19] al-Marzūqī, *Azmina*, 2:162, *Kānū yukrihūna fatayātihim ʿalā 'l-bighā'*, echoing Quran 24: 33, "Do not force your maidservants into prostitution if they desire chastity." See also al-Afghānī, *Aswāq*: 236-7.

[20] al-Bakrī, *Muʿjam*, 4:97; Yāqūt, *Muʿjam*, 5:134-5, citing Ibn al-Faqīh. See also al-Afghānī, *Aswāq*: 197-9, 240-51; *EI*[2], s.v. "al-Mushaḳḳar" (C.E. Bosworth), 7:671.

[21] al-Muqaddasī, *Aḥsan al-taqāsīm* (Leiden: E. J. Brill, 1967): 70-1, 92-3; Yāqūt, *Muʿjam*, 2:435, 3:394; al-Afghānī, *Aswāq*: 261-5.

ruler, al-Julandā, appointed or confirmed by the Sasanians, and taking tithes or customs dues from the markets. At Ṣuḥār, the tradition tells of local Arabian wares. At Dabā, we have the arrival of "the merchants of India and Sind...also of China and the people of the East."

Next came al-Shiḥr, on the coast of Ḥaḍramawt. Since al-Shiḥr was not under the control of any king or polity (*arḍ mumlaka*), visitors there had to "seek the protection" of the Banū Yathrib, a fraction (*taqallul*) of the dominant clan in the area, the Banū Mahra. Items of commerce included tanned hides, fabrics and other goods probably meant for local distribution; and frankincense, myrrh and other aromatics, destined for markets far away.

Then came the market of ʿAdan (Aden), described by the geographer al-Hamdānī as "foremost of the markets of the Arabs."[22] Unlike al-Shiḥr, Aden was "territory under rule and jurisdiction" (*arḍ mumlaka wa-amr muḥkam*): formerly that of the kings of Ḥimyar and more recently, of the *abnāʾ*, the Arabized Persians who ruled Yemen after them. This ruling elite is praised, especially for its abstaining from participation in the market.[23] Commodities here included perfumes which were then transported overland to Persia and Byzantium. After Aden came Ṣanʿāʾ in central Yemen,[24] where many products were traded, including cotton, saffron, dyestuffs and iron. The political regime of Ṣanʿāʾ was similar to Aden's. Next came Rābiya, now impossible to locate,[25] but somewhere in the mountains of Ḥaḍramawt, beyond the control of any ruler or state. As at al-Shiḥr, those who went to Rābiya had to seek the protection of a local clan, the Āl Masrūq b. Wāʾil al-Ḥaḍramī.

ʿUkāẓ, the culminating point in the cycle, receives more attention than any other market. Pre-Islamic ʿUkāẓ had no fixed site, and may have changed place from year to year.[26] ʿUkāẓ lay beyond anyone's

---

[22] al-Hamdānī, *Ṣifat Jazīrat al-ʿArab* (Leiden: E. J. Brill, 1881-1903): 53. See also Yāqūt, *Muʿjam*, 4:89-90; al-Afghānī, *Aswāq*: 268-70.

[23] al-Afghānī, *Aswāq*: 270, thinks that this abstention on the part of the *abnāʾ* had the result of making the ʿAdan market "freer" than those of Dūma and Ṣuḥār.

[24] al-Bakrī, *Muʿjam*, 3:118-19; Yāqūt, *Muʿjam*, 3:425-31; al-Afghānī, *Aswāq*: 271-4.

[25] Rābiya is not mentioned in any geographical source of which I am aware. Al-Afghānī, *Aswāq*: 275-6, describes it as a "local market," but without citing evidence.

[26] Kh. al-Muaikel, "Sūq ʿUkāẓ in al-Ṭāʾif: Archaeological Survey of an Islamic Site," *al-ʿUṣūr al-Wusṭā* 7.1 (1995): 1-7. On the fair of ʿUkāẓ, see al-Bakrī, 3:218-21;

control, imposing "neither tithes nor protection."[27] In other words, it had no greedy "kings" and no extorting tribesmen. The tradition on the markets makes little mention of commercial transactions at ʿUkāẓ. Instead, this was an occasion for giving gifts (see below) and a pan-Arab peace. Here the Arabs formed alliances and marriages, were alerted to the presence of traitors,[28] and instigated wars. After ʿUkāẓ came Majanna and Dhū ʾl-Majāz, located just to the west. These provided a link to the yearly pilgrimage. It seems, in fact, that ʿUkāẓ, Majanna and Dhū ʾl-Majāz together formed what amounted to a large, single fair. Finally, the different versions of the tradition on the markets disagree on the end of the sequence. The most plausible version is that of Ibn Ḥabīb,[29] who has it conclude in central Arabia, at Nuṭāt Khaybar,[30] and then in Ḥajr of al-Yamāma,[31] the very heart of Arabia.

Forms and Techniques of Trade in the "Markets of the Arabs"

Within this sequence, the tradition on the markets describes several forms and methods of sale. On analysis, these boil down to three main categories. One of these, mentioned for Dabā, is *musāwama*, "bargaining," "haggling," "negotiating a price." This is just the sort of activity that Islamic law would later expect and encourage,[32] and at the time it was already the norm in the Byzantine and Sasanian empires, and no doubt also in much of Arabia. The other two methods of sale described in the tradition correspond to what we have

---

Yāqūt, 4:142; Wellhausen, *Reste arabischen Heidentums* (Berlin, 1897): 88-91; al-Afghānī, *Aswāq*: 277-343.

27 al-Marzūqī, *Azmina*, 2:165.

28 al-Marzūqī, *Azmina*, 2:170.

29 Ibn Ḥabīb, *Muḥabbar*: 268.

30 Yāqūt, *Muʿjam*, 5:291, has difficulty identifying Nuṭāt Khaybar, saying that it refers to a fortification (*ḥiṣn*) in Khaybar, or alternatively, a spring which watered palm groves and villages.

31 al-Hamdānī, *Ṣifat*: 139, 153-4, 180; *EI*², s.v."al-Yamāma" (G.R. Smith), 11:269. Ḥajr al-Yamāma should not be confused with Hajar (the region where al-Mushaqqar was located) or with al-Ḥijr (Madāʾin Ṣāliḥ), in northwestern Arabia.

32 Mālik, *Muwaṭṭaʾ*, 2:216-18, Buyūʿ 45, nos. 1994-8, *mā yunhā ʿanhu min al-musāwama waʾl-mubāyaʿa*, condemns certain activities such as bargaining before the caravan has arrived at the market. Bargaining in itself is permitted and expected, as when Mālik says (no. 1996), "There is nothing wrong with bargaining over merchandise for sale that is set up on display, [so long as] more than one person can bargain for it."

already seen in Islamic law, namely sale by touching, and sale by casting stones.

Sale by touching is mentioned in passing for Ṣanʿāʾ, and described more fully for al-Mushaqqar. We should remember that al-Mushaqqar was a place where people arrived from all over Arabia and beyond in order to trade and even, in some cases, to settle down.

> They used to sell there by touching [one another] with their hands (*mulāmasa*), by murmuring and grunting (*hamhama*), and by moving their heads (*īmāʾ*) as they gestured at one another. In this way they would conduct their business without speaking, until they had reached a bargain. This was so that none of the parties could make a false oath, by asserting that the owner of the merchandise had agreed to a deal (*an yazʿuma annahu badhala lahu ṣāḥib al-silʿa*).[33]

Nothing here suggests that the buyer may not view, unfold, or otherwise examine the merchandise. Instead, the underlying principle is that bargaining must be conducted in silence. This technique is thought to protect participants from fraud and false oaths. If we are looking for a functionalist basis for this practice, then this attempt to avoid false oaths does indeed seem like a compelling rationale. At the same time, these ways of business also seem to have a certain ritualistic character. At any rate, we can confirm that here the parties to the transaction do not touch the merchandise, as they do in the *mulāmasa* described in Islamic law. Instead they touch one another.

We find "casting stones" in the tradition on the markets at Dūmat al-Jandal, Ṣuḥār and al-Shiḥr, described in more detail than it is in books of Islamic law and *ḥadīth*.

> The way they did commerce in [Dūma] was by casting stones, namely, that a group of them would gather around an item for sale, bargaining over it with its owner. Whenever one of them was content [with the price], he would cast a stone. It might happen that several of them would decide [to purchase] the same item of merchandise, and in that case they might find no alternative to sharing [it], even if they were unwilling to do so. And it might happen that they all cast their stones at the same time. In that case, if they made common cause against the item's owner, they might compel him to accept a low price.[34]

---

[33] al-Marzūqī, *Azmina*, 2:162. Ibn Ḥabīb, *Muḥabbar*: 265, has: "The purpose of the murmuring was to avoid false oaths from any of them, in case the purchaser claimed he had changed his mind," *annahu qad badā lahu*.

[34] al-Marzūqī, *Azmina*, 2:162, *fa-yūkisūna ṣāḥib al-silʿa idhā taẓāharū ʿalayhi*; Ibn Ḥabīb, *Muḥabbar*: 265.

Al-Nawawī's third interpretation of sale by casting stones (see above) comes closest to this description: the act of casting the stone constitutes the sale, like the handshake in Islamic law. Note, however, that the buyers can get the better of the seller, especially when they join forces against him. This transaction, as described here, does seem constrained, and from the perspective of Islamic law there is good reason for condemning it.

Now we may outline a possible trajectory over time of these forms of sale. In pre-Islamic Arabia, as reported in the tradition on the markets, one method of concluding a sale was to do it non-verbally, with gestures, murmuring, and touching, perhaps using a system of sign language of which we have no further record. "Touching," *mulāmasa*, here meant touching the other person's arm or tugging at his clothing, and did not mean touching the object of sale. After the coming of Islam, there was a recollection that *mulāmasa* used to involve a mutual touching of the parties during their negotiations. Soon, however, the original context—the silence imposed on these transactions—became obscure, and all that remained was a memory of the gesture of touching. At first tentatively, and then with increasing confidence, it was stated that the touching and negotiation had all been directed at the object of sale. It was also stated that in the pre-Islamic marketplace, the buyer had been allowed only to touch this object, and that he had been forbidden to view, unfold, or otherwise examine it.

Meanwhile, there was also a method of sale that involved casting pebbles or stones, a way of signaling agreement to a bargain. Like sale by touching, this method compelled (or allowed) the participants to retain a degree of silence. Here again, the original context became obscure in early Islamic legal texts, while the stones became lost to memory and only the gesture of throwing remained. Now it was thought that the two parties used to throw the object of sale at one another, and—in accordance with the parallel practice of *mulāmasa*—that this object of sale was the very garment that they had on their backs at that moment. *Mulāmasa* and *munābadha*, always considered together, thus became reduced to the absurd image of two men in a busy marketplace, doffing their robes and swapping them, sight unseen.

With the passage of time, the context and meaning of sale by touching and casting became ever more obscure. For the jurists, however, the point of all this had to do with the indeterminate, aleatory element of *gharar*, the rejection of which is a fundamental principle for the Islamic law of sale. Their insistence on this principle came together with a forgetting of much of the old practice, and a misreading of what they did remember. The result was the rather incoherent construction of "*jāhilī* sale" that we find in classical Islamic law.[35]

Silent Trade

What these practices of trade by casting stones, tugging at clothing, gesturing, murmuring, grunting and the like all have in common is that they impose silence or near-silence on the parties to the transaction. Anyone who has been to a market anywhere knows that silence on these occasions goes against the grain of basically the entire human race. However, there are many examples, from many times and places, of something that the ethnographic literature calls "silent trade." The most famous, and earliest example comes in Herodotus's account of the activity of Carthaginian traders somewhere on the coast of West Africa.

> The Carthaginians also tell us that they trade with a race of men who live in a part of Libya beyond the Pillars of Heracles. On reaching this country, they unload their goods, arrange them tidily along the beach, and then, returning to their boats, raise a smoke. Seeing the smoke, the natives come down to the beach, place on the ground a certain quantity of gold in exchange for the goods, and go off again to a distance. The Carthaginians then come ashore and take a look at the gold; and if they think it represents a fair price for their wares, they collect it and go away; if, on the other hand, it seems too little, they go back on board and wait, and the natives come and add to the gold until they are satisfied. There is perfect honesty on both sides; the Carthaginians never touch the gold until it equals in value what they have offered for sale, and the natives never touch the goods until the gold has been taken away.[36]

A similar practice is attested by the tenth-century Arabic writer al-Masʿūdī, regarding exchanges between Muslim North Africans

[35] If this argument is correct, then the tradition on the markets represents historical reality more closely than do the accounts of the matter in Islamic law. I think this is so, even though the tradition on the markets was subject to the vagaries of literary transmission, just like any other narrative. See "The Tradition on the Markets of the Arabs."

[36] Herodotus, *Histories*, 4:196; trans. A. de Sélincourt (Hammondsworth: Penguin, 1996): 336.

and people "on the other side of the great river," in a "land of gold" beyond Sijilmāsa. Al-Mas'ūdī also describes silent trade of this kind at the other end of the known world, "in the most remote region of Khurāsān, at the limits of the country inhabited by the Turks," practiced by a people who also "live on the banks of an immense river."[37] Ibn Baṭṭūṭa in the early fourteenth century likewise describes a people inhabiting a region forty days beyond the Volga Bulgars, in an ice-bound "land of darkness." Here the traveler deposits his goods and waits for the natives to leave their furs. If he is satisfied, he takes the furs and leaves. Otherwise he waits, and the inhabitants then either add more furs, or take away their goods and leave the merchant's goods untouched. "Those who go there do not know whom they are trading with or whether they be *jinn* or men, for they never see anyone."[38]

Silent trade along these lines—what we will call here the "classic" or "pure" silent trade—is attested in many other places in historical and ethnographical literature.[39] In the descriptions that we have of it, it tends to be highly organized; it does not permit face-to-face contact or bodily gestures between trading partners; it involves a step-by-step, turn-by-turn process of iteration; and it includes no third-party mechanism to govern the transaction.[40] Moreover, this "classic" or "pure" silent trade occurs during contacts between groups separated by high barriers of language and culture. More precisely, it seems to be typical of contacts between inhabitants of city-states, empires or kingdoms (Carthaginians, Chinese, subjects of the Caliphate and its successor states) and people living in tribes or bands. According to John Price, it was preferred and, in effect, imposed by the "civilized" merchants, since it allowed them to avoid the ceremonies and gift-giving that accompany exchanges with

---

[37] al-Mas'ūdī, *Murūj al-dhahab*, ed. C. Pellat (Beirut: Manshūrāt al-Jāmi'a al-Lubnānīya, 1965-79), 2:408, § 1420.

[38] Ibn Baṭṭūṭa, *Travels in Asia and Africa, 1325-1354*, translated by H.A.R. Gibb (London: Routledge, 1929): 151; J.A. Price, "On Silent Trade," in *Research in Economic Anthropology*, vol. 3, ed. G. Dalton (Greenwich: JAI Press, 1980): 77.

[39] The classic study in English is P.J.H.Grierson, "The Silent Trade" (Edinburgh: W. Green and Son, 1903), repr. in *Research in Economic Anthropology*, vol. 3, ed. G. Dalton (Greenwich: JAI Press, 1980). Objections and corrections to Grierson are summarized in Price, "On Silent Trade" (see previous note). See also K. Polanyi, "Ports of Trade in Early Societies," *Journal of Economic History* 23 (1963): 30-45; A.H. David, "Trade, Language and Communication" (http://www.nyu.edu/econ/dept/austrian/Trade&Comm.pdf, Dec. 14, 2004): esp. 52-69.

[40] David, "Trade, Language and Communication": 56-60.

"primitive" peoples.[41] However that may be, silent trade of this kind was reported "on the remote fringes of civilization in the Old World, northern Siberia, northern Europe, a broad zone across Africa, and Southeast Asia, and beyond that fringe, rarely or not at all.[42] In the New World it apparently did not occur, at least not in this form.[43]

Here we may pause and take some distance. All these examples of silent trade, beginning with Herodotus, are reported as hearsay: "the Carthaginians tell us," "they say," "it is said," and so on. Reliable eyewitnesses are scarce or nonexistent. For these and other reasons, anthropologists now discuss this topic less than they did a few decades ago, and when they do so, it is often to express skepticism.[44] After all, this "classic" silent trade may well be a myth of the frontier: out there where civilization and Empire come to an end, relations with the barbarians assume this reassuring form, which emphasizes our common humanity, while still furthering the interests of civilization and Empire. Even if this is so, however, it is still remarkable that the idea (or myth) of "silent trade" should be shared so widely, in so many languages and across such extents of time and space.

The "classic" form of silent trade that we have been discussing until now—described in Herodotus, al-Masʿūdī and so on—has generally been considered as the "true" or "pure" type.[45] But in fact, we can identify a broad spectrum of situations in which trading and marketplaces have been—and are—conducted in silence. The "classic, pure" silent trade is only one of these. The most widespread and familiar practice is the "dumb barter" which occurs between individuals who are separated by high barriers of language and culture. Many of us have practiced this, when traveling, by using gestures and sign language in order to make a purchase or trade. In more technical terms, dumb barter involves pointing (indexical representa-

---

[41] Price, "On Silent Trade": 90. "Silent trade was an exchange that was in many ways the opposite of the usual primitive trade...an almost exclusively utilitarian exchange, something that was very unusual to the primitive and favored by the long distance trader."

[42] Price, "On Silent Trade": 93.

[43] Price, "On Silent Trade": 77, 93, thinks this is because the New World had less social differentiation than the Old.

[44] L. Vajda, "'Stummer Handel' im alten Afrika?" in *Mundus Africanus... Festschrift für Karl-Ferdinand Schaedler*, ed. A. Roehreke: 173-8 (Rahden: Verlag Marie Leidorf, 2000).

[45] Price, "On Silent Trade": 75, criticizes Grierson for imprecision, especially for including too many "peripheral forms": "It is not uncommon to barter without words, and silent trade is different from just that."

tion) and mimicry (iconic representation), with all the ambiguities and misunderstandings these can lead to.[46] Dumb barter is attested for many situations, including early contacts between European explorers and the natives of the Pacific and the Americas. In the modern literature, this activity of dumb barter has been characterized as "utilitarian," a way of allowing both parties to satisfy their needs as efficiently as possible.[47]

Between or beyond these extremes of "pure," collective silent trade and "utilitarian," individualistic dumb barter, trading without words or sounds has been reported and described in a variety of circumstances. For instance, it may be that silence in the marketplace helped to create an "institutional island of neutrality" between states or peoples, similar to the "port of trade" that (according to Polanyi and his disciples) was characteristic of more developed commerce, and perhaps it was indeed used to avoid costly, time-consuming contacts with tribal peoples.[48] Another reason could be the desire of a royal or religious establishment to impose order and awe on the marketplace, while taking a share of the proceeds for itself. According to Theophrastus (371-286 BCE) this is what happened in the ancient South Arabian monarchy of Saba: myrrh and frankincense were sold in the temple of the sun according to a technique approaching that of "pure" silent trade—with the parties organized in groups, and with no visual or other contact between them—and with a third of the price levied as a tax for the god.[49] Yet another reason for observing silence could be the desire of individuals, especially in a tribal society, to avoid direct communication in order to maintain status, to avoid shame, or something of the sort. These individuals would need to have recourse to third parties in order to transact their business; and so we may find, in these cases, an intermediary figure who may also be described as a kind of merchant. Transactions along these lines

[46] Harper, "Trade, Language and Communication": 61-5.

[47] Price, "On Silent Trade": 90.

[48] Price, "On Silent Trade": 92.

[49] Theophrastus, *Enquiry into Plants*, 9:4 (London and Cambridge, MA: Wm. Heinemann and Harvard University Press, 1961), 2:236-9; Grierson, "The Silent Trade": 25. Frankincense and myrrh were brought to the temple of the sun; each owner set out a heap with a tablet stating quantity and price. Merchants came, set down the required amount, and then the priest took a third for the god. The sellers then came and took what remained.

were observed (apparently at first hand) among the Aleuts in early nineteenth-century Alaska.[50]

All this shows that the concept of "silent trade" can apply to a spectrum of transactions (including "dumb barter" between individuals), and not just the "pure," collectively organized type.[51] We must add here that not all these forms and examples are reliably attested: perhaps the only one of whose existence we can be absolutely sure is the individualistic "dumb barter." But the fact that these practices come up in so many literary sources, from so many different times and places, indicates that silence in the marketplace must often have answered to real economic and social needs, beyond the requirements or inventions of literary narratives.

Pre-Islamic Arabia is a case in point. The circumstances of its silent trade remain mysterious, in part because of the ways in which Islamic jurists subsequently misread the practice. The "pure," "classic," collective silent trade does not describe what went on there, but neither, for all that, does the one-on-one, *ad hoc* bargaining of "dumb barter." After all, in Arabia most market-goers spoke Arabic, and for those who did not, some sort of *lingua franca* must have been available. It seems that buyers and sellers avoided doing the easy, natural thing, which would have been talking and shouting while trading. Silence prevailed in the "markets of the Arabs," and we still do not understand why.

---

[50] The source of this information is the priest I. Veniaminov, afterward [Saint] Innokentiĭ, Metropolitan of Moscow and Kolomna (1797-1879), in his *Notes on the Islands of the Unalashka District* (trans. L. Black and R.H. Geoghegan, Fairbanks and Kingston: Limestone Press, 1984): 212. See also R.G. Liapunova, *Essays on the Ethnography of the Aleuts* (Fairbanks: University of Alaska Press, 1966): 150-1; W.N. Dall, *Alaska and Its Resources* (Boston, 1894): 394; Grierson, "The Silent Trade": 30. "The Aleuts do not trade in person, face to face, but always through an agent...chosen from among the young Aleuts. Someone who has a superfluous or not very necessary article sends it with the [agent] and instructs him to ask for tobacco or some other thing....[The agent enters the dwelling and says:] 'Here is [a thing] for sale.' The name of the person to whom this thing belongs, however, is never stated even if everybody recognizes him by the article." The agent then goes back and forth until both parties are satisfied. "No matter how long such trading or, it is better to say, this barter, is kept up, the owner and buyer never meet. This custom of trading is very ancient among the Aleuts, hardly changed even to the present time, and takes place very often."

[51] This is borne out by the variety of types in medieval and early modern Japan, described in Kurimoto, "Silent Trade in Japan." Note the existence there of "halfway houses" (*nakayado*), situated on ecological borders (mountain passes), facilitating exchange between mountain people and lowland villagers.

Silent Trade at 'Ukāẓ

We may recall that the "markets of the Arabs" formed an annual sequence in which the culminating point was the fair of 'Ukāẓ. Within this entirely Arab meeting-place, with zero barriers of language and culture, we find another kind of silent trade, which may hold a key to understanding the entire situation for Arabia at the turn of the seventh century.

> They did their selling there [at 'Ukāẓ] in secret (*bi'l-sirār* or *bi'l-sarār*). If it was necessary to sell when a merchant had in his presence a thousand men wishing to buy, and he did not wish to do so, then he had a right to a share in the profit.[52]

To a modern reader this seems strange. Why should a merchant, besieged by eager customers, not want to sell just when he stands to receive a favorable price for his entire stock? From whom does he claim "a share in the profit"? What is the connection between this "share in the profit" and the "selling in secret" imposed on the marketplace? Above all, why is secrecy—a form of silence—imposed here?

As a commercial practice, *al-bayʿ bi'l-sirār* is unknown to texts of Islamic law,[53] but it does occur fleetingly in Arabic lexicography. There we are told that it consisted of two parties to a sale racing to pull their seal rings off their fingers (or out of their sleeves); whoever produced his seal first got to conclude the bargain on his own terms,[54] an absurd technique if there ever was one, and unlikely to have been used in pre-Islamic Arabia or anywhere else.

First we must ask what *al-bayʿ bi'l-sirār* really means. *Sirār* or *sarār* can mean "the last night of the lunar month."[55] If this were to apply here, then we would have: "They did their selling [at 'Ukāẓ] in the last day of the month": a crush of customers doing their shopping in a brief time and overwhelming the merchant, whose reluctance to sell may be aggravated by the tendency of buyers to gang up against

[52] al-Marzūqī, *Azmina*, 2:165. *Fa-idhā wajaba al-bayʿ wa-'inda al-tājir alf rajul mimman yurīdu al-shirā' wa-lā yurīduhu fa-lahu al-sharika fi'l-ribḥ*.

[53] I have not found it in any legal text, and neither did al-Afghānī: see *Aswāq*: 53-4.

[54] al-Muṭarrizī, *al-Mughrib*: s.v.; cf. al-Afghānī, *Aswāq*: 54.

[55] E. Lane, *An Arabic-English Lexicon* (London: Williams and Norgate, 1863-1893), 1:1399.

him.[56] Such a severe constriction of time for commerce at ʿUkāẓ is far-fetched, and goes against other evidence that we have.[57] The only modern scholar who ventured a solution to this problem, F. Krenkow, thought that *al-bayʿ bi'l-sirār* indeed meant "selling in secret," as if it were *al-bayʿ bi'l-sirr*. He reasoned that because the tribes came together at ʿUkāz while still in a state of war, they concealed themselves even as they traded. Proof for this came, Krenkow thought, in a passage in the tradition on the markets in which the Arab nobles are said to have veiled themselves at ʿUkāẓ out of fear of being recognized by their enemies.[58]

If Krenkow was right—and no other solution has been proposed—then we have at ʿUkāẓ a "selling in secret" which echoes the Arabian silent practices that we have already seen. Even so, however, the passage just quoted on "selling in secret" still makes little sense. Before we assign the blame to generations of transmitters and copyists for garbling the text, we should recall that "profit" also occurs in several other texts relating to pre-Islamic Arabia, specifically in narratives about the activity of the Quraysh—the dominant tribal group in Mecca—going back for several generations, beginning with Muḥammad's ancestor Hāshim b. ʿAbd Manāf.

Hāshim is said to have established a series of commercial networks, associated with something called *īlāf*. This term appears in the Quran,[59] and there has been disagreement, both in medieval and modern scholarship, over its meaning and context. Much of the discussion has been exegetical, aimed at understanding the Quranic passage. In general, *īlāf* has been understood to mean "reconciliation," "pact," "safe-conduct." Several of the extra-Quranic narratives that touch on this matter state that Hāshim and his brothers concluded pacts with the rulers of Byzantium, Ethiopia, Yemen and

[56] al-Marzūqī, *Azmina*, 2:162; above, n. 34.

[57] For instance, Abū 'l-Faraj, *Kitāb al-Aghānī* (Cairo: al-Hay'a al-Miṣrīya al-ʿĀmma li'l-Kitāb, 1992-4), 22:57, describing ʿUkāẓ as open for most or all of the month of Dhū 'l-Qaʿda. See Bonner, "'Time Has Come Full Circle.'"

[58] al-Marzūqī, *Azmina*, 2:166. Krenkow expressed this view in a personal communication to al-Afghānī, reported by the latter at *Aswāq*: 54, n. 2. al-Afghānī himself dismissed Krenkow's view.

[59] Quran 106 (Quraysh): "For the *īlāf* of Quraysh, their *īlāf* for the winter and summer caravan. So let them serve the Lord of this House who has fed them against hunger and secured them from fear." (Arberry translation, with modifications).

Persia.[60] Some narratives also describe the networks that Hāshim developed closer to home, to enable his caravans to reach those far-away places.[61] The third/ninth-century author al-Jāḥiẓ wrote that Hāshim "let the chiefs of the Arab tribes share in his commerce...and made over a *ribḥ* (profit) to them, together with [the *īlāf*]."[62] Al-Thaʿālibī in the fifth/eleventh century similarly wrote that *īlāf* was a sum that Hāshim granted to the heads of several tribes as *ribḥ*, while he undertook the transportation of their wares together with his own.[63] In this view of Hāshim's activity, *ribḥ* is not only "gain," but also a kind of gift (or protection money) made to a *sayyid*, a tribal chief, in order to conciliate him and to facilitate the movement of Quraysh's caravans through his territory. It differs from the extorted payment, the *khifāra*, that we find in the tradition on the "markets of the Arabs" regarding al-Shiḥr and Rābiya: Hāshim's *īlāf* and *ribḥ* are used in a wide network that has a single center (Mecca) and a single leader (Hāshim), whereas *khifāra* (protection) must be established anew each time on a person-to-person (or predator-to-victim) basis. At any rate, the *ribḥ* associated with Hāshim, Quraysh and the *īlāf* permits the movement of the caravans, while confirming the noble status of its recipient.

There are reasons for doubting the literal historicity of these narrative traditions about Hāshim and his commercial networks.[64]

---

[60] al-Ṭabarī, *Ta'rīkh al-Rusul wa'l-mulūk* (Leiden: E.J. Brill, 1879-1901), 1:1089-90. Ibn Hishām, *Sīra al-Nabawīya* ed. M. al-Saqqā and others (Cairo, 1955), 1:143, does not mention Hāshim's pacts with foreign potentates, but does associate Hāshim with the summer and winter journeys named in Qur'ān 106. Al-Masʿūdī, *Murūj*, 2:177, § 971, connects *īlāf* with Quraysh's treaties with foreign kings and their foreign journeys, but does not mention Hāshim. Other early sources (such as al-Azraqī's *Akhbār Makka*) do not mention this story at all. It is modern scholars who have connected the dots to form a unified picture: al-Afghānī, *Aswāq*: 147-61; M.J. Kister, "Mecca and Tamim," *JESHO* 8:2 (1965): 113-63, repr. in *Studies in Jahilīya and Early Islam* (Alsdershot: Ashgate, 1980); R. Simon, *Meccan Trade* (Budapest: Akadémiai Kiadó, 1989): 63-70. See the critique of this unified picture in P. Crone, *Meccan Trade and the Rise of Islam* (Princeton: Princeton University Press, 1987).

[61] Ibn Ḥabīb, *Muḥabbar*: 162-4; other sources indicated in Crone, *Meccan Trade*: 109-14, 117-18, 206-8.

[62] al-Jāḥiẓ, *Faḍl Hāshim ʿalā ʿAbd Shams*, in *Rasā'il al- Jāḥiẓ*, ed. al-Sandūbī (Cairo: al-Maṭbaʿa al-Raḥmānīya, 1933): 70. *Wa-sharika fi tijāratihi ru'asā' al-qabā'il min al-ʿarab...wa-jaʿala lahum maʿahu ribḥan....* Cf. Kister, "Mecca and Tamim": 119.

[63] al-Thaʿālibī, *Thimār al-qulūb* (Damascus: Dār al-Bashā'ir, 1994), 1:215; Kister, *loc. cit.*

[64] Crone, *Meccan Trade*: 109-14.

However, there may also be reasons for doubting the literal historicity of the traditions on the "markets of the Arabs." The point here is that these two groups of traditions have different notions, not only regarding what happened in sixth-century Arabian tribal politics, but also regarding the meaning of "profit" and "nobility." In what follows, we will examine what the tradition on the markets has to say about these matters, and draw some consequences.

In both cases—in (at least some of) the traditions on Hāshim and the *īlāf*, and in the tradition on the markets—*ribḥ* is different from what it usually means in classical Arabic, which is the difference between what a person spends in acquiring something and what he sells it for, or in other words, his gain or profit.[65] Instead, as we have already seen, *ribḥ* here is a gift made to a prominent person, confirming his status as a *sayyid* or tribal chief. At the same time, this *ribḥ* strengthens the giver's peninsular networks and enables his caravans to pass through territory that the *sayyid* controls.

Unlike the Hāshim/*īlāf* traditions, the tradition on the markets never mentions *īlāf* and does not connect *ribḥ* (profit, gain) to Hāshim or any of the Quraysh. It does, however, emphatically connect *ribḥ* (or *rabaḥ*) and its plural, *arbāḥ*, to a process of evaluating and rewarding nobility.

> The nobles (*ashrāf*) of the Arabs used to appear at these markets together with the merchants. The reason for this was that the kings gave presents to the nobles, awarding each of them a share of the profits (*kānat tarḍakhu li'l-ashrāf bi-sahm min al-arbāḥ*).[66]

Here the tradition is discussing not only 'Ukāẓ, but the entire sequence of markets. In several of these markets there were local "kings" (Ukaydir at Dūma, Julandā in 'Umān, etc.) who levied taxes while exercising the right to sell merchandise on their own account, before anyone else.[67] Apparently all these revenues together constituted these petty rulers' "profits." And here we see how they spent them: on gifts for the great men of the tribes. Of course they made these gifts with an eye to their own political and commercial advan-

---

[65] It is also different from the older meaning of *ribḥ* (or *rabaḥ*), namely the "excess fat of young weaned camels," distributed (at games of *maysir*) to the tribe and to guests (Lane, *Lexicon*, 1:155, 1009), which is to say, "surplus."

[66] al-Marzūqī, *Azmina*, 2:166.

[67] Ibn Ḥabīb, *Muḥabbar*: 264; al-Marzūqī, *Azmina*, 2:161.

tage; however, the heart of the matter is confirmation of the recipients' noble status.

Unlike other markets in the sequence of the "markets of the Arabs," 'Ukāẓ had no ruler and allowed "neither tax nor protection." In former days, however, the South Arabian monarchs used to intervene there:

> One of the kings of Yemen used to send a beautiful sword, a fine suit of clothes (*ḥulla ḥasana*), and a swift mount; [the king's envoy] would stand in [the market] and announce it, [saying:] "let the most valiant of the Arabs take it" (*li-ya'khudhhu a'azzu al-'arab*). The intent of this was to find out who was the noble and the chief, and [the king] would order [his envoy] to treat him with deference, to cultivate a relationship with him, and to make presents to him (*jā'izatihi*).[68]

The Yemeni monarch advanced his interests by acting in the manner of the petty "kings" of northern and eastern Arabia, by providing gifts for the *sayyid*s. Noble status thus became confirmed at the fairs through the bestowal of royal gifts.

Meanwhile, these processes of gift-giving, taxation and selling in the markets also involve merchants. In the tradition on the markets, the merchants often do not act independently of the nobles and kings: this is the plain sense of the passage just quoted,[69] and consistent with the logic of the entire situation, as we shall see a little later on.

Secrecy, Honor and Prestige

In the narratives about Quraysh, Hāshim, Mecca and the *īlāf*—but not in the tradition on the "markets of the Arabs"—Hāshim and his descendants play a role similar to that of the kings, including the South Arabian monarchs, mentioned in the passages just quoted from the tradition on the markets. That is, they confirm the status of tribal chiefs through gift-giving (*ribḥ*), while extending their own political and trading networks (*īlāf*). However, Hāshim and his successors make no claim of royalty for themselves. The *sayyid*s in these

---

[68] al-Marzūqī, *Azmina*, 2:165. This bit of information stands out in that it describes circumstances before the Ethiopian invasion of Yemen in the early sixth century. For the most part, the tradition on the markets describes the situation in Arabia ca. 600-10.

[69] See above, n. 66: "The nobles...used to appear at these markets together with the merchants."

narratives, for their part, accept their alliance with Quraysh and the *ribḥ* that it brings, without facing any accusations of ignoble behavior or greed. For after all, this *ribḥ* that Hāshim bestows is demystified, not far removed from what *ribḥ* will become soon afterward under Islam: "profit" pure and simple, an "economic" fact which is not, in itself, reprehensible or problematic.

By contrast, *ribḥ* in the tradition on the "markets of the Arabs" is anything but demystified: it is a gift made in recognition of a person's nobility and valor. However, while noble status is confirmed by accepting gifts from kings, it is not acquired that way. Nobility emerges from constant competition, especially in the extent of one's own generosity. This competitive requirement inevitably creates tension vis-à-vis the royal bestower of the *ribḥ*. After all, it is better to be seen as a giver than a receiver. And the king, the bestower of *ribḥ*, has accumulated his wealth ("profits," *arbāḥ*) through means that are less than noble, including the levying of taxes in the market and the sale of commodities that may, as at Dūmat al-Jandal, include human beings.

For these reasons, both the *sayyid* and the king, the recipient and the bestower of *ribḥ*, are likely to feel uneasy, even ashamed of their gains. To assuage these feelings, the marketplace imposes a decorous silence. This silence also helps to preserve the participants' anonymity, making it easier for tribes in a state of war to interact with one another, as Krenkow suggested. Here the anonymity that needs preserving is not that of the tribe or clan, but rather of its leader:

> No nobleman would appear there [at 'Ukāẓ] unless he had covered his face with a veil (*burqa'*), for fear that he might be taken prisoner and held for a large ransom. The first to cast off the veil was Ṭarīf al-'Anbarī: when he saw them studying his face carefully and trying to divine his features, he said, "It is vile to accustom oneself to anything but nobility" (*qabuḥa man waṭṭana nafsahu illā 'alā sharafihi)*. And so he cast away the veil and uncovered his face.[70]

In their arduous quest for status and for wealth to bestow on others, the Arab nobles and kings observe "secrecy" (*sirār*, *sarār* or *sirr*) in their marketplaces. Meanwhile, as we have already seen, they make use of the services of merchants. In the southeastern ('Umānī) part of the sequence of the "markets of the Arabs," merchants arrive by sea and then move about the peninsula, apparently operating on their

[70] al-Marzūqī, *Azmina*, 2:166: above, n. 58.

own account. In the sequence as a whole, however, it appears that many merchants belong to the rulers' bureaucracies or households: in the language of Karl Polanyi, these are functionaries, "factors" and "status traders," rather than independent entrepreneurs.[71] We see this especially in the northern parts of the sequence (Dūma, al-Mushaqqar), where the ruler "does whatever he likes" with the market and sells his own wares there before anyone else: which means that directly or indirectly, he dictates prices. In other words, prices in these Arabian markets were not what we would call "free," but were calculated to promote the interests of local rulers. Naturally, the rulers did not perform this demeaning work themselves, but relegated it to their merchants.

The structure and rules of these Arabian markets—apparently including ʿUkāẓ—thus favored the contestants for noble status and their "royal" patrons. Even if the polities in question were simple, even crude, at least some of the trade within them was still, again in the language of Polanyi, "administered" or "tied."[72] But if this is so, then why does the tradition on the markets describe all the procedures for bargaining (casting stones, gesturing, haggling, etc.) that we have mentioned? The answer must be that such bargaining did take place, but on the periphery of price structures that were already established: or in other words, in a secondary, derivative trading zone. And within that zone the bargaining was even further constricted, by virtue of its being conducted in silence.

Now we may return to the conundrum that this strange material has presented. To our way of thinking, a merchant who finds himself surrounded by a thousand customers, all eager to buy, is in an enviable position. But in the tradition on the markets, this merchant closes shop and demands a subsidy from the authorities. Why does he do this? In fact he has at least two reasons for feeling anxious. The first is the tendency, mentioned earlier on, of groups of buyers to gang up against sellers and to force them to accept an unfavorable price.[73] The other reason is that the ruler, through his merchant-

---

[71] K. Polanyi, "Traders and Trade," in *Ancient Civilization and Trade*, ed. J. A. Sabloff and C. C. Lamberg-Karlovsky (Albuquerque: University of New Mexico Press, 1975): 138. Here I cannot enter into the debates over Polanyi and his legacy, but his views on "status traders" and "tied trade" seem useful in this context.

[72] K. Polanyi, "The Economy as Instituted Process," in *Trade and Market in the Early Empires*, ed. K. Polanyi (Glencoe: Pree Press, 1957).

[73] al-Marzūqī, *Azmina*, 2:162; above, n. 34.

bureaucrats, has already established a price structure, crude perhaps, but a structure nonetheless. In the case of our besieged merchant, the throng of buyers will tend to move prices; and since even here the law of supply and demand will still apply, this movement of prices will be in an upward direction. At this point, however, what the merchant fears most is a confrontation with the authorities. Accordingly, he closes shop and demands a share of the ruler's revenues ("profits"), very likely after he has handed over his stock of goods to the ruler's stores.

Then we have the added complication that this event is described as taking place at 'Ukāẓ, where there is no single ruler. However, someone there was charged with supervision in some form.[74] More broadly and more importantly, we can only make sense of this material if we focus on the entire sequence of markets, and on the roles of the "kings" (whether these are petty rulers such as Julandā in 'Umān, or rulers with long dynastic traditions such as the earlier kings of Ḥimyar), and of the *sayyid*s who compete for royal patronage at 'Ukāẓ and elsewhere.

In some ways this "administered" or "tied" trade of the Arabian markets resembled the situation of the Byzantine and Sasanian empires of this era. However, there were also differences. Sixth-century Byzantium struck large quantities of coins, which it used to pay its army and bureaucracy, and then took back into its coffers in the form of taxes. This circulation of money had consequences for other, "private" sectors of the economy, but in the eyes of the state these were incidental or ignored altogether.[75] By contrast, in the "markets of the Arabs," there is little evidence for the presence of much coined money in circulation. Craftsmen and agriculturalists produced much of what was traded in these Arabian markets, but these markets remained, in large part, places that regulated tensions between the desert and the sown, as has been known for a long time. What needs to be emphasized here is the domination of trade—at least within the sequence of the "markets of the Arabs"—by ambitious, competing rulers and nobles.

---

[74] al-Marzūqī, *Azmina*, 2:167, "control over the fair and the judgeship of 'Ukāẓ," *amr al-mawsim wa-qaḍā' 'Ukāẓ*.

[75] M.F. Hendy, "Economy and State in late Rome and Early Byzantium," in *Economy, Fiscal Administration and Coinage of Byzantium* (Northampton: Variorum, 1989): 1-23; Simon, *Meccan Trade*: 92f.

At the same time, these Arabian markets, like Arabia as a whole, were undergoing a transition and crisis. We see this in the way that redistributive processes, namely the collecting of taxes and the fixing of prices on the part of the ruler for his own commercial benefit, led to an accumulation of wealth which was then expended in the mode of reciprocity, or in other words, in the acquisition and expression of patronage through lavish gift-giving. None of this is particularly unusual, and in early Islam we find it on a far vaster scale. However, we can perceive that different ways of doing commerce and setting prices were clashing in Arabia at this time, together with different ways of claiming leadership within the towns and tribes.

When Islam arrived, the memory of these old Arabian markets became negative and vague. For the disapproving Muslim jurists, the pre-Islamic marketplace provided the perfect example of *gharar*, the indeterminate or aleatory element that renders a transaction void and reprehensible. We can see now that the Muslim jurists were not being merely dogmatic and closed-minded on this point. For trading in pre-Islamic Arabia did sometimes take place in conditions which resembled games of chance—conditions which were roundly condemned in the Quran and early Islam. Afterward, under Islam, it was the merchants, rather than the nobles, kings or caliphs, who ultimately took charge of the modes and techniques of trade, while the market became, much more than previously, a price-setting mechanism on its own. These later developments obscured the fact that the "markets of the Arabs" used to have their own purposes in their own time.

We may conclude with a final look at the silence of the Arabian markets. The earliest examples of silent trade are reported from Africa.[76] It is afterward that it is said to appear around the Indian Ocean and Southeast Asia, as well as the northern fringes of Eurasia. It has been suggested that it was the Arabs (or more correctly, the traders of the Caliphate and its successor states) who carried the practice eastward and northward.[77] However, this will require detailed

[76] Vajda, "'Stummer Handel' im alten Afrika": 174.

[77] Price, "On Silent Trade": 93. This assertion is incompatible with the *Periplus of the Erythraean Sea* (trans. and ed. by G.W.B. Huntingford, London: Hakluyt Society, 1980): Chap. 65, p. 56. In this Greek text, composed by an anonymous author around 100 CE, we read of people "of a wild nature" who come every year to the borders of Thina [China], leave their goods on display and then withdraw, after which the Chinese arrive and collect the items. This is, in other words, an instance of "pure" silent trade in Asia, long before the coming of the Arabs and Islam.

research. What we can affirm now is that silent trade in some form was practiced in Arabia at the turn of the seventh century. The evidence for this consists of the tradition on the markets of the Arabs, together with the theme of "*jāhilī* trade" in Islamic law.

Some nine centuries previously, silent trade had reportedly existed within the Sabaean monarchy in South Arabia, which used it in its own internal frankincense market (and not in its dealings with tribal peoples), for the benefit of its monarchy and priesthood.[78] Subsequently, there seems to be no direct evidence for survival of this practice in South Arabia.[79] However, in the sixth century CE, silent trade of the "pure" type is described between trading agents of the Ethiopian monarchy of Axum and tribal peoples in the Horn of Africa.[80] If there is any truth at all to this account, then given the close connections between Axum and Ḥimyar, it is plausible that some form of the practice was known in South Arabia as well. From there the northward migrations out of Yemen in the centuries before Islam could have made it known all over the Arabian Peninsula.

At all events, silent trade in the "markets of the Arabs" is associated with rulership and prestige, and assumes two forms. First, as a set of bargaining techniques, it allows local rulers to exert control over external commerce, heaping up treasure (or "profit") and increasing their power. Second, as a code of secrecy imposed at 'Ukāẓ, it allows the Arab nobles to avoid reprobation and shame in

---

[78] Above, n. 49.

[79] Pliny, *Natural History* (Cambridge, MA and London: Harvard University Press and Wm. Heinemann, 1986), 12:30-40, while discussing frankincense, myrrh and other South Arabian aromatics, describes the harvesting and marketing of these products, but with no hint of "silent trade" (*pace* Grierson, *The Silent Trade*, 25).

[80] Cosmas Indicopleustes, *Christian Topography*, trans. J.W. McCrindle (London: Hakluyt Society, 1897): 52-3. "The King of the Axomites...sends agents to bargain for the gold, and these are accompanied by many other traders—upwards, say, of five hundred...[bearing] oxen, lumps of salt, and iron....[T]hey...form an encampment, which they fence round with a great hedge of thorns....[H]aving slaughtered the oxen, they cut them in pieces, and lay the pieces on the top of the thorns, along with the lumps of salt and the iron. Then come the natives bringing gold in nuggets like peas...and lay one or two or more of these upon what pleases them...and then they retire to some distance off. Then the owner of the meat approaches, and if he is satisfied he takes the gold away, and upon seeing this its owner comes and takes the flesh or the salt or the iron. If, however, he is not satisfied, he leaves the gold, when the native seeing that he has not taken it, comes and either puts down more gold, or takes up what he had laid down, and goes away. Such is the mode in which business is transacted with the people of that country, because their language is different and interpreters are hardly to be found...."

the course of their endless struggles among themselves. In these ways, the Arabian silent trade transforms the wealth accumulated from commerce and taxation into prestige-enhancing gifts.

Bibliography

Primary sources

ʿAbd al-Razzāq b. Ḥammām al-Ṣanʿānī. *al-Muṣannaf*. Beirut: al-Maktab al-Islāmī, 1983-87.

Abū Dāʾūd Sulaymān b. al-Ashʿath. *Sunan*. Cairo: Maṭbaʿat al-Saʿāda, 1950.

Abū ʾl-Faraj al-Iṣfahāni. *Kitāb al-Aghāni*. Cairo: al-Hayʾa al-Miṣrīya al-ʿĀmma lil-Kitāb, 1992-94.

al-Azraqī, A.al-Walīd M. *Akhbār Makka*. Mecca: Dār al-Thaqāfa, 1965.

al-Baghdādī, ʿA.al-Qādir b. ʿUmar. *Khizānat al-adab*. Beirut: Dār al-Kutub al-ʿIlmīya, 1967.

al-Bakrī, A. ʿU.al-Andalusī. *Muʿjam mā istaʿjam*. Beirut: Dār al-Kutub al-ʿIlmīya, 1998.

al-Bukhārī, M. b. Ismāʿīl. *al-Jāmiʿ al-ṣaḥīḥ*. Leiden: Brill, 1862-1908.

Cosmas Indicopleustes. *The Christian Topography*. Translated by McCrindle, J.W. London: Hakluyt Society, 1897.

al-Hamdānī, A. M. al-Ḥasan. *Ṣifat Jazīrat al-ʿArab*. Leiden: Brill, 1881-1901.

Herodotus, *The Histories*. Translated by A. de Sélincourt. Harmondsworth: Penguin, 1996.

Ibn Baṭṭūṭa, *Travels in Asia and Africa, 1325-1354*. Translated and selected by Gibb, H.A.R. London: Routledge, 1929.

Ibn Ḥabīb, M. *al-Muḥabbar*. Hyderabad: Dāʾirat al-Maʿārif al-ʿUthmānīya , 1941.

Ibn Qudāma, ʿA.A. b. Aḥmad. *al-Mughnī*. Cairo: Dār al-Manār, 1948.

al-Jāḥiẓ, ʿA.b. Baḥr. *Rasāʾil al-Jāḥiẓ*, edited by H. al-Sandūbī. Cairo: al-Maṭbaʿa al-Raḥmānīya, 1933.

Mālik b. Anas. *al-Muwaṭṭaʾ*. Beirut: Dār al-Gharb al-Islāmī, 1996.

al-Marzūqī, A.ʿA.A. *Kitāb al-azmina wal-amkina*. Hyderabad: Dāʾirat al-Maʿārif, 1914.

al-Masʿūdī, ʿA.b. al-Ḥusayn. *Murūj al-dhahab wa-maʿādin al-jawhar*. Edited by Pellat, Ch. Beirut: Manshūrāt al-Jāmiʿa al-Lubnānīya, 1965-79.

al-Muqaddasī, S.D. *Aḥsan al-taqāsīm li-maʿrifat al-aqālīm*. Edited by De Goeje, M.J. *Bibliotheca Geographorum Arabicorum*, vol. 3. Leiden: Brill, 1967.

Muslim b. al-Ḥajjāj. *Ṣaḥīḥ Muslim bi-sharḥ al-Nawawī*. Beirut: Dār Iḥyāʾ al-Turāth al-ʿArabī, 1984.

al-Muṭarrizī, N.b.ʿA.S. *al-Mughrib fī tartīb al-muʿrib*. Beirut: Maktabat Lubnān, 1999.

al-Nawawī. See above, Muslim b. al-Ḥajjāj.

The Periplus of the Erythraean Sea. Translated and edited by Huntingford, G.W.B. London: The Hakluyt Society, 1980.

Pliny. *Natural History*. Cambridge, MA and London: Harvard University Press and Wm. Heinemann Ltd., 1986.

al-Qalqashandī, A.b.ʿA. *Ṣubḥ al-aʿshā*. Cairo: al-Muʾassasa al-Miṣrīya al-ʿĀmma liʾl-Taʾlīf waʾl-Tarjama waʾl-Ṭibāʿa waʾl-Nashr, 1964.

al-Ṭabarī, A.J. *Taʾrīkh al-rusul waʾl-mulūk*. Leiden: Brill, 1879-1901.

al-Tawḥīdī, A.Ḥ. *al-Imtāʿ waʾl-muʾānasa*. Beirut: Manshūrāt Dār Maktabat al-Ḥayāt, 1965.

al-Thaʿālibī, ʿA.M. b. Muḥammad. *Thimār al-qulūb fī 'l-muḍāf wa'l-mansūb*. Damascus: Dār al-Bashā'ir, 1994.
Theophrastus. *Enquiry into Plants*. Translated by Hort, A. London and Cambridge, MA: Wm. Heinemann and Harvard University Press, 1961.
al-Yaʿqūbī. *Ta'rīkh*. Beirut, 1960.
Yāqūt b. ʿAbd Allāh al-Ḥamawī al-Rūmī. *Muʿjam al-buldān*. Beirut: Dār Ṣādir, 1955-7.

Secondary Sources

al-Afghānī, S. *Aswāq al-ʿArab fī l-jāhilīya wal-Islām*. Damascus: Dār al-Fikr, 1960.
al-Muaikel, Kh.I. "Sūq ʿUkāẓ in al-Ṭā'if: Archaeological Survey of an Islamic Site." *al-ʿUṣūr al-Wusṭā* 7, no. 1 (1995): 1-7.
Blachère, R. *Histoire de la littérature arabe des origines à la fin du XVe siècle de J.-C.* 3 vols. Paris: Maisonneuve, 1952-66. Reprint, Paris: Maisonneuve, 1980-90.
Bosworth, C.E. "al-Mushaḳḳar. In *Encyclopaedia of Islam*, second edition (*EI*[2]), 7: 671 Leiden: E.J. Brill, 1993.
Crone, P. *Meccan Trade and the Rise of Islam*. Princeton: Princeton University Press, 1987.
Dall, W.N. *Alaska and its Resources*. Boston: Lee and Shepherd, 1870.
David, A. Harper, "Trade, Language and Communication" (http://www.nyu.edu/econ/dept/austrian/Trade&Comm.pdf , Dec. 14, 2004).
Grierson, P.J.H. *The Silent Trade*. Edinburgh: W. Green and Son, Ltd., 1903. Repr. in *Research in Economic Anthropology*, vol. 3, edited by George Dalton, 1-74. Greenwich, CT: JAI Press, 1980.
Hendy, M.F. "Economy and State in Late Rome and Early Byzantium: An Introduction." In *Economy, Fiscal Administration and Coinage of Byzantium*, 1-23. Northampton: Variorum, 1989.
Kawar, I. "The Arabs in the Peace Treaty of A.D. 561." *Arabica* 3 (1956): 181-213.
Kister, M.J. "The Market of the Prophet." *Journal of the Economic and Social History of the Orient* 8 (1965): 272-6. Repr. in *Studies in Jahiliyya and Early Islam*. Aldershot: Ashgate, 1980.
——. "Mecca and Tamīm (Aspects of their Relations)." *Journal of the Economic and Social History of the Orient* 8 (1965): 113-63. Repr. in *Studies in Jahiliyya and Early Islam*.Aldershot: Ashgate, 1980.
Kurimoto, S. "Silent Trade in Japan." In *Research in Economic Anthropology*, Vol. 3, edited by Dalton, G. 97-108. Greenwich: JAI Press, 1980.
Lane, E. *An Arabic-English Lexicon*. London: Williams and Norgate, 1863-1893.
Lecker, M. "On the Markets of Medina (Yathrib) in Pre-Islamic and Early Islamic Times." *Jerusalem Studies in Arabic and Islam* 8 (1986): 133-47.
Liapunova, R.G. *Essays on the Ethnography of the Aleuts*. Translated by Shelest, J. Vol. 9, *Rasmuson Library Historical Translation Series*. Fairbanks: University of Alaska Press, 1996.
Periplus of the Erythraean Sea. Translated and edited by G.W.B. Huntingford. London: Hakluyt Society, 1980.
Polanyi, K. "The Economy as an Instituted Process." In *Trade and Market in the Early Empires*, edited by Karl Polanyi, 243-70. Glencoe: Free Press, 1957.
——. "Ports of Trade in Early societies." *Journal of Economic History* 23 (1963): 30-45.
——. *Trade and Market in the Early Empires: Economies in History and Theory*. Glencoe: Free Press, 1957.

——. "Traders and Trade." In *Ancient Civilization and Trade*, edited by Jeremy A. Sabloff and C.C. Lamberg-Karlovsky, 133-54. Albuquerque: University of New Mexico Press, 1975.

Price, J.A. "On Silent Trade." In *Research in Economic Anthropology*, vol. 3, edited by George Dalton, 75-96. Greenwich, CT: JAI Press, 1980.

Santillana, D. *Istituzioni di diritto musulmano malichita, con riguardo anche al sistema sciafiita*. Rome: Istituto per l'Oriente, 1926-38.

Simon, R. *Meccan Trade and Islam*. Budapest: Akadémia Kiadó, 1989.

Smith, G.R. "al-Yamāma," EI[2] 11:269.

Vaglieri, L.V. "Dūmat al-Djandal," *EI*[2], 2:624-6. Leiden: E.J. Brill, 1965.

Vajda, L. "'Stummer Handel' im alten Afrika?" In *Mundus africanus: Ethnologische Streifzüge durch sieben Jahrtausende afrikanischer Geschichte. Festschrift für Karl-Ferdinand Schaedler zum 70. Geburtstag*, edited by Roehreke, A. Rahden: Verlag Marie Leidorf, 2000.

Veniaminov, I. *Notes on the Islands of the Unalashka District*. Translated by Lydia T. Black and R.H. Geoghegan. Vol. 27, *Alaska History*. Fairbanks and Kingston: Elmer E. Rasmuson Library Translation Program and the Limestone Press, 1984.

Wellhausen, J. *Reste arabischen Heidentums*. Berlin: Walter de Gruyter, 1927.

Wensinck, A.J. *Concordance et indices de la tradition musulmane*. Leiden: E.J. Brill, 1892.

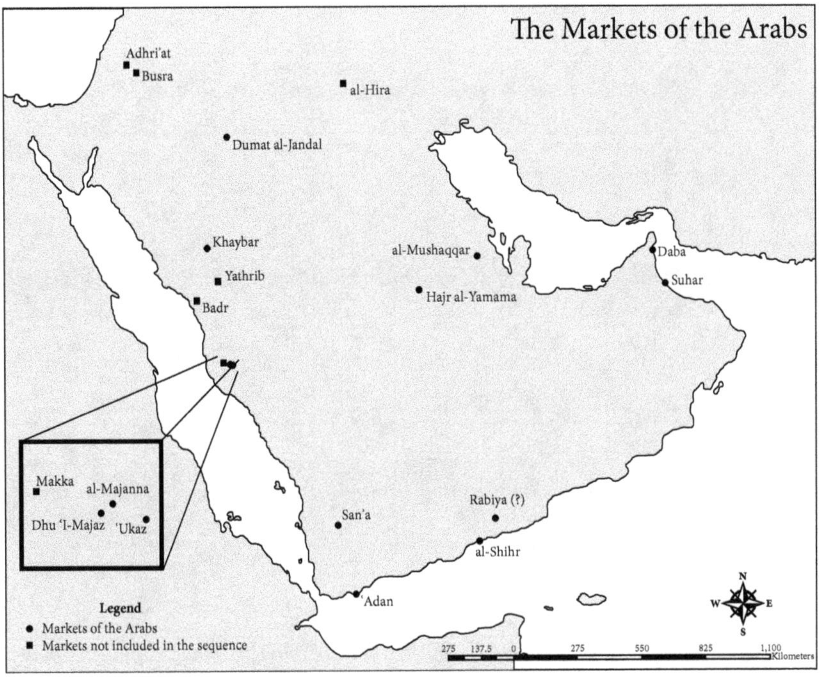
The Markets of the Arabs
Adhri'at
Busra
al-Hira
Dumat al-Jandal
Khaybar
Yathrib
Badr
al-Mushaqqar
Hajr al-Yamama
Daba
Suhar
Makka
al-Majanna
Dhu 'l-Majaz
'Ukaz
San'a
Rabiya (?)
al-Shihr
'Adan
N
W
E
S
Legend
Markets of the Arabs
Markets not included in the sequence
275 137.5 0 275 550 825 1,100
Kilometers

RINGING BELLS IN ḤAFṢID TUNIS: RELIGIOUS CONCESSIONS TO CHRISTIAN *FONDACOS* IN THE LATER THIRTEENTH CENTURY

Olivia Remie Constable

On July 29, 1287 (18 Jumāda al-ākhira, 686), amidst political troubles in both of their realms, the Aragonese king Alfonso III and the Ḥafṣid claimant ʿAbd al-Wāḥid b. al-Wāthiq drew up a treaty of mutual support that promised—among other things—extensive religious freedoms for western Christians living in the European *fondacos* in Tunis.[1] This treaty is especially interesting because it survives in both Arabic and Latin versions, the latter probably being a translation of the former since the document was issued in the voice of ʿAbd al-Wāḥid. Both versions are preserved in the archives of the Crown of Aragón in Barcelona, and each has been edited.[2] The section relating to *fondacos* and religious concessions reads as follows:

> ...We grant to you that you shall have a *funduq* [*alfundicum*] in Tunis with all of the freedoms and good customs that pertain to this *funduq* which tradition has consecrated since the reign of the illustrious Don James, king of Aragón,[3] your grandfather, may God have mercy on him, according to the best of the freedoms and good customs of the aforementioned *funduq* during the reign of the aforementioned illustri-

---

[1] I use the Romance word *fondaco* for both the Arabic *funduq* and the Latin *alfundicum*. By the later thirteenth century, there would have been many western Christians living in North Africa, not only merchants (who generally lived in *fondacos*) but also mercenaries, captives, slaves, renegades, fugitives, and others. Contemporary sources make clear that popes and other churchmen (especially members of the preaching orders), as well as European rulers, were concerned with the spiritual welfare of these Christians overseas. For more on *fondacos* and western communities, see O.R. Constable, *Housing the Stranger in the Mediterranean World: Lodging Trade, and Travel in Late Antiquity and the Middle Ages* (Cambridge: Cambridge University Press, 2003).

[2] Arabic version edited by M.A. Alarcón y Santón, *Los Documentos árabes diplomáticos del Archivo de la Corona de Aragón* (Madrid: Publicaciones de las Escuelas de Estudios Árabes de Madrid y Granada, 1940): 394-400 (doc. 155). The Latin version was edited by G. La Mantia, *Codice diplomatico dei Re Aragonesi* (Palermo: Società siciliana di storia patria, 1917; reprint Palermo: Ristampa Anastatica, 1990): 377-86 (doc. 167).

[3] The Arabic spelling of James' name, *Jaqmī*, reflects its medieval Catalan pronunciation.

ous ruler, Don James, your grandfather. We also grant and concede to you and to your aforementioned leader[4] and to the Christians who are with him, that they may have a church in Tunis and they will be permitted to bring with them priests [Latin: and other clerics] to lead them in church services and the worship of Jesus Christ. And it is permitted to them that they carry the body of Jesus Christ at the signal of a bell [Latin: or a small bell] as is the custom among the Christians in all of the *funduqs* and habitations[5] of the Christians. And they may give this body of Jesus Christ to those Christians who ask for it. And it is permitted for these priests to carry the cross and censer to the bodies of dead Christians for their burial, according to the dictates of custom among the Christians, without opposition or resistance from Us or anyone else.

Arabic version

ونعم لكم ان يكون لكم في تونس فندق بجميع ها ولائك الحريات وعوائد جياد التي كانت لذالك الفندق
وجرت به العادة في دولة المعظم المرحوم دون جقمي ملك ارغون جدكم على احسن ما كانت الجريات
والعوايد الجيدة للفندق المذكور في دولة السلطان المعظم المذكور دون جقمي جدكم و ايضا نعطي
ونعم لكم و للمذكور قائدكم وللنصارى الذين يكونوا معه لان يكون لهم في تونس كنيسية ويكون مباح
لهم ان يحبسوا اقسة ان ياذنوا لهم عبادة الكنيسية او عبادة جاشو قريشط ويكون مباح لهم ان يحملوا
جسد جاشو قريشط بعلامة ناقوس علي ما جرت به العادة بين النصارى في جميع الفندق ورحائل
النصارى و يسلموا ذلك الجسد متاع جاشوقريشط للنصارى الذين يطلبونه و يكون مباح لها ولائك
الاقسة ان يحملوا صليب و مبخر لاجساد النصارى الموتى الى ان يدفنوا على ما جرت به العادة بين
النصارى دون عناد و اعراض منا ومن غيرنا

Latin version

... Item damus et concedimus vobis quod habeatis apud Tunicium alfundicum, cum omnibus illis libertatibus et bonis consuetudinibus, quas ipse alfundicus habuit et consuevit habere et possidere tempore illustris Iacobi bone memorie, regis Aragonum avi vestri, prout melius ipsas libertates, bonas consuetudines aliquo tempore habuit, tenuit et possedit tempore predicti illustris regis Iacobi avi vestri. Item damus et concedimus vobis quod predictus Alcaldus vester et omnes Cristiani, qui cum eo erunt, possint apud Tunicium habere ecclesiam, et quod possint secum tradere sacerdotes et alios clericos, qui celebrent eis in ipsa ecclesia officium ecclesiasticum sive domini Iesu Christi, et qui

[4] Presumably the consul; Arabic: *qā'id*; Latin: *Alcaldus*.

[5] Way-stations, or places where Christians stay; the Arabic plural form *raḥā'il* is listed as a Sicilian usage (R. Dozy, *Supplément aux dictionnaires arabes* [Leiden: Brill, 1881], 1:517). The Latin text translates these as *vassallos*, which has a more proprietary sense.

> possint portare corpus Cristi cum signo campane sive squille, prout moris est Cristianorum per omnes alfundicos et vassallos Cristianorum, et tradere ipsum corpus Cristi Cristianis hoc requirentibus. Et quod ipsi clerici possint portare crucem et turibula corporibus Cristianorum decedencium, donec fuerint traditi sepulturi, secundum quod hoc consuevit fieri inter Cristianos, sine omni contradicione et impedimento nostri et cuiuscumque persone.

Although all of the religious concessions mentioned in this document can be found in other texts and treaties relevant to European activities in Tunis, this statement in 1287 is unusually generous and comprehensive. Not only may the Catalan community have a church or chapel in their *fondaco*, but they may signal the celebration of mass with the ringing of a bell, and priests in the *fondaco* may offer the host to those Christians who request it.[6] The bells in question may either have been large church bells or smaller hand bells; the Latin version of the text allows for both (*campane sive squille*), while the Arabic simply mentions *nāqūs*. The document went on to promise that priests could minister to the dead, and could carry a cross and incense to western Christians who had died. The suggestion here is that this license included ministering to Christians living (and dying) outside the walls of the Catalan *fondaco*. Although these religious concessions were granted to Alfonso III, with repeated reference to precedents set in the time of his grandfather, James I, it appears that they were not necessarily intended to be limited to the Catalan community. Certainly, the text claims that churches and bells were common in other Christian *fondacos* and properties.

Nevertheless, the permissions granted in this text directly conflict with commonly stated regulations for Christians living within the *dār al-Islām*, both *dhimmīs* and foreigners. For example, in a twelfth-century version of the so-called "Pact of 'Umar" transmitted by the Andalusī jurist Abū Bakr al-Ṭurṭūshī (d. 520/1126), Christians promised that "we shall not show our crosses or our books in the roads of the Muslims or their markets. We shall only ring our bells in our churches very gently. We shall not raise our voices during recitations in our churches or in the presence of Muslims, nor shall we raise our voices when following our dead ... we shall not walk past [the

[6] Although the treaty was negotiated with Alfonso III, as king of the Crown of Aragón, the facility in Tunis is more properly referred to as the Catalan *fondaco*, since most of the merchants in this community would have been Catalan speakers from eastern Iberia.

Muslims] with our dead."[7] Evidently, these were ongoing issues of concern in the western Muslim world during the twelfth and thirteenth centuries.

The treaty of 1287 raises a number of questions, not only about Christian religious freedoms in Tunis in the later thirteenth century, and but also about the political context that produced this rather unusual document. The latter is easier to explain, and may help to illuminate the former. Western Mediterranean politics in the later thirteenth century played out between the Crown of Aragón, the Ḥafṣid sultanate, the kingdom of France, the Italian city states of Genoa, Pisa, and Venice, and the island of Sicily (which shifted from Hohenstaufen, to Angevin, and then to Aragonese control). Although the crusade of the French king Louis IX to Tunis in 1270 marked a rallying moment for Christian religious fervor against Islam, this military effort achieved little in terms of real religious, political, or economic change in the region. Instead, western Mediterranean hostilities were more consistently aimed by Christian powers against each other, while European rulers and merchants often worked out advantageous political and economic relationships with the Ḥafṣids and other contemporary Muslim states.

Alfonso III was the third king of Aragón to be deeply invested in the political affairs of the western Mediterranean, following in the footsteps of his grandfather, James I (d. 1276), called "the Conqueror," and his father, Peter III (d. 1285). James had vastly expanded his kingdom's territorial extent during the first half of the thirteenth century, with the conquest of the Muslim island of Mallorca in 1228 and of the kingdom of Valencia in 1238. Thereafter, these combined territories, along with the older realms of Aragón and Catalonia, are collectively (if somewhat inaccurately) referred to as the Crown of Aragón. Meanwhile, James' interests also reached eastwards into the central Mediterranean, where he pursued military engagements and diplomatic relations with the Ḥafṣids. These resulted in numerous concessions for Catalan merchants in Tunis and Bougie, including rights to establish Catalan *fondacos* in these cities. Strikingly, James invariably referred to these facilities as *nostri fondaci*, suggesting a degree of foreign oversight and royal control of these *fondacos* and

[7] al-Ṭurṭūshī, *Sirāj al-mulūk* (Alexandria, 1289/1872): 230; I translate the word *nawāqīs* as "bells," since this was its understanding in the western Islamic world by the central middle ages. In earlier eastern versions of the Pact of 'Umar, this word would have referred to wooden clappers.

their funds that is not found for other European facilities in Ḥafṣid lands.[8] After James' death in 1276, his extensive kingdom was divided between his two sons, Peter (who received the mainland territories in eastern Spain) and James (who inherited Mallorca and regions in what is now south-western France).

Peter III continued to pursue his father's Mediterranean interests, and in March 1282, he wrested Sicily from Angevin control, basing his claim on the interests of his wife, Constance, the daughter of the last Hohenstaufen king, Manfred (who had lost the island to the French prince, Charles of Anjou, in 1266). The island was subsequently held by Peter's vassal, Roger of Lauria, who further expanded Aragonese domains in the central Mediterranean by capturing Jerba in October 1284 and threatening other Ḥafṣid territories. Six months later, in June 1285, Peter III received emissaries from the Ḥafṣid ruler, Abū Ḥafṣ 'Umar, and concluded a wide-ranging treaty that was very favorable to Aragonese interests. These included matters of trade and security, concessions for Christian religious practice in Tunis, and the right to name the head of the Christian militia,[9] together with an annual tribute of 33,333 and one third bezants to be paid to Peter in his capacity as king of Sicily.[10]

Although this agreement was meant to last for fifteen years, it had little opportunity to be effective, since Peter III died the following November, only a few months after the treaty was signed. He left his mainland Iberian territories to his older son, who took the throne as Alfonso III, and the kingdom of Sicily to his younger son, James (who later ruled a recombined Crown of Aragón, as James II, after the death of his brother Alfonso in 1291). After his accession in late 1285, Alfonso III did not immediately follow up on his father's diplomatic policies, instead pursuing negotiations with the Marinids in

---

[8] Constable, *Housing the Strange*: 192-9.

[9] There is considerable evidence of Christian mercenary forces serving in North Africa, and these included soldiers from the Crown of Aragón. See R.I. Burns, "Renegades, Adventurers, and Sharp Businessmen: The Thirteenth-century Spaniard in the Cause of Islam," *Catholic Historical Review* 58 (1972): 341-66. Also M. Lower, "Tunis in 1270: A Case of Interfaith Relations in the Late Thirteenth Century," *International History Review* 28 (2006): 507-8.

[10] L. de Mas Latrie, *Traités de paix et de commerce et documents divers concernant les relations des chrétiens avec les arabes de l'Afrique septentrionale au moyen âge* (Paris: Henri Plon, 1865): 286-90; Ch.E. Dufourcq, *L'Espagne catalane et le maghrib aux XIIIe et XIVe siècles* (Paris: Presses Universitaires de France, 1966): 271-4; R. Brunschvig, *La Berbérie orientale sous les Ḥafṣides des origines a la fin du XVe siècle* (Paris: Adrien-Maisonneuve, 1940): 94-6.

Morocco, supporting the emerging ʿAbd al-Wādid state in central North Africa (based in Tlemcen after 1283), and allowing Roger of Lauria to resume raids on Ḥafṣid territories in 1286-1287. Meanwhile, in Ifrīqīya, Abū Ḥafṣ ʿUmar had further troubles of his own, as disputes over power and succession created political schisms. In 1285, his nephew, Abū Zakarīyā al-Muntakhab, seized control of the western part of the Ḥafṣid domains, including Bougie and Constantine. At the same time, ʿAbd al-Wāḥid, the son of another nephew, Abū Zakarīyā al-Wāthiq (who had ruled from 1277 to 1279), also claimed the Ḥafṣid throne. It was this claimant, ʿAbd al-Wāḥid b. al-Wāthiq, who was party to the July 1287 treaty with Alfonso III.

Both Alfonso III and ʿAbd al-Wāḥid had important things to gain from their negotiations in 1287. The latter hoped to acquire Aragonese support for his claims against those of his great uncle, Abū Ḥafṣ ʿUmar, while the former wanted concessions—especially the 33,333 bezants of annual tribute to Sicily—that had been negotiated in the 1285 treaty between Tunis and the Crown of Aragón. Strictly speaking, this tribute was now due to Alfonso's younger brother James, as king of Sicily, not to the ruler of mainland Aragonese territories. However, the 1287 treaty arranged that the entire sum of 33,333 would be paid to Alfonso, with an additional payment of 16,000 bezants to go to his brother James. The document went on to list other concessions to the Aragonese, including the religious freedoms cited in the passages translated above.

Given the complex political context of the 1287 treaty, and the fact that ʿAbd al-Wāḥid never became the Ḥafṣid sultan, it seems reasonable to consider this document as merely a list of desiderata rather than as a statement of items for implementation. In this light, it is not surprising that the list of religious concessions granted to Christians in Tunis seems more generous and extensive than what is found in other roughly contemporary Christian treaties with Ḥafṣid rulers. Nevertheless, data from a variety of other sources suggest that the individual concessions regarding Christian practice in the treaty—the rights to churches, priests, services, burial for the dead, and possibly even bells—were indeed available to Christians in Tunis during the later thirteenth century. Thus, in large part, the 1287 treaty was probably a synthesis and confirmation of current practice, and a statement of the expectation of its continuity, even if the document itself was never activated. In order to clarify the situation of Christians in Ḥafṣid Tunis, it will be useful to consider the contents of the 1287 treaty in comparison with other sources.

It is noteworthy that the section in the 1287 treaty relating to the Catalan *fondaco* in Tunis and to Christian religious practice emphasized prior precedents set in the time of James I, Alfonso's grandfather. Custom and tradition are strongly stressed in this passage, and there is no admission of any intention of innovation. The mention of James I makes perfect sense, since the Aragonese *fondaco* in Tunis was first established during his reign, in the early 1250s, and that king took a special interest in its supervision and fiscal management. Early consuls were directly appointed by James, who leased the position in return for a substantial rent, while still retaining royal control of certain aspects of the facility.[11] Among these was oversight of the religious affairs of the *fondaco* and appointment of a chaplain (*capellano*) *in capella alfundici nostri Tunicii*. In May 1261, James made a donation to the chapel in the Catalan *fondaco* to pay for the construction of two small rooms for the chaplain, one that this man could live in himself and the other that he could either use or rent out. In the same document, James named Gerald of Argileto as priest (*presbitero*) of the *fondaco*, with a life appointment, and with the expectation that he would celebrate mass and other divine offices in the chapel (*quam capellam nostram alfundici predicti damus et concedimus Geraldo de Argileto, presbitero, diebus omnibus vite sue, et ipse teneatur in eadem capella celebrare et alia divina officia facere consueta*).[12]

In fact, it was standard practice for European *fondacos* in Muslim cities to contain a church or chapel where members of the foreign Christian community could worship. From the twelfth century onwards, treaties between Muslim and Christian states routinely granted *fondacos* together with a cluster of other facilities, including churches, bath houses, cemeteries, ovens, and gardens, in Alexandria, Tunis, and elsewhere. [13] Indeed, the concession of churches to western merchant communities probably predated the evolution of the

[11] Ch.E. Dufourcq, "Les consulats Catalans de Tunis et de Bougie au temps de Jacques le Conquérant," *Anuario de Estudios Medievales* 3 (1966): 469-79.

[12] A.H. Miranda and M.D. Pecourt, eds. *Documentos de Jaime I de Aragon* (Zaragoza: Anubar, 1982), 4:306 (doc. 1232).

[13] Constable, *Housing the Stranger*: 119-26.

fondaco.[14] The link between European *fondacos* and churches may also have had roots in the fact that Muslim *funduqs* and *khāns* often contained a small mosque or a room for prayer.[15] As early as 1229, Pisa was promised the right to a *fondaco*, church, cemetery, bath, and oven in Tunis, and this commitment was repeated in later negotiations in 1264.[16] In 1259, the archbishop of Pisa appointed a priest "for the care and administration of the church of Santa Maria in Tunis" (*curam et administrationem ecclesie Sancte Marie de Tunithe*).[17] By the second half of the thirteenth century there were also chapels in the Genoese, Venetian, French, and Sicilian *fondacos* in Tunis, as well as the *capella* in the Catalan *fondaco*. Notarial records from Tunis in 1289 mention both a church in the Genoese *fondaco*, also dedicated to the Virgin (*eclesie Sancte Marie*), and an *eclesia fondicis Sicilianorum*.[18]

A church or chapel needed a priest in order to conduct services, and there is considerable evidence beyond the 1261 grant by James I to confirm the presence of Christian religious functionaries in Tunis during the later thirteenth century.[19] Two decades earlier, in 1240, the podestá of Pisa had made similar provisions for the chaplain of the Pisan community in Tunis to have a room in the *fondaco* for his use and lodging (*dictus sacerdos potest habitare in una apotheca suprascripti fundaci*). The text refers to this man as both *sacerdos* and *presbiter Pisanorum de Tunithi*.[20] Another priest, identified as *presbitero Opitho*, was appointed in Tunis by the Pisan

[14] V. Slessarev, "*Ecclesiae Mercatorum* and the Rise of Merchant Colonies," *Business History Review* 41 (1967): 177-97.

[15] Constable, *Housing the Stranger*: 98-9.

[16] Mas Latrie, *Traités de paix et de commerce*: 32-3. The date on this treaty, which mentions that *in quolibet fontico, fieri debet ecclesia et cimeterium*, is in doubt. It was issued in 1229 or 1234, but either date represents the earliest treaty mentioning a church in Tunis. A similar phrase in Italian, *debbia a loro essere facto in ciascheduno fondacho una ecclesia et uno cimiterio*, appeared in the 1264 treaty, together with mention of a bath and oven (M. Latrie, *Traités de paix et de commerce*: 44).

[17] Mas Latrie, *Traités de paix et de commerce*: 37.

[18] G. Pistarino, ed., *Notai genovesi in Oltremare. Atti rogati a Tunisi da Pietro Battifoglio (1288-1289)* (Genoa: Università di Genova, 1986); There are many references to the church in the Genoese *fondaco* (see index page 238); Sicilian *fondaco* (doc. 5).

[19] On priests in *fondacos* in places other than Tunis, see Constable, *Housing the Stranger*: 138-9; also Dufourcq, *L'Espagne catalane*: 104-6.

[20] Mas Latrie, *Traités de paix et de commerce*: 36. Such provisions were probably normal; a text relating to Acre in 1244 mentioned that the *sacerdos* in the Venetian *fondaco* had his own room (Constable, *Housing the Stranger*: 228).

archbishop in 1259.[21] The attempted crusade of Louis IX to Tunis, in the summer of 1270, appears to have had both positive and negative consequences for Christian priests in Ḥafṣid lands. Although the crusade disrupted western Christian life in Ifrīqīya, affairs soon resumed their pre-war status. Another document issued by the archbishop of Pisa, in April 1271, recorded both the forced flight of Jaffaro, the priest in the Pisan *fondaco* in Bougie, because of the crusade, and his subsequent reinstatement as chaplain in this church (*presbiterum Jafferum pro cappellano ipsius ecclesie remisit*).[22]

After the failure of the French crusading effort, Christian diplomats still managed to negotiate favorable terms with the Ḥafṣid state, including expanded privileges for Christian religious practice. An Arabic treaty signed in November 1270 between France (including Sicily under Charles of Anjou) and the sultan al-Mustanṣir, and intended to be in force for fifteen years, included a section relating to Christian monks or priests (*ruhbān al-naṣārī aw qusūsihim*), who were allowed "to stay in the lands of the Amīr al-Muʿminīn, who will give them space where they may build monasteries and churches and bury their dead. These monks and priests may preach publicly in their churches, and they may serve God according to the rites of their religion and the customs of their own country."[23] Three months later, in February 1271, James I of Aragón also signed a ten-year peace treaty with Tunis, but this document contained no mention of churches or priests. Possibly this omission was because earlier arrangements concerning the Catalan *fondaco* in Tunis were still in place.[24]

---

[21] Mas Latrie, *Traités de paix et de commerce*: 37.

[22] Ibidem: 47-8.

[23] The Arabic text and French translation by S. De Sacy were published by P. Grandchamp (« P.G.G. ») in "Documents divers relatifs à la croisade de Saint Louis contre Tunis (1270)," *Les Cahiers de Tunisie* 25 (1977): 245-82. This is an updated version of an article originally published in the *Revue Tunisienne* 91 (1912). De Sacy's French translation, without the Arabic text, also appears in Mas Latrie, *Traités de paix et de commerce*: 94.

[24] Mas Latrie, *Traités de paix et de commerce*: 280-4. Unlike other contemporary treaties, which were translated into Latin or romance vernacular languages from an Arabic original, this treaty was originally drawn up in Catalan, then translated into Arabic; see R.A. Messier, "The Christian Community of Tunis at the Time of St. Louis' Crusade, AD 1270," in *The Meeting of Two Worlds: Cultural Exchange between East and West during the Period of the Crusades*, ed. V.P. Gross and C.V. Bornstein (Kalamazoo: Medieval Institute Publications, 1986): 248.

It is probable that the monks mentioned in the 1270 treaty with France were Franciscans or Dominicans. Since the early thirteenth century, members of these two orders had been interested in visiting Tunis to preach and spread their message.[25] Although some of these preachers explicitly hoped to convert Muslims, even including the sultan himself, it is more realistic to assume that their efforts were mainly aimed at the variety of western Christians—including merchants, mercenaries, captives, and renegades—who were living in Ḥafṣid lands. In 1219, Giles of Assisi, an early follower of St. Francis, journeyed to Tunis to preach, but he was quickly sent home by the local Christian community. There are also papal letters from 1226 and 1233 mentioning Franciscans and Dominicans in Morocco, and the latter notes the appointment of a Franciscan as bishop of Fez.[26] Another letter, sent by pope Gregory IX to the Ḥafṣid sultan in 1235, mentioned the arrival in Tunis of a certain brother Joannus, who was a member of the Franciscan community in Morocco (*ordinis Minorum de Barbaria*).[27] A decade later, in 1246, pope Innocent IV begged the rulers of Tunis, Ceuta, and Bougie to afford protection to Franciscans (*fratres Minores*) who had been sent to minister to Christians in their lands.[28] Later in the thirteenth century, several famous names appear among those who traveled to Tunis, including the Catalan Dominican Ramon Martí, who encouraged Louis IX's crusading aspirations and who had himself gone to preach in Tunis (without any notable success) in 1268-1269.[29] Later, the prolific preacher and author Ramon Llull, also a Catalan, would travel to Tunis with similar intentions in 1293, and for a second time shortly before his death in 1316.[30] But alongside these visits by illustrious personalities, ordinary Franciscans also continued to be a presence in Tunis. On June 9, 1287, roughly two months before the treaty between Alfonso III and ʿAbd al-Wāḥid b. al-Wāthiq, a trade agreement drawn up in Tunis between the Genoese ambassador and

[25] Dufourcq, *L'Espagne catalane*: 106-10, 490-1. See also R. Vose, *Dominicans, Muslims, and Jews in the Medieval Crown of Aragon* (Cambridge: Cambridge University Press, 2009).

[26] Mas Latrie, *Traités de paix et de commerce*: 9-10.

[27] Ibidem: 11.

[28] Ibidem: 13.

[29] A. Bonner, ed. *Doctor Illuminatus: a Ramon Llull Reader* (Princeton: Princeton University Press,1993), 76; J. Tolan, *Saracens, Islam in the Medieval European Imagination* (New York: Columbia University Press, 2002): 203.

[30] Tolan, *Saracens*: 259-60.

representatives of the Ḥafṣid sultan Abū Ḥafṣ 'Umar, was witnessed by two Franciscans, *fratres Pelegrinus et Bernardus de ordine Fratrum minorum*.[31]

Also appearing on the same witness list was Tealdus, the chaplain of the church of Santa Maria in the Genoese *fondaco* in Tunis (*presbiter Tealdus capellanus ecclesie Sancte Marie de fondico Januensium in Tunexi*).[32] This might have been our only knowledge of this Tealdus, were it not for the survival of the notarial records of Pietro Battifoglio, who served as notary in the Genoese *fondaco* in Tunis, covering the years 1288 and 1289. Tealdus appears in no less than twenty-six documents, usually as a witness but often in a more active capacity.[33] In most of these, he is referred to by the title *presbiter Tealdus, capellannus eclesie Sancte Marie fondicis veteri Ianuensium*, or some slight variant of this phrase. Tealdus was apparently considered trustworthy and impartial, and when there was an altercation with local Muslim authorities over sales of wine in the *fondaco*, Tealdus was entrusted with the keys to the wine store until the dispute could be resolved.[34] Tealdus also frequently acted as the local executor (*fidecummisario in Tunexi*) for western merchants who had died in Tunis, and he held their goods in safe-keeping until they could be delivered to the proper recipient as stated in the will.[35] Documents drawn up in 1289 might record the delivery or dispute of goods entrusted several years earlier. In one case, the dead man was a merchant from Mallorca who had died in Tunis in December 1287.[36] Since his will was written by Pietro Battifoglio, and his belongings were entrusted to Tealdus, both men must also have been present in Tunis at that time. It is perhaps odd that a Mallorcan would have chosen a Genoese notary and priest for these roles, but maybe

---

[31] Mas Latrie, *Traités de paix et de commerce*: 127.

[32] Ibidem: 127.

[33] Pistarino, *Notai genovesi in Oltremare*; Tealdus appears as a witness in twenty documents (numbers 1, 3, 8-11, 14, 18-19, 35-36, 51-52, 55, 60, 78, 92, 97, 124, and 131).

[34] Pistarino, *Notai genovesi in Oltremare*: 3-4 (doc. 1).

[35] Provision for the safe transfer of a dead person's goods to the heirs was always of concern, but it could be especially difficult when a merchant died far from home. In such a case, it was common for the consul of the *fondaco*, its priest, or another merchant to be entrusted with their safe-keeping. A clause in a Venetian treaty with Tunis, dated April 1251, provided detailed protections to prevent a dead person's belongings from being commandeered by local authorities (Mas Latrie, *Traités de paix et de commerce*, 201).

[36] Pistarino, *Notai genovesi in Oltremare*: 90-1 (doc. 61).

illness or accident had forced expediency. Alternately, political issues between Mallorca and Barcelona may have discouraged the dying man from turning to inhabitants of the Catalan *fondaco*, or possibly there was no priest currently appointed to that facility. A few months earlier, on August 7, 1287, Pietro and Tealdus had also performed similar roles for a dying merchant from Chiavari, but in this case his choice of the Genoese *fondaco* was more straightforward since the man came from a town just down the Ligurian coast from Genoa.[37] This document locates both the notary and the priest in Tunis within days of the treaty signed between Alfonso III and ʿAbd al-Wāḥid b. al-Wāthiq on July 29, 1287.

Tealdus' role as executor indicates that he was present when wills were made by western merchants dying in Tunis. By extension, we may assume Tealdus' presence, in his capacity as a priest, at their deathbeds and funerals. One document records such an event, in the last testament of Giovanna Zenogia, whose will was dictated to Pietro Battifoglio as she lay dying in the Marseille *fondaco* in Tunis in January 1289.[38] Either there was no priest or notary available in this building, nor a church or cemetery, or she deliberately chose to turn to the Genoese for these last services. Giovanna wished that her body should be buried by the church of the old Genoese *fondaco*, and she left money for the funeral with the stipulation that Tealdus, the chaplain of that church, was to preside over her internment (*volo et iubeo corpus [meum se]peliri ad eclesiam Sancte Marie fondi[ci]s veteri Ianuensium; item lego pro sepultura mea et pro funeris mei [presbite]ro Tealdo, capellanno dicte eclesie, dublerium unum boni auri de Miro et iusti ponderis*).[39] She did not, however, nominate Tealdus as her executor.

The giving of last rites was one of the most important sacraments, and it is no surprise that western Christian communities in Muslim cities were concerned to provide for this necessity. As suggested by the data on Tealdus, it may be that there was sometimes only one Latin priest available, who would have visited Christians in various

[37] Three separate documents relate to a dispute over this will: Pistarino, *Notai genovesi in Oltremar*: 91-2 (doc. 62), 114-15 (doc. 79), and 119-22 (doc. 83). Another document relating to a different will (150-2 [doc. 104]) also names Tealdus as *fidecummisarius*. G. Jehel has studied the different nationalities of people mentioned in P. Battifoglio's notarial register; G. Jehel, "Catalans et majorquins à Tunis en 1289," *Cuadernos de historia económica de Cataluña* 20 (1979): 125-30.

[38] A correction in the original text substitutes *Marsiliorum* for *Sicilianorum*.

[39] Pistarino, *Notai genovesi in Oltremare*: 11-13 (doc. 6).

different *fondacos*. This would explain the phrase in the 1287 treaty that permitted "priests to carry the cross and censer to the bodies of dead Christians for their burial." Even in Alexandria, where there was a relatively large western Christian population, the fifteenth-century German pilgrim Felix Fabri went to hear mass at one of the Venetian *fondacos*, because there was no priest available in the Catalan *fondaco* where he was staying. Likewise, the Venetian chaplain attended the death of Felix's companion, the Count de Solm, who died and was buried in Alexandria.[40]

Christian burials abroad often appear in passing, in accounts like Felix Fabri's pilgrim narrative or the notarial materials of Pietro Battifoglio, but diplomatic treaties also frequently included clauses granting cemeteries to western *fondaco* communities in Islamic cities. Cemeteries were granted in conjunction with *fondacos*, but it is unclear if they were located inside or outside the walls of the main building. Giovanna Zenogia's last wish to be buried by the church (*ad eclesiam*) of the old Genoese *fondaco* suggests a location within, or very close to, the *fondaco's* church. Pisa was promised a *cimeterium* in Tunis by 1234, and a *cimiterio* was referred to again in the Pisan-Ḥafṣid treaty of 1264.[41] In 1270, French diplomats likewise negotiated for rights to a place where they could bury their dead in Tunis.[42] There must also have been a Pisan cemetery in Bougie by 1271, along with a church, because the priest, Jaffaro, had the right "to excommunicate anybody who desecrated the church or the cemetery" (*potestatem excommunicandi omnes qui dictam ecclesiam vel ejus cimiterium invaderint*).[43] The sentence of excommunication indicates that the concern related to violations by Christians, not Muslims.

Perhaps the most problematic issue relating to Christian practice in western *fondacos* concerned the ringing of bells to signal services. This makes the mention of bells in the 1287 treaty between Alfonso III and ʿAbd al-Wāḥid b. al-Wāthiq especially noteworthy. Even the provision of wine in *fondacos* (both for the celebration of mass and

---

[40] F. Fabri, *Evagatorium in terrae sanctae, Arabiae et Egypti peregrinationem*, ed. C.D. Hassler (Stuttgart: Soc. Lit. Stuttgardiensis, 1843-1849), 3:22 [81b]; 32, [85b]; 199-200 [142b-143a]; French translation by J. Masson, *Le Voyage en Egypte de Félix Fabri, 1483* (Cairo: Institut français d'archéologie orientale, 1975), 2:406, 428, 764-7.

[41] Mas Latrie, *Traités de paix et de commerce*: 32, 44.

[42] Ibidem: 94.

[43] Ibidem: 48.

for general consumption) seems to have been more straightforward and openly regulated.[44] Muslim concerns about the audible aspects of Christian religious practice go back to the earliest *dhimmī* regulations, with prohibitions against the use of clappers or bells (*nawāqīs*) and loud chanting.[45] Although early Islamic regulations related to the wooden clapper (*nāqūs*) used in eastern Christian church services, later medieval texts employed the same word for bells. The section from the "Pact of 'Umar," quoted by Abū Bakr al-Ṭurṭūshī (noted above), indicates that the issue of bells and Christian noise remained alive in the Muslim West during the central medieval period. Andalusī *ḥisba* texts also testify to the same ongoing concerns. The early twelfth-century text of Ibn 'Abdūn, describing Seville, ruled that the ringing of bells (*ḍarb al-nawāqīs*) should be suppressed in all Muslim territories and the sound should only be heard in the lands of the Christians."[46] A century later, al-Saqaṭī, writing in Malaga, warned that nobody should go about ringing a bell (*jaras*) to alert people to something.[47] Al-Wansharīsī also recorded an undated *fatwa* from Tunis that addressed the fact that foreign Christians had built a new church with a tower (*ṣawmaʿa*) in their *funduq*. No bells were mentioned, although these may have been a factor in the dispute. Instead, the Christians argued that the tower was needed to provide light to the church, and they presented Muslim authorities with the text of a treaty stating that nobody should stop them from building a place of worship.[48]

Bells were a potent element within the medieval discourse on religious power. They were both a signal and a symbol. Like the voice of the muezzin, the ringing of bells both defined and announced the presence of a religious community to all those who heard them. Bells could be an auditory symbol of conquest, and in thirteenth-century

[44] Constable, *Housing the Stranger*: 138-44, 276-8.

[45] A.S. Tritton, *The Caliphs and their Non-Muslim Subjects* (London: Humphrey Milford, 1930): 100-14.

[46] Ibn ʿAbdūn, *Documents arabes inédits sur la vie sociale et économique en occident musulman au moyen âge. Trois traités hispaniques de ḥisba*, ed. E. Lévi-Provençal (Cairo: Institut français d'archéologie orientale, 1955): 55.

[47] Al-Saqaṭī, *Un manuel hispanique de ḥisba*, ed. E. Lévi-Provençal (Paris: Librerie Ernest Leroux, 1931): 67. The late thirteenth-century Andalusī *ḥisba* text of al-Jarsīfī also associated Christians with bells, although in this case ruling that Christian women should wear small bells (*juljul*) as an identifying aspect of their costume (in *Documents arabes inédits sur la vie sociale*, ed. E. Lévi-Provençal: 122).

[48] al-Wansharīsī, *Miʿyār al-muʿrib wa al-jāmiʿ al-maghrib* (Rabat: Wizārat al-awqāf, 1981), 2: 215-16.

Spain, it was common for them to be installed immediately in the new church towers of recently conquered towns. According to al-Maqqarī, when Valencia was besieged by James I, the Muslim ruler Ibn Zayyān sent an emissary to Tunis, asking for assistance and warning that the mosque call could soon be replaced by the sound of bells (*jaras*), and the geographer al-Ḥimyarī likewise recorded that "the bell overcame the sound of the call to prayer" (*abṭala al-nāqūs ṣawt adhānihā*) after the conquest of Valencia in 1238.[49] In Segorbe, near Valencia, the first ringing of bells after its transfer to Christian control in 1244 provoked a riot in the local Muslim community.[50] Even without their being sounded, the symbolism of bells was played out in historical actions. For example, when the Umayyad regent, al-Manṣūr, attacked Santiago de Compostela in 997, he took the bells of the church back to Córdoba, where—according to the thirteenth-century Castilian *Primera crónica general*—they were transformed into lamps for the mosque (*las canpanas ...servieran y en logar de lanparas*). Over two centuries later, after the Christian conquest of Córdoba in 1236, Ferdinand III of Castile returned these bells to the Compostela shrine. Bell-capture remained symbolically important in the later medieval period, when the Almohads also took bells from churches in Christian Spain, including nine bells captured from the town of Úbeda in 1180. The bells were subsequently taken to Morocco and installed—silenced and redesigned—as lamps in the Qarawīyīn Mosque in Fez. These bell-lamps provide a valuable insight into how the bells taken from Santiago de Compostela might have been hung as lamps in the Córdoba mosque.[51] The events in Úbeda, Valencia,

---

[49] al-Maqqarī, *Khurūj al-Andalus min yad al-Muslimīn* (Kuwait: Dār al-awrad, 1993): 145; on this embassy to Tunis see also H. Kennedy, *Muslim Spain and Portugal* (London: Longman, 1996): 270-1 (my thanks to A.A. Alibhai for these two citations); Al-Ḥimyarī, *La Péninsule ibérique au moyen-age d'après le Kitāb ar-rawḍ al-mi'ṭar fī ḫabar al-akṭār d'Ibn 'Abd al-Mun'im al-Ḥimyarī*, ed. and transl. E. Lévi-Provençal (Leiden: Brill, 1938): 50 (trans. 63). Both al-Maqqarī and al-Ḥimyarī cited the work of the thirteenth-century scholar Ibn al-'Abbār (d. 1260), who served as Ibn Zayyān's ambassador to Tunis.

[50] R.I. Burns, *The Crusader Kingdom of Valencia. Reconstruction on a Thirteenth-century Frontier* (Cambridge, MA: Harvard University Press, 1967), 1:48, 56.

[51] E. Lévi-Provençal, *Histoire de l'Espagne musulmane* (Paris: Maisonneuve, 1950), 2:250; *Primera crónica general de España*, ed. R.M. Pidal (Madrid: Editorial Gredos, 1977), 2:734. The bell-lamps have been discussed by A.A. Alibhai, in "Silent Declarations: Bells in Transition in Medieval Iberia," a paper delivered at the 42nd Annual Medieval Congress, Kalamazoo MI, May 2007. There are photographs of the Úbeda bells hanging as lamps in the Qarawīyīn mosque (together with another example of a bell-lamp, taken from Gibraltar by the Marinids in 1333) in

and Córdoba would still have been very much part of Christian and Muslim memory during diplomatic negotiations in the later thirteenth century, and any reference to bells would have been highly charged with meaning.

Bells are striking in their absence from Christian diplomatic negotiations with Tunis except for a sudden cluster of references to them in the final decades of the thirteenth century.[52] This small group of texts makes clear that the rulers of Aragón, at least, pressed for the right to ring bells for Christian religious services in Tunis during this period. Perhaps the military ascendancy of the Crown of Aragón at this time, in combination with the political troubles of the Ḥafṣid state, suggested that this was an opportune moment to broach this normally taboo request. It is also worth keeping in mind that James I and his heirs had always treated the Catalan *fondacos* in Tunis with a more directly proprietary attitude (referring to them as *nostri fondaci*, keeping close royal control of their revenues, and personally overseeing the leasing of these buildings) than was the case for other European facilities in Ḥafṣid lands.

The 1285 treaty between Peter III of Aragón and Abū Ḥafṣ ʿUmar seems to have been the first document of its kind to deal with the issue of bells in Christian *fondacos*. It promised that Christian churches and bells for Christian religious services (*les esgleyes dels Crestians, les esquelles els oficis dels Crestians*) would be permitted in Tunis.[53] This unusual agreement apparently sparked a brief and optimistic flurry of Aragonese diplomacy on the subject of bells in this Ḥafṣid city. In early 1287, Alfonso III instructed Conrad Lancia, his ambassador to Tunis, to insist that "the body of Christ should be allowed to be carried through all of the Christian neighborhoods and *fondacos* at the signal of a bell" (*quel Corpus Christi puscha portat ab seyal de campaneta per tots los ravals e los fondechs de les*

Al-Andalus: The Art of Islamic Spain, ed. J.D. Dodds (New York: Metropolitan Museum of Art, 1992): 272-3, 278-9.

[52] I have found no references to bells in *fondacos* in other Muslim cities. In 1277, however, the Venetian community in Tyre was permitted to build a church with a bell tower (Constable, *Housing the Stranger*: 232). Tyre was still a Christian city at this point, and would remain so until its capture by the Mamluks in 1291. Bells would have been an auditory reminder of the ongoing crusader control of this city.

[53] Mas Latrie, *Traités de paix et de commerce*: 289. The Catalan *esquelles* is cognate to the Latin *squille* (small bell).

Crestians).[54] Within a few months, these requests were granted by the Ḥafṣid pretender, ʿAbd al-Wāḥid b. al-Wāthiq, in the clause allowing priests to "carry the body of Jesus Christ at the signal of a bell as is the custom among the Christians." Of course, this permission had no force, since ʿAbd al-Wāḥid was never in a position to grant actual concessions. Perhaps because of this, three years later, in 1290, Alfonso III reminded his next ambassador to Tunis, Bernard de Belvis, that he should be sure to negotiate the right for Christians to "have churches, where they may be married and bury their dead, and that they may sound bells to signal church services" (*quels crestians ajen esgleyes e y pusquen soterrar e fer matrimonis e sonar campanes e usar doffici desgleya*).[55] It is noteworthy that although all of these documents dealt with the same topic, they did not directly quote each other. Their differences in wording suggest repeated requests rather than the rote repetition of diplomatic phrases.

Did these negotiations result in the ringing of bells in Ḥafṣid Tunis in the later thirteenth century? It is hard to know, but it seems unlikely, especially because this sudden expression of Aragonese interest in bells was not followed up in subsequent diplomacy. Later sources relating to western Christian activities in Tunis continued to mention *fondacos*, churches, priests, and cemeteries, but they made no reference to bells. So this handful of references dating between 1285 and 1290 seems to be an anomaly in the diplomatic record. Certainly, there is little to suggest that the citizens of Ḥafṣid Tunis experienced the ringing of Christian bells on a regular basis.

Yet bells were sometimes heard in the region during the later thirteenth century. When the Moroccan pilgrim al-ʿAbdarī passed through the small town of Zawāra, on the Libyan coast west of Tripoli, in 688/1289, he reported hearing the sound of bells ringing (*dāwā aṣwāt al-nawāqīṣ* [sic]) and associated this with other Christian practices.[56] Four years later, a letter dated 1293, sent from Charles, the Angevin king of Hungary, to Frederick (brother of James II of Aragón and later Frederick III of Sicily) and Roger of Lauria, mentioned a Catalan ship carrying two bells (*campanas duas*) to Jerba,

[54] Ch.E. Dufourcq, "La Couronne d'Aragon et les Hafsides au XIIIe siècle (1229-1301)," *Analecta Sacra Tarraconensia* 25 (1952): 50, 61.

[55] L. Klüpfel, *Die äussere Politik Alfonsos III. Von Aragonien (1285-1291)* (Berlin: W. Rothschild, 1911): 174.

[56] al-ʿAbdarī, *Riḥlat al-ʿAbdarī* (Rabat: Jāmiʿat Muḥammad al-Khāmis, 1968): 76. The author also mentioned the sale of pork to Christians in the same passage.

which was still in Christian hands.[57] Once these bells were mounted, their sound would have been a potent auditory announcement of the Christian presence on the island. The repeated prohibitions in *ḥisba* texts and other legal materials likewise suggest that Christian bells were not completely unknown in Ḥafṣid domains and elsewhere in the Islamic West.

In conclusion, it is clear that although the religious concessions granted in 1287 were especially generous, and never enforceable, the individual elements noted in this text all fitted comfortably within a broader diplomatic pattern of Christian requests and Ḥafṣid promises in this period. There was nothing out of line here either with contemporary diplomacy or actual practice in western *fondacos* in thirteenth-century Tunis. Most of the Christian communities had churches and cemeteries as part of their *fondaco* complexes, and these churches were staffed, at least sporadically, by resident Latin priests, who conducted services and attended to the religious needs of the western Christian population. Sometimes, they may even have rung bells.

Bibliography

al-ʿAbdarī, *Riḥlat al-ʿAbdarī*. Rabat: Jāmiʿat Muḥammad al-Khāmis, 1968.

Alarcón y Santón, M.A. *Los Documentos árabes diplomáticos del Archivo de la Corona de Aragón*. Madrid: Publicaciones de las Escuelas de Estudios Árabes de Madrid y Granada, 1940.

(Alfonso X). *Primera crónica general de España*. Edited by Ramón Menéndez Pidal. Madrid: Editorial Gredos, 1977.

Alibhai, A.A. "Silent Declarations: Bells in Transition in Medieval Iberia," unpublished paper, 42nd Annual Medieval Congress. Kalamazoo MI, May 2007.

Bonner, A. ed. *Doctor Illuminatus: a Ramon Llull Reader*. Princeton: Princeton University Press, 1993.

Burns, R. I. *The Crusader Kingdom of Valencia. Reconstruction on a Thirteenth-century Frontier*, 2 volumes. Cambridge, MA: Harvard University Press, 1967.

——. "Renegades, Adventurers, and Sharp Businessmen: The Thirteenth-century Spaniard in the Cause of Islam." *Catholic Historical Review* 58 (1972): 341-66.

Brunschvig, R. *La Berbérie orientale sous les Ḥafṣides des origines a la fin du XVe siècle*. Paris: Adrien-Maisonneuve, 1940.

Cerone, F. "A proposito di alcuni documenti sulla seconda spedizione di Alfonso V contro l'isola Gerba." *Anuari d'Institut d'Estudis Catalans* 3 (1909-1910): 51-87.

[57] F. Cerone, "A proposito di alcuni documenti sulla seconda spedizione di Alfonso V contro l'isola Gerba," *Anuari d'Institut d'Estudis Catalans* 3 (1909-10): 54, 80.

Constable, O. R. *Housing the Stranger in the Mediterranean World: Lodging, Trade, and Travel in Late Antiquity and the Middle Ages*. Cambridge: Cambridge University Press, 2003.

Dodds, J.D. ed. *Al-Andalus: The Art of Islamic Spain*. New York: Metropolitan Museum of Art, 1992.

Dozy, R. *Supplément aux dictionnaires arabes*. Leiden: Brill, 1881.

Dufourcq, Ch.E. "Les consulats Catalans de Tunis et de Bougie au temps de Jacques le Conquérant." *Anuario de Estudios Medievales* 3 (1966): 469-79.

——. "La Couronne d'Aragon et les Hafsides au XIIIe siècle (1229-1301)." *Analecta Sacra Tarraconensia* 25 (1952): 1-63.

——. *L'Espagne catalane et le maghrib aux XIIIe et XIVe siècles*. Paris: Presses Universitaires de France, 1966.

Fabri, F. *Evagatorium in terrae sanctae, Arabiae et Egypti peregrinationem*, edited by C.D. Hassler, 3 volumes. Stuttgart: Soc. Lit. Stuttgardiensis, 1843-9. French translation by Jacques Masson, *Le Voyage en Egypte de Félix Fabri, 1483*. Cairo: Institut français d'archéologie orientale, 1975.

Grandchamp, P. "Documents divers relatifs à la croisade de Saint Louis contre Tunis (1270)." *Les Cahiers de Tunisie* 25 (1977): 245-82.

al-Ḥimyarī, *La Péninsule ibérique au moyen-age d'après le Kitāb ar-rawḍ al-mi'ṭar fī ḫabar al-akṭār d'Ibn 'Abd al-Mun'im al-Ḥimyarī*, edited and translated by E. Lévi-Provençal. Leiden: Brill, 1938.

Ibn 'Abdūn, in *Documents arabes inédits sur la vie sociale et économique en occident musulman au moyen âge. Trois traités hispaniques de ḥisba*, edited by E. Lévi-Provençal, 3-65. Cairo: Institut français d'archéologie orientale, 1955.

(James I). *Documentos de Jaime I de Aragon*, edited by Ambrosio Huici Miranda and M. Desamparados Pecourt, volume 4, Zaragoza: Anubar, 1982.

al-Jarsīfī, in *Documents arabes inédits sur la vie sociale et économique en occident musulman au moyen âge. Trois traités hispaniques de ḥisba*, edited by E. Lévi-Provençal, 119-128. Cairo: Institut français d'archéologie orientale, 1955.

Jehel, G. "Catalans et majorquins à Tunis en 1289." *Cuadernos de historia económica de Cataluña* 20 (1979): 125-30.

Kennedy, H. *Muslim Spain and Portugal*. London: Longman, 1996.

Klüpfel, L. *Die äussere Politik Alfonsos III. Von Aragonien (1285-1291)*. Berlin: W. Rothschild, 1911.

La Mantia, G. *Codice diplomatico dei Re Aragonesi*. Palermo: Società siciliana di storia patria, 1917; reprint Palermo: Ristampa Anastatica, 1990.

Lévi-Provençal, E. *Histoire de l'Espagne musulmane*, 3 volumes. Paris: Maisonneuve, 1950.

Lower, M. "Tunis in 1270: A Case of Interfaith Relations in the Late Thirteenth Century." *International History Review* 28 (2006): 504-14.

al-Maqqarī, *Khurūj al-Andalus min yad al-Muslimīn*. Kuwait: Dār al-awrad, 1993.

Mas Latrie, L. de. *Traités de paix et de commerce et documents divers concernant les relations des chrétiens avec les arabes de l'Afrique septentrionale au moyen âge*. Paris: Henri Plon, 1865.

Messier, R.A. "The Christian Community of Tunis at the Time of St. Louis' Crusade, AD 1270." In *The Meeting of Two Worlds: Cultural Exchange between East and West during the Period of the Crusades*, edited by V.P. Gross and C.V. Bornstein, 241-55. Kalamazoo: Medieval Institute Publications, 1986.

Pistarino, G. ed. *Notai genovesi in Oltremare. Atti rogati a Tunisi da Pietro Battifoglio (1288-1289)*. Genoa: Università di Genova, 1986.

al-Saqaṭī, *Un manuel hispanique de ḥisba*, edited by E. Lévi-Provençal, Paris: Librerie Ernest Leroux, 1931.

Slessarev, V. "*Ecclesiae Mercatorum* and the Rise of Merchant Colonies." *Business History Review* 41 (1967): 177-97.
Tolan, J. *Saracens. Islam in the Medieval European Imagination.* New York: Columbia University Press, 2002.
Tritton, S. *The Caliphs and their Non-Muslim Subjects.* London: Humphrey Milford, 1930.
al-Ṭurṭūshī, A.B. *Sirāj al-mulūk.* Alexandria, 1289/1872.
Vose, R. *Dominicans, Muslims, and Jews in the Medieval Crown of Aragon.* Cambridge: Cambridge University Press, 2009.
al-Wansharīsī, *Mi'yār al-mu'rib wa al-jāmi' al-maghrib.* Rabat: Wizārat al-awqāf, 1981.

AN OVERVIEW OF THE SLAVES' JURIDICAL STATUS AT SEA IN ROMANO-BYZANTINE, AND ISLAMIC LAWS

Hassan S. Khalilieh

Slavery, which constituted an inseparable part of the Romano-Byzantine and Islamic societies, played an integral role in the social, economic, military, and political life. Although many studies deal with these aspects of life, the available data regarding the treatment and carriage of slaves by sea is still unsatisfactory in quantity and quality. The manner in which they were transported, sheltered on ships, treated and supplied with food and water by their slavers and masters has received inadequate attention in modern scholarship. For example, it is unclear if a slave, acting as a ship's master, could be held liable for damage and loss resulting from his own acts, or the acts of his slave-sailors and human cargo? When did Byzantine and Islamic laws apply strict liability and vicarious liability on an individual slave for a tortious act or omission that caused loss to a third party? In terms of internal arrangements, where were slaves accommodated, how much space was available for each one on shipboard, and were male and female slaves divided? When danger was imminent, could slaves be thrown overboard? Did Byzantine legal codices and Islamic jurisprudence discriminate among slaves as crews and those purchased for commercial and private purposes? Based on the scattered legal and historical data available at hand, this paper attempts to portray slave life and experience at ports and at sea in periods when the overseas slave trade had increasingly been flourishing.[1]

---

[1] Destinations to which the slaves were transported, countries of supply, volume of slave trade, trunk routes merchantmen plied, purposes for which they were purchased, *etc.* have been extensively treated by some of the secondary sources utilized and cited in the current paper. Therefore, the author has deemed it appropriate not to re-address such issues here, but to focus on the slaves' legal status and conditions between the embarkation and debarkation ports.

Slaves as Ships' Masters, Sailors, and Servants

1. *Sustenance*

A full complement of officers and crew on board a large-sized seagoing and river vessel could number as many as eleven men, including the ship's servants, who were the personal attendants of the ship's officers and crew.[2] Salaried sailors, servants, and the ship's slaves generally enjoyed a similar legal status on board the vessel.[3]

As part of the seamen's labour and human rights, those in charge of the vessel—her owners and/or masters—had to load on board sufficient quantities of food, water, and other drinks for daily consumption for the outward voyage at least.[4] From the Roman through-

[2] R.L. Sargent, "The Use of Slaves by the Athenians in Warfare," *Classical Philology* 22 (1927): 264-79; L. Casson, "Galley Slaves," *Transactions and Proceedings of the American Philological Association* 97 (1966): 35-44; idem, *Ships and Seamanship in the Ancient World* (Princeton: Princeton University Press, 1971): 322; J.M. Libourel, "Galley Slaves in the Second Punic War," *Classical Philology* 68 (1973): 116-19; H. Ahrweiler, *Byzance et la mer: la marine de guerre, la politique et les institutions maritimes de Byzance aux VIIe-XVe siècles* (Paris: Presses universitaires de France, 1966), esp.: 405; H.I. Bell, "Two Official Letters of the Arab Period," *Journal of Egyptian Archaeology* 12 (1926): 265-81. Some contemporary historians assume that slaves of the Greco-Roman period were not enlisted as sailors since this profession was considered the privilege of freemen. V. Christides, "Raid and Trade in the Eastern Mediterranean: A Treatise by Muḥammad Ibn ʿUmar, the Faqīh from Occupied Moslem Crete, and Rhodian Sea Law, Two Parallel Texts," *Graeco-Arabica* 5 (1993): 86; H.S. Khalilieh, *Islamic Maritime Law: An Introduction* (Leiden: E. J. Brill, 1998): 42-7; M.A. Ṭāher (ed.), *Kitāb Akriyat al-Sufun wal-Nizāʿ bayna Ahlihā, Cahiers de Tunisie* 31 (1983): 32, 36; al-Yaḥṣubī, *Madhāhib al-Ḥukkām fī Nawāzil al-Aḥkām* (Beirut: Dār al-Gharb al-Islāmī, 1994): 235, 238; al-Qarāfī, *Anwār al-burūq fī anwāʾ al-Furūq* (Tūnis: 1885), 4:11; 5:488; idem, *Al-Dhakhīra* (Beirut: Dār al-Gharb al-Islāmī, 1994), 5:487; al-Wansharīsī, *Al-Miʿyār al-Muʿrib wal-Jāmiʿ al-Mughrib ʿan Fatāwā Ahl Ifrīqiya wal-Andalus wal-Maghrib* (Beirut: Dār al-Gharb al-Islāmī, 1981), 8:311. On slaves as seafarers and their engagement in the shipping business under Roman law, refer to Digest IV: 9, 3, 3; Digest IV: 9, 6, 1; Digest IV: 9, 6, 2; Digest IV: 9, 7; Digest IV: 9, 7, 3; Digest IV: 9, 7, 4; Digest IV: 9, 7, 6; Digest V: 3, 29; Digest IX: 4, 19, 21; Digest XIII: 6, 18; Digest XIII: 6, 55; Digest XIV: 1, 1, 4; Digest XIV: 1, 1, 16; Digest XIV: 1, 1, 21; Digest XIV: 1, 1, 22; Digest XIV: 1, 4, 2; Digest XIV: 1, 4, 3; Digest XIV: 1, 4, 4; Digest XIV: 1, 5; Digest XIV: 1, 5, 1; Digest XIV: 1, 6; Digest XIV: 1, 7, 2.

[3] Salaried sailors are described by the *Nomos Rhodion Nautikos* (Rhodian Sea Law) as "slaves," who are under obligation to execute all commissions professionally. See W. Ashburner, *The Rhodian Sea-Law* (Oxford: Clarendon Press, 1909): 121. Appendix D, Article III, states: "If a sailor hires himself out, let him know that he is a slave and has sold himself, and that he is to execute every commission."

[4] L. Casson, "The Feeding of the Trireme Crews and an Early in IG ii 2 1631," *Transactions of the American Philological Association* 125 (1995): 261-9; Ashburner,

out the Islamic Mediterranean, legal, documentary, and historical evidence show that the supply typically consisted of wheat for bread, barely, butter, oil, salt, dates,[5] and other staple foodstuffs that seamen "need for nourishment and survival."[6] Ibn Ḥazm urged slavers and slaveowners to feed their slaves "from the same kind of food his city residents consume (*mimmā ya'kul ahlu baladihi*)."[7] Citing one of the Prophet's final injunctions, al-Ghazālī appealed to his fellow Muslims urging them to feed their slaves "with what they eat," and cover them with what they wear: "The right of the slave is that his master should share his food and clothing with him."[8] However, although the amount of food and water each slave-sailor consumed per day is unclear, it stands to reason that the quota each one would receive was fixed prior to the departure schedule, or as mandated by the service contract and/or maritime custom.[9] Obviously, the presence of a cook and the existence of a caboose on seagoing vessels and river crafts constitute a clear evidence for serving hot meals in various stages of the maritime journey; hot meals were served once a day.[10]

Rhodian Sea-Law, clxxiv: 102, 103. The Rhodian maritime treatise makes two references to the diet of seamen though it does not prescribe the quality and quantity of food. Article III: 22 requires the ship master to supply seamen with food and water: "Let the captain take nothing but water and provisions … ." Article III: 25 requires merchants to provide seamen with drink and victuals if they were delayed in loading.

[5] K. Bradley, *Slavery and Society at Rome* (Cambridge: Cambridge University Press, 1994): 81-4; M.A. Fahmy, *Moslem Naval Organization* (Cairo: National Publication and Printing House, 1966): 109-11.

[6] Ṭāher ed.), *Akriyat al-Sufun*: 39.

[7] 'A.I. Bin-Maliḥ, *Al-Riqq fī Bilād al-Maghrib wa'l-Andalus* (Beirut: Dār al-Intishār al-'Arabī, 2004): 366; Bāzmūl, *Aḥkām al-Khadam fī al-Sharī'a al-Islāmīya* (Beirut: Dār al-Bashā'ir al-Lubnāniyya, 2008): 215-18.

[8] B. Lewis, *Race and Slavery in the Middle East: An Historical Inquiry* (Oxford: Oxford University Press, 1990): 146-7. For the original Arabic text see al-Ghazālī, *Iḥyā' 'Ulūm al-Dīn* (Cairo, 1967), 2: 281. Regarding the divine law on the treatment of slaves, refer to *Qur'ān*, 2:221; 4:36; 9:60; 16:71; 24:58; 30:28; 76:8; N.K. Kīrah, *Al-Jawārī wal-Ghulmān fī Miṣr fī al-'Aṣrayn al-Fāṭimī wal-Ayyūbī (358-648/969-1250)* (Cairo: Maktabat al-Zahrā', 2007): 28-36.

[9] R.H. Barrow, *Slavery in the Roman Empire* (New York: Barnes & Noble, 1968): 101; H.S. Khalilieh, *Admiralty and Maritime Laws in the Mediterranean Sea (ca. 800-1050): The Kitāb Akriyat al-Sufun vis-à-vis the Nomos Rhodion Nautikos* (Leiden: E. J. Brill, 2006): 66-7.

[10] Casson, "Feeding of the Trireme Crews": 264; D. Sperber, *Nautica Talmudica* (Leiden: E.J. Brill, 1986): 98-9. Cooking utensils and equipment connected with food carried on board were excluded by Islamic law from the general average contribution in case of jettison and loss at sea. See Yaḥṣubī, *Madhāhib al-Ḥukkām*: 236; Ṭāher ed. *Akriyat al-Sufun*: 52.

Like food, ship owners and masters were required to designate a space for sleeping and storing the crews' personal belongings,[11] and to outfit them with uniform dress to distinguish them from shippers and ordinary passengers.[12] Slaves were not necessarily dressed in poor clothing although they did have distinctive clothing that evidently indicated their hierarchical status on board the ship.[13] Justinian's Digest XV, 1, 25 states:

> Clothing begins to be part of the *peculium* if the master gave it that the slave might always want to use it, and the master handed it over on the understanding that no one else was to use it, and that the slave could keep it with a view to that use. But clothing that a master gave to a slave to use, not that he might always use it, but for certain times, for instance when in attendance upon him or when serving him at table, that clothing is not *peculium*.[14]

2. *Liability*

Regardless of whether the sailors as employees were either free-persons, slaves, or freedmen, Romano-Byzantine and Islamic laws alike did not absolve them from liability when they committed a delict. In some situations the law applied strict liability, whereas under other circumstances legal authorities applied vicarious liability for a slave-seaman's negligence or infliction of harm to a third party. The issue to be addressed is this: when was the ship owner and/or master himself held strictly liable and could be sued for a particular tort action caused by his slave-employee? And, when was the tortfeasor him-

---

[11] M. McCormick, *Origins of the European Economy: Communications and Commerce A.D. 300-900* (Cambridge: Cambridge University Press, 2001): 427; Baghdādī, *Al-Ifāda wa'l I'tibār*, ed. and trans. K.H. Zand *et al.* (London: George Allen and Unwin, 1965): 189; D. al-Nukhaylī, *Al-Sufun al-Islāmīya 'alā Ḥurūf al-Mu'jam* (Alexandria: Alexandria University Press, 1974): 42. This space is known in Arabic as *khunn*, a place in the ship's hull where seamen store their personal effects.

[12] A.'A.M. b. Abī al-Qāsim al-Tanūkhī, *Al-Faraj ba'da al-Shiddah* (Cairo: Dār al-Ṭibā'a al-Muḥammadīya, 1955), 1:388; Y.K. Stillman, *Arab Dress from the Dawn of Islam to Modern Times: A Short History* (Leiden: E. J. Brill, 2000): 50. It is called *jibāb* (sing. *jubba*, a long outer garment, open in front, with wide sleeves), or *tubbān*, (a small under-drawer or a brief).

[13] Bin-Malīḥ, *Al-Riqq fī Bilād al-Maghrib wa'l-Andalus*: 367-74.

[14] A. Watson, *Roman Slave Law* (Baltimore: The Johns Hopkins University Press, 1987): 99; Bradley, *Slavery and Society*: 87-9, 96-9. As a matter of fact, there were no clothes that were uniquely associated with slaves. In certain occasions, domestic slaves were well dressed, especially when their owners intended to project their wealth. By contrast, another segment of slaves wore distinctive clothes, reflecting their low esteem social status.

self—if he happened to be a slave—the only person to be blamed and sued for damages and loss resulting from his acts?

As a matter of principle, a ship owner takes full responsibility for the safekeeping and delivery of cargo in the state it is received at the embarkation point until it arrives at its destined port in the absence of any disclaimer.[15] The potential liability of the *exercitor navis* (ship owner) for safekeeping of property begins when it is placed on board.[16] Carriers are responsible for the safety of their craft and cargo, as well as for the behavior of the crew. An unprofessional performance, a wrongful or negligent act on the carrier's part, and/or those of his officers and crew, on board or possibly even ashore, make him accountable for any resulting loss or damage.[17] Since, he is held responsible for loss or damage to the cargo resulting from his crew's or officers' misconduct felonies.[18] The *exercitor navis*, who appoints the *magister navis*,[19] is required to hire trustworthy seamen to operate and manage the ship.[20]

---

[15] D.S. Bogen, "Ignoring History: The Liability of Ships' Masters, Innkeepers and Stablekeepers under Roman Law," *American Journal of Legal History* 36 (1992): 349-52.

[16] A. Watson, *The Digest of Justinian* (Philadelphia: University of Pennsylvania Press, 1998), Digest IV, 9, 1, 8; S.P. Scott, *The Civil Law* (Cincinnati: The Central Trust Company, 1932), 3:134, Digest IV, 9, 1; Bogen, "Liability under Roman Law," 334, 341. The Digest further rules that the *exercitor navis* may be held liable not only for the acts of the crew, but also for the passengers. This liability applies to merchandise, to the passengers' personal effects and provisions, as well as to merchandise accepted as a pledge on account of money loaned for the voyage.

[17] Whether the *culpa* or *dolus* is confined to acts of seamen on board the ship or includes also misconduct on land is unresolved in the Digest. For instance, Digest IV, 9, 3 states: "... where the property has not yet been placed on board a ship, but has been lost on land, it is at the risk of the owner of the vessel who at first took charge of it." By contrast, Digest IV, 9, 7 rules: "The owner of a vessel shall be responsible for the acts of all of his sailors, whether they are freemen, or slaves, and not without reason, for he himself employed them at his own risk. But he is not responsible, except where the damage has been committed on board the vessel; for where it happens off the vessel, even though it was committed by the sailors, he will not be liable." Furthermore, where Digest XLVII, 5, 1, 6 relieves ship owners of liability for damages committed by travelers, Digest IV, 9, 7, 2 rules out any liability of a ship owner for acts done by one seaman against another: "Where any of the sailors cause damage to the property of one another, this does not affect the owner of the ship."

[18] Scott, *Civil Law*, 3:134, Digest IV, 9, 1, 2.

[19] Master, captain or the person in charge of the care of the entire ship.

[20] Scott, *Civil Law*, 3:135-6, Digest IV, 9, 1, 6-8; Bogen, "Liability under Roman Law": 345. The Digest justifies action against the ship master by faulting him for using the services of "bad men"; thus, he is held liable in respect to his fault of employing such persons.

The Digest draws a clear distinction as to when the *exercitor navis*, rather than the wrongdoer, becomes liable, and vice versa. In principle, the *exercitor navis* has to cover the acts of the crew and of other persons on board.[21] Nevertheless, the Digest further states that if a crewmember commits theft or assault, the aggrieved person has two means of redress: he may either sue the *exercitor navis* or the wrongdoer; occasionally he has the legal right to sue both for the same felony or transgression.[22] He can opt to bring an action for damages against the *exercitor navis* only, in which case, if the person in charge of the vessel is acquitted, the injured party can then bring suit against the actual culprit. The Digest entitles the *exercitor* to cross-claim against a seaman who steals goods that the former has undertaken to transport,[23] or, if damages against him are recovered, he can bring an *ex conducto* suit against the seaman who committed the felony.[24] If, however, the culprit happens to be the *exercitor*'s slave-seaman, the *exercitor* can avoid liability by surrendering him to the claimant.[25] Similarly, the Rhodian treatise refers to the judicial outcomes of robbery in various charters. Article III:1 relates to a thief, not necessarily a seaman, who stole anchors from a ship moored in port or on a beach. If the thief was convicted, the law condemned him to corporal punishment, besides twofold restitution. Article III:2 applies to seamen who stole anchors of another vessel anchored in the port at the command of their captain. It rules that if it was conclusively confirmed that the captain ordered the robbery, he would be held liable for the forfeiture and would have to make good the loss to the ship and those on board. However, according to Article III:2, if anyone, including seamen, stole the ship's tackle or other equipment, the thief had to pay twofold restitution if convicted. Whereas the previous article refers to robbery of the ship's rigging and equipment, Article

---

[21] Scott, *Civil Law*, 3:134, Digest IV, 9, 7; 10:79, Digest XLIV, 7, 5, 6: "The master of a ship ... is held to be responsible for a quasi criminal offense for any damage or theft which may be committed on board the ship", 10:286, Digest XLVII, 5, 1: "An action is granted against those who have control of ships ... where anything is alleged to have been stolen by any one of them, or by persons in their employ; whether the theft was committed with the aid and advice of the proprietor himself, or the owner of the ship, or of those who were on board for the purpose of navigation."

[22] Scott, *Civil Law*, 3:137, Digest IV, 9, 4; 10:286, Digest XLVII, 5, 1, 4.

[23] Watson, *Digest of Justinian*, Digest IV, 9, 3, 5; Digest XLVII.

[24] Scott, *Civil Law*, 3:138, Digest IV, 9, 6, 4.

[25] Ibid., 3:139, Digest IV, 9, 7, 4; 10:286, Digest XLVII, 5, 1, 5.

III:3 presents the legal consequences of a theft committed by a crewmember from a shipper or a passenger by orders of the captain. In such a case, the captain had to make twofold restitution to those who were robbed, while the seaman who committed the robbery would receive a hundred lashes. However, if the seaman committed the theft on his own initiative and was caught or convicted by witnesses, he would be grievously tortured and beaten, especially if the stolen object was gold, and he had to make restitution to those who were robbed.[26] Regardless of whether or not the crewmember committed the theft from the shipper, the latter, as established in the Digest, has the right to sue the ship owner. This right stems from the lading contract negotiated between the shipper and ship owner, which stipulates safekeeping and transportation of the cargo.[27]

Robbery could occur because an untrustworthy captain and seamen were employed. Article III:8 states that, if the employees set sail and made off with the ship and her contents, the offenders' possessions—movable, immovable, and self-moving—should be seized and sold to refund the value of the ship with damages and charges. If the value of such properties and possessions did not suffice to make good the loss, the offenders had to be hired out to work as servants and pay compensation out of their earnings until they gave full satisfaction for the damage they caused, upon returning into their dominion, *i.e.*, their port of origin. To avoid legal altercations, then, Rhodian lawyers advised depositors, shippers, and even ship owners under Article III:12 to make deposits of merchandise, gold, ships, or anything else of value with trustworthy seamen, in writing and before three witnesses.[28] In addition to risking fines and lost wages, a sea-

---

[26] Ashburner, *Rhodian Sea-Law*: 77-81. R. Dareste, "La *Lex Rhodia*," *Revue de Philologie* 29 (1905): 7; A. Justice, *General Treatise of the Dominion of the Sea* (London: Printed for the executors of J. Nicholson, 1724): 87-8; E.H. Freshfield, *A Manual of Later Roman Law: The Ecloga* (Cambridge: Cambridge University Press, 1927): 195-6; D.G. Letsios, *Das Seegesetz der Rhodier: Untersuchungen zu Seerecht und Handelsschiffahrt in Byzanz* (Rhodos: Institouto Aigaiou tou Dikaiou tes Thalassas kai tou Nautikou Diakiou, 1996): 128, 141, 211, 258.

[27] The issue regarding the ship owner's liability for damages caused by seamen, servants, and slaves on board his vessel is well addressed in the Fourth Book of the Justinianic Digest, especially Digest IV, 9, 1, 3; Digest IV; 9, 3, 1, Digest IV; 9, 3, 3; Digest IV, 9, 4, 1; Digest IV, 9, 5; Digest IV, 9, 5, 1; Digest IV, 9, 6; Digest IV, 9, 6, 1; Digest IV, 9, 6, 2; Digest IV, 9, 7; Digest IV, 9, 7, 2; Digest IV, 9, 7, 3; Digest IV, 9, 7, 4; Digest IV, 9, 7, 5; Digest IV, 9, 7, 6. See Scott, *Civil Law*, 3:135-9.

[28] Ashburner, *Rhodian Sea-Law*: 83-5; Dareste, "*Lex Rhodia*," 9; A. Justice, *General Treatise*: 89; Freshfield, *Manual of Later Roman Law*: 196-7; Letsios, *Das Seege-*

man who steals may risk his freedom and become a slave. If a master does not order the slave-seaman to steal, but a theft is committed and then the slave-seaman runs away, "the theft and the flight and the death are to be made up by the master out of his wages."[29]

Whether a shipper is granted the right to sue the ship's master or not depends on the terms of the master's contract of employment as well as the authority invested in him by the owner. Where a ship owner appoints a master but limits his authority, the latter must comply with the restrictions imposed by the former. That is to say, authority is the limit of liability.[30] For instance, if the owner appoints a master only for the purpose of collecting the freight, but not leasing the ship, the owner will not be liable for damage that occurs on a charter contracted by his ship master. Likewise, if the ship master was appointed to contract with passengers but not to offer the use of the ship for merchandise, or vice versa, and exceeds his instructions, he does not bind the owner.[31] Put another way, liability for loss and injury to cargo and humans is upon the owner rather than the master of the ship if the latter is proved to have followed the owner's instructions and fulfilled his duty professionally. Thus, he is not authorized to cancel the charter, to alter its terms or the vessel's course, or the freight charges without the consent of the vessel's owner/s. However, where a master enjoys all-inclusive authority, he can carry out transactions on behalf of the owner, including borrowing money for the repair of the ship.[32] Here too, shippers and passengers have the right to sue him or his employer in case of loss or

---

setz der Rhodier: 127-8, 198-9, 259, 260; S. Leder, *Die arabische Ecloga* (Frankfurt: Forschungen zur byzantinischen Rechtsgeschichte, 1985): 116-19, Articles, 28:10-13.

[29] Ashburner, *Rhodian Sea-Law*: 122-4, Appendix D:III, IV.

[30] W.W. Buckland, *The Roman Law of Slavery* (New York: AMS Press, 1969): 174; Watson, *Roman Slave Law*: 94. Digest XIV, 1, 1, 4: "If a slave acts as ship master without the authorization of his own owner, then if the owner is aware of this he is liable as if on the *actio tributoria*, if unaware on the *actio de peculio*."

[31] Scott, *Civil Law*, 4:202; Watson, *Roman Slave Law*: 94-5, Digest XIV, 1, 1, 12: "Therefore it is the appointment itself which lays down the terms that bind the contracting parties. Therefore if one put him in charge of a ship on the understanding that he was only to collect the freight but not that he was to let out space on the vessel (the *exercitor* himself letting out the space), the *exercitor* will not be liable if the ship master lets out space ... We may add that if the master was appointed so that he should hire out the ship for the carriage of certain goods, for instance vegetables or hemp, and he hires it out for marble or other material, the *exercitor* will not be liable."

[32] Scott, *Civil Law*, 4:201, Digest XIV, 1, 1, 9; 4:205, Digest XIV, 1, 7.

damage to their goods and personal effects.[33] Furthermore, there is redress for harm to the belongings and cargo of passengers: "If something is thrown out from a ship an *actio utilis* (direct action) will be granted against the person in charge of the ship."[34] This applies even if the claimant paid no fare.[35] Ultimately, the Digest absolves the *exercitor navis* or *magister navis* from liability if he warns a shipper or a passenger accompanying his shipment to look after his goods.[36]

Islamic jurisprudence distinguishes between three types of liability: strict liability, vicarious liability, and liability based on fault. The *Sharīʿa* divides strict liability into two categories: that of a common carrier (*ajīr mushtarak*, lit. independent contractor or general agent/employee) and that of a private carrier (*ajīr khāṣṣ*, lit. private agent or exclusive employee).[37] *Ajīr mushtarak* is defined as a person with whom a contract is made for a specific task such as transporting a thing to a specified destination provided that his wages are paid when the work is done.[38] Properties delivered to a common carrier are classified as a deposit (*wadīʿa*) or as a trust (*amāna*), and the common carrier is termed an *amīn* (trustee).[39] From the *Sharīʿa* point of view, the trustee is not accountable for the loss of or damage to the shipped property unless it results from misconduct or negligence on his part. Therefore, the common carrier must take all practical steps to ensure that the cargo entrusted to him is delivered safely to its destination. In principle, where there has been no negligence or transgression on the part of the ship owner or master, there can be no liability for loss or damage. However, liability can be incurred by either if the damage or loss arises from carelessness or neglect.[40] As

---

[33] Bogen, "Liability under Roman Law": 334-6; Scott, *Civil Law*, 4:204, Digest XIV, 1, 1, 24.

[34] Watson, *Digest of Justinian*, Digest IX, 3, 6, 3.

[35] Ashburner, *Rhodian Sea-Law*, clx.

[36] Scott, *Civil Law*, 3:138, Digest IV, 9, 7: "If he (shipmaster) gives warning that every passenger must be responsible for his own property, and that he will not be liable for damage, and the passengers agree to the terms of the warning, he cannot be sued."

[37] A.B. Bin-Muhamad, "Vicarious Liability: A Study of the Liability of Employer and Employee in the Islamic Law of Tort," *Arab Law Quarterly* 15 (2000): 200.

[38] Ibid.: 201; D.R. Noble, "The Principles of Islamic Maritime Law" (Ph.D. diss., University of London, 1988): 150-1; M.M. Rajab, *Al-Qānūn al-Baḥrī al-Islāmī ka-Maṣdar li-Qawāʿid al-Qānūn al-Baḥrī al-Muʿāṣir* (Alexandria: Al-Maktab al-ʿArabī al-Ḥadīth, 1990): 109-10.

[39] Bin-Muhamad, "Vicarious Liability": 204.

[40] Noble, "Principles of Islamic Maritime Law": 152-7; ʿA.R. b. Aḥmad Ibn Fāyiʿ, *Aḥkām al-Baḥr fī al-Fiqh al-Islāmī* (Jedda: Dār al-Andalus al-Khaḍrāʾ, 2000): 356-9;

a result, placing absolute liability in the leasing contract on either party is legally forbidden. Mālik Ibn Anas (97-179/715-795) rules: "If the ship owners/carriers stipulate not to be held liable for the foodstuffs, but for that which is not guaranteeable, then their stipulation is invalid and the contract is void. Had they concluded (such a deal), they assume liability for foodstuffs only and the ship owner/carrier collects a comparable freight disregarding the contract stipulations."[41] The ship owner's/carrier's liability is limited to wrongful acts and transgressions. Unforeseeable damages from such irresistible forces such as hostile attacks or rough seas, preclude liability on the part of the ship owners.

A ship owner, as an *ajīr mushtarak*, is normally held responsible not only for his own negligence, but also for that of the *ajīr khāṣṣ*—master, crew, or servants, including slave-sailors—if the wrongdoer committed his act in the course of his employment. This is vicarious liability because it follows from the ship owner's capacity as employer.[42] The principle of vicarious liability is derived from the Prophetic tradition stating that "profit follows responsibility."[43] Specifically, the ship owner is fully liable for acts of his crew if they followed their employer's instructions and orders and, in so doing, caused damage to the goods shipped. Accordingly, a plaintiff need not prove negligence on the part of the ship owner, but only that a contract of employment existed between the wrongdoer and the ship owner.[44] In sum, responsibility follows ownership. For that reason, the *Kitāb Akriyat al-Sufun* enjoins shippers not to entrust their cargoes to untrustworthy carriers, but to deliver them to faithful and professional ship owners, who must ensure that: (a) their ships are well

Ṭāher (ed.) *Akriyat al-Sufun*: 39, the ship owner is held liable for intentional damage to cargo based on market prices at his most distant destination, providing the lessee pays the whole freight.

[41] Ṭāher (ed.) *Akriyat al-Sufun*: 41; al-Tanūkhī, *Al-Mudawwana al-Kubrā* (Cairo: Maṭba'at al-Sa'āda, 1905), 4:491; Qarāfī, *Al-Dhakhīra*, 5:529. Mālik's judgment apparently relies on Qur'ānic prohibition, which enjoins people not to exert themselves. *Qur'ān* 2:286 ordains: "On no soul doth Allāh place a burden greater than it can bear. It gets every good that it earns." (Pray:) "Our Lord! Condemn us not if we forget or fall into error…."

[42] Bin-Muhamad, "Vicarious Liability": 202-3.

[43] Noble, "Principles of Islamic Maritime Law": 163: "*Al-kharāj bi'l-ḍamān aw al-ghurm bi'l-ghurm* ('Gain accompanies liability for loss—or entitlement to return is justified by taking risks.')."

[44] Ibid.: 162. On p. 164, she argues that the Ḥanafite jurists lay the liability for the damage to or loss from the cargo upon the hireling who committed the wrongdoing rather than the employer.

equipped and seaworthy and (b) they hire experienced and trustworthy crew to navigate them.[45] In a case where two or more persons own a ship, they are held answerable for the wrong acts of their seamen in proportion to their shares.[46] The only circumstance where a shipmaster is solely accountable for loss or damage is when he improperly takes over a ship and subsequently collides with another. This rash act on his part exempts the ship owner from liability.[47]

With regard to liability based on fault, the law distinguishes between liability arising from an act contrary to a contract (*ḍamān al-ʿaqd*), and liability arising from an unlawful act (*ḍamān al-fiʿl*).[48] The ship owner is not liable for the losses caused by forces of nature.[49] Intentional wrongdoing on his part or that of the crew, however, obliges him to remunerate the shipper. If the ship owner can prove that the damage was unavoidable, he is absolved of responsibility.[50] Similar to the edict established by Digest IV, 9, 7, a ship owner can also free himself from responsibility if the shipper or his agent accompanies the shipment or sails on another ship in the convoy.[51] Nevertheless, the ship owner is bound by law to carry the shipment safely and deliver it at the journey's end in the state in which he received it and must not sell or steal any part of the shipment. If he does, the merchant is either entitled to receive goods of the same kind, quality and quantity, or an equivalent sum of money based on market price at the destination.[52]

---

[45] Ṭāher (ed.), *Akriyat al-Sufun*: 38.

[46] Noble, "Principles of Islamic Maritime Law": 166.

[47] Ibid., 170; Ibn Fāyiʿ, *Aḥkām al-Baḥr*: 381-4.

[48] Noble, "Principles of Islamic Maritime Law": 170-1; Bin-Muhamad, "Vicarious Liability": 198.

[49] Noble, "Principles of Islamic Maritime Law": 176-9; Rajab, *Al-Qānūn al-Baḥrī al-Islāmī*: 112-4; Ibn Fāyiʿ, *Aḥkām al-Baḥr*: 360-7.

[50] Ṭāher (ed.), *Akriyat al-Sufun*: 38-9; al-Tanūkhī, *Al-Mudawwana*, 4:494-5; Ibn Rushd, *Al-Bayān wa'l-Taḥṣīl wa'l-Sharḥ wa'l-Tawjīh wal-Taʿlīl fī Masā'il al-Mustakhraja* (Beirut: Dār al-Gharb al-Islāmī, 1984), 9:58.

[51] al-Tanūkhī, *Al-Mudawwana*, 4:494; al-Wansharīsī, *Al-Miʿyār*, 8:322; Ibn Fāyiʿ, *Aḥkām al-Baḥr*: 372-4.

[52] Ṭāher (ed.), *Akriyat al-Sufun*: 38-9; Ibn Rushd, *Al-Bayān wal-Taḥṣīl*, 9:135-7. On theft on board Islamic ships, consult Khalilieh, *Islamic Maritime Law*: 157-9; Noble, "Principles of Islamic Maritime Law": 89-90; Ibn Fāyiʿ, *Aḥkām al-Baḥr*: 573-9. In a letter dated 1010, ʿAlūsh Ibn Joshuʿa al-Andalusī describes to Ismāʿīl Ibn Abraham how some bales were stolen from a merchant ship, whose owner paid the value of the stolen bales to their owners. Subsequently, when the bales were recovered, the merchant refunded the ship owner and paid the shipping charges in full. See M. Gil, *In the Kingdom of Ishmael: Texts from the Cairo Geniza* (Tel Aviv: Tel Aviv University Press, 1997) (Hebrew), 2:618-19 [212], JNUL 4°577.3, f. 12.

A total or partial damage or loss, unlawful act, or intentional negligence a crewmember committed made him liable to indemnify the injured person. Where cargo was lost or damaged through the act or oversight of a crewmember in the navigation or management of the ship, or in the loading, carriage or discharge of her cargo, the negligent party was liable for compensation to the shipper. Islamic and Byzantine laws agree that the seaman incurs liability if he commits a wrongful or negligence act, unless it is not established that he has done so.[53]

Slaves as Ordinary Passengers and Human Cargo

1. *Slave's Eligibility for Boarding a Ship*

It stands to reason that the passengers' identity and character could not necessarily be known to the ship owner and captain when the contract of hire was signed. However, the ship owner's and captain's actual assessment of the passengers' behavior began when they awaited boarding on the pre-boarding area and continued throughout the journey so as to avoid serious consequences. Thus, it's not surprising to observe that distinguished pilots and authors like Ibn Mājid cautioned masters and captains of commercial ships to "look thoroughly at all the passengers and the crew and assess them carefully," in order to recognize and pre-empt any evil in them.[54] The twelfth-century C.E. Andalusian jurist Ibn ʿAbdūn warned ship owners not to transport suspicious passengers, particularly mercenaries

---

[53] Tāher (ed.), *Akriyat al-Sufun*: 43; Saḥnūn, *Al-Mudawwana*, 4:494-5; M. b. Idrīs al-Shāfiʿī, *Al-Umm* (Beirut: Dār al-Maʿrifa li'l-Ṭibāʿa wa'l-Nashr, 1973), 6:86; M. b. Amad al-Sarakhsī, *Al-Mabsūṭ* (Cairo: Maṭbaʿat al-Saʿāda, 1906), 16:10; Ibn Rushd, *Al-Bayān wa'l-Taḥṣīl*, 15:447-8; 16:76-7; al-Wansharīsī, *Al-Miʿyār*, 8:332-25; Ibn Aḥmad Ibn Qudāma, *Al-Mughnī* (Cairo: Dār Hajar li'l-Ṭibāʿa wa'l-Nashr, 1986), 7:432; ʿĀ. B. ʿAlī al-Shammākhī, *Al-Īḍāḥ* (Beirut, 1970), 3:602-9; Noble, "Principles of Islamic Maritime Law": 170-85; Khalilieh, *Islamic Maritime Law*: 48-9, 68-70, 87; Christides, "Raid and Trade": 83, 85; Ashburner, *Rhodian Sea-Law*: 91, 105-6, 108, 112; Articles 3:10, 3:26, 3:27, 3:31, and 3:38; Freshfield, *Manual of Later Roman Law*, 197, 201, 202, 203; A.Justice, *General Treatise*: 93, 102, 104, 109; Dareste, "Lex Rhodia": 19, 21, 23; Letsios, *Das Seegesetz der Rhodier*: 206, 259-60, 262-3, 264; Leder, *Die arabische Ecloga*: 116-17, Article 28:8.

[54] S.D.A. Ibn Mājid, *Kitāb al-Fawāʾid fī Uṣūl ʿIlm al-Baḥr wa'l-Qawāʿid* (Damascus, 1971): 245.

of barbarian origin, black slaves (*'abīd*), and people of ill repute.[55] He further advised ship owners and crews to avoid carrying women—including maidservants and female slaves—and freaks aboard their vessels for the pleasure of the exposition of their charms.[56] In addition, he strongly cautioned city authorities against allowing ship owners to ferry women who bore immoral and vicious characteristics across the Guadalquivir; if a ship owner intended to do so, he had to inform the port superintendent.[57]

Indeed, the precautionary measures set up by market *muḥtasib*s (market superintendents) aimed at preventing improper and immoral behavior on board the ship in any stage of the maritime journey. Jurists were concerned about fornication committed during the maritime journey, a matter which led Muslim jurists in the Far East to introduce laws that applied to sexual intercourse at sea, although in the Mashriq and Maghrib their fellow jurists applied land laws to the sea issuing rulings solely on the basis of analogy. By all accounts, Islamic law distinguished between fornication between freemen and freewomen, a freeman and a female slave, and male and female slaves.[58] Imām Mālik Ibn Anas decrees:

> "What is done in our community about the man who rapes a woman, virgin or non-virgin, if she is free, is that he must pay the bride-price of someone like her. If she is a slave, he must pay what he has diminished of her worth. The *ḥadd* punishment in such cases is applied to the rapist, and there is no punishment applied to the woman raped. If the rapist is a slave, that is against his master unless he wishes to surrender him."[59]

---

[55] Muḥammad Ibn Aḥmad Ibn 'Abdūn al-Tujībī, *Seville Musulmane au debut du XIIe Siecle, Le traité d'Ibn 'Abdūn sur la vie urbaine et les corps des métiers*, ed. E. Levi-Provençal (Paris: Maisonneuve, 1947): 64; E. Lévi-Provençal, "Un document sur la vie urbaine et les corps de métiers à Séville au début du XIIe siécle: Le traité d'Ibn 'Abdūn," *Journal Asiatique* 224 (1934): 247.

[56] E. Lévi-Provençal, "Le traité d'Ibn 'Abdūn": 247-8.

[57] E. Lévi-Provençal, *Trois traités hispaniques de Ḥisba* (Cairo: IFAO, 1955): 56-7.

[58] Bāzmūl, *Aḥkām al-Khadam fī al-Sharī'a al-Islāmīya*: 188-91. The maritime code of Islamic Malaya—dated from 695/1296—established that a freeman committing adultery with a sailor's wife must be put to death. As to the wife, her husband could put her to death; if he did not wish to do so, she became the captain's irredeemable slave If a freeman fornicated with a female slave, he had to pay a fine equal to the slave's price. See Raffles, "Maritime Code of the Malays," 82; Winstedt and Josselin, "Maritime Laws of Malaca": 52.

[59] M. Ibn Anas, *Al-Muwaṭṭa' of Imām Mālik Ibn Anas*, trans. by A. Bewley (London: Kegan Paul International, 1989): 303, chapter 36.16: This ruling is partially compatible with that established in Islamic Far East, which states that Mālik's edict

Mālik further rules that if an unmarried woman is pregnant and claims to have been raped, unless there is physical evidence, she is presumed guilty of fornication and therefore punished.[60] But if this was a female slave so long in her master's possession that she was like his wife, the master could claim either a fine or the death penalty. However, if a male and female slave committed fornication, they were to be whipped in public. If a woman accused a man of raping her and he denied it, she was in essence confessing to illicit sexual contact and therefore punishable, in the very likely event that she had no evidence to support her testimony. Since the captain served as a judge on board, he supervised the punishment, usually administered by the crew.[61] Generally, the woman was made to suffer for a crime committed by another because the focus was on the sexual act and not on rape as violence. Last but not least, al-Māwardī tended to mitigate the *ḥadd* against slaves stating that they should incur only half the penalty decreed for the freeborn "due to their low-esteem status as slaves."[62] Romano-Byzantine judicial literature remains silent as to the treatment of sexual misconduct committed by slaves at sea, probably because the jurists did not differ between the application of punishment on land and at sea.

2. *Carriage and Accommodation*

The internal arrangements and the average space reserved for human cargo depended on the ship's structural design, the number, age, and body-size of the transported slaves, the quantity of cargoes, the distance between the embarkation and debarkation points, and most importantly the slave's human status and social affiliation. Slaves were divided into two categories: slaves purchased for personal services (including servants and merchants' agents), and classified as ordinary passengers,[63] and slaves acquired for commercial purposes

---

that if a man is convicted of rape, he receives the punishment mentioned for adultery and also must pay a bride-price to the victim. See Raffles, "Maritime Code of the Malays," 82; Winstedt and Josselin, "Maritime Laws of Malaca": 52.

[60] Ibn Anas, *Al-Muwaṭṭa'*: 347, chapter 41.4.

[61] H.S. Khalilieh, "Women at Sea: Modesty, Privacy and Sexual Misconduct of Passengers and Sailors Aboard Islamic Ships," *Al-Qanṭara* 27 (2006): 145-7.

[62] A. H. b. Muḥammad Ibn Ḥabīb al-Māwardī, *Al-Aḥkām al-Sulṭānīya wa'l-Wilāyāt al-Dīnīya* (Beirut: Dār al-Kutub al-'Ilmīya, 1978): 341; Bin-Malīḥ, *Al-Riqq fī Bilād al-Maghrib wal-Andalus*: 333-9.

[63] Barrow, *Slavery in the Roman Empire*: 101; Bradley, *Slavery and Society*: 57-80, esp. 75. In spite of differences in times, slaves in Islamic Mediterranean enjoyed

and classified as human cargo.[64] As far as the first category is concerned, their legal status on ships did not significantly differ from that of ordinary and freeborn passengers. A master accompanied by his slave could not accommodate him/her wherever he saw fit except if the leasing terms so specified. For instance, maidservants and slaves sailing with their masters on luxurious commercial ships—with private cabins, lavatories, closets, and occasionally projecting balconies—could also be placed in private cabins.[65] However, on small or medium-sized ships with one deck, females had to be segregated from males; segregation between the sexes applied to male and female slaves as well even if they were transported on the same level of the ship. To minimize interactions between male and female passengers, al-Māwardī strongly urged *muḥtasib*s to ensure that large, roomy ships should have separate toilets for women "so that they are not exposed to view when they need to use them."[66] The desire to avoid mingling arose from fears of encouraging illicit sexual conduct.

Most of the multi-level ships contained special rooms above the deepest hold for the carriage of slaves. Whereas the deepest hold was reserved for heavy cargoes (grain, iron, metals, etc.) the middle level was outfitted for women, maids, and segregated male/female slave sections, and the highest level, the deck superstructure, housed the men (the captain, crew, merchants, and passengers) and their personal servants.[67] Islamic legal inquiries and sources confirm that human cargoes were carried in limited quarters on sailing ships.[68]

comparable social and legal to those prevailed in the Roman Empire; in certain occasions, they held high ranking positions in governmental offices and military. For further details, consult Goitein, *Mediterranean Society*, 1:130-47; Kīrah, *Al-Jawārī wal-Ghulmān*: 185-228; Bin-Malīḥ, *Al-Riqq fī Bilād al-Maghrib wal-Andalus*: 92-114, 475-550.

[64] Slaves' legal status from private to human cargo could be transacted in any stage of the maritime journey provided it had to take place when the danger was unforeseeable and on the condition that such a transaction had to be concluded in conformity with the shipmaster and registered in the cargo-book.

[65] al-Minhājī, *Jawāhir al-'Uqūd wa-Mu'īn al-Quḍā wal-Muwaqqi'īn wal-Shuhūd* (Cairo, 1955), 1:95; M. al-Nuwayrī, *Kitāb al-Ilmām bi'l-I'lām fi-mā Jarat bi-hi al-Aḥkām wa'l-Umūr al-Muqḍiya fī Waq'at al-Iskandariyya* (Hyderabad: Osmania Oriental Publications Bureau, Osmania University, 1969), 2:234-5; 'A.L. al-Baghdādī, *Al-Ifāda wa'l I'tibār*: 183.

[66] al-Māwardī, *Al-Aḥkām al-Sulṭānīya*: 257.

[67] al-Minhājī, *Jawāhir al-'Uqūd*, 2:94-6.

[68] A late thirteenth-century C.E. Islamic maritime code from Malay reveals the proportional space a slave was granted during the maritime journey: "Where slaves

Also, they dictated that Muslim ship owners set aside enough space for performing prayers; this suggests that designated slave space was associated with body size, but not age or sex.[69] The average space a worshipper could occupy is six feet long and two feet wide, a rate which is comparable to that fixed in Article II:9 of the Rhodian Sea-Law.[70]

3. *Sustenance*

Since the dawn of ancient civilizations until the early years of the modern age, ordinary sea travellers were required to supply themselves and their servants and slaves with bread, food, water, cloths, mattresses and blankets and dried food for the voyage.[71] Although Romano-Byzantine and certain Islamic maritime customs required ship owners and carriers to supply water for their voyagers, neither the latter, nor their servants and/or slaves had free access to the water tank, *i.e.*, ship owners and carriers did not provide them with more than the share stipulated in the contract of carriage.[72] As to the questions what kind of food and how many meals were served to human cargo aboard Roman, Byzantine, and Islamic ships remain vague. Nonetheless, it stands to reason that slave cargo enjoyed two

---

are purchased at Java, the duty shall be calculated on twelve men for each division of the hold." See Sir S. Raffles, "The Maritime Code of the Malays," *Royal Asiatic Society of Great Britain and Ireland; Malayan Branch* (1879): 74.

[69] ʿA. A. Ibn Yāsīn al-Shamarānī, *Isʿāf Ahl al-ʿAṣr bi-Aḥkām al-Baḥr* (Riāḍ: Dār al-Waṭan li'l-Nashr, 1999): 207-14, 222-8; Khalilieh, *Islamic Maritime Law*: 163.

[70] Ashburner, *Rhodian Sea-Law*: 59, 61; Freshfield, *Manual of Later Roman Law*: 206, reads: "Space occupied by a passenger is three cubits length by one cubit broad. A woman passenger shall be entitled to a space of a cubit, and a child, not fully grown, shall have a half of that space."

[71] L. Casson, *Travel in the Ancient World* (Baltimore: The Johns Hopkins University Press, 1994): 153; idem, *Ships and Seamanship*: 90; Bāzmūl, *Aḥkām al-Khadam fī al-Sharīʿa al-Islāmīya*: 215-18, Khalilieh, *Islamic Maritime Law*: 54-7; Ṭāher (ed.), *Akriyat al-Sufun*: 38-43; ʿA. b.Yaḥyā al-Jazīrī, *Al-Maqṣad al-Maḥmūd fī Talkhīṣ al-ʿUqūd* (Madrid: Consejo Superior de Investigacioens Científicas Agencia Española de Cooperación Internacional, 1998): 224-5; S.D. Goitein, *A Mediterranean Society: The Jewish Communities of the Arab World as Portrayed in the Documents of the Cairo Geniza: Economic Foundations* (Berkeley: University of California Press, 1967), 1:316; idem, "The Tribulations of an Overseer of the Sultan's Ships," in *Arabic and Islamic Studies in Honor of Hamilton A.R. Gibb*, ed. G. Makdisi (Cambridge: Cambridge University Press, 1965): 275, 280, doc. TS 24. 78, ll. 49-53; idem, *Letters of Medieval Jewish Traders* (Princeton: Princeton University Press, 1973): 334, doc. Mosseri, L 101.

[72] Casson, *Travel in the Ancient World*: 153; Sperber, *Nautica Talmudica*: 36-7, 96-7; Ashburner, *Rhodian Sea-Law*, cl-clii; Khalilieh, *Islamic Maritime Law*: 55.

meals a day, probably of the same food they used to consume in their home-countries.

4. *Injury and Death*

The Corpus Juris Civilis required the shipmaster and his crew to deliver the human cargo safely to the prescribed destination. Where the shipmaster failed to do so, or injured the transported persons, he and his crew would, on accepted principles, be liable for the losses.[73] In the absence of dereliction, however, the captain and his crewmen were absolved of liability.[74] Thus, if a slave was injured in transit—even if the injury healed—the captain was held accountable to the merchant. If the slave's injury was chronic or permanent, the captain was held liable for his/her price. Even though the value of slaves differed according to the purpose for which they were purchased, Romano-Byzantine lawyers fixed the exact amount of the slaves' contribution in the Digest. However, they make the legal distinction between slaves as commodities and slaves as private possessions by exempting the owner who buys a slave or slaves for private use from import duties at ports.[75]

In order to ensure the safe-delivery of human cargo at the destination, several factors had to be taken into consideration: the slaves' health condition, the quantity and quality of food and water which had to be taken aboard ship, weather conditions, voyage duration, speed of the ship, and construction and design of the vessels (ventilation ports, internal division, and the slaves' sleeping and living arrangements). Digest XIV, 2, 10 states:

> "If you have made a contract for the transportation of slaves, freight is not due to you for a slave who died on the ship. Paulus says that, in fact, the question is what was agreed upon, whether freight was to be paid for those who were loaded on the ship, or only for those who were carried to their destination? And if this cannot be established, it will

[73] Scott, *Civil Law*, 4:211, Digest XIV, 2, 10.

[74] Ibid., 4:185, Digest XIII, 6, 18: "... the deaths of slaves which occur without malice or negligence on his part, attacks by robbers and enemies, the strategems of pirates, shipwrecks, fires, and the escape of slaves whom it is not usual to keep under guard ..."; ibid., 4:209, Digest XIV, 2, 2, 5: "No estimate should be made of slaves who are lost at sea, any more than where those who are ill die on the ship, or throw themselves overboard."

[75] Ibid., 11:288-9, Digest L, 16, 203; 9:23, Digest XXXIX 4, 16, 3 & 10.

> be enough for the master of the ship to prove that the slave was placed on board."[76]

Inasmuch as the ship owner could prove that the death of a slave did not result from his dereliction, but occurred from disease, accident, rebellion, suicide, or natural disasters in any stage of the maritime journey, the slaveowner would have to pay the entire transportation fees.[77] The carrier-shipper mutual interest necessitated that both parties to the contract of carriage look after the slaves' welfare from the moment they were brought to the loading berth and handed over to the captain until their safe disembarkation at the destined terminal.[78]

Although ancient writings and Romano-Byzantine legal codices deal with death on board ships,[79] none of these sources describes the procedure for treating the body of a deceased passenger and/or slave in the course of the voyage. All we know is that, if a person died during the maritime journey the corpse had to be cast overboard.[80] By contrast, legal sources, historical accounts, and documentary evidence from the Muslim world describe at length the funeral practice at sea. If the deceased slave happened to be a Muslim,[81] the corpse had to be washed, shrouded, embalmed, and buried at sea in accordance with Islamic ceremonial and burial rites.[82]

5. *Newborn Slaves*

Digest XIX, 2, 19, 7 rules:

> "Where anyone makes a contract for the transportation of a woman by sea, and afterwards a child is born to her on the ship, it has been established that nothing is due on account of the child; for the trans-

[76] Ibid., 4:211.

[77] Ibid., 4:185, Digest XIII, 6, 18; 4:209, Digest XIV, 2, 2, 5.

[78] R. Winstedt and P.E. de Josselin de Jong, "The Maritime Laws of Malacca," *Journal of the Malayan Branch of the Royal Asiatic Society-Singapore* 29 (1956): 55: "If a passenger is hurt when boarding a ship through the galley collapsing, the captain must pay his medical expenses."

[79] Digest IV, 9, 7, 4; Digest IV, 9, 7, 6; Digest XIII, 6, 18; Digest XIV, 1, 4, 3; Digest XIV, 1, 4, 4; Digest XIV, 2, 2, 5; Digest XIV, 2, 10; Digest XXXIX, 4, 11, 2.

[80] Casson, *Travel in the Ancient World*: 156.

[81] Ṭāher (ed.), *Akriyat al-Sufun*: 24; Bin-Malīḥ, *Al-Riqq fī Bilād al-Maghrib wal-Andalus*: 327-33.

[82] Khalilieh, *Islamic Maritime Law*: 168-71; idem, *Admiralty and Maritime Laws*: 81; Ibn Fāyiʿ, *Aḥkām al-Baḥr*: 165-77; al-Shamarānī, *Isʿāf Ahl al-ʿAṣr*: 330-44.

portation was not more expensive, nor did the child consume anything which was provided for the use of those navigating the vessel."[83]

Like the Romano-Byzantine maritime tradition, which provided that a ship owner was not entitled to collect a fee of carriage of a baby born in the voyage, thus exempting slavers/slaveowners from paying an extra shipping fee for an "unexpected" increase of shipment,[84] Muslim jurists did apparently apply this principle as in the case of the birth of a human baby on-board, but not on the carriage of domestic animals.[85] All slaves intended for commercial purposes, including newly born babies, had to be registered by the ship's scribe in the cargo-book, which contained full description of the slave's age, height, race, physical features, and distinguishing characteristics to make each slave individually identifiable. This log was chiefly used to settle cases of negligence by the captain or crew, liability for jettison, or loss of human cargoes and commercial commodities at sea.[86] As a result, the transfer of a slave ownership at sea could not be transacted without the approval of the captain and scribe of the vessel, who had to register all commercial transactions in the log.[87]

Human Jettison and Contribution

The problem of human jettison has been treated in my previous studies and can be summed up as follows. The Justinianic Digest made a distinction between slaves acquired for commercial purposes and those for private services: the latter were worth more. For example, a slave who served as a *peculium* (manager/operator) on board ship had the status as a captain. He and other operators of the vessel, were they freemen or slaves, could not be cast into the sea because the vessel could not sail without them and their nautical knowledge. The

---

[83] Scott, *Civil Law*, 5:86.

[84] J.C. Thomas, "Juridical Aspects of Carriage by Sea and Warehousing in Roman Law," *Recueils de la Société Jean Bodin pour l'Histoire Comparative des Institutions* 32 (1972): 127.

[85] al-Wansharīsī, *Al-Mi'yār*, 8:64.

[86] Customs officials also referred to the cargo-book/logbook when appraising the value of commodities at the disembarkation point.

[87] Khalilieh, *Islamic Maritime Law*: 46, 94, 96, 104; idem, *Admiralty and Maritime Laws*: 74, 97, 112, 159, 183, 186, 187-8; A.H al-Makhzūmī, *Kitāb al-Minhāj fī 'Ilm Kharāj Miṣr* (ed. by C. Cahen and Y. Rāghib. Caire: Institut Français d'Archéologie Orientale, 1986): 20-2.

Digest authorizes the *peculium*, after consultation with the parties involved, to cast cargo and passengers overboard for the safety of the ship. If an altercation arose between the *peculium* and the shipper, legal allegations were brought against the ship owner rather than his employed slave.[88] However, a slaver or a slave master could claim contribution only if his human cargo was jettisoned for the general safety of the ship, her crewmen and freemen. The inclusion of slaves in the general average contribution was made possible since they fell under the heading of *res* "things."[89]

Islamic law provides more details on the issue of forcing human beings to abandon ship under extreme danger. Al-Qāḍī ʿIyāḍ condenses the Islamic legal points of view by stating:

> Aside from commercial commodities, if there were only passengers left, they were, after (the victims) had been chosen by lot,[90] indiscriminately subjected to being thrown overboard, regardless of their social status and allegiance, whether they were males or females, slaves or freemen, Muslims or *dhimmīs*.[91]
>
> Abū al-Ḥasan al-Lakhmī (d. 478/1080) decreed: Concerning the jettison of possessions (including slaves), regardless of whether they were purchased for commercial or private purposes, all of them are subject to contribution. If they sailed in the vicinity of the coast, or the vessel was shaken fiercely by the wind and the ship owner manages to face it up, then it is prohibited (to jettison a slave). Had they sailed far from the shore and the slave's owner cannot swim well or his overweight cannot keep him afloat, the slaves should be considered for jettison. Muḥammad (Ibn al-Mawwāz 180-269/796-882) decreed: On the basis of this precept, one should take into account the distance of a vessel from the shore, as well as the capability or incapability of slaves to swim; the same rule is pertinent to freemen for those jurists who apply this ruling to them.
>
> Al-Lakhmī stated: The law school jurists agreed upon the exclusion of freemen in the calculation of the general average. Moreover, the

---

[88] Scott, *Civil Law*, 4:200-5, Digest XIV, 1, 1, 1; Digest XIV, 1, 1, 3; Digest XIV, 1, 1, 22; Digest XIV, 1, 4, 2; Digest XIV, 1, 4, 3; Digest XIV, 1, 4, 4; Digest XIV, 1, 5, 1; Digest XIV, 1, 6; G. Chowdbaray-Best, "Ancient Maritime Law," *The Mariner's Mirror* 62 (1976): 89.

[89] H.S. Khalilieh, "Human Jettison, Contribution for Lives, and Life Salvage in the Byzantine and Early Islamic Maritime Laws in the Mediterranean," *Byzantion* 75 (2005): 226-7.

[90] B. Ibn Shahriyār, *Kitāb ʿAjāʾib al-Hind*, ed. and compiled by Y. al-Sharouni (London: Riad el-Rayyis, 1989): 58-9. Even if the victims were chosen by lot, it was most likely that the captain and crew were the last to relinquish the vessel since they were "bound by oaths not to abandon her."

[91] al-Yaḥṣubī, *Madhāhib al-Ḥukkām*: 235.

> responsibility for the losses does not rest on their shoulders, regardless of whether they have cargo on board or not. However, some jurists embraced by analogy the doctrine that they are held liable for the losses since jettisoning someone's cargo saved the lives of those who did not have commodities on board. Ibn Yūnus (d. 361/972) also ruled that this is the correct legal reasoning. Al-Lakhmī said too: It is more appropriate to include these slaves who were acquired for private possession and commercial purposes. If it were a female slave, her master has no other choice, either by converting her (through marriage), or keeping her as an infidel.
>
> Ibn al-Jahm dictated: Slaves shall not be thrown overboard, even if they were acquired for commercial purposes, due to the tacit prohibition of Islamic law. Were the law to allow the sacrifice of slaves, it would be necessary to consider freemen.[92]

Although the subject remained controversial, most Muslim jurists opposed the practice, and condemnation of human jettison was widespread. A group of jurists opposed throwing any human being overboard in any circumstance, even if the matter dealt with captives of the polytheists. Another one approved of sacrificing some lives if it would save a larger number, regardless of the ethnic, religious, or social allegiance of the individuals on board. However, when there was no choice but to force some passengers to abandon ship, they had to be treated equally and chosen by lot. And the third group of Muslim jurists determined that if human jettison were necessary, pagans would be thrown overboard before Muslims, men before women, and war captives before slaves. They further suggested that two factors had to be considered before throwing a slave overboard: (a) his/her ability to swim ashore; and (b) the distance of the ship from the coast. Strong swimmers amongst the slaves were to be thrown overboard if the coast was in sight.[93]

The Rhodian Sea-Law clarifies the assessment of human lives better than the Digest, distinguishing between slaves carried for private services and those transported as commercial goods. The value of domestic slaves is fifty-percent [50%] higher than slaves who are merely merchandise. Article III:9 decrees that a slave or a ship servant not being carried for sale should be valued at three *minas*, while one who is bought for commercial purposes, has a value of two

[92] al-Yaḥṣubī, *Madhāhib al-Ḥukkām:* 238.
[93] Khalilieh, "Human Jettison": 227-9.

minas.[94] The amount of contribution for a slave bought for private use was thus higher than for one who was merely merchandise.[95] Although market value obviously depended on the slaves' build, sex, age, and ethnic origin, the maritime treatise of Rhodes dealt with the slave issue in a very general sense, not with its specifics.

The legal status of slaves depended on whether they were purchased for commercial or private use. In the latter case, they were not subject to contribution, a legal consideration presented by the *qāḍī* Ibn Abī Maṭar (d. 337/948):

> "Humans, be they freemen or slaves bought for a private possession, except for those who were purchased for commercial purposes, are not included in the calculation of the general average. Neither are the vessel's servicemen, be they freemen or white slaves [*mamālīk*], nor those who travel without cargo, subject to contribution."[96]

Commercial slaves were treated like other commodities and articles on board. They were subject to general average contribution so that their owners had to share the losses with other merchants who were owners of the jetsam, in proportion to their value. Following the principle of the general average, a slaver whose slaves remained safe was obliged to pay proportionately to cover the losses of those whose goods and slaves were jettisoned.[97] Obviously, the assessment of the monetary value of a jettisoned slave depended on his/her place of origin, gender, age, appearance, physical condition and abilities.[98] The

---

[94] Ashburner, *Rhodian Sea-Law*: 87; Alexander Justice, *General Treatise*: 91-3; Dareste, "*Lex Rhodia*": 11.

[95] Ashburner, *Rhodian Sea-Law*: 90.

[96] Khalilieh, "Human Jettison": 230; Qarāfī, *Al-Furūq*, 4:10; idem, *Al-Dhakhīra*, 5:487: "Neither the ship owner, nor the vessel's servicemen, be they freemen or white slaves—except for those purchased for commercial purposes—are included in the calculation of the general average contribution. Likewise, those who do not have commodities are classified in the same category. However, all means by which those traveling by sea aim to profit from commercial transactions are subject to contribution." Al-Nuwayrī, *Al-Ilmām*, 2:243: "... Likewise, the value of property one is forbidden to jettison such as slaves and slave-girls intended for commercial purposes is included in the apportionment [of losses]."

[97] Khalilieh, "Human Jettison": 230-1; A.L. Udovitch, "An Eleventh Century Islamic Treatise on the Law of the Sea," *Annales Islamologiques* 27 (1993): 49; Ashburner, *Rhodian Sea-Law*, cclxxv; Freshfield, *Manual of Later Roman Law*: 211; O.R. Constable, "The Problem of Jettison in Medieval Mediterranean Maritime Law," *Journal of Medieval History* 20 (1994): 217.

[98] *EI*^{2}, s.v. "ʿAbd" (R. Brunschvig), 1:32-3; Goitein, *Mediterranean Society*, 1:130-47; idem, "Slaves and Slave-girls in the Cairo Geniza Records," *Arabica* 9 (1962): 1-20. According to documents from the Cairo Geniza, female slaves were far more

slave's price was calculated the moment he/she was taken on board. Again, when the monetary value of the jettisoned slaves and commercial articles was calculated, taxes paid at the point of embarkation had to be excluded as a non-refundable official prerogative.[99] Finally, the jettison of goods and human cargo led to a right of contribution from the freight upon slaves; the cost of shipping had to be reduced proportionately to the extent of the reduction in the value of the jettisoned slaves. A shipper or slaver whose mercantile slaves were jettisoned had the right to recover the freight charges for them.[100]

Conclusion

Slaves experienced a unique legal position at sea maintaining the status of humans and objects as well. Slaves serving in the ship were an integral part of the crew, and were, therefore, merited the same rights and duties granted to freeborn employees by Romano-Byzantine and Islamic admiralty laws. Both of these separate legal systems required ship owners to provide them with sufficient amounts of food, water, and other drinks, spaces for sleeping and storing the slaves' personal belongings, and outfit them with uniform dress. It follows that ship owners were, for the most part, held liable for the acts of their crews and servants except if the latter intentionally disobeyed the owner's orders. This principle is firmly established in a *ḥadīth* attributed to Prophet Muḥammad stating:

> "Everyone of you is a guardian and is responsible for his charge, the *imām* (ruler) is a guardian and is responsible for his subjects, the man is a guardian in the affairs for his family and responsible for his charges, a woman is guardian of her husband's house and responsible for her charges, and the servant is a guardian of his master's property and is responsible for his charges."[101]

numerous and costly than male slaves. A descending order of value made whites more costly than blacks; young slaves more expensive than older ones, and some slaves were more valuable because they were less available. Moreover, almost all transactions in this documentary evidence were made for cash, even though business was commonly conducted on credit. Finally, contracts commonly required a sales tax (literally, the dues of the market) to be paid.

[99] al-Yaḥṣubī, *Madhāhib al-Ḥukkām*: 238.

[100] Khalilieh, "Human Jettison": 231-2.

[101] Bin-Muhamad, "Vicarious Liability": 199.

As passengers, Romano-Byzantine and Islamic laws both drew a clear-cut distinction between slaves purchased as merchandise, and those bought for household. The former category includes slaves serving in the ship, who were an integral part of the crew, and ordinary slave-travellers, who either accompanied their masters,[102] or sailed alone in the service of their masters.[103] Those slaves were excluded from the general average contribution and loss. Contrariwise, slaves purchased for commercial purposes were considered by jurists and assessors as "*res*" (things). They were treated as human cargo and evaluated on the basis of their market value when calculating the general average contribution.

Unlike the Justinianic Digest and the Nomos Rhodion Nautikos, which barely shed light on the social behavior and norms of slaves at sea, documentary and legal evidence from the Muslim world seemed to have set up the guidelines the port superintendents, ship owners, and masters had to follow when slaves had to be transported by sea. Since Islamic law required segregation between sexes, ships had to contain separate sections for male and female slaves. In roomy ships, shipwrights installed separate toilets for women to minimize interactions between men and women.

Slaves' life and legal status at sea and on ports in the Mediterranean world from the rise of Islam until the mid-eleventh century relatively remains vague. Although our essay has added to our understanding of the slaves' daily life on Romano-Byzantine and Islamic ships, there are other themes that need to be developed, such as their engagement in the overseas trade and military expeditions. These and other topics are beyond the scope of the current short essay and might be brought up and expanded in future studies.

---

[102] Fahmy, *Muslim Naval Organization*: 113-14. It is reported that slaves, be they males or female, who accompanied their masters and traders could not move from one territory or province to another without a separate passport for each one. For instance, during the reign of Aḥmad Ibn Ṭūlūn (254-270/868-884) a trader accompanied by his slave could not pass through the customs of al-ʿArīsh, a coastal frontier town between Palestine and Egypt, unless the governmental authorities there obtained an official instruction from Fusṭāṭ.

[103] Goitein, *Letters*: 13, 186, 190; Bin-Malīḥ, *Al-Riqq fī Bilād al-Maghrib wa'l-Andalus*: 358-63.

Bibliography

Primary Sources

al-Baghdādī, A.L. (557-629/1162-1231). *Al-Ifāda wa'l I'tibār*, Edited and translated by Kamal H. Zand *et al.* London: George Allen and Unwin, 1965.
al-Ghazālī, A.Ḥ.M.(450-505/1058-1111) *Iḥyā' 'Ulūm al-Dīn*, 5 vols. Cairo, 1967.
Ibn Anas, M. (97-179/715-795). *Al-Muwaṭṭa' of Imām Mālik Ibn Anas*, Translated by A. Bewley. London: Kegan Paul International, 1989.
Ibn Mājid, A. (840-906/1436-1500). *Kitāb al-Fawā'id fī Uṣūl 'Ilm al-Baḥr wa'l-Qawā'id.* Damascus, 1971.
Ibn Qudāma, A.A.(541-620/1146-1223). *Al-Mughnī*, 15 vols. Cairo: Dār Hajar li'l-Ṭibā'a wa'l-Nashr, 1986.
Ibn Rushd, A.W.M.(450-520/1058-1126). *Al-Bayān wa'l-Taḥṣīl wa'l-Sharḥ wa'l-Tawjīh wal-Ta'līl fī Masā'il al-Mustakhraja*, 20 vols. Beirut: Dār al-Gharb al-Islāmī, 1984.
Ibn Shahriyār, B. (10th Century C.E.). *Kitāb 'Ajā'ib al-Hind*, Edited and compiled by Yousef al-Sharouni. London: Riad el-Rayyis, 1989.
al-Jazīrī, A.(d. 585/1189). *Al-Maqṣad al-Maḥmūd fī Talkhīṣ al-'Uqūd.* Madrid: Consejo Superior de Investigacioens Científicas Agencia Española de Cooperación Internacional, 1998.
al-Makhzūmī, A.Ḥ.(d. 585/1189). *Kitāb al-Minhāj fī 'Ilm Kharāj Miṣr*, Edited by. Claude Cahen and Yūsuf Rāghib. Cairo: Institut Français d'Archéologie Orientale, 1986.
al-Māwardī, A.Ḥ.(364-450/974-1058). *Al-Aḥkām al-Sulṭānīya wa'l-Wilāyāt al-Dīnīya.* Beirut: Dār al-Kutub al-'Ilmīya, 1978.
al-Minhājī, M.(d. 880/1475). *Jawāhir al-'Uqūd wa-Mu'īn al-Qu·ā wal-Muwaqqi'īn wal-Shuhūd.* 2 vols. Cairo, 1955.
al-Nuwayrī, M. (d. 775/1372). *Kitāb al-Ilmām bi'l-I'lām fī-mā Jarat bi-hi al-Aḥkām wa'l-Umūr al-Muq·iya fī Waq'at al-Iskandarīya*, 6 vols. Hyderabad: Osmania Oriental Publications Bureau, Osmania University, 1969.
al-Qarāfī, A.A. (d. 684/1285). *Al-Dhakhīra*, 11 vols. Beirut: Dār al-Gharb al-Islāmī, 1994.
———. *Al-Furūq.* 4 vols. Tūnis, 1885.
al-Sarakhsī, M. (11th century C.E.). *Al-Mabsūṭ.* 31 vols. Cairo: Maṭba'at al-Sa'āda, 1906.
al-Shāfi'ī, Muḥammad Ibn Idrīs (150-204/767-820). *Al-Umm.* 8 vols. Beirut: Dār al-Ma'rifa li'l-Ṭibā'a wa'l-Nashr, 1973.
al-Shammākhī, Ā. (d. 793/1390). *Al-Īḍāḥ*, 4 vols. Beirut, 1970.
Ṭāher, M.A. (ed.), "Kitāb Akriyat al-Sufun wa'l-Nizā' bayna Ahlihā", *Cahiers de Tunisie* 31 (1983): 5-54.
al-Tanūkhī, Abū 'Alī Muḥassin Ibn Abī al-Qāsim (160-240/776-854). *Al-Faraj ba'da al-Shiddah.* Cairo: Dār al-Ṭibā'a al-Muḥammadīya, 1955.
al-Tanūkhī, S. (160-240/776-854). *Al-Mudawwana al-Kubrā*, 6 vols. Cairo: Maṭba'at al-Sa'āda, 1905.
al-Wansharīsī, A.A. (834-914/1430-1508), *Al-Mi'yār al-Mu'rib wal-Jāmi' al-Mughrib 'an Fatāwā Ahl Ifrīqiyya wal-Andalus wal-Maghrib.* Beirut: Dār al-Gharb al-Islāmī, 1981.
al-Yaḥṣubī, Q.I. (476-544/1083-1149). *Madhāhib al-Ḥukkām fī Nawāzil al-Aḥkām.* Beirut: Dār al-Gharb al-Islāmī, 1994.

Secondary Sources

Ahrweiler, H. *Byzance et la mer: la marine de guerre, la politique et les institutions maritimes de Byzance aux VIIe-XVe siècles*. Paris: Presses universitaires de France, 1966.

Ashburner, W. *The Rhodian Sea-Law*. Oxford: Clarendon Press, 1909.

Barrow, R.H. *Slavery in the Roman Empire*. New York: Barnes & Noble, 1968.

Bāzmūl, M. *Aḥkām al-Khadam fī al-Sharī'a al-Islāmīya*. Beirut: Dār al-Bashā'ir al-Lubnāniyya, 2008.

Bell, H.I. "Two Official Letters of the Arab Period." *Journal of Egyptian Archaeology* 12 (1926): 265-81.

Bin-Malīḥ, A.I. *Al-Riqq fī Bilād al-Maghrib wa'l-Andalus*. Beirut: Dār al-Intishār al-'Arabī, 2004.

Bin-Muhamad, A.B. "Vicarious Liability: A Study of the Liability of Employer and Employee in the Islamic Law of Tort." *Arab Law Quarterly* 15 (2000): 197-205.

Bogen, D.S. "Ignoring History: The Liability of Ships' Masters, Innkeepers and Stablekeepers under Roman Law." *American Journal of Legal History* 36 (1992): 326-60.

Bradley, *Slavery and Society*. Cambridge: Cambridge University Press, 1994.

Brunschvig, R. "'Abd." *The Encyclopaedia of Islam*. Leiden: E.J. Brill, 1960. 1: 32-3.

Buckland, W.W. *The Roman Law of Slavery*. New York: AMS Press, 1969.

Casson, L. *Travel in the Ancient World*. Baltimore: The Johns Hopkins University Press, 1994.

——. "The Feeding of the Trireme Crews and an Early in IG ii 2 1631." *Transactions of the American Philological Association* 125 (1995): 261-9.

——. *Ships and Seamanship in the Ancient World*. Princeton: Princeton University Press, 1971.

——. "Galley Slaves." *Transactions and Proceedings of the American Philological Association* 97 (1966): 35-44.

Chowdbaray-Best, G. "Ancient Maritime Law." *The Mariner's Mirror* 62 (1976): 81-91.

Christides, V. "Raid and Trade in the Eastern Mediterranean: A Treatise by Muḥammad Ibn 'Umar, the Faqīh from Occupied Moslem Crete, and Rhodian Sea Law, Two Parallel Texts." *Graeco-Arabica* 5 (1993): 61-102.

Constable, O.R. "The Problem of Jettison in Medieval Mediterranean Maritime Law." *Journal of Medieval History* 20 (1994): 207-20.

Dareste, R. "La *Lex Rhodia*." *Revue de Philologie* 29 (1905): 1-29.

Fahmy, M.A. *Moslem Naval Organization*. Cairo: National Publication and Printing House, 1966.

Freshfield, E.H.A. *Manual of Later Roman Law: The Ecloga*. Cambridge: Cambridge University Press, 1927.

Gil, M. *In the Kingdom of Ishmael: Texts from the Cairo Geniza*. 4 vols. Tel Aviv: Tel Aviv University Press, 1997. (Hebrew)

Goitein, S.D. *Letters of Medieval Jewish Traders*. Princeton: Princeton University Press, 1973.

——. *A Mediterranean Society: The Jewish Communities of the Arab World as Portrayed in the Documents of the Cairo Geniza*, 6 vols. Berkeley: University of California Press, 1967-93.

——. "The Tribulations of an Overseer of the Sultan's Ships." In *Arabic and Islamic Studies in Honor of Hamilton A.R. Gibb*. Ed. George Makdisi. Cambridge: Cambridge University Press, 1965: 270-84.

——. "Slaves and Slave-girls in the Cairo Geniza Records." *Arabica* 9 (1962): 1-20.

Ibn Fāyiʿ, A.R. *Aḥkām al-Baḥr fī al-Fiqh al-Islāmī*. Jedda: Dār al-Andalus al-Khaḍrāʾ, 2000.

Justice, A. *A General Treatise of the Dominion of the Sea*. London: Printed for the executors of J. Nicholson, 1724.

Khalilieh, H.S. *Admiralty and Maritime Laws in the Mediterranean Sea (ca. 800-1050): The Kitāb Akriyat al-Sufun vis-à-vis the Nomos Rhodion Nautikos*. Leiden: E.J. Brill, 2006.

——. *Islamic Maritime Law: An Introduction*. Leiden: E.J. Brill, 1998.

——. "Women at Sea: Modesty, Privacy and Sexual Misconduct of Passengers and Sailors Aboard Islamic Ships." *Al-Qanṭara* 27 (2006): 135-51.

——. "Human Jettison, Contribution for Lives, and Life Salvage in the Byzantine and Early Islamic Maritime Laws in the Mediterranean." *Byzantion* 75 (2005): 225-35.

Kīrah, N.K. *Al-Jawārī wal-Ghulmān fī Miṣr fī al-ʿAṣrayn al-Fāṭimī wal-Ayyūbī (358-648/969-1250)*. Cairo: Maktabat al-Zahrāʾ, 2007.

Leder, S. *Die arabische Ecloga*. Frankfurt: Forschungen zur byzantinischen Rechtsgeschichte, 1985.

Letsios, D.G. *Das Seegesetz der Rhodier: Untersuchungen zu Seerecht und Handelsschiffahrt in Byzanz*. Rhodos: Institouto Aigaiou tou Dikaiou tes Thalassas kai tou Nautikou Diakiou, 1996.

Lévi-Provençal, E. *Trois traités hispaniques de Ḥisba*. Cairo: Institut français d'archéologie orientale, 1955.

——. *Seville Musulmane au debut du XIIe Siecle, Le traité d'Ibn ʿAbdūn sur la vie urbaine et les corps des métiers*. Paris: Maisonneuve, 1947.

——. "Un document sur la vie urbaine et les corps de métiers à Séville au début du XIIe siécle: Le traité d'Ibn ʿAbdūn." *Journal Asiatique* 224 (1934): 193-252.

Lewis, B. *Race and Slavery in the Middle East: An Historical Inquiry*. Oxford: Oxford University Press, 1990.

Libourel, Jan M. "Galley Slaves in the Second Punic War." *Classical Philology* 68 (1973): 116-19.

McCormick, M. *Origins of the European Economy: Communications and Commerce A.D. 300-900*. Cambridge: Cambridge University Press, 2001.

Noble, D.R. "The Principles of Islamic Maritime Law." (Ph.D. diss., University of London, 1988.

Nukhaylī, D. *Al-Sufun al-Islāmīya ʿalā Ḥurūf al-Muʿjam*. Alexandria: Alexandria University Press, 1974.

Raffles, S.S. "The Maritime Code of the Malays." *Royal Asiatic Society of Great Britain and Ireland; Malayan Branch* (1879): 62-84.

Rajab, M.M. *Al-Qānūn al-Baḥrī al-Islāmī ka-Maṣdar li-Qawāʿid al-Qānūn al-Baḥrī al-Muʿāṣir*. Alexandria: Al-Maktab al-ʿArabī al-Ḥadīth, 1990.

Sargent, R.L. "The Use of Slaves by the Athenians in Warfare." *Classical Philology* 22 (1927): 264-79.

Scott, S.P. *The Civil Law*. Cincinnati: The Central Trust Company, 1932.

Shamarānī, A.A. *Isʿāf Ahl al-ʿAṣr bi-Aḥkām al-Baḥr*. Riāḍ: Dār al-Waṭan li'l-Nashr, 1999.

Sperber, D. *Nautica Talmudica*. Leiden: E.J. Brill, 1986.

Stillman, Y.K. *Arab Dress from the Dawn of Islam to Modern Times: A Short History*. Leiden: E.J. Brill, 2000.

Thomas, J.A. "Juridical Aspects of Carriage by Sea and Warehousing in Roman Law." *Recueils de la Société Jean Bodin pour l'Histoire Comparative des Institutions* 32 (1972): 117-59.

Udovitch, A.L. "An Eleventh Century Islamic Treatise on the Law of the Sea." *Annales Islamologiques* 27 (1993): 37-54.

Watson, A. *The Digest of Justinian*. Philadelphia: University of Pennsylvania Press, 1998.

——. *Roman Slave Law*. Baltimore: The Johns Hopkins University Press, 1987.

Winstedt, R. and de Josselin de Jong, P.E. "The Maritime Laws of Malacca." *Journal of the Malayan Branch of the Royal Asiatic Society-Singapore* 29 (1956): 22-59.

MARITIME CITYSCAPES: LESSONS FROM REAL AND IMAGINED TOPOGRAPHIES OF WESTERN INDIAN OCEAN PORTS

Roxani Eleni Margariti

Introduction

In his article "Medieval Alexandria," published in the proceedings of a conference credited with sparking new interest in the study of the great Egyptian port,[1] Abraham L. Udovitch discusses the historical and historiographical gap between medieval Alexandria and its illustrious earlier (Hellenistic, Roman and late antique) and later (19th- and early 20th-century) incarnations. His point of departure is Alexandria's "incontestable status as Egypt's *second* city" in medieval times.[2] Indeed the Latin appellation "Alexandria ad Aegyptum" and its suggestion of autonomy, centrality, and exceptionality seem to have no longer obtained after the Arab conquest of the 1st/7th century. As Udovitch and other scholars in the 1993 conference pointed out, in Graeco-Roman times the port was not of Egypt, but by Egypt, perceived as a virtual island, free-floating, oriented towards a multiple yet familiar foreland, and only marginally attached to an essentially foreign hinterland. Conversely, in medieval times the city was subordinated to and overshadowed by an ever expanding inland capital city.[3]

---

[1] See M.S. Venit, Review of *Alexandria and Alexandrianism: Papers Delivered at a Symposium Organized by the J. Paul Getty Museum and by the Getty Center for the History of Art and the Humanities and Held at the Museum, April 22-25, 1993. American Journal of Archaeology* 102 (1998): 453.

[2] A.L. Udovitch, "Medieval Alexandria: Some Evidence from the Cairo Genizah Documents," *Alexandria and Alexandrianism: Papers Delivered at a Symposium Organized by the J. Paul Getty Center for History of Art and the Humanities and Held at the Museum, April 22-25, 1993* (Malibu, CA: Getty Museum, 1996): 273-4. In a later article Udovitch notes that "medieval Alexandria has been a stepchild of both Egyptian and of general history": "Alexandria in the 11th and 12th Centuries; Letters and Documents of the Cairo Geniza Merchants: an Interim Balance Sheet," in *Alexandrie médiévale* 2, ed. by Ch. Décobert (Cairo: Institut Français d'Archéologie Orientale, 2002): 99.

[3] Udovitch, "Medieval Alexandria": 274, 282-3.

In the fourteen years since the Alexandria conference, the path of devoting more research to the medieval port has lead to the breaking of important new ground.[4] In addition, a wealth of new research on ports of the Islamic world in general puts us today in a unique place to ponder the nature of port cities of the medieval Islamic world as centers of economic, social, and even political life.[5] What characterized ports as urban centers, and how did they function vis-à-vis their foreland and their hinterland? What were the main features of their physical make-up and how did these relate to the organization of social, economic, and even political life?

The purpose of this paper is to contribute to the last question with regard to port cities of the Western Indian Ocean which stood at multiple crossroads of the transoceanic trade connecting South Asia, Africa, the Middle East, and the Mediterranean world. Since the early 1970's research on pre-10th/16th-century port towns of the western shores of the Indian Ocean has made big strides. My goal here is to highlight and juxtapose the findings that relate to the topographies of ports investigated so far, and more importantly to outline questions that these findings raise concerning the nature of littoral states and societies of the Indian Ocean world before the early modern period and the arrival of new players in the region's commercial arena.

---

[4] Two symposia in 1996 and 1999, held in Cairo and Alexandria respectively, were explicitly devoted to the medieval city and resulted in two publications, *Alexandrie médiévale* 1 and 2, ed. by J.-Y. Empereur and Ch. Décobert. For a systematic treatment of Alexandria's port's continued significance, and often primacy, and a presentation of invaluable documentary evidence on the subject, see P.M. Sijpesteijn, "Travel and Trade on the River," in *Papyrology and the History of Early Islamic Egypt*, ed. by P.M. Sijpesteijn and L. Sundelin (Leiden: E. J. Brill, 2004): 119-24. For an important study of the Jewish community of medieval Alexandria, see M. Frenkel's work on the port's Jewish community, *The Compassionate and the Benevolent: The Leading Elite in the Jewish Community of Alexandria in the Middle Ages* (in Hebrew) (Jerusalem: Yad Izhak Ben Zvi and Hebrew University, 2006). The book is based on Frenkel's dissertation "The Jewish Community of Alexandria under the Fatimids and the Ayyubids: Portrait of a Leading Elite" [in Hebrew]. Ph.D. diss., Hebrew University 2001.

[5] On a remarkable database of ports and maritime routes of the Islamic world discussed below, see C. Hardy-Guilbert, M. Kervran, Ch. Picard, H. Renel and A. Rougeulle, "Ports et commerce maritime islamiques: Présentation du programme APIM (Atlas des ports et itinéraires maritimes du monde musulman)," in *Ports maritimes et ports fluviaux au Moyen Âge: XXXV Congrès de la Société des Historiens Médiévistes de l'Enseignement Public (SHMESP) (La Rochelle 5 et 6 juin 2004)* (Paris: Publications de la Sorbonne, 2005): 79-97.

Much of what I argue here stems from my recently published work on the medieval port of Aden in Yemen between the 5th/11th and the 7th/13th centuries. In order to avoid making overly broad generalizations from material that is necessarily of limited geographical and chronological scope, I will generally limit my comments to the westernmost reaches of the Indian Ocean. These ports can be said to form a subgroup of the much more extensive "archipelago of world cities" of trade to use Janet Abu-Lughod's felicitous phrase,[6] by virtue of their relative mutual proximity and strong interconnectedness, their location on important corridors of the inter-oceanic trade linking the Indian Ocean and Mediterranean worlds, and their shared extended forelands that included the East African and Indian littorals. Even so, my choice is somewhat arbitrary and partly dictated by the constraints of empirical research; it is my hope that what I have to say here, circumscribed as it is by the artificial boundaries I draw for the sake of manageable analysis, will stimulate comments and responses from a number of differing perspectives that will transcend these limits and perhaps delineate different maritime terrains.

"Real" and "Imagined"

Whether supplementing or standing in for archaeological evidence, the writings of geographers and travelers, who visited western Indian Ocean ports or collected information about them between the 4th/10th and the 10th/16th centuries, have been used as a major source and have guided historical and archaeological research on the ports of the region. I will focus primarily on material written in Arabic, which in any case constitutes the majority of sources relating to our subject. What do I mean by "imagined" topographies? In reading through the early geographical descriptions of Western Indian Ocean ports, I argue that the reader is left with the vague impression of the region's model port city. Sīrāf, Ṣuḥār, Aden, and Jeddah, are all described as populous, densely built, endowed with impressive architecture, and vestiges of an earlier, Iranian maritime presence.[7]

---

[6] J. Abu-Lughod, *Before European Hegemony: The World System, A.D. 1250-1350* (New York: Oxford University Press, 1989): 353.

[7] For example according to al-Muqaddasī, Jeddah is *madīna muḥaṣṣana*, fortified, *'āmira*, densely built, and, *āhila*, populous; *Aḥsan al-taqāsīm fi ma'rifat*

The hot climate, lack of water, and water supply solutions are also routinely noted.

This is not to say that the reports are identical. In fact, there are apparent disagreements on the relative status of these ports, and the disparity is partly attributable to timing of the report, and, perhaps more crucially, bias of the reporter. Aden, for example, is a small place, famous only because of its position but in fact less expansive than other Yemeni cities according to al-Iṣṭakhrī and his follower Ibn Ḥawqal.[8] Al-Muqaddasī (d. ca. 380/990), on the other hand, writing only slightly later devotes a long section to what he immediately identifies as a *balad jalīl* (splendid town), and later dubs "the anteroom of China, entrepôt of Yemen, treasury of the West, and mother lode of trade wares."[9] It is likely that Aden was experiencing growth and urban development in the course of the 4th/10th century, when the ascendancy of the Fatimids in Egypt and the concomitant boost of the Red Sea route, in addition with the Yemeni-Fatimid nexus brought the port's already strategic position even greater prominence. Conversely, al-Muqaddasī's predecessors' reports may reflect the port's earlier, more modest phase of development.

Still, the difference in tone is dramatic, and begs the question of the observers' point of view. While it is unknown whether al- Iṣṭakhrī and Ibn Ḥawqal actually passed through Aden, al-Muqaddasī makes a point of emphasizing his visit there and reporting information he obtained from local sailors.[10] Rather than photographically recording

---

al-aqālīm (Leiden: E. J. Brill, 1967): 79. Aden, receives a longer description, and is *balad jalīl*, a splendid town, *ʿāmir, āhil, ḥaṣīn*, fortified, and *khafīf*, pleasant (ibid., 85); Ṣuḥār, also merits a long description, and is *ʿāmir, āhil, ḥasan*, beautiful, *ṭayyib*, salubrious, *nazih*, pure, and unsurpassed by other cities in various respects, *laysat ʿalā baḥr al-ṣīn al-yawm balad ajall minhu*, "no town on the sea of China is more splendid than it" (ibid.: 92); finally, Sīrāf's buildings are extensively described, the town itself said to have been admired *li-shiddat ʿimāratihā wa-ḥusn duwurihā wa-ẓarf jāmiʿihā wa-labāqat aswāqihā*, "the strength of its architecture, the beauty of its houses, the elegance of its mosque, and the refinement of its markets" (ibid.: 426).

[8] al-Iṣṭakhrī, *Al-Masālik wa'l-mamālik* (Leiden: E. J. Brill, 1967): 25. Ibn Ḥawqal, *Al-Masālik wa'l-mamālik* (Leiden: E. J. Brill, 1873): 32.

[9] al-Muqaddasī, *Aḥsan al-taqāsīm fi maʿrifat al-aqālīm*, 85: *dihlīz al-ṣīn wa-furḍat al-yaman wa-khizānat al-maghrib wa-maʿdin al-tijārāt kathīr al-quṣūr mubārik ʿalā man dakhalahu muthīr li-man sakanahu.*

[10] al-Muqaddasī, *Aḥsan al-taqāsīm fi maʿrifat al-aqālīm*: 10-11. In addition to consulting captains, sailors, navigational astronomers (*riyāḍīyīn*; E. Fagnan, *Additions aux dictionnaires Arabes*, Beirut: Librairie du Liban, 1982, provides the definition "astronomer"), agents, and merchants, the author speaks to leading merchant, and "most knowledgeable of people" Abū ʿAlī b. Ḥāzim, *bi-sāḥil ʿAdan*, on the Aden

an actual multitude of forts and a richly built city, however, his account perhaps conveys the excitement of a Levantine over his arrival at a distant shore. It also reflects his perspective on the region of the *Jazirat al-ʿarab*: this for him was the quintessential place of trade, the locus of *furḍatay al-dunyā*, the two entrepots of the world, Yemen and Oman.[11] In this scheme, major ports of this region were the openings through which the riches of world trade were channeled: the description of Aden's topography is a formula meant to reflect that reality.

A second example that speaks to the intertwined issues of accuracy and positionality of descriptive reports pertains to the Omani port of Ṣuḥār on the eastern end of the southern Arabian shores. In his meticulous and thoughtful study of Ṣuḥār, archaeologist Andrew Williamson, addresses the remarkably favorable image of the city as it emerges from the accounts of the 4th/10th-century geographers discussed earlier, as well as from later accounts of the city's passed glory. His analysis suggests that although these accounts appear "extravagant", they are nonetheless meaningful because the reporters "are not given to exaggerated claims and are generally highly regarded for their accuracy."[12] This assessment requires elaboration; indeed, the reports are meaningful but not in the sense that they can be relied upon for an absolute assessment of either the stage of development of any one port at any one period, or of the relative importance of different ports. Indeed, although al- Iṣṭakhrī enthuses that "no other city on the shores of the sea of Fars in all the lands of Islam is known to be richer in buildings and wealth than Ṣuḥār,"[13] he also devotes

seaboard. This is a remarkable passage for what it tells us about the transmission of navigational knowledge and about the author's account of his methodology and experience.

[11] al-Muqaddasī, *Aḥsan al-taqāsīm fi maʿrifat al-aqālīm*: 97-8. This section, devoted to the trade of the Arabian Peninsula, opens with the statement that "trade in this *iqlīm* is beneficial because it contains the entrepots of the world": *wa'l-tijārāt hādhā al-iqlīm mufida lianna bihi furḍatay al-dunyā*. On the translation of *furḍa* as entrepot, see below. Only one manuscript identifies these as Oman and Yemen, but it seems safe to assume that. The author then notes that the sea here connects to China, that the ports of the Hijaz are connected to Egypt, to Yemen, and to Iraq, and continues that a description of all merchandise to be found here would be too unwieldy.

[12] A. Williamson, *Sohar and Omani Seafaring in the Indian Ocean* (Muscat: Petroleum Development Oman Ltd, 1973): 3, 11-12.

[13] al-Iṣṭakhrī, *Al-Masālik wa'l-mamālik*: 25: *wa-lā takād tuʿaraf ʿalā shāṭī baḥr fāris bi-jamīʿ bilād al-islām madīna akthar ʿimāra wa-mālan min Ṣuḥār*. See also Ibn Ḥawqal, *Al-Masālik wa'l-mamālik*: 32; his report mirrors that of al-Iṣṭakhrī with only

more book space and greater detail of topographical and architectural description to Sīrāf; compared to his Sīrāf comments, in fact, the Ṣuḥār praise is rather vague.[14]

Thus, it is doubtful that his statement of Ṣuḥār's primacy was meant literally as an assessment of its importance vis-à-vis other ports. Instead, his reports and those of his colleagues in the geographical tradition are best understood as conveying the overall status that major ports on the India route enjoyed in the eyes of outsiders, as most of these writers were to most of the maritime places they describe. In other words, we should consider their descriptions for what they tell us about a port imaginary, or perhaps a literary *topos* encapsulating the image of an urban center located both physically and conceptually at the borderland of the Indian Ocean littoral.

Travelers sometimes give more detailed information about the lay of the land they visit than do geographers. Here too, while combing their accounts for glimpses of port topographies, we should not lose sight of the authors' predispositions, as these are shaped by their biographies, their experiences, and the goals of their journeys, as much or more than by the journeys themselves. For example, Ibn al-Mujāwir (fl. ca. 626/1228), a Central Asian traveler and possibly merchant who visited the Arabian peninsula in the beginning of the 7th/13th century, left such a detailed account of Jeddah and Aden in his *Ta'rīkh al-mustabṣir*, that in later times authors Ibn Faraj of Jeddah (d. 1010/1602) and Abū Makhrama of Aden (870-947/1465-1540) folded the traveler's observations into their books dedicated to their respective home towns.[15] The Andalusian Ibn Jubayr (540/1145-614/1217) proves to be a keen observer of navigational

minor differences. The reports do not contain the level of detail on building construction or topography that the authors devote to Sīrāf.

[14] al-Iṣṭakhrī, *al-Masālik wa'l-mamālik*: 127-8, 154. Sīrāf is here said to be almost as big as Shiraz and among the largest cities of Fars. The author seems particularly impressed with the construction of its multistory buildings.

[15] On Ibn al-Mujāwir, see G.R. Smith, "Ibn al-Mujāwir's Ta'rīkh al-mustabṣir: A Source for the Historical Geography and of the Economic and Social History of Medieval Yemen." Paper Presented at the Middle East Studies Association 29th Annual Meeting, Washington, D.C. 6-10 December 1995; G.R. Smith, "Ibn al-Mujāwir on Dhofar and Socotra," Proceedings of the Seminar for Arabian Studies 25 (1995): 127-40; Idem, "Ibn al-Mujāwir's 7th/13th-century Guide to Arabia: The Eastern Connection," *Occasional Papers of the School of Abbasid Studies* (1990): 71-89. On Ibn Faraj, *Al-Silāḥ wa'l-'uddah fī ta'rīkh thaghr Juddah/Bride of the Sea: a 10th/16th-Century Account of Jeddah*, ed. G.R. Smith and A.U. al-Zayla'ī (Durham,

practice and, to some extent, of port topography as well. His relatively dispassionate description of Jeddah's residential architecture—understated yet fascinating for what it reveals about the use of thatch structures and their juxtaposition with stone-and-mortar edifices—should be measured against the vehement distaste with which he recounts his experiences at ʿAydhāb.[16] The Maghrebi Ibn Baṭṭūṭa (703/1304-770 or 779/1368-69 or 1377) on the other hand, more interested as he was in rubbing shoulders with, and receiving lavish hospitality from, scholars and dignitaries, provides an impressionistic and rather hyperbolic view of Aden's port.[17]

At the liminal space between reality and imagination lies language. A brief survey of some of the terms that geographers and travelers use to designate the ports in question is instructive. Originally denoting an opening in the bank of a river, an opening that offers access to the water, the term *furḍa*, routinely applied to Aden and other ports of the region, conveys the sense of clearing house, entrepôt; in further metaphor, it also came to mean a port's customs house.[18] Less frequently used descriptive terms, such as al-Muqaddasī *khizāna* and *dihlīz*, literally meaning treasury and vestibule respectively, also convey the sense of mercantile depot-cum-transit hall.[19] As applied to Indian Ocean ports, the term *thaghr* like *furḍa*, conveys the sense of opening, but with the added sense of border. Its history is interesting:

UK: Center for Middle Eastern and Islamic Studies, 1984): i-iii. On Abū Makhrama, see *EI*², s.v. "Makhrama" (O. Löfgren), 6:132-3.

[16] Ibn Jubayr, *Riḥla* (Leiden: E. J. Brill 1907): 73, 75-6.

[17] Ibn Baṭṭūṭa, *Riḥlat Ibn Baṭṭūṭa* (Beirut: Dār Ṣādir, 1960): 194-5.

[18] Ibn Manẓūr, *Lisān al-ʿarab* (Beirut: Dār Ṣādir, 1955) offers notch of a bow, a place where water is drawn from a river, a break or gap in the river, and a river landing-place for boats. Geographers use the term in the sense of a maritime landing-place, and a clearing house of merchandise for a broader hinterland. Thus Aden is *furḍat al-yaman* (al-Muqaddasī, *Aḥsan al-taqāsīm fī maʿrifat al-aqālīm*: 85), *furḍa ʿalā al-baḥr* (al-Iṣṭakhrī, *Al-Masālik wa'l-mamālik*: 25; Ibn Ḥawqal, *Al-Masālik wa'l-mamālik*: 32); Jeddah is *furḍa li-makka* (Ibn Ḥawqal, *Al-Masālik wa'l-mamālik*: 27) and Sīrāf is *al-furḍat al-ʿaẓīma li-fāris* (al-Iṣṭakhrī, *Al-Masālik wa'l-mamālik*: 34, 154; Ibn Ḥawqal, *Al-Masālik wa'l-mamālik*: 39). Ibn al-Mujāwir records the application of the term to Aden in the above sense (Ibn al-Mujāwir, *Ta'rīkh al-mustabṣir*: 129: *wa-tusammā furḍat al-yaman*) but also to describe Aden's customs house both as a building and as an institution (ibid.: 157-8). On this latter definition see also R.E. Margariti, *Aden and the Indian Ocean trade: 150 years in the Life of a Medieval Arabian port* (Chapel Hills, NC: The University of North Carolina Press, 2007): 94-6, 114-19.

[19] al-Muqaddasī, *Aḥsan al-taqāsīm fī maʿrifat al-aqālīm*: 79 (*Judda khizānat makka, miṣr*), 85 (*ʿAdan dihlīz al-ṣīn khizānat al-maghrib*), 92 (*Ṣuḥār dihlīz al-ṣīn khizānat al-sharq*).

it does not appear in the early geographers' descriptions of Indian Ocean ports, but on the other hand has a long history of designating borderlands between the Islamic and non-Islamic realms, and by extension ports on the Mediterranean Sea. Geographical sources describe Alexandria as a *thaghr* for the first time in the 7th/13th century, although the usage is attested earlier in Judeo-Arabic Geniza documents.[20] In the 10th/16th century, Aden and Jeddah too are *thughūr* according to their native authors Abū Makhrama and Ibn Faraj respectively, but the term appears to be interchangeable with the term *sāḥil*, and simply means "coastal settlement" or "port"; thus while Aden is designated simply as "*thaghr ʿAdan*", Jeddah is said to be "*thaghr li-Makkah*" and later "*sāḥil li-Makkah.*"[21]

Do these designations suggest that ports were substantively dependent on inland cities? In the Latin-based and Latin-related languages of Northern Europe "le terme de port renvoie en effect a celui de porte."[22] We should be careful, however, not to make the philological point too rigidly, and to watch out for possible semantic shifts that at some point disassociate the terms from some of the essential elements of their original meaning. Thus, in the Northern European medieval context the sense of the port as a "doorway" may have spoken directly to a reality in which a port was a transportation hub but not a locus of extensive economic, social, and political life, and was organically disconnected from the city proper.[23] The usage of the parallel terms in the Arabic sources, however, is different in nature, as it is not exclusive of other terminology. Thus, in their description of the Indian Ocean world, the early geographical authors frequently

---

[20] For the use of the term *thaghr* in geographical sources to denote a fortress town on a border zone, see R.W. Brauer, *Boundaries and Frontiers in Medieval Muslim Geography* (Philadelphia: The American Philosophical Society, 1995): 19, 25-6. Brauer's data suggests that Alexandria was first designated as a *thaghr* in geographical writings in the 7th/13th century (by Yāqūt). Udovitch notes the application of the term to ports, as well as to Alexandria, and Ibn Khaldūn's justification of this usage; "Medieval Alexandria": 276-7. For the application of the term *thaghr* to Alexandria in the Geniza documents, see S.D. Goitein, *A Mediterranean Society: The Jewish Communities of the Mediterranean World as Portrayed in the Cairo Geniza* (Berkeley: University of California Press, 1983), 4:7.

[21] See Abū Makhrama, *Ta'rīkh thaghr ʿAdan*, ed. O. Lofgren (Leiden: E. J. Brill, 1936-1950): 1; Ibn Faraj, *Al-silāḥ wa'l-ʿuddah fī ta'rīkh thaghr Juddah*: 13.

[22] M. Tranchant, "Les ports maritimes en France au moyen âge," in *Ports maritimes et port fluviaux au Moyen Âge*: 25.

[23] Tranchant, "Les ports maritimes": 25. "En revanche, le port n'était pas nécessairement un lieu où se réalisaient les transactions. La ville, siège des notaires et des changeurs demeurait privilegiée pour cela."

use such as terms *madīna*, *qaṣba*, and *balad*.[24] In other words, the constellation of terms applied by the medieval authors to any one of the ports under consideration here, conveys the sense of door as a nodal location, a hub of transportation, and a clearing house of merchandise, the additional meanings of borderland and line of defense, and the more general import of urban locus of economic activities—including but not exclusively customs collection—and even of center of social and political life, that is, the sense of city.

In addition to offering a key to the conceptualization of Indian Ocean ports in literary and perhaps to some extent popular medieval imagination, the geographies and especially the accounts of travelers like Ibn al-Mujāwir, and city-centered histories by native sons, like Abū Makhrama for Aden and Ibn Faraj for Jeddah, taken together, map out the contours of an otherwise invisible body of maritime folklore emanating from and focused on maritime cities. Al-Iṣṭakhrī tells us of a Sīrāfī man who became so invested in his trading that he abandoned the town and lived on a ship, changing vessel each time that the older one fell apart.[25] Ibn al-Mujāwir tells of customs evaders that led to the construction of the fortification wall in Aden, and of magic talismans built into the gate of Jeddah's circuit wall which revealed the names of anyone having committed theft in town.[26] Ibn Faraj tells of special processions to Eve's tomb just outside Jeddah, where sailors' clairvoyant trances would divine the fate of Jeddah ships missing on the high seas.[27] Stories like these would not have been out of place in the delightful collection of salty dog tales recounted by Buzurg b. Shahriyār in his *'Ajā'ib al-Hind*.[28] The difference is that Iṣṭakhrī, Ibn al-Mujāwir, and Ibn Faraj are chiefly

[24] Jeddah is *madīna* (al-Muqaddasī, *Aḥsan al-taqāsīm fi ma'rifat al-aqālīm*: 69, 79); Aden is *balad* and *madīna* as well as *furḍat al-yaman* (ibid.: 70, 85). Ṣuḥār is *qaṣbat 'Umān* and *madīna* (ibid.: 70, 92; al-Iṣṭakhrī, *Al-Masālik wa'l-mamālik*: 25; Ibn Ḥawqal, *Al-Masālik wa'l-mamālik*: 32). Sīrāf is *qaṣbat Ardashīr Khurra* and *madīna* (al-Muqaddasī, *Aḥsan al-taqāsīm fi ma'rifat al-aqālīm*: 420, 422, 426; al-Iṣṭakhrī, *Al-Masālik wa'l-mamālik*: 34, 97, 106, 127, 128; Ibn Ḥawqal, *Al-Masālik wa'l-mamālik*: 39, 179, 197).

[25] al-Iṣṭakhrī, *Al-Masālik wa'l-mamālik*: 138

[26] Ibn al-Mujāwir, *Ta'rīkh al-mustabṣir*: 146-7 (on Aden); 56 (on Jeddah).

[27] Ibn Faraj, *Al-Silāḥ wa'l-'uddah fī ta'rīkh bandar Juddah*: 15 (English): 50-1 (Arabic).

[28] Buzurg, *Kitāb 'ajā'ib al-Hind*, ed. M.S. al-Ṭurayḥī (Abu Dhabi, UAE: Al-mujamma' al-thaqafī, 2000). For an English translation see G.S.P. Freeman-Grenville, ed., *The Book of the Wonders of India: Mainland, Sea, and Islands* (London: East-West Publications, 1981).

concerned with narratives connected to specific cities, and pertaining to the shared themes of managing risks on the high seas from the safety of an urban haven, and containing unruliness and transgression at port.

The Promise of Documentary Sources

Documentary sources are rare for the pre-modern western Indian Ocean, but in two remarkable cases they have significantly elucidated the topography and workings of Western Indian Ocean ports Aden and Quṣayr. Preserved in the Cairo Geniza and now scattered in libraries in Europe and the United States, letters, accounts, and legal depositions of Jewish Yemeni and Mediterranean traders speak directly or indirectly to life and trade in the Yemeni port from the late 5th/11th to the early 7th/13th century. A comparable range of documents is now available from the Egyptian port of Quṣayr, where the University of Chicago excavations between 1978 and 1982, and more recently the University of Southampton excavation starting in the late 1990s, unearthed remarkable deposits of written materials.[29]

Select corpuses from these two assemblages constitute the pivotal historical sources in two recent monographs on maritime and commercial life in the two medieval ports of the Red Sea and Gulf of Aden respectively.[30] What did we learn about port topographies from the documentary material, and how does the information dovetail with literary, archaeological, and environmental data? Unlike travelers, authors of commercial letters were not self-consciously articulate about the sea- and cityscapes that surrounded them and the daily life

[29] The general affinity of the Quṣayr assemblage with that of the Geniza documents is noted in the 2001 interim report on the excavations at the Egyptian port site; see "2001-Arabic Fragments," http://www.arch.soton.ac.uk/Research/Quseir. M.R. Cohen has suggested that the Quṣayr deposit in the Shaykh's House might in fact be an Islamic *geniza*: M.R. Cohen, "Goitein, Magic, and the Geniza," *Jewish Studies Quarterly* 13 (2006) 301-4. An impressive new study of the documents' archaeological context, on the other hand, emphasizes the contrast between geniza-like deposits and the documentary assemblage at Quṣayr, where documents were scattered throughout all strata of the building in question; see K.S. Burke, "Archaeological Texts and Contexts on the Red Sea: The Sheikh's House at Quseir al-Qadim," (Ph.D. Diss., University of Chicago, Illinois, June 2007): 224.

[30] L. Guo, *Commerce, Culture, and Community in a Red Sea Port in the Thirteenth Century: The Arabic Documents from Quseir* (Leiden: E. J. Brill, 2004). R.E.Margariti, *Aden and the Indian Ocean Trade: 150 Years in the Life of a Medieval Arabian Port* (Chapel Hill, NC: University of North Carolina Press, 2007)

they took for granted. Precisely because their lives and livelihoods were embedded in those topographies, however, glimpses of mooring, breakwater, customs house, storeroom, market, and even private residence, invariably shine through their writings.

Consider, for example, an Adenī Jewish merchant's description of the blockade of his home port by an expeditionary naval force from Persian Gulf island-state of Kish/Qays around 529/1134-35. Remarkably, this is one of two fortuitously preserved contemporary accounts of the dramatic events of the blockade communicated by local merchants to their partners overseas, and as such, it vividly conjures both the events themselves and the topographical scene within which they were enacted:

> "They [the enemies] were in the sea and we [the Adenī people] were on land. No one was left behind in the city, neither old nor young, except in the forts, and below the forts the houses were empty...the enemy was in the anchorage and the people had fled their houses."[31]

Faintly but promisingly the lines of the medieval city's topography begin to emerge here, especially when the fragments of the 6th/12th-century eyewitness accounts are juxtaposed to Ibn al-Mujāwir's description of the city and to the rocky landscape of the Aden peninsula that constitutes the port's *longue durée*: a harbor town nesting in the crater of an extinct volcano, a protected anchorage known to the locals as *al-mukallā* within the broader harbor described as

[31] TS18J5, f. 5/India Book 149 and II.46, lines 9-16: *hum fī al- baḥr wa-naḥnu fī al-barr wa-lam yabqā fī al-balad kabīr wa-lā ṣaghīr illā fī al-ḥuṣūn wa-taḥt al-ḥuṣūn illā buyūt fārigha...wa-al-ʿadūw fī al-mukallā wa-al-nās qad harabū min buyūtihim.* This letter was first published by Goitein, "Two Eyewitness Reports on an Expedition of the King of Kish (Qais) against Aden," *Bulletin of the School of Oriental and African Studies* 16 (1954): 247-57. In 1954 Goitein was in the process of collecting material for his "India Book," a study of the India Trade through the testimony of Geniza documentary material. He later sidelined this project, when it became clear that the India Trade material in the Cairo Geniza was only a small segment of a much larger corpus the majority of which pertained to the social and economic history of Jewish communities of the Mediterranean. He thus completed his *opus magnus*, the five-volume *A Mediterranean Society: The Jewish Communities of the Arab World as Portrayed in the Documents of the Cairo* Geniza, and returned to his India Book shortly before his death in 1985; the book was recently published under the care of M.A. Friedman (*India Traders of the Middle Ages: Documents from the Cairo Geniza*, Leiden: E. J. Brill, 2008). I consulted the document I discuss here in the copy of Goitein's research archive deposited at Princeton University and forming the centerpiece of the University's S.D. Goitein Laboratory for Geniza Research at Princeton. I discuss the implications of the episode and its description for Aden's topography in *Aden and the Indian Ocean Trade*: 76-85.

al-bandar, forts located on the upper reaches of the craters sides, and houses on lower ground facing the water.[32]

In the case of Quṣayr, the remarkable documentary material found "in nearly all strata of the building, occupation, and abandonment"[33] of an archaeologically investigated structure did not only provide a name for the excavated complex—dubbed "the Shaykh's house" in reference to the many mentions of various "shaykhs" in the documents[34]—but also enriched our understanding of the port's topography in multiple ways. The unearthed remains were suggestive enough: a complex consisting of living quarters and storage rooms, with staircases leading to a usable roof or a second story.[35] Obviously a trader's house? Without the documents found *in situ* other possibilities might have been contemplated. As it is, the commercial nature of a large number of the documents, the central role of a certain Abū Mufarrij and his family in their contents, and the reference to a "*shūna*" or warehouse suggest that the building was indeed the "major workstation which functioned as both living quarters and warehouse" of this man and his extended family of traders.[36] In other words, the documents' contents as well as their archaeological context itself indicate that the Quṣayr traders were conducting business from home. Katherine Strange Burke's detailed new study of the stratigraphy and associations of the documents with other artifacts furthers this conclusion by proposing specific uses of space in different parts of the complex.[37] As we shall see below, all this contributes to a developing discussion on public and domestic space in Indian Ocean ports.

Can we expect to find similar caches in other ports? The new document finds at Quṣayr by the Southampton team are greatly encouraging for those of us who want to answer in the affirmative to the above question. If the written material found in the "Shaykh's House" indeed represent the remnants of a merchant's papers, then I do not see why excavations at other medieval sites, such as Sharma, Shiḥr,

---

[32] For a detailed account of the land and marine topography of Aden, see Margariti, *Aden and the Indian Ocean Trade*: 34-53, 68-105.

[33] Burke, "Archaeological Texts and Contexts": 224.

[34] Guo, *Commerce, Culture, and Community:* xii, 1.

[35] Guo, *Commerce, Culture, and Community*: xi-xii, 1-2; D.Whitcomb and J. Johnson, "1982 Season of Excavation at Qusayr al-Qadim," *American Research Center in Egypt Newsletter* 120 (1982): 24-30.

[36] Guo, *Commerce, Culture, and Community*: 1-11.

[37] Burke, "Archaeological Texts and Contexts."

Qalhāt,[38] Kish, or Dahlak, might not lead to further documentary finds. That such finds would be a boon for our understanding of Arabian and Indian Ocean ports in general is an understatement. However faint, the voices of the people who lived there could supplement, amend, and ultimately enrich the testimonies of literary texts and material remains.

Harbor Works, Small City States, and the Indian Ocean Shipping Tradition

Since the very early days of underwater archaeological surveys, ancient Mediterranean harbors and harbor works have been studied extensively; the results of these studies highlight the technological expertise and investment of labor involved in maintaining functional harbor facilities.[39] The study of medieval ports has been more checkered but has recently picked up speed. The basic contours of the investigation of built harbor infrastructure and other anchorage solutions in the Islamic world were outlined already in the 1993 *Encyclopedia of Islam* entry "Mīnā'" by Svat Soucek.[40] A remarkable example of the proliferation of port studies since then, and in this first decade of the 21st century, is the ambitious collaborative project on the maritime culture of medieval Islam initiated in France under the auspices of Centre National de la Recherche Scientifique. The output of this project includes the building of an impressive database on ports and maritime routes entitled *Atlas des ports et itinéraires*

---

[38] On the archaeological potential at Qalhāt see T. Vosmer, D. Agius, P. Baker, J. Carpenter and S. Cave, *Oman Maritime Heritage Project: Field Report 1998*, Western Australian Maritime Museum Report No. 144 (Freemantle: Western Australia Maritime Museum 1998): 1-47.

[39] On the significance of the earliest surveys of harbors, such as that of Antoine Poidebard in Tyre and Sidon, see G. Bass, *Archaeology Under Water* (New York: Frederick A. Praeger, 1966): 88-90. See also Blackman's programmatic "Ancient Harbours of the Mediterranean," *International Journal of Nautical Archaeology and Underwater Exploration* 11 (1982): 79-104, 185-211; E. Hadjidaki's survey, "Harbour Studies," *Encyclopedaea of Underwater and Maritime Archaeology*, ed. by J.P. Delgado (London: British Museum Press, 1997): 187-9. For the research stemming from the large-scale excavation of Caesaria, see Oleson et al., "The Caesaria Ancient Harbor Excavation Project (C.A.H.E.P.): Preliminary Report on the 1980-1983 Seasons," *Journal of Field Archaeology* 11 (1984): 281-305.

[40] *EI*[2], s.v. "Mīnā'" (S. Soucek), 7:66-72.

maritimes du monde musulmane (APIM).[41] Discrete recent studies, such as Andrew Petersen's comprehensive survey of the archaeological record of Palestine,[42] Tasha Vorderstrasse's archaeologically inflected investigation of the 'river seaport' of al-Mina,[43] and most recently Yumna Masarwa's pioneering work on the *ribāṭ* of the Syro-Palestinian coast,[44] while not focusing exclusively on harbor works, also take up the issue of the nature of Muslim settlement patterns and maritime investment on the Mediterranean shores.

In the western Indian Ocean too, research on medieval harbor arrangements is growing. The foundations laid by earlier archaeological projects at Sīrāf, Ṣuḥār, and the East African seaboard (Kilwa, Manda, Shanga), are now being expanded by the work at such sites as Quṣayr, the south Arabian ports of the Hadramawt, the renewed project centered on Kilwa in Tanzania, and tentatively the Omani port of Qalhāt. The picture that emerges from just these projects is of a variety of solutions to berthing needs. Indeed, harbor arrangement in the Indian Ocean can be said to be as diverse as the environments and cultural assemblages present on its shores. And while input of labor and expertise in the building and maintenance of harbors is here too a meaningful index of state and merchants' involvement in fostering trade and developing a coastal city's trade interests, we should not presume that lack of built harbor works implies an indifference to trade or a passive attitude towards the potential of maximizing a city's mercantile participation. Alternative solutions to built harbor works can be efficient, even ingenious responses to marine topography and shipping technology.

Below I give some examples of harbor arrangements in the region under consideration here. In highlighting the diversity of Indian

---

[41] http://www.islam-medieval.cnrs.fr/apim.htm. See C.Hardy-Guilbert, M. Kervran, Ch. Picard, H. Renel and A. Rougeulle, "Ports et commerce maritime islamiques: Présentation du programme APIM (Atlas des ports et itineraries maritimes du monde musulman)," in *Ports maritimes et port fluviaux au Moyen Âge*: 79-97. The project was publicized in a conference which in itself showcased the developments on medieval port studies in general: *Ports maritimes et ports fluviaux au Moyen Âge* (Paris: Publications de la Sorbonne, 2005).

[42] A. Petersen, *The Towns of Palestine under Muslim Rule, 600-1600*. B.A.R. International Series, no. 1381 (Oxford: Archaeopress, 2005).

[43] T. Vorderstrasse, *Al-Mina: a Port of Antioch from Late Antiquity to the End of the Ottomans* (Leiden: Nederlands Instituut voor het Nabije Oosten, 2005).

[44] Y. Masarwa, "From a Word of God to Archaeological Monuments: a Historical-Archaeological Study of the Umayyad Ribāṭs of Palestine," Ph.D. Dissertation, Princeton University, 2006.

Ocean harbor outlines, I hope to make two points. On the one hand, each case requires separate investigation in order to fully assess the connection between harbor arrangement and the degree to which merchants and the state participated in maritime trade. On the other hand, this very diversity marked the experience of Indian Ocean seafaring in medieval times. The occasional glimpses of travelers at sea teach us that the wide range of conditions and arrangements required of western Indian Ocean captains considerable skill and extensive local knowledge.

Aden, an easily accessible anchorage directly in front of the walled city is protected on its southeastern side by the islet of Ṣīra. To shield it from the Northeasterlies, city officials or merchants at some point built a breakwater extending from the northern end of the islet, probably in a northwestern direction, and thus mitigating the effect of the swells caused by the winter monsoon. This feature is spoken of only once, in Abū Makhrama's history of the city where it is described under the term "*shiṣna.*" Its presence, however, may be inferred by the descriptions of the port's naval blockage in the middle of the 6th/12th century, and, remarkably, the single effort at an extensive survey of the old harbor area, conducted by Edward Prados in the early 1990s, uncovered remains that may, in fact, correspond to Abū Makhrama's *shiṣna.* An additional bay and anchorage south of the islet may also have been used.[45] To the best of my knowledge, the construction of a breakwater is not attested at any other harbor.

If breakwaters were lacking in other ports, and if in the famous cases of Ṣuḥār and Sīrāf anchorage consisted chiefly of open roadsteads, other manmade harbor features are attested in the region. At the Persian Gulf island of Kish, where the site of the main town on the northern coast boasts no protected anchorage, galleries dug out of the rocky coastline may have served as bays to receive small boats, perhaps lighters.[46] It should be noted here that similar structures,

---

[45] Margariti, *Aden and the Indian Ocean Trade*, 72-85. See also E. Prados, "An Archaeological Investigation of Sira Bay, Aden, Republic of Yemen," *International Journal of Nautical Archaeology* 23.4 (1994): 297-307; and V. Porter, "The Ports of Yemen and the Indian Ocean Trade during the Tahirid Period (1454-1517)," in *Studies on Arabia in Honour of Professor G. Rex Smith*, ed. J.F. Healey and V. Porter (Oxford: Oxford University Press, 2002): 171-89.

[46] On the general lack of sheltered anchorage at Kish, except perhaps off the island's northeast point at times other than winter, see A. Wilson, *The Persian Gulf* (Oxford: Clarendon Press, 1928): 97. On the rock-cut galleries and their possible use for sheltering boats, see Whitehouse, "Kīsh," *Iran* 14 (1976): 147.

albeit it built up as walls, may also have been used at the island port of Manda in the Lamu archipelago.[47]

Elsewhere, inlets or *khawr*s may have served as anchorages and may have been combined with open roadsteads. At Ṣuḥār, Andrew Williamson posited that wadi outlets may have issued to the sea in the Middle Ages, thus forming creeks or inlets that could have been dredged and used for sheltering boats.[48] At the site of al-Balid, identified with medieval Ẓafār, inlets on either side of the site are joined to form a kind of defensive moat. Rex Smith has argued that the port of Ẓafār must have been 15 km away, at Raysut, but that the inlets surrounding the town may have been used to shelter small craft, especially lighters ferrying merchandise from ships stationed at the distant port.[49] Perhaps a similar arrangement obtained in Jeddah: according to Ibn al-Mujāwir's report repeated later by local author Ibn Faraj, the town was surrounded by a moat filled with sea water, and the inhabitants could launch their ships, presumably directly from within the town, to escape a landward siege.[50]

Keeping such inlets serviceable would presumably require periodic dredging. Some evidence of underwater work and dredging exists for the Mediterranean,[51] but to the best of my knowledge, written sources do not offer insights into the extent and nature of underwater operations in the harbors of Indian Ocean ports, with the exception of Ibn Faraj: his account of the building of the sea wall of Jeddah in Mamluk times contains an exciting glimpse of divers working underwater to construct the base of the wall's towers.[52] Further surveys and excava-

---

[47] See Chittick, *Manda: Excavations at an Island Port on the Kenya Coast* (Nairobi: British Institue in Eastern Africa, 1984): 21, 36, 41.

[48] A. Williamson, *Sohar*: 17. Also see Williamson, "Harvard Archaeological Survey in Oman, 1973: Sohar and the Sea Trade of Oman in the 10th Century A.D," *Proceedings of the Seminar for Arabian Studies* 4 (1974): 82, 88-90.

[49] G.R. Smith and V. Porter, "The Rasulids in Dhofar in the VII-VIIIth/XIII-XIVth-Centuries," The Journal of the Royal Asiatic Society of Great Britain and Ireland (1988): 26

[50] Ibn al-Mujāwir, *Ta'rīkh al-mustabṣir*: 56, 59. Ibn Faraj, *Al-Silāḥ wa'l-'uddah fī ta'rīkh Juddah*: 14-15 (Arabic): 5 (English).

[51] Al-Muqaddasī writes of his grandfather's building of partly underwater walls in Acre for Ibn Ṭulūn; see al-Muqaddasī, *Aḥsan al-taqāsīm fī ma'rifat al-aqālīm*. On dredging operations in the canal linking the Nile with Alexandria, see Sijpesteijn, "Travel and Trade on the River": 117-18.

[52] Ibn Faraj, *Al-Silāḥ wa'l-'uddah fī ta'rīkh Juddah*: 30 (Arabic): 9 (English): *wa-ammā al-burjān al-baḥrīyān fa-qad nazala bihimā al-ghawwāṣūn fī al-baḥr ithnā 'ashara dhirā'an ka-a'lāhā.*

tions may add to the admittedly slim record of harbor construction.

While the unique combination of literary, documentary, and archaeological sources produce a veritable harbor panorama in the case of Aden, this is clearly not the case elsewhere. Often, however, we can know a lot about the maritime approaches to a port. To Ibn Jubayr, for example, the maritime route to Jeddah was terrifyingly riddled with hidden reefs which only the crew's most impressive demonstration of skill could ford.[53] By looking beyond harbor works and harbor arrangements at coastal waters and the conditions for entering and leaving a harbor, we get a better feel for the obstacles that city-centered commercial enterprise faced, and the kinds of networks of local expertise and maritime resources that must have necessarily formed to overcome them.

Fortifications and the Historiographical Trope of an Indian Ocean Utopia

Reflecting on the nature of the extant written sources that pertain to ports, the scholars of the APIM project observe that medieval Arab authors pay more attention to fortifications, customs houses, and arsenals than to other kinds of port infrastructure; this is because fortifications, customs houses and arsenals are "structures that mark the presence of the state," and writers are often aligned with, sponsored by, or generally preoccupied with state power and institutions.[54] Literary and institutional biases aside, the presence of walls around several Indian Ocean ports, as attested by medieval writers and con-

---

[53] Ibn Jubayr, *Riḥla*: 74: *wa-dukhūl hādhihi al-marāsī ṣaʿb al-marām bi-sabab kathrat al-shiʿāb wa-iltifāfihā wa-abṣarnā min ṣinaʿat haʾulāʾ al-ruʾsāʾ waʾl-nawātiya fī al-taṣarruf biʾl-jalba athnāʾhā amran ḍakhman yudkhilūnahā ʿalā maḍāyiq wa-yuṣrifūnahā khilālahā taṣrīf al-fāris liʾl-jawād al-raṭb al-ʿinān al-salis al-qiyād* ("entering these harbors is very difficult because of the multitude of reefs and the need to bypass them; we witnessed great things of the craft of those captains and sailors in steering the *jalba* through the reefs; they would lead the boat into narrows and would steer her just like the horseman steers a steed subtle to the reins and obedient to the bridle"). While the risks are different and have to do with dangerous coastal waves, the harbor layout well known, and the record more extensive in general, Alexandria harbor was also known for its perilous access. The Geniza documents give ample evidence of shipwrecks within view of the Pharos; see Goitein, *A Meditteranean Society*, 1:319, 482 notes 43 and 44.

[54] Hardy-Guilbert, Kervran, Picard, Renel and Rougeulle, "Ports et commerce maritime islamiques": 89.

firmed by archaeology, requires explanation. The received wisdom on the ports of the region is that the relative peace and quiet reigning before the entrance of Portuguese, Ottomans, and the host of other western adventurers who followed them onto the Indian Ocean stage, rendered built defenses largely unnecessary. The following comments are meant to modify this view.[55]

Walls appear to have functioned to keep enemies outside as much as to keep taxes inside the city. The foundational story of Aden's defensive wall as recorded by Ibn al-Mujāwir, and later by Abū Makhrama, is instructive in this respect.[56] One day, a trader from the West arrived by sea and sought to hide his merchandise from the customs house or, as he put it, from the port's governor. He disembarked in the city at night and went straight to an impressive house that he took to be a fellow merchant's home. The owner of the house received him and, when asked, offered him a place to hide his valuable merchandise. The next day the foreigner awoke to a nasty surprise: his host of the night before was no fellow trader but the governor himself. However, instead of punishing the intruder, the governor offered him gifts—and here comes the story's punchline—as a reward for alerting him to the kind of exposure and loss of tax revenue that lack of walls entailed. Soon thereafter the governor had walls built, thus securing the city's control over and exploitation of the incoming and outgoing trade.[57]

If defending the port against prospective smugglers and transgressors who sought to defy the ports' customs regime was a major goal, shielding it from intruders from its own hinterland was also important, more important perhaps than guarding against attacks from the sea. Thus, at al-Balīd (the site identified with the ancient city of Ẓafār in Dhofar) the *khawr*s flanking the urban space and possibly used for mooring may also have served a defensive purpose: they were apparently linked to surround the town entirely, in a moat-like fash-

[55] Since writing the present article, I have discussed the issues pertaining to conflict and competition in the pre-modern Indian Ocean in R. E. Margariti, "Mercantile Networks, Port Cities, and "Pirate States": Conflict and Competition in the Indian Ocean World of Trade Before the Sixteenth Century," *Journal of Economic and Social History of the Orient* 51 (2008): 543-77.

[56] Ibn al-Mujāwir, *Ta'rīkh al-mustabṣir*: 127-8. Abū Makhrama, *Ta'rīkh thaghr 'Adan*, 1:13.

[57] For a more detailed analysis of the story and its implications, see Margariti, *Aden and the Indian Ocean Trade*: 87-8.

ion.[58] In Jeddah, the early Iranian settlers credited with building a wall around the city, are said to have further reinforced the defenses similarly, with a perimeter moat, encircling the city with sea water and rendering it a virtual island. These were clearly measures to keep out the nomads who lived on the margins of and often threatened urban settlements. Accounts of conflict between nomads and city dwellers are numerous and come from sources ranging chronologically, and in the case of Jeddah the connection between the Jeddah defenses and a threatening hinterland is made explicitly by Ibn al-Mujāwir and Ibn Faraj, as noted earlier.[59]

Finally if walls were built for containing the city's tax revenues and for repulsing its hinterland enemies, could they also have functioned as defenses against attacks from the sea? At Aden, the seaward walls separated the defenders of the city and the attackers from Kish in the 529/1134-35 episode described earlier, and the subsequent Ayyubid administration is said to have renewed the seaward wall. The archaeologically attested seawalls at Sīrāf, Manda, and the comprehensive fortification of Sharma certainly seem to have served a defensive function.[60] Partly problematizing the image of a pre-modern Indian Ocean as a system of laissez-faire and multiethnic shipping established over long centuries of relative peace and tolerance,"[61] these walls suggest that port city rulers were wary of their foreland colleagues and competitors. The case of Aden's blockade by forces from the island state of Kish may be exceptional, but it still highlights a poorly-understood and little-known aspect of Indian Ocean trade. In the 6th/12th century, at least, polities like Aden and Kish, virtually independent from their hinterlands and endowed with increased maritime capability, engaged in open competition for maritime

---

[58] Smith, "The Rasulids in Dhofar": 26

[59] Ibn al-Mujāwir, *Ta'rīkh al-mustabṣir*: 56, 59. Ibn Faraj, *Al-Silāḥ wa'l-'uddah fī ta'rīkh Juddah*: 14-15 (Arabic): 5 (English); infra, note 50.

[60] Whitehouse describes a massive wall with buttresses: "Excavations at Sīrāf: First Interim Report," *Iran* 6 (1968): 5, 10; Whitehouse, "Excavations at Sīrāf: Fourth Interim Report," *Iran* 9 (1971): 10. In a later report, he notes a 4th/10th century "curtain wall" connecting waterfront buildings, perhaps in an effort to avert attack from the sea: Whitehouse, "Excavations at Sīrāf: Sixth Interim Report:" 18-21. Excavating the port of Manda in the Lamu Archipelago, Neville Chittick also reported seawalls dating to the 4th/10th-5th/11th centuries; Chittick, *Manda*: 17-35. In Sharma, excavator Axelle Rougeulle notes the hasty erection of a seaward wall; "Le Yemen entre Orient et Afrique: Sharma, un entrepot du commerce médiéval sur la côte sud de l'Arabie," *Annales Islamologiques* 38 (2004): 210-12.

[61] J. Abu-Lughod, *Before European Hegemony*: 276.

terrain, and even armed conflict. If the historiographical trope of a largely peaceful Indian Ocean before the 16th century is closely linked to post-colonial assessments of the changes brought about by the period of increasing European intrusion into Indian Ocean economies and societies, studies of maritime violence in medieval times will contribute to Indian Ocean historiography as a whole.[62]

Commercial Space, Port City Society, and the Riddle of Indian Ocean Diversity

Past urban layouts and the physical ordering of city space are elusive in places with multiple lives like many of the ports of the Indian Ocean. Layering and organic transformation often conceal or completely erase the architectural traces of earlier phases of development. Thus, very little survives of medieval Aden, where the 19th- and 20th-century transformation of the town into a thriving colonial port obliterated earlier topography, and the efforts at restoration of select monuments rendered them almost unintelligible.[63] Somewhat paradoxically, sites that suffered from catastrophic events, or were abandoned and forgotten by the outside world shortly after a major *floruit*, are more likely to yield physical vestiges of urban topographies. Perhaps the most well-known example of that is the port city of Sīrāf.

Since the ports under discussion here lived primarily for and from trade, the structuring of commercial space is central to our understanding of their urban character and the nature of the communities that inhabited them. Where did merchants conduct business? Was there spatial segregation along occupational, functional, or denominational lines? Were different architectural idioms used and did they signal or correlate with the ordering of established social hierarchies?

---

[62] For an excellent account of the link between the construct of a relatively harmonious Indian Ocean trading realm before the 16th century and post-colonial nostalgia for an era different from the one wrought with the advent of westerners on the Indian Ocean scene, see G. Desai, "Old World Orders: Amitav Ghosh and the Writing of Nostalgia," *Representations* 85 (2004): esp. 134-7.

[63] The heavy-handed restoration of the medieval city's water supply system by the British colonial administration was noted already in colonial times by British archaeologists, and has been discussed in detail by local Adeni historian ʿAbdallāh Aḥmad Muḥayriz, *Ṣahārīj ʿAdan* (Aden: Dār al-Hamdānī, 1987): esp. 5-7, 61. See also Margariti, *Aden and the Indian Ocean trade*: 12, 50, 235 note 69.

Interesting in themselves, these questions can be pursued also for what they tell us about the character of the diverse and complex yet highly functioning trading communities that studded the shores of the Indian Ocean before and to some extent even after the establishment of modern national states.

Nancy Um's recent work on the early modern Red Sea port of al-Mukhā makes an important contribution by investigating the interrelation of public and domestic space in the great port on the Tihama, and thus introducing the issue in the study of Indian Ocean ports. At 18th-century al-Mukhā mercantile and private space overlap in the residences of great merchants, public mercantile spaces are relatively rare, and merchants appear to have inhabited spaces with a wide range of functions and to have conducted a large part of their business at home.[64] In my own work on medieval Aden, I found a comparable relative dearth of public commercial buildings, as well as compelling evidence that the residences of prominent merchants constituted centers of mercantile activity.[65] The comparative assessment of these two cases of important port cities of the region at different historical periods suggests an Indian Ocean phenomenon that perhaps did not obtain in the Mediterranean world. Indeed, medieval Cairo exhibits a different functional pattern of urban space: in the Egyptian city most business was conducted in buildings of the *dār al-wakāla* type, and residential units were generally discrete.[66]

Additional evidence about the articulation of mercantile space is now available from Quṣayr. By virtue of its floor plan, consisting a series of rooms and storage areas with access to an upper level, and of the general import and specific references of the documents discovered on its floors, the "Shaykh's house" is convincingly identified as a merchant's residence but also as his warehouse and place of business. In her rigorous account of the stratigraphical contexts of the Quṣayr texts, Katherine Strange Burke highlights the close

---

[64] N. Um, *A Red Sea Society in Yemen*: 108-18; Idem, "Spatial Negotiations in a Commercial City: The Red Sea Port of Mocha, Yemen, during the First Half of the Eighteenth Century," *Journal of the Society of Architectural Historians* 62 (2003): 181-3. See also *The Merchant Houses of Mocha: Trade and Architecture in an Indian Ocean Port* (Seattle: University of Washington Press, 2009), Um's monograph which appeared while the current article was already in press.

[65] Margariti, *Aden and the Indian Ocean Trade*: 100-2, 192-4.

[66] On the functions of the *dār al-wakāla* in Cairo, see Goitein, *Mediterranean Society*, 1:186-92 and 4:26. On residential and domestic space, see *Mediterranean Society*, 4:15-24.

association of finds of domestic and commercial character in different parts of the complex.[67] Li Guo, whose exhaustive study of documents from the building paints a fascinating portrait of mercantile life at the port, argues that Abū Mufarrij's complex may be identified as a *dār al-wakāla*, and may have housed traveling merchants and other mercantile transients.[68] Without challenging Guo's conclusion in its essence, i.e. that the complex in question was, among other things, a business center, I draw attention to the difference between this kind of *dār al-wakāla*, that served as its owner's primary residence, at least during the periods when he was present at the port,[69] and the typical such building in the Mediterranean world as noted above. On the question of transient, semi-permanent, and permanent accommodation, an important contribution can be made through on-going research on the buildings at the southern edge of the town of Qusayr, which excavators have tentatively identified as a *wakāla* or caravanserai, with storage facilities and temporary accommodations for incoming travelers.[70]

There are two other ways in which the ports in question may have differed from those of the Mediterranean. One has to do with use of building materials. The early occupants of Aden, Ibn al-Mujāwir and later sources suggest, built their habitations out of palm-frond thatch (*khūṣ*), and an inland section of town was still replete with them in the days of the reports.[71] A little earlier, Ibn Jubayr witnessed what he describes as a combination of stone-and-mortar architecture with thatch construction; according to him, however, palm-frond was not only used in building huts, but stone and mortar houses were topped with thatch structures, perhaps as shades for the inhabitable roof.[72] Extensive construction in such perishable materials may have also characterized the town of 4th/10th-century Ṣuḥār according to

---

[67] Burke, "Archaeological Texts and Contexts": esp. 246-7, 264.

[68] Guo, *Commerce, Culture, and Community*: 11, 97.

[69] It is important to note here the suggestion, attributed by Guo to the archaeologists of the Quṣayr project, that the the "Shaykh's House" was not Abū al-Mufarrij's family's primary residence, and that their permanent home was instead in the Nile Valley; see Guo, *Commerce, Community, and Culture*: 11 note 11.

[70] See D. Peacock and L. Blue, eds, *Myos Hormos-Quseir al-Qadim: Roman and Islamic Ports on the Red Sea* (Oxford: Oxbow Books, 2006): 103-4 (discussion by L. Blue, E. Beadsmoore and J. Phillips). The identification of the site as a caravanserai is noted in Guo, *Commerce, Culture, and Community*: 97 note 20.

[71] Ibn al-Mujāwir, *Ta'rīkh al-mustabṣir*: 117. Abū Makhrama, *Ta'rīkh thaghr 'Adan*: 9.

[72] Ibn Jubayr, *Riḥla*: 76.

Williamson's archaeological assessment.[73] It appears, then, that at least in some Indian Ocean ports, humble parts of town were built in material and style similar to *barasti* construction, a vernacular architectural medium prevalent to this day around the coasts of Arabia, but that the same material was perhaps used for lighter structures topping stone-and-mortar buildings. The difference between affluent and poor habitations was not only one of materials, however. Location mattered too. Since my focus here has been on cityscapes mingling with seascapes, I will close with a topographical note on the real estate value of the waterfront. In his anthropological study of Ṣuḥār in the 1970s, Fredrik Barth found that "Wealth tends to concentrate along the beach waterfront."[74] A similar phenomenon appears to have been at work in the pre-modern era. In 5rd/11th-7th/13th-century Aden, overlooking the harbor was strategically crucial, humbler residences of *barasti* construction were delegated to the inland part of the city, and maritime views were declaratively enjoyed by all.[75] Considering such factors in the development of the ports' urban landscape may prove fruitful for our understanding of Indian Ocean city topographies and the ways in which they differed from their peers in the Mediterranean.

Bibliography

Abu-Lughod, J. *Before European Hegemony: The World System, A.D. 1250-1350*. New York: Oxford University Press, 1989.

Abū Makhrama, Abū Muḥammad 'Abdallāh. *Ta'rīkh thaghr 'Adan*, 2 vols. In *Arabische Texte zur Kenntnis der Stadt Aden im Mittelalter*, edited by L. Oscar Löfgren. Leiden: E. J. Brill, 1936-50.

Barth, F. *Sohar: Culture and Society in an Omani Town*. Baltimore, MD: The Johns Hopkins University Press, 1983.

Bass, G.F. *Archaeology Under Water*. New York: Frederick A. Praeger, 1966.

Blackman, D.J. "Ancient Harbours in the Mediterranean." *International Journal of Nautical Archaeology and Underwater Exploration* 11 (1982): 79-104, 185-211.

---

[73] Williamson, *Sohar*: 16.

[74] F. Barth, *Sohar: Culture and Society in an Omani Town* (Baltimore, MA: The Johns Hopkins University Press 1983): 68. I use the anthropological and ethnographical work of F. Barth not to claim some sort of continuity between present and past, and thereby risk ascribing monolithic character to the cultures generated in Indian Ocean ports, but as a source of a productive model to be used in a comparative framework that seeks to makes sense out of the patterns visible in the earlier much more fragmentary material and documentary record.

[75] Margariti, *Aden and the Indian Ocean Trade*: 71, 100-3.

Brauer, R.W. *Boundaries and Frontiers in Medieval Muslim Geography*. Transactions of the American Philosophical Society, Vol. 85.6 (Philadelphia: The American Philosophical Society, 1995).
Burke, K.S. "Archaeological Texts and Contexts on the Red Sea: The Sheikh's House at Quseir al-Qadim." Ph.D. Diss. University of Chicago, Illinois. June 2007.
Buzurg, b. Shahriyār *Kitāb ʿajāʾib al-Hind*, edited by Muḥammad Saʿīd al-Ṭurayḥī. Abu Dhabi, UAE: Al-Mujammaʿ al-Thaqāfī, 2000.
Chittick, N. *Manda: Excavations at an Island Port on the Kenya Coast*. Memoir, no. 9. Nairobi: The British Institute in East Africa, 1984.
Cohen, M.R. "Goitein, Magic, and the Geniza." *Jewish Studies Quarterly* 13 (2006): 294-304.
Desai, G. "Old World Orders: Amitav Ghosh and the Writing of Nostalgia," *Representations* 85 (2004): 125-48.
Empereur, J-Y. and Décobert, Ch. *Alexandrie Médiévale 1 et 2*. Etudes Alexandrines, vols. 3 and 8. Cairo: Institut Français d' Archéologie Orientale, 1998.
Fagnan, E. *Additions aux dictionnaires Arabes*. Beirut: Librairie du Liban, 1982.
Freeman-Grenville, G.S.P., ed. *The Book of the Wonders of India: Mainland, Sea, and Islands*. London: East-West Publications, 1981.
Frenkel, M. *The Compassionate and the Benevolent: The Leading Elite in the Jewish Community of Alexandria in the Middle Ages* (in Hebrew). Jerusalem: Tad Izhak Ben Zvi and Hebrew University, 2006.
——. "The Jewish Community of Alexandria under the Fatimids and the Ayyubids: Portrait of a Leading Elite." [in Hebrew]. Ph.D. dissertation, Hebrew University, 2001.
Goitein, S.D. *A Mediterranean Society: The Jewish Communities of the Arab World as Portrayed in the Documents of the Cairo Geniza*, 6 Volumes. Berkeley and Los Angeles: University of California Press, 1967-93.
——. "Two Eyewitness Reports on an Expedition of the King of Kish (Qais) against Aden." *Bulletin of the School of Oriental and Africal Studies* 16 (1954): 247-57.
Guo, L. *Commerce, Culture, and Community in a Red Sea Port in the Thirteenth Century: The Arabic Documents from Quseir*. Leiden: E. J. Brill, 2004.
Hadjidaki, E. "Harbour Studies." In *Encyclopedaea of Underwater and Maritime Archaeology*, edited by James P. Delgado, 187-9. London: British Museum Press, 1997.
Hardy-Guilbert, C., Kervran, M., Picard, Ch., Renel, H. and Rougeulle, A. "Ports et commerce maritime islamiques: Présentation du programme APIM (Atlas des ports et itineraries maritimes du monde musulman)," in *Ports maritimes et port fluviaux au Moyen Âge*. XXXV Congress of the Société des Historiens Médiévistes de l'Enseignement Public (SHMEP) (La Rochelle 5 et 6 Juen, 2004), 79-97. Paris: Publications de la Sorbonne, 2005.
Ibn Baṭṭūṭa, Muḥammad b. ʿAbdallāh. *Riḥlat Ibn Baṭṭūṭa*. Beirut: Dār Ṣādir, 1960.
Ibn Faraj, ʿAbd al-Qādir b. Aḥmad. *Al-Silāḥ wa'l-ʿuddah fī taʾrīkh thaghr Juddah/ Bride of the Red Sea: A 10th/16th Century Account of Jeddah*, edited by G. Rex Smith and Aḥmad ʿUmar al-Zaylaʿī. Occasional Papers Series No. 22. Durham: Center for Middle Eastern and Islamic Studies, 1984.
Ibn Ḥawqal, Muḥammad. *Kitāb al-masālik wa'l-mamālik*, edited by Michael Jan de Goeje, Bibliotheca geographorum Arabicorum, no. 2. Leiden: E. J. Brill 1873.
Ibn Jubayr, Muḥammad b. Aḥmad. *Riḥla*. Leiden: E. J. Brill, 1907.
Ibn Manẓūr, Muḥammad b. Mukarram. *Lisān al-ʿarab*. Beirut: Dār Ṣādir, 1955.
Ibn al-Mujāwir, Abū Bakr b. Muḥammad. *Taʾrīkh al-Mustabṣir*. Cairo: Maktabat al-thaqāfa al-dīnīya, 1997.

al-Iṣṭakhrī, Ibrāhīm b. Muḥammad. *Kitāb al-masālik wa'l-mamālik*, edited by Michael Jan de Goeje, Bibliotheca geographorum Arabicorum, no. 1. Leiden: E. J. Brill, 1967.

Löfgren, O. "Makhrama." *The Encyclopaedia of Islam, new ed.*, 6:132-3. Leiden: E. J. Brill, 1991.

Margariti, R.E. *Aden and the Indian Ocean Trade: 150 Years in the Life of a Medieval Arabian Port*. Chapel Hill, NC: The University of North Carolina Press, 2007.

———. "Mercantile Networks, Port Cities, and "Pirate States": Conflict and Competition In the Indian Ocean World of Trade Before the Sixteenth Century." *Journal of Economic and Social History of the Orient* 51 (2008): 543-77.

Masarwa, Y. "From a Word of God to Archaeological Monuments: a Historical-Archaeological Study of the Umayyad Ribāṭs of Palestine." Ph.D. Dissertation, Princeton University, 2006.

Muḥayriz, A.A. *Ṣahārīj ʿAdan*. Aden: Dār al-Hamdānī, 1987

al-Muqaddasī, Muḥammad b. Aḥmad. *Kitāb aḥsan al-taqāsīm fī maʿrifat al-aqālīm*, edited by Michael Jan de Goeje. Bibliotheca geographorum Arabicorum, no. 3. Leiden: E. J. Brill, 1967.

Oleson, J.P., Hohlfelder, R.L., Raban, A., and Vann, R.L.. "The Caesaria Ancient Harbor Excavation Project (C.A.H.E.P.): Preliminary Report on the 1980-1983 Seasons." *Journal of Field Archaeology* 11 (1984): 281-305.

Peacock, D. and Blue, L., eds. *Myos Hormos-Quseir al-Qadim: Roman and Islamic Ports on the Red Sea. Survey and Excavations 1999-2003*. Oxford: Oxbow Books, 2006.

Petersen, A. *The Towns of Palestine under Muslim Rule, 600-1600*. B.A.R. International Series, no. 1381. Oxford: Archaeopress, 2005.

Porter, V. "The Ports of Yemen and the Indian Ocean Trade during the Tahirid Period (1454-1517)." In *Studies on Arabia in Honour of Professor G. Rex Smith*, edited by John F. Healey and Venetia Porter, 171-189. Journal of Semitic Studies Supplement, no. 14. Oxford: Oxford University Press, 2002.

Prados, E. "An Archaeological Investigation of Sira Bay, Aden, Republic of Yemen." *International Journal of Nautical Archaeology* 23.4 (1994): 297-307.

Rougeulle, A. "Le Yemen entre Orient et Afrique: Sharma, un entrepôt du commerce médiéval sur la côte sud de l'Arabie." *Annales Islamologiques* 38 (2004): 201-53.

Sijpesteijn, P. "Travel and Trade on the River," in *Papyrology and the History of Early Islamic Egypt*, edited by Petra M. Sijpesteijn and Lennart Sundelin, 119-24. Leiden: E. J. Brill, 2004.

Smith, G.R. "Ibn al-Mujāwir's Ta'rīkh al-mustabṣir: A Source for the Historical Geography and of the Economic and Social History of Medieval Yemen." Paper Presented at the Middle East Studies' 29th Annual Meeting, Washington, D.C. 6-10 December 1995.

———. "Ibn al-Mujāwir on Dhofar and Socotra," *Proceedings of the Seminar for Arabian Studies* 25 (1995): 127-40.

———. "Ibn al-Mujāwir's 7th/13th-century Guide to Arabia: The Eastern Connection," *Occasional Papers of the School of Abbasid Studies* (1990): 71-89.

Smith, G.R., and Porter, V."The Rasulids in Dhofar in the VII-VIIIth/XIII-XIVth-Centuries," *The Journal of the Royal Asiatic Society of Great Britain and Ireland* (1988): 26-44.

Smith, G.R., and al-Zaylaʿī, A.U. eds. *Bride of the Sea: a 10th/16th-Century Account of Jeddah*. Durham, UK: Center for Middle Eastern and Islamic Studies, 1984.

Soucek, S. "Minā'." *The Encyclopaedia of Islam, New Edition*, 7:66-72. Leiden: Brill, 1993.

Tranchant, M. "Les ports maritimes en France au moyen âge," in *Ports maritimes et port fluviaux au Moyen Âge*, XXXV Congress of the SHMESP (La Rochelle, 5 and 6 June 2004): 21-31. La Rochelle: Publications de la Sorbonne, 2005.
Udovitch, A.L. "Alexandria in the 11th and 12th Centuries, Letters and Documents of the Cairo Geniza Merchants: an Interim Balance Sheet." In *Alexandrie médiévale* 2. Edited by Christian Décobert (Cairo: Institut Français d'Archéologie Orientale, 2002): 99-112.
——. "Medieval Alexandria: Some Evidence from the Cairo Genizah Documents," in *Alexandria and Alexandrianism*. Papers Delivered at a Symposium Organized by the J. Paul Getty Museum and the Getty Center for History of Art and the Humanities and Held at the Museum, April 22-25, 1993, 273-83. Malibu, CA: J. Paul Getty Museum, 1996.
Um, N.A. "A Red Sea Society in Yemen: Architecture, Urban Form and Cultural Dynamics in the Eighteenth-Century Port City of al-Mukhā." Ph.D. Dissertation, University of California, Los Angeles, 2001.
——. *The Merchant Houses of Mocha: Trade and Architecture in an Indian Ocean Port*. Seattle: University of Washington Press, 2009.
——. "Spatial Negotiations in a Commercial City: The Red Sea Port of Mocha, Yemen, during the First Half of the Eighteenth Century." *Journal of the Society of Architectural Historians* 62 (2003): 178-90.
Venit, M.S. Review of *Alexandria and Alexandrianism: Papers Delivered at a Symposium Organized by the J. Paul Getty Museum and by the Getty Center for the History of Art and the Humanities and Held at the Museum, April 22-25, 1993*. *American Journal of Archaeology* 102 (1998): 453-5.
Vordestrasse, T. *Al-Mina: a Port of Antioch from Late Antiquity to the End of the Ottomans*. Leiden: Nederlands Istitutuut voor het Nabije Oosten, 2005.
Vosmer, T., Agius, D., Baker, P., Carpenter, J., and Cave, S. *Oman Maritime Heritage Project: Field Report 1998*, Western Australian Maritime Museum Report No. 144. Freemantle: Western Australia Maritime Museum, 1998.
Whitcomb, D.S. and Janet Johnson. "1982 Season of Excavation at Qusayr al-Qadim." *American Research Center in Egypt Newsletter* 120 (1982): 24-30.
Whitehouse, D. "Kīsh." *Iran* 14 (1976): 146-7.
——. "Excavations at Sīrāf: First Interim Report," *Iran* 6 (1968): 1-22.
——. "Excavations at Sīrāf: Fourth Interim Report," *Iran* 9 (1971): 1-67.
——. "Excavations at Sīrāf: Sixth Interim Report," *Iran* 12 (1974): 1-30.
Williamson, A. *Sohar and Omani Seafaring in the Indian Ocean*. Muscat, 1973.
——. "Harvard Archaeological Survey in Oman, 1973: Sohar and the Sea Trade of Oman in the 10th Century A.D." *Proceedings of the Seminar for Arabian Studies* 4 (1974): 78-96.
Wilson, A. *The Persian Gulf*. Oxford: Clarendon Press, 1928.

DEMONIZING ZENOBIA: THE LEGEND OF AL-ZABBĀ' IN ISLAMIC SOURCES

*David S. Powers**

Cenobia, of Palymerie Queene
As writen persiens of hir noblesse,
So worthy was in armes and so keene,
That no wight passed hire in hardynesse
Ne in lynage, ne in oother gentillesse.
Chaucer, *The Canterbury Tales*

Introduction

Since the beginnings of recorded history, most Near Eastern polities have been ruled by kings, although women have on occasion risen to positions of power and authority. Some of these women are legendary,[1] others historical.[2]

* I thank Z. Maghen, P. Sijpesteijn, and A. Silverstein for helpful comments on drafts of this essay, the writing of which was made possible by my appointment as a Carnegie Scholar in 2007 and a grant from the Carnegie Corporation of New York. The statements and views expressed are solely my responsibility.

[1] After hearing of the wisdom of King Solomon, the unnamed queen of the land of Sheba traveled to Israel bearing gifts of spices, gold and precious stones (I Kings 10:1-13; cf. II Chronicles 9:1-12); Josephus adds that she held power over Ethiopia and Egypt. A woman named Nitocris—if she existed—was reportedly the last Pharaoh of the sixth Egyptian dynasty, possibly the first known queen regnant in recorded history, and the first of three women who assumed the title of Pharaoh. She is mentioned in the *Histories* of Herodotus and writings of Manetho. According to Herodotus (*Histories* ii), following the assassination of her brother, the king of Egypt, Nitocris invited the murderers to a banquet and killed them by sealing the room and flooding it with water drawn from the Nile; so as not to be killed by additional conspirators, she committed suicide. Alas, there is no mention of Nitocris in any Egyptian inscriptions and historians now think that she has been confused with the male king Netjerkare Siptah I, about whom documentary evidence does exist. Another legendary figure is Elissa/Dido, who according to Junianus Justinus (3d century BCE) and Virgil (d. 19 BCE), fled Tyre and made her way to North Africa, where ca. 800 BCE she founded the city of Carthage and became its first queen.

[2] In the ancient Near East, many women served as regents for their sons and some of them eventually took power in their own names. Among the Hittites of Anatolia (ca. 1300 BCE) the queen ruled for life, first as crown princess and, after the death of her husband, in the office called *Tawananna*. Among the Assyrians, the

Prior to the rise of Islam, the Arabs would have been familiar with several queens whose existence is a matter of historical record.[3] Arguably the best-known and most famous Arab queen was Zenobia, who ruled the city-state of Palmyra as its queen from 267-72 CE. During this period, armies commanded by the Arab queen conquered Egypt and much of Asia Minor. In response to this threat, the Roman emperor marched across Anatolia to Syria, where he defeated the queen's forces in two major battles, first at Antioch and then at Palmyra. Zenobia was captured and transported to Rome, where she ended her days under house arrest.[4]

Famous in life, Zenobia was even more famous in death. From Palmyra, accounts of her exploits spread outwards. In the West she came to be known for her beauty, valor, and chastity.[5] In Syria and Iraq the local population never forgot that imperial forces once marched under the flag of an Arab queen. In the middle of the 6th century CE Zenobia was known to the inhabitants of al-Ḥīra. That she was known to Muḥammad and the early Muslim community in the Hijaz is suggested by the fact that two of Muḥammad's wives and one of his daughters bore the name Zaynab, which is the Arabic

West Semitic "palace woman" Zakutu, wife of Sennacherib (706-681 BCE) and mother of Esarhaddon (r. 681-669 BCE), ruled as queen during her son's minority; as did Adad-Guppi mother of Nabonidus (r. 556-539 BCE). See *A History of Ancient Near Eastern Law*, ed. R. Westbrook, 2 vols. (Leiden and Boston: E. J. Brill, 2003), 1:435, 569, 597, 627-8; R. Stoneman, *Palmyra and its Empire: Zenobia's Revolt against Rome* (Ann Arbor: The University of Michigan Press, 1992): 118-21.

[3] Assyrian records mention Zabibi queen of Aribi, a mighty Arab warrior queen who revolted and was subdued in 738 BCE. Queen Šamsi the Midianite (r. 740-20 BCE) fought the Assyrian king Tiglath-Pileser III and was eventually defeated and forced to pay tribute. She was succeeded by Queen Yatie (r. ca. 730 BCE) who, in turn, was succeeded by Queen Telkhanu, who controlled the deserts of eastern Syria and Jordan from her capital at ʿAdurna. In the last half of the first century CE, Shaqilath ruled the Nabateans for five years during the minority of her son al-Rabil (r. 70-106). Al-Rabil's sister Gamilath also was queen of the Nabateans. See N. Abbott, "Pre-Islamic Arab Queens," *The American Journal of Semitic Languages and Literatures*, 58:1 (1941): 1-22.

[4] On Zenobia, see Stoneman, *Palmyra and its Empire*; Bowersock, *Roman Arabia* (Cambridge and London: Harvard University Press, 1983): 129-37.

[5] For a brief summary of the representation of Zenobia in Western literature by the likes of Boccaccio, Chaucer, Lord Tennyson, and others, see Stoneman, *Palmyra and its Empire*, 197-200. *Re* Zenobia's chastity: It is said that she limited her sexual liaisons with her husband to the days immediately following the completion of her menstrual cycle, when she could be certain that she was fertile; once she became pregnant, she would not engage in sexual relations with her husband until after the child was born, and even then, according to the same rules (ibid.: 113-14).

equivalent of Zenobia.[6] In the aftermath of the Arab conquests, accounts relating to Zenobia were picked up and no doubt transformed by Muslim (and non-Muslim) storytellers. The process whereby the Syro-Iraqi and Arabo-Islamic accounts were fused together may be beyond the reach of historical investigation. Suffice it to say that by the end of the 3d/9th century, a distinctive Islamic narrative had assumed a relatively fixed and stable shape. In the monumental *Ta'rīkh* of Ṭabarī (d. 310/923), Zenobia—or al-Zabbā', as she is known to Muslims—plays a central role in the historian's portrayal of events in Iraq, Syria and northern Arabia between the 3d and 6th centuries CE.[7] Drawing upon sources preserved a century earlier by Ibn al-Kalbī (d. 204-206/819-21),[8] Ṭabarī skillfully integrates al-Zabbā' into his historical narrative.

The profile of al-Zabbā' preserved by Ṭabarī diverges widely from the profile of the Queen of Palmyra found in non-Islamic sources. As has long been recognized, the Islamic narrative is part historical, part legendary. A generation ago Charles Pellat proposed that "the task of scholarship is to disentangle fact from fiction in the Islamic sources and so reach the kernel of historical truth which they undoubtedly have."[9] Without discounting the merits of this approach, I propose to address the issue in a different manner. In this essay, my concern is precisely the *interface* between history and legend: How did Muslim storytellers transform the Zenobia of history into the Zabbā' of legend? Why was the powerful Arab queen turned into a demon? What function does the Arabo-Islamic legend play in Ṭabarī's *History*? By raising these questions, I seek to shed light on the art of Arabic storytelling and the craft whereby stories were incorporated into historical narratives. To this end, it will be necessary to engage in a good measure of my own storytelling. Perhaps it

---

[6] *EI*², s.vv. "Zaynab bt. Jaḥsh" (C.E. Bosworth); "Zaynab bt. Khuzayma" (C.E. Bosworth); "Zaynab bt. Muḥammad" (V. Vacca).

[7] al-Ṭabarī, *Ta'rīkh al-rusul wa'l-mulūk*, ed. Muḥammad Abū al-Faḍl Ibrāhīm, 11 vols (4th ed. Cairo: Dār al-ma'ārif, 1960-77), 1:606-28; *The History of al-Ṭabarī, vol. iv, The Ancient Kingdoms*, trans. M. Perlmann (Albany: State University of New York Press, 1987), 126-50. For other versions, see al-Mas'ūdī (d. 345/956), *Murūj al-dhahab wa-ma'ādin al-jawhar*, ed. Ch. Pellat, 4 vols (Beirut: Dār al-Andalus, 1965-6), 2:213-30; Ibn al-Athīr (d. 630/1233), *al-Kāmil fī al-Ta'rīkh*, 13 vols (Beirut: Dār Bayrūt, 1992), 1:342-51; al-Nuwayrī (d. 733/1333), *Nihāyat al-arab fī funūn al-adab*, 33 vols (Cairo: al-Mu'assasa al-miṣrīya al-'āmma li'l-ta'līf wa'l-tarjama, 1964), 15:316-23.

[8] al-Kalbī, better known as Ibn al-Kalbī, was a prolific writer who was the author of books in many fields, especially Arab history. See *EI*², s.v. "al-Kalbī" (W. Atallah).

[9] *EI*², s.v. "al-Zabbā'" (Ch. Pellat).

would be more accurate to say that I shall re-tell several stories from the perspective of my personal understanding of their meaning and significance. One level of meaning is manifest, another latent. My goal is to expose the meaning of the story that lies immediately below the smooth linguistic surface of the narrative by drawing attention to literary devices that are the stock-in-trade of storytellers around the world: themes, motifs, *topoi*, linguistic creativity (names, maxims, and proverbs), and rhetorical devices (metaphors, parallels, and inversions). After identifying these literary devices, I shall compare the legend of al-Zabbā' to legends and stories that manifest these same literary devices—including a curious episode in the career of the Prophet Muḥammad. I begin with a summary of what is known about the historical Zenobia.[10]

Zenobia Batzabbai, Queen of Palmyra

Zenobia was the wife of Septimius Odenathus (ca. 220-67 CE), son of Hairan and grandson of Vaballath Nasor.

The names of Odenathus, his father and his grandfather suggest that he was of mixed Arab and Aramean descent: Odenathus is the Greek equivalent of *udhayna* ("little ear"), while Hairan and Nasor are Aramaic names. It is not certain when or under what circumstances his family settled in Palmyra. They may have been tribal sheikhs who amassed great wealth as landowners and organizers of the caravan trade; or they may have been among those bands of Arameans driven across the Euphrates by Ardashir I (r. 226-41), founder of the Sassanian dynasty.[11] Odenathus had two wives. His

[10] The literary-critical approach to Arabic historical texts was pioneered by A. Noth in his "Quellenkritische Studien zu Themen, Formen und Tendenzen frühislamischer Geschichtsüberlieferung, I. Themen und Formen" (Ph.D. thesis, University of Bonn, 1973). The thesis was translated into English by M. Bonner as *The Early Arabic Historical Tradition: A Source-Critical Study* (2nd ed., Princeton: Darwin Press, 1994). Also important is J. Wansbrough, *The Sectarian Milieu: Content and Composition of Islamic Salvation History* (Oxford and New York: Oxford University Press, 1978). See also J. Lassner, *Islamic Revolution and Historical Memory* (New Haven: American Oriental Society, 1986); El-Tayyib al-Hibri, *Reinterpreting Islamic Historiography* (Cambridge: Cambridge University Press, 1999); S. Leder, "al-Madā'inī's Version of *Qiṣṣat al-Shūra*: The Paradigmatic Character of Historical Narration," in *Ideas, Images, and Methods of Portrayal: Insights into Classical Arabic Literature and Islam*, ed. Sebastian Günther (Leiden: E.J. Brill, 2005): 379-98.

[11] Stoneman, *Palmyra and its Empire*: 76-7.

first wife, whose name is unknown, gave birth to Herodes, who accompanied his father into battle and is credited with defeating the Persians in one military encounter. His second wife, Zenobia, gave birth to Wahballath ("Gift of Allat") and Herodianus.[12] In an inscription indicted ca. 271 CE, Zenobia is identified as Septimia Bathzabbai. *Septimia* is Latin and *Bathzabbai* is Aramaic. Both mean "daughter of seven."[13] The inscription suggests that Zenobia regarded herself as a latter-day Bathsheba, the biblical queen who was the wife of King David and mother of King Solomon.[14]

Odenathus was a military leader and political figure. Inscriptions written in Greek and Palmyrene identify him as *ras tadmor* or Chief of Tadmor. Some time before 254 he acquired the rank of Roman *senator*. By 258 Rome had made him a *consularis*.[15] In the middle of the 3d century CE, the Roman emperors were unable to maintain their hold over the empire for any length of time. In the West, the Gauls threatened, in the East the Persians. Between 230 and 256, Shapur I (r. ca. 239-73) carried out three campaigns against Roman provinces in Asia Minor. In 256 he destroyed Dura-Europus, in 257 he captured Antioch, and in 259 he captured the Roman co-emperor Valerian (who reigned together with his son Gallienus from 253-60). Several pretenders now sought to seize control of the weakened Roman empire. It was Odenathus who championed Roman resistance to Persian aggression. In 261 the Arab *consularis* defeated two of these pretenders in the name of Gallienus (who reigned as sole emperor from 260 until 268). As a reward for his efforts, the emperor made him *strategos* of all the East, that is to say, ruler of Syria, Asia Minor and Egypt. After recovering Carrhae from the Persians in 262, Odenathus was widely regarded as the savior of the empire, and Gallienus now conferred upon him the titles of *dux Romanorum* and *restitutor totius Orientis*. He called himself king and lord.[16]

In 267 Odenathus and his son Herodes carried out a second campaign against the Sassanians, driving the Persian army back to the gates of Ctesiphon. Although the temptation to claim the title of

---

[12] Ibid.: 116-18.

[13] Ibid.: 118; Bowersock, *Roman Arabia*: 134, note 46.

[14] Stoneman, *Palmyra and its Empire*: 150. On Zenobia's possible attachment to Judaism, see ibid.: 151-3.

[15] Ibid.: 78.

[16] Stoneman, *Palmyra and its Empire*: 105-6; Bowersock, *Roman Arabia*: 130, note 32.

emperor must have been strong, Odenathus demonstrated remarkable restraint and caution, which may have cost him his life. On their way back to Palmyra after defeating the Persians, Odenathus and Herodes stopped at Emessa, where both men were murdered by Maeonius, a cousin of Odenathus. Historians have speculated that Maeonius was put up to the deed by a rival to the throne or by a group of conspirators unhappy with the close ties between Odenathus and Rome. In Rome itself, rumors spread implicating Zenobia in the murders on the grounds that she had much to gain from the elimination of her cautious husband and his son by his first wife.[17] It was against a background of assassination, suspicion and intrigue that Zenobia seized power in the name of her son Wahballath. For the next six years, she ruled Palmyra and its surroundings from a magnificent palace to which she invited philosophers and other scholars and intellectuals.[18]

With the support of mobile Bedouin soldiers, Zenobia challenged the sovereignty of Rome. Her immediate objective was to secure the commercial interests of the Palmyrenes that were threatened by unrest along the frontier zones. But historians have speculated that she aspired to become either empress of Rome itself or ruler of a third polity that would dominate Rome and Persia. Be that as it may, she conquered Egypt and proclaimed herself queen, claiming now descent from Cleopatra and Mark Antony, on the one hand, and Dido, on the other. In 271—the same year in which the inscription identifying Zenobia as Septimia Bathzabbai was carved—Wahballath assumed the title of *Augustus*. By the end of the year, Zenobia's forces had seized most of Syria and Asia Minor and she controlled approximately one-third of the Roman Empire.[19]

In response to the threat posed by the Arab queen, Aurelian dispatched his general Probus to Egypt while the emperor himself led his armies across Anatolia and down the eastern coast of the Mediterranean. It took the Roman army an estimated 124 days to reach the Orontes, near Antioch, where Zenobia was waiting for him with forces estimated at 70,000 soldiers. When the two armies met on the battlefield, the Roman cavalry tricked the Palmyrenes by pretending to flee, continuing their feigned retreat until they were sure

[17] Stoneman, *Palmyra and its Empire*: 107-8.
[18] Ibid.: 109, 129 ff; Bowersock, *Roman Arabia*: 135.
[19] Stoneman, *Palmyra and its Empire*: 158-63.

that their pursuers had been exhausted by the heat and the weight of their weapons. At this point, the Roman forces—reportedly encouraged by the appearance of a "divine form"—turned and fell upon the Palmyrene forces, causing great loss of life.[20]

After the Romans had inflicted another defeat on the Arabs at Emessa, the remnants of Zenobia's army retreated across the Syrian desert to Palmyra. To prepare the city for the upcoming siege, Zenobia ordered the construction of a circuit wall. Aurelian led his forces—six legions plus auxiliaries or approximately 40,000 men—across seventy-five miles of rugged desert terrain. Upon reaching Palmyra, the Romans pounded the newly fortified city with ballista, "scorpions," siege engines, battering rams, and fire-darts. In the midst of diplomatic exchanges, the siege dragged on. Eventually, Roman shock and awe had its intended affect. After the Armenian allies of the Palmyrenes went over to the Roman side, the city capitulated, but not before Zenobia and Wahballath had escaped and fled toward Persia seeking reinforcements. Shortly thereafter, Zenobia was captured and brought to Rome, where she was paraded, bound in gold chains, in front of Aurelian. Impressed by her beauty and character, the emperor freed her and granted her a villa in Tibur, where she is said to have spent the rest of her life discussing philosophy and hosting banquets.[21]

From Zenobia Batzabbai to ʿAdī B. Zayd

In the Arabic literary tradition, the legend of Zenobia is closely linked with a pre-Islamic Arab by the name of ʿAdī b. Zayd. To ʿAdī is attributed the *qaṣīda*-poem that contains what may be the earliest

[20] Ibid.: 165-72.

[21] Ibid.: 172-9. Certain elements of the encounter between Gallienus and Zenobia bring to mind events associated with the Battle of the Trench in 5/627. The construction of a circuit wall around Palmyra recalls the digging of a trench around Medina; the appearance of divine forms who spurred Roman soldiers on to victory recalls the appearance of angels who fought together with the Muslims; and the behavior of the Armenians recalls that of the Medinese hypocrites. In addition, the Roman emperor's march across the desert brings to mind Khālid b. al-Walīd's famous march from Iraq, across the Syrian desert, to Damascus.

reference to Zenobia in Arabic literature.[22] For this reason he merits attention. We begin with his father.

Zayd b. Ḥammād was an educated and cultured Nestorian who lived in al-Ḥīra, capital of the Lakhmid kingdom which was a vassal state of the Persians. Zayd was on good terms with the Persian *dihqān* Farrukh-māhān, who helped his friend to secure the coveted position of Postmaster,[23] normally reserved for the sons of Persian provincial governors. Ca. 575 CE Zayd saved the throne for the Lakhmids by convincing the people of al-Ḥīra to accept as their king al-Mundhir IV, the third and last son of al-Mundhir III to serve as king.[24] Al-Mundhir IV reigned from 575 until 580. He had two wives, Salma bt. al-Ṣā'igh, a Jewess captured at Fadak in the Hijaz, and Māriya bt. al-Ḥārith, a Christian of the tribe of Taym al-Rabīʿ. Together, his two wives produced twelve sons. Salma was the mother of al-Nuʿmān,[25] and Māriya was the mother of al-Aswad. The rivalry between these two half-brothers would have fatal consequences for Zayd's son ʿAdī.[26]

ʿAdī b. Zayd was born in al-Ḥīra in the middle of the 6th century CE and educated together with the son of the above-mentioned Persian *dihqān*. At school he mastered Persian and Arabic. The young man, who was not only handsome, clever and eloquent, was also an accomplished archer, horseman and polo-player. Eventually, his talents came to the attention of the Persian emperor Anūshirwān (r. 531-79), who appointed ʿAdī as his secretary and interpreter. Shortly thereafter, the emperor sent ʿAdī on a diplomatic mission to Constantinople, capital of Byzantium, where he acquired valuable knowledge of the empire and its strategic resources. ʿAdī was an important and influential figure in the Lakhmid kingdom.[27]

Some time before 580 CE, ʿAdī b. Zayd married a woman named Hind—a name borne by several Arab queens—the young and beautiful daughter of al-Nuʿmān b. al-Mundhir. The narrative account of

---

[22] For biographical details, see *Dīwān ʿAdī b. Zayd al-ʿIbādī*, ed. M.Ḥ. al-Muʿība (Baghdad: Shirkat Dār al-Jumhūrīya li'l-nashr wa'l-ṭabʿ, 1965): 9-19.

[23] On the postal service, see A.J. Silverstein, *Postal Systems in the pre-modern Islamic World* (Cambridge: Cambridge University Press, 2007).

[24] *EI*², s.v. "al-Mundhir IV" (I. Shahid).

[25] *EI*², s.v. "al-Nuʿmān (III) b. al-Mundhir" (I. Shahid).

[26] A.F. al-Iṣfahānī, *Kitāb al-Aghānī*, 25 vols (Beirut: Dār al-thaqāfa, 1955), vol. 2, part 1, 80-3; al-Nuwayrī, *Nihāyat al-arab*: 15:321; R.A. Nicholson, *A Literary History of the Arabs* (Cambridge: Cambridge University Press, 1909): 45.

[27] al-Iṣfahānī, *Kitāb al-Aghānī*, vol. 2, part 1: 83-5; *EI*², s.v. "ʿAdī b. Zayd" (F. Gabrieli).

this marriage merits attention because several of its themes and literary devices bear a striking resemblance to themes and literary devices found in the Arabo-Islamic legend of al-Zabbā'. In brief, the story is as follows: Hind was tall, shapely and beautiful—one of the most beautiful women of her tribe and time (*min ajmal nisā' ahlihā wa-zamānihā*). One day, when she was eleven years old, she entered a church, accompanied by several female attendants, including a certain Māriya who secretly was in love with ʿAdī. As fate would have it, ʿAdī entered the church and caught sight of Hind, who was unaware of his presence (*fa-ra'āhā ʿAdī wa-hiya ghāfilat*[un]). It was love at first sight, although ʿAdī said nothing to Hind and kept his feelings a secret for an entire year. One year later, Hind (who was now twelve), Māriya and ʿAdī once again found themselves in the same church. Mistakenly thinking that ʿAdī had forgotten about Hind, Māriya drew her mistress' attention to the man with whom she herself was secretly in love. In an effort to get a better look, Hind approached ʿAdī and was immediately struck dumb by his beauty (*fa-dhahilat lamma ra'athu wa-bahitat tanẓuru ilayhi*). Again, it was love at first sight. Māriya, however, was not going to give up on ʿAdī before ensuring that her needs had been satisfied. The next day, the servant girl confronted ʿAdī and told him that if he agreed to have sexual relations with her, she would devise a scheme that would make it possible for him to marry Hind. ʿAdī complied. After the deed was done, Māriya arranged an encounter between the would-be lovers, following which Hind announced that if she could not have ʿAdī she surely would die. But Hind was the daughter of a Lakhmid prince whereas ʿAdī was merely a commoner. How to arrange such a union? Leave it to Māriya, the now satisfied female attendant, who devised another scheme. She instructed ʿAdī to invite al-Nuʿmān to a dinner party and, after the prince had become intoxicated, to ask for the hand of his daughter in marriage. ʿAdī did exactly as instructed. No sooner had al-Nuʿmān fallen under the influence of the wine than ʿAdī asked for permission to marry his daughter. The intoxicated prince agreed, and the marriage was consummated before three days had passed. Thus it was that ʿAdī b. Zayd became the son-in-law of al-Nuʿmān b. al-Mundhir.[28]

---

[28] al-Iṣfahānī, *Kitāb al-Aghānī*, vol. 2, part 1: 87-8, 106-9; Nicholson, *A Literary History of the Arabs*: 46-7.

Following the death of al-Mundhir IV in 580, the Persian emperor Hurmuz IV (r. 579-90) summoned all twelve of the Lakhmid king's sons to Ctesiphon so that he might choose one of them as the new king of al-Ḥīra. Like his father before him, ʿAdī played the role of kingmaker. Working behind the scenes, ʿAdī instructed each of the Lakhmid princes—with the exception of al-Nuʿmān, that if the emperor were to ask if he was capable of keeping the Arabs in order, the proper reply would be, "All except al-Nuʿmān." And he instructed al-Nuʿmān that if the emperor were to ask if he was capable of keeping his brothers in order, the proper reply would be, "If I cannot manage them, who can I manage?" Pleased with al-Nuʿmān's response, Hurmuz chose him as king and celebrated his accession by placing a magnificent crown on his head. Al-Nuʿmān b. al-Mundhir reigned as king of al-Ḥīra from 580 until 602. He was the last Lakhmid king of al-Ḥīra—an historical detail to which we shall return.[29]

ʿAdī's support for al-Nuʿmān (the son of Salmā the Jewess) stirred up resentment among al-Mundhir's other children, especially al-Aswad (the son of Māriya the Nestorian). Disappointed at having been passed over, al-Aswad sought to take revenge against ʿAdī. With the help of co-conspirators, al-Aswad succeeded in raising al-Nuʿmān's suspicions about the loyalty of his son-in-law, the very man who had secured the throne for him. The king forced ʿAdī to divorce Hind and threw his former son-in-law into prison, where he languished for a decade or more, composing poetry—including the verses that would memorialize Zenobia/al-Zabbāʾ. Ca. 590, Hurmuz IV died and was succeeded by his son Parvīz, who ruled as Khusraw II (r. 591-628). The new Persian emperor interceded on behalf of ʿAdī and arranged to secure his release from prison; immediately prior to his release, however, an agent working on behalf of al-Nuʿmān strangled ʿAdī and suffocated him to death. As for Hind, she is said to have retired to the Convent of Hind the Younger, where she lived into Islamic times.[30]

---

[29] al-Masʿūdī, *Murūj al-dhahab*, 2:225-30; al-Iṣfahānī, *Kitāb al-Aghānī*, vol. 2, part 1: 88-90; al-Nuwayrī, *Nihāyat al-arab*, 15:322-3.

[30] al-Iṣfahānī, *Kitāb al-Aghānī*, vol. 2, part 1: 90-2, 95-7, 99, 110; al-Nuwayrī, *Nihāyat al-arab*, 15: 323-6. It is reported that Hind received a visit from the governor of Kufa, al-Mughīra b. Shuʿba (r. 643-5). The Muslim storytellers relate that the governor proposed to marry Hind—despite her being 90 years old—so that he might boast of having married the daughter of al-Nuʿmān III. She refused. See Abbot, "Pre-Islamic Arab Queens," 20; *EI*^{2}, s.v. "al-Mug͟hīra b. S͟huʿba" (H. Lammens).

Outwardly al-Nuʿmān made a public display of grief; inwardly he was pleased with the outcome. One day, while the Ḥīran king was on a hunting expedition, he encountered one of ʿAdī's sons, a clever youth named Zayd (who would have been a contemporary of the Prophet Muḥammad's). The king took a special interest in his grandson. Some time later, he sent Zayd to the court of Khusraw II with the recommendation that the emperor appoint him as a replacement (*khalaf*) for his father. Khusraw II accepted the recommendation, and Zayd became Secretary of Arab Affairs. Outwardly Zayd b. ʿAdī pretended to be reconciled with al-Nuʿmān—who was his maternal grandfather; inwardly he was waiting for the right moment to take revenge against the man responsible for his father's murder. The opportunity presented itself when the need arose to replenish the royal harem in Ctesiphon, hitherto stocked exclusively with Persian women, the most beautiful and talented in the realm. Whenever the number of women in the harem declined, the emperor would circulate a public announcement detailing the physical and personal characteristics sought in new recruits. Previously, it is said, the Persian emperors had never expressed any interest in Arab women. This was the opening for which Zayd b. ʿAdī had been waiting. He now approached Khusraw II and advised him that several women in al-Nuʿmān's family possessed the desired qualifications. He asked the emperor to send him to the Lakhmid king in al-Ḥīra, accompanied by a Persian bodyguard who spoke Arabic, albeit poorly—a critical narrative detail. In the Lakhmid capital Zayd was granted an audience with al-Nuʿmān and came face-to-face with the man who only recently had ordered the murder of his father. When he explained the purpose of his mission to al-Nuʿmān, the king retorted, "Are not the gazelles of Persia sufficient for your needs?" The Persian bodyguard, who did not understand the meaning of the Arabic word *gazelle*, asked Zayd to explain it to him. Zayd dissembled, saying that the word means *cow*. Upon returning to Ctesiphon, the bodyguard informed the Persian emperor that the Arab king had said, "Are not the *cows* of Persia sufficient for your needs?" The emperor was furious, and al-Nuʿmān understood that his fate had been sealed. The Lakhmid king fled al-Ḥīra but later surrendered to the emperor, who ordered that he be trampled to death by elephants.[31]

---

[31] al-Masʿūdī, *Murūj al-dhahab*, 2:225-7; al-Iṣfahānī, *Kitāb al-Aghānī*, vol. 2, part 1: 99-106; al-Nuwayrī, *Nihāyat al-arab*, 15:326-30; *EI*², s.vv. "ʿAdī b. Zayd"

History remembers ʿAdī b. Zayd as an educated and accomplished Nestorian Arab, fluent in Persian and Arabic, who rose to the height of power in the Lakhmid kingdom as a diplomat, political strategist, and kingmaker. In the end, ʿAdī was a victim of his own success. His clever political machinations triggered powerful feelings of resentment among the king's brothers, and he himself was the victim of a plot that undermined his relationship with his father-in-law, the man whom he had made king. This plot set in motion a cycle of violence that resulted in the deaths of both ʿAdī and al-Nuʿmān. Before ʿAdī was murdered, however, he succeeded in composing the poems for which he is remembered, including a *qaṣīda* about an Arabian queen named al-Zabbā'—which brings us to Ṭabarī and his *History.*

Ṭabarī on the Ancient Kingdoms

Ṭabarī's account of the ancient kingdoms begins with Kaykāwus, the mythical second king of the Kayānid line, followed by the Israelites after Solomon down to the destruction of the First Temple, the Persians after Alexander, and the Arsacids.[32]

Ṭabarī returns to events in Palestine in his chapter on the life of Jesus, which is followed by a chapter in which the historian records the names and reigns of the Roman and Byzantine emperors who controlled Palestine, beginning with Gaius son of Tiberius (d. 37 CE) and ending with Heraclius (d. 641). The list, he explains, was based on unidentified Christian sources. According to these same sources, he adds, a thousand years passed from the rebuilding of the Temple in Jerusalem to the Hijra. It was during the eighth year of the reign of Ardashīr b. Bābak that John the Baptist was killed "at the hands of the Israelites." And—on the authority of Ibn al-Kalbī—it was just prior to the reign of Ardashīr that several Arab tribes left Iraq and settled in al-Ḥīra and al-Anbār.[33] At about that time, tribesmen of Azd were settling in al-Baḥrayn, where they allied themselves with

(F. Gabrieli), al-Nuʿmān (III) b. al-Mundhir (Irfan Shahid); Nicholson, *A Literary History of the Arabs*: 45-8.

[32] al-Ṭabarī, *Ta'rīkh al-rusul wa'l-mulūk*, 1:488 ff.; *The History of al-Ṭabarī*, 4:1-150.

[33] al-Ṭabarī, *Ta'rīkh al-rusul wa'l-mulūk*, 1:606; *The History of al-Ṭabarī*, 4:126-7; Ibn al-Athīr, *al-Kāmil fī al-Ta'rīkh*, 1:340, 342. On Ibn al-Kalbī, see above, note 8.

the Tanūkh who, in turn, were allied with the Numāra b. Lakhm.[34] The focus of Ṭabarī's narrative now shifts from events in Palestine to events in southern Iraq and northern Arabia. In a chapter devoted to the history of al-Ḥīra and al-Anbār, he singles out for attention several historical figures who would have been well-known to his immediate audience but who no doubt are unknown to mine: Jadhīma b. al-Abrash, ʿAdī b. Naṣr and the latter's son ʿAmr b. ʿAdī, ʿAmr b. Ẓarib, and, finally, al-Zabbā'. Although the presentation is history-like, the narratives have a distinctive literary quality. The individual sections, beginning with Jadhīma and ending with al-Zabbā', are clearly part of a single narrative cycle. Only at the end of this cycle does Ṭabarī explain why these historical figures are important to him.

The Legend of Al-Zabbā'

Jadhīma b. al-Abrash

The literary cycle begins with a man named Jadhīma. According to the Latin maxim, *nomen est omen*, a person's name determines his or her fate. This is true not only of Jadhīma but also of other characters in the narrative cycle. In Arabic, the transitive verb *jadhama* signifies *to cut off or amputate*, viz., a hand or arm; and the intransitive verb *jadhuma* signifies *to be afflicted with the disease called* judhām, i.e., leprosy, a disease which, as the ancients mistakenly believed, causes the fingers and toes of its victims to atrophy and fall off.[35] Jadhīma was indeed a leper but a powerful one. In fact, he was such a powerful and awe-inspiring figure that the Arabs preferred not to refer to him by his real name—about which more below; instead they called him Jadhīma al-Waḍḍāḥ—the Luminous Leper, or Jadhīma al-Abrash—the Bespeckled Leper. The medical condition

---

[34] An inscription from the first half of the 3ᵈ century CE describes the northeastern sector of the Arabian peninsula as "provinces of Persia and the land of Tanūkh." This suggests that it was the interference of the Persians in the affairs of Arabia that caused the Tanūkh to move northwards in the direction of Iraq. See Bowersock, *Roman Arabia*: 132-3.

[35] E.W. Lane, *An Arabic-English Lexicon*, 8 parts (London and Edinburgh: Williams and Norgate, 1863-93; reprinted 1984, The Islamic Texts Society), s.v. j-dh-m. On attitudes to leprosy in Muslim society, see Jāḥiẓ, *al-Burṣān wa'l-ʿurjān wa'l-ʿumyān wa'l-ḥūlān*, ed. M.M. al-Khūlī (Cairo: Dār iʿtiṣām li'l-ṭabʿ wa'l-nashr, 1972); M.W. Dols, "The Leper in Medieval Islamic Society," *Speculum*: 58:4 (1983): 891-916.

did not hamper Jadhīma's career. He possessed the powers of prophecy and divination; he was a pagan priest who was responsible for two Dayzans, two idols housed in al-Ḥīra, to which people would bring gifts in an effort to secure either water or aid against an enemy; and he aspired to political power.[36] The combination of leprosy, divination, cultic practices, and political aspirations brings to mind the biblical figure of Ahitophel ("brother of impiety"), one-time trusted advisor of King David who, at the end of his life, switched his political allegiance, throwing his support in favor of Absalom, who led a revolt against his father. When the revolt failed, Ahitophel committed suicide. The rabbis taught that Ahitophel "beheld but did not see," that is to say, he beheld the eruption of leprosy on his body and interpreted the appearance of the disease, albeit mistakenly, as a sign that he would rule over Israel.[37] In fact, it was not Ahitophel but his granddaughter Bathsheba who would rule over Israel as the wife of King David. Although the similarities between Jadhīma and Ahitophel are not obvious, they may have been noticed by the more learned and knowledgeable members of Ṭabarī's audience.[38]

Arab genealogists divide the inhabitants of the Arabian peninsula into two groups: original inhabitants and later waves of immigrants from the north and south. It is thought that the original inhabitants of the peninsula were tribesmen who spoke a pure form of the Arabic language. At some point in antiquity, other tribal groups known as the proto-Arabs (*al-ʿāriba al-ūlā*) migrated to the peninsula, where they learned to speak the Arabic language and adopted the manners and customs of the pure Arabs.[39] These proto-Arabs are said to have been descendants of the biblical Ishmael, and Jadhīma was one of them. His genealogy indicates that his forefathers had been living in the Arabian peninsula for only four generations. He was Jadhīma b. Mālik b. Fahm b. Ghānim b. Daws al-Azdī. It is noteworthy that the upper segment of his genealogy—which the pure Arabs preferred not to mention—connected him with biblical Israel: He was one of the Banū Wabar b. Umaym b. Lūdh b. Shem b. Nūḥ. In addition to his

---

[36] *EI²*, s.v. "D̲j̲ad̲h̲īma al-Abras̲h̲ or al-Waḍḍāḥ" (I. Kawar).

[37] Babylonian Talmut, *Sanhedrin*, 101b.

[38] al-Ṭabarī, *Taʾrīkh*, 1:613-14; *The History of al-Ṭabarī*, 4:132-4; al-Nuwayrī, *Nihāyat al-ʿarab*, 15:316. An inscription discovered at Umm Jamāl written in Nabataean and Greek refers to "Jadhīma the king of the Tanūkh" (*gdymt mlk tnwḥ*). See Bowersock, *Roman Arabia*: 133.

[39] *EI²*, s.vv. "Mustaʿriba" (Ilse Lichtenstädter), "Mutaʿarriba" (idem); Lane, *An Arabic-English Lexicon*, s.v. ʿ-r-b.

resemblance to Ahitophel, Jadhīma was also a lineal descendant of Noah. He and his fellow tribesmen were thus collateral relatives of the Israelites.[40]

Jadhīma and his people lived along the west bank of the Euphrates River between al-Anbār and al-Ḥīra. Known as *the Arabs of the unwalled area*, these proto-Arabs reportedly were tent-living nomads who had little contact with house-dwelling townsmen. Jadhīma did realize his ambition to become king. He was the first proto-Arab to rule in Iraq and he was one of the greatest of the proto-Arab kings. His power extended over the territory that circumscribed the Euphratian towns of al-Ḥīra, al-Anbār, Baqqa and Hīt. Known for his decisiveness and resolution, he was called *rajul mijdhām* (literally: *a decisive man*). Note the word-play: the adjective *mijdhām* and the name *Jadhīma* are both derived from the same root: *j-dh-m*.[41]

ʿAdī b. Naṣr and Raqāsh

After introducing Jadhīma, Ṭabarī makes an effortless segue to a second key figure in his narrative: ʿAdī b. Naṣr al-Lakhmī, a handsome and graceful youth who was a member of the tribe of ʿIyād.[42] When the ʿIyādīs were attacked by Jadhīma's forces, they responded by plying the guardians of the two Dayzans with wine and stealing the idols. They sent a message to Jadhīma, promising to return the king's cherished idols if he would agree not to raid them again. Jadhīma accepted their proposal but only on the condition that they send him ʿAdī b. Naṣr. They agreed, and Jadhīma left the ʿIyādīs in peace. ʿAdī became Jadhīma's trusted slave, and the king put him in charge of his wine—a decision that would come back to haunt him.[43]

Jadhīma's sister was Raqāsh bt. Mālik. In Arabic, the Form II verb *raqqasha* means *to occasion discord or dissension* and the noun *raqāsh* means *serpent*.[44] Her name signals her character: the Snake, i.e., someone slippery and untrustworthy. One day Raqāsh caught sight

---

[40] al-Ṭabarī, *Ta'rīkh*, 1:613.

[41] Ibid.; *The History of al-Ṭabarī*, 4:132; cf. al-Masʿūdī, *Murūj al-dhahab*, 2:213; Ibn al-Athīr, *al-Kāmil fī al-Ta'rīkh*, 1:341.

[42] His full name was ʿAdī b. Naṣr b. Rabīʿa b. ʿAmr b. al-Ḥārith b. Saʿūd b. Mālik b. ʿUmam b. Numāra b. Lakhm. See al-Ṭabarī, *Ta'rīkh*, 1:614; *The History of al-Ṭabarī*, 4:134.

[43] al-Ṭabarī, *Ta'rīkh*, 1:614-15; *The History of al-Ṭabarī*, 4:134; Ibn al-Athīr, *al-Kāmil fī al-Ta'rīkh*, 1:342-3.

[44] Lane, *Lexicon*, s.v. r-q-sh.

of ʿAdī and immediately fell in love with him (*abṣarathu … fa-ʿashiqathu*). According to established social conventions, however, even a handsome and trusted slave could not marry a royal princess. Raqāsh was determined. "O ʿAdī," she said, "speak to the king about your marrying me, for you are a man of lineage and status." Curiously, ʿAdī was reluctant to pursue the matter, protesting that he did not want to marry her and—more to the point—that he dare not raise the issue with the king (he would have done well to listen to his inner voices). Undeterred, Raqāsh now devised a scheme that she ordered Adī to execute:

> When the king sits over his wine, and his boon companions arrive, serve him pure wine, but offer his boon companions wine that has been diluted with water. When he becomes intoxicated, talk to him about marrying me. He will not refuse you (*lan yaruddaka*) or decline. When he agrees to marry you to me, make sure that his boon companions bear witness.[45]

As the overseer of the king's wine, ʿAdī was well-positioned to carry out the plan. He did exactly as instructed. When the wine had done its work, ʿAdī asked Jadhīma for the hand of Raqāsh. The king agreed, transferring his authority over his sister to his slave. The marriage was consummated that very night. The next day, Jadhīma noticed that ʿAdī had a red spot on his face caused—unbeknownst to the king—by the bride's make-up. "What is that?" he asked his slave. "It is from the wedding," ʿAdī responded. "What wedding?" the king demanded. "The wedding with Raqāsh," ʿAdī replied. "Woe is you!," Jadhīma exclaimed. And he asked, "Who married her to you?" "The king did," ʿAdī replied. When he heard this, Jadhīma pummeled his face and threw himself on the ground, thinking that he had been betrayed by his trusted slave. The king's reaction signaled to ʿAdī that his life was in danger and he fled to his fellow tribesmen, the ʿIyādīs, among whom he lived out the rest of his life, never again to be seen by his wife, by her brother, or by anyone else in al-Ḥīra. In fact, ʿAdī's life was cut short by an accident. One day, while he was out hunting, he was fatally wounded by a stray arrow shot from the bow of one of his hunting companions.[46]

---

[45] al-Ṭabarī, *Taʾrīkh*, 1:615; *The History of al-Ṭabarī*, 4:134; Ibn al-Athīr, *al-Kāmil fī al-Taʾrīkh*, 1:343.

[46] al-Ṭabarī, *Taʾrīkh*, 1:615; *The History of al-Ṭabarī*, 4:135; cf. al-Masʿūdī, *Murūj al-dhahab*, 2:214; Ibn al-Athīr, *al-Kāmil fī al-Taʾrīkh*, 1:343.

Meanwhile Jadhīma summoned Raqāsh and gave his sister a merciless tongue-lashing in verse that culminated with the following lines:

> Tell me, and do not lie,
> did you fornicate with a noble man or an ignoble one?
> Was it a slave?
> Then you are worthy of a slave.
> Perhaps a worthless man?
> Then a worthless man you deserve.[47]

Only after Jadhīma had finished his barrage of verbal insults did Raqāsh relate her version of events, cleverly shifting all responsibility for the inappropriate marriage from herself to her brother. It was the king, she insisted, who had married her "to an Arab who is well known and of noble birth. You did not ask me if I wanted to marry, and I had no authority over myself." If Raqāsh was to be believed, then it was the king who had decided to marry his sister to a slave, and she had no choice but to accept his decision. The gullible king did believe his sister and, duly chastened, he refrained from punishing her. As it happened, Raqāsh was carrying ʿAdī's child, a son whose father never knew that he even existed. Nine months later she gave birth to a boy whose name, ʿAmr ("Life"), suggests that his prospects were good. Thus did Raqāsh become Umm ʿAmr—although there was no need for the storyteller to say so (and he does not). Raqāsh raised the infant by herself without the knowledge of the king. When ʿAmr reached boyhood, his mother dressed him in fine clothes, perfumed him, and presented him to his maternal uncle. No sooner did Jadhīma lay eyes on his nephew than he was smitten by the boy and showered him with love. The boy played with the king's children, and they played with him. As a sign of his affection, the king instructed his jeweler to make a silver necklace for ʿAmr, who thus became the first Arab to wear a necklace—hence, his nickname Dhū al-Ṭawq ("the neck-ringed youth")—a key narrative detail. Jadhīma attached the boy to himself and assumed responsibility for him. Although the storyteller does not say so, the relationship

[47] al-Ṭabarī, *Taʾrīkh*, 1:615; *The History of al-Ṭabarī*, 4:135; cf. al-Masʿūdī, *Murūj al-dhahab*, 2:215; Ibn al-Athīr, *al-Kāmil fī al-Taʾrīkh*, 1:343.

between the two was like that between a father and his son—and a beloved son at that.[48]

Lost and found

If Jadhīma did regard ʿAmr as his beloved son, then ʿAmr would succeed him as king of Iraq. But just as ʿAmr's biological father was denied the pleasure of ever seeing his son, so too his surrogate father was denied the pleasure of raising the boy and grooming him for royal office. One day while ʿAmr was in his teens, jinn appeared, lured the boy away from his home, and spirited him away from his family. Jadhīma searched far and wide but to no avail. When salvation came, it would emerge from an unexpected quarter.[49]

Some time after ʿAmr's disappearance, two brothers, Mālik and ʿAqīl the two sons of Fāriḥ (or Fārij or Qāliḥ), set out from Syria en route to Iraq bearing precious gifts for Jadhīma, the king of Iraq. The brothers were accompanied by a songstress named Umm ʿAmr. More word play. The threesome made their way to Iraq, stopping *en route* at a rest house where the songstress prepared food and served it to her masters. As the men were eating, a young man appeared out of nowhere. He was naked and haggard, his hair was tangled and dirty, and his nails had not been cut for a long time. He was hungry and appeared to be sick. The wild-looking youth sat down beside the two brothers and, without saying a word, extended his hand, signaling his desire for food. The songstress gave him a wing, which he immediately devoured. But when he extended his arm a second time, asking for more, she exclaimed, "Give a slave a wing and he will take the whole arm"—an expression that became proverbial. She then offered her masters some wine and tied up the skin, eliciting a protest from the still-thirsty youth (who, we will soon learn, is none other than ʿAmr). Just as his uncle previously had rebuked Raqāsh—the real Umm ʿAmr—it was now ʿAmr's turn to rebuke a woman with the same name:

---

[48] al-Ṭabarī, *Taʾrīkh*, 1:615-16; *The History of al-Ṭabarī, vol. iv, The Ancient Kingdoms*: 135; cf. al-Masʿūdī, *Murūj al-dhahab*, 2:215; Ibn al-Athīr, *al-Kāmil fī al-Taʾrīkh*, 1:343-4. N.B.: I. Shahid refers to ʿAmr as Jadhīma's *adopted* son (*EI*[2], s.v. "al-Zabbāʾ").

[49] al-Ṭabarī, *Taʾrīkh*, 1:616; *The History of al-Ṭabarī, vol. iv, The Ancient Kingdoms*: 136; cf. al-Masʿūdī, *Murūj al-dhahab*, 2:215; Ibn al-Athīr, *al-Kāmil fī al-Taʾrīkh*, 1:344; al-Nuwayrī, *Nihāyat al-ʿarab*, 15:316.

Pass round from left to right! Why do you allow, Umm ʿAmr
me and my comrades thirst,
Yet you will not serve me this morning, Umm ʿAmr
Am I the worst of us three?[50]

"Who are you, young man?," Mālik and ʿAqīl demanded. "Indeed, you don't know me or my genealogy. I am ʿAmr b. ʿAdī," he replied, "son of a Tanūkh woman, from the tribe of Lakhm." ʿAmr now made the following prediction, "You will see me tomorrow, among the clans of Numāra, having been denied the staff of royal authority (*ghayr muʿaṣṣan*, from the root *ʿ-ṣ-w*)."[51] There was no need to explain the reference to ʿAmr's political misfortune, for the storyteller's audience surely would have made the connection between ʿAmr and the biblical Ishmael, whose father cast him into the wilderness with his mother. Whereas in the biblical narrative Hagar "filled the skin with water and let the boy drink" (Gen. 21:19), here Umm ʿAmr ties up the wineskin and refuses to satisfy the boy's thirst—thereby inverting the biblical motif.

Upon hearing the youth's name, Mālik and ʿAqīl immediately recognized him as the son of Raqāsh, the boy who had been captured by jinn. The two men stood up and embraced the youth, marveling at their own good fortune, for they had recovered the beloved nephew (and surrogate son) of the powerful king whom they would be visiting on the morrow. What better gift could they bestow upon Jadhīma than his long lost nephew! By reuniting the youth with the king, they would be carrying out the will of God. First, however, the wild-looking youth had to be domesticated. The brothers washed ʿAmr's head, clipped his nails, shampooed his hair, and dressed him in fresh clothes. By the end of the next day, the group had reached the gates of al-Ḥīra. They entered the city and made their way to the king. When he heard the good news, Jadhīma was beside himself with joy. Curiously, the king did *not* recognize the youth. The two gift-bearing brothers tried to reassure the king, saying, "Bless you, a man in his

[50] al-Ṭabarī, *Ta'rīkh*, 1:616; *The History of al-Ṭabarī*, 4:136; cf. al-Masʿūdī, *Murūj al-dhahab*, 2:216; Ibn al-Athīr, *al-Kāmil fī al-Ta'rīkh*, 1:344; al-Nuwayrī, *Nihāyat al-ʿarab*, 15:316. The English translation of the poem is that of M. Perlmann, based on Nicholson's translation in his *Literary History of the Arabs*, 111. The verse is from the *Muʿallaqa* of ʿAmr b. Kulthūm.

[51] al-Ṭabarī, *Ta'rīkh*, 1:616; *The History of al-Ṭabarī*, 4:136; cf. al-Masʿūdī, *Murūj al-dhahab*, 2:216; Ibn al-Athīr, *al-Kāmil fī al-Ta'rīkh*, 1:345; al-Nuwayrī, *Nihāyat al-arab*, 15:317. It is also possible to read this expression as *ghayr maʿṣiyyan*, which would signify, "not having been disobeyed."

state will change." Jadhīma now sent ʿAmr to spend some time with his mother, the *real* Umm ʿAmr. A few days later, she sent him back to the king who, still harboring suspicions that the youth was an imposter, devised a test. The king said, "On the day on which the boy disappeared, he was wearing a necklace. Since that day I have been unable to get him out of my heart or mind." On cue, the brothers produced the necklace and presented it to the king, who declared, "ʿAmr has outgrown the necklace"—another proverbial expression. The king then turned to the two brothers and promised them whatever they wanted as a reward for their gift. "Our reward is to be your boon companions as long as we and you are alive."[52] More wine. Some people never learn.

Jadhīma slays ʿAmr b. Ẓarib

At this time, "the ruler of the Arabs in the Jazīra and the Syrian highlands"—that is to say, the king of Palmyra and its surrounding territories, was another man named ʿAmr: ʿAmr b. Ẓarib b. Ḥassān b. Udhayna b. al-Samaydaʿ b. Hawbar al-ʿAmlaqī (or al-ʿAmlīqī).

Three elements of this ʿAmr's name merit attention. First, Ẓarib is derived from the root *ẓ-r-b*. From the same root is derived the word *ẓaribān*, which signifies *a small stinking animal that resembles a cat, Chinese dog, ape or monkey that often emits a noiseless wind from the anus*; this animal is also *small and has short ears* (*aṣlamu al-udhnayn*).[53] This ʿAmr was the son of a foul-smelling animal with short ears. Second, *udhayna* (the diminutive form of *udhn* or ear, i.e., *small-eared*) is the Arabic equivalent of the Greek Odenathus. This ʿAmr clearly is connected to Odenathus, King of Palmyra and husband of Zenobia. Third, the king was al-ʿAmlīqī, a member of the Canaanite tribe of Amalek that was destroyed by the Israelites. Thus ʿAmr b. Ẓarib is recognizable as an historical figure with biblical associations. His name may have been ʿAmr ("Life"), but as Udhayna = Odenathus the Amalekite, his chances of survival were nil.

When Jadhīma the Leper learned that ʿAmr b. Ẓarib ("the small stinking animal") the Amalekite had left his base in Syria and was

---

52 al-Ṭabarī, *Taʾrīkh*, 1:617; *The History of al-Ṭabarī*, 4:137; cf. al-Masʿūdī, *Murūj al-dhahab*, 2:216-17; Ibn al-Athīr, *al-Kāmil fī al-Taʾrīkh*, 1:345; Nuwayrī, *Nihāyat al-arab*, 15:317.

53 Lane, *Arabic-English Lexicon*, s.v. ẓ-r-b.

leading his forces in the direction of Iraq, the king of Iraq gathered a large army composed of Arabs and set off to confront the invaders. The two armies met at an unidentified location. During the ensuing battle, 'Amr b. Ẓarib was slain (just as Odenathus was murdered) and his army scattered (just as the Amalekites were destroyed). Jadhīma now found himself on the wrong side of two men named 'Amr: his nephew 'Amr b. 'Adī—for the death of whose father he was indirectly responsible, and the late king of the Jazīra and Syria 'Amr b. Ẓarib—for whose death he was directly responsible.[54]

Al-Zabbā' Seeks Revenge

The slaying of 'Amr b. Ẓarib brings us, finally, to Zenobia, whose character undergoes a remarkable transformation in Islamic sources. As Nicholson noted a century ago, the Muslim storytellers played freely with the details of history to the point that Zenobia is barely recognizable:

> ... the legend, as told in their traditions, has little in common with reality. Not only are the names and places freely altered—Zenobia herself being confused with the Syrian general Zabdai—but the historical setting, though dimly visible in the background, has been distorted almost beyond recognition.[55]

Nicholson was correct to point out the gap between legend and history, although it is regrettable that he did not pay greater attention to the significance of the transformation undergone by the Palmyrene queen. Let us begin with her name. It is curious that the Muslim storytellers who gave shape to and transmitted the legend chose not to refer to the queen of Palmyra, the heroine who almost conquered Rome in the 3d century CE, as Zaynab—the Arabic equivalent of Zenobia. Zaynab is a common name among Muslims. As noted above, Muḥammad married two women named Zaynab and gave this name to one of his daughters.[56] The association of the name Zaynab with the Prophet may explain the onomastic transformation: Whereas in non-Islamic sources Zenobia is remembered for her beauty, bravery and chastity, in Islamic sources she is portrayed as

---

[54] al-Ṭabarī, *Ta'rīkh*, 1:617-18; *The History of al-Ṭabarī*, 4:138; Ibn al-Athīr, *al-Kāmil fī al-Ta'rīkh*, 1:345.

[55] Nicholson, *A Literary History of the Arabs*: 34.

[56] See above, note 6.

a sexually brazen, vengeful and blood-thirsty demon—as will soon become clear. No Muslim storyteller in his right mind would dare to use the name of one of the Prophet's wives or daughters to refer to a figure—historical or fictional—associated with sex, murder and mayhem. For this reason, the Queen of Palmyra was given a new name: Nā'ila al-Zabbā'. *Pace* Nicholson, however, the Muslim storytellers did not confuse Zenobia with the Syrian general Zabdai; rather, they focused on another element of the Palmyrene queen's name, Bathzabbai—as documented on the above-mentioned inscription of 271 CE. The name Bathzabbai brings to mind the biblical figure of Bathsheba, the beautiful wife of King David. The Aramaic *zabbai* became in Arabic *al-Zabbā'*, which signifies *a woman with much or long hair*.[57] Once again, a name defines a character—although, as we shall learn, not for the reasons that immediately come to mind. The name change was accompanied by a curious adjustment to the historical record: Whereas the Zenobia of history was the *wife* of Odenathus, in the Islamic legend al-Zabbā' is the *daughter* of ʿAmr b. Ẓarib b. Ḥassān b. Udhayna (= Odenathus). One wonders if the transformation of the wife of a king into his daughter is one of the inevitable vagaries of the transmission of a folktale from one culture to another, or if there may not be another explanation for the change of status. Be that as it may, despite the onomastic and genealogical transformations, the identity of the two women is unmistakable: al-Zabbā' is the Arabo-Islamic equivalent of Zenobia.[58]

The literary cycle that begins with Jadhīma ends with al-Zabbā'. After ʿAmr b. Ẓarib (= Odenathus) was slain in battle by Jadhīma, he was succeeded as ruler of the Arabs in the Jazīra and Syria by his daughter al-Zabbā'. Thus it was that an Arab woman became the Queen of Palmyra, a major achievement and a potential historical precedent that the early Muslim community could not—and did not—ignore. One of al-Zabbā''s first acts upon taking power was to order the construction of a fortress on the west bank of the Euphrates, where she would spend the winter months; with the arrival of spring, the queen would move to Baṭn al-Najjār, and from there to Palmyra.

[57] Lane, *An Arabic-English Lexicon*, s.v. z-b-b.

[58] As support for the identity of Zenobia and al-Zabbā', Nicholson (*A Literary History of the Arabs*: 35) cites Ibn Qutayba's statement that "Jadhīma sought in marriage al-Zabbā', the daughter of the king of Mesopotamia, who became queen after her *husband*" (emphasis in Nicholson). This identification has been accepted by P. Hitti, E. Littman, and Bowersock. See Bowersock, *Roman Arabia*: 134, note 46.

After consolidating her power, al-Zabbā' resolved to take revenge on Jadhīma for the death of her father. But she was dissuaded from pursuing a military option by her thoughtful and clever sister Zabība (both names are derived from the root *z-b-b*).[59] Zabība warned al-Zabbā' that the military option was a double-edged sword: Victory might yield sweet vengeance but defeat would result in the breakup of her polity. Al-Zabbā' wisely accepted her sister's advice. Unlike Zenobia, whose use of military force resulted in her downfall and the destruction of Palmyra, al-Zabbā' would use trickery, deception, and cunning—what the Greeks call *métis*.[60] Al-Zabbā' wrote a letter to Jadhīma in which she conceded that women are weak rulers and inept administrators. She also flattered the king, writing that no one but he was her peer and equal. "Come to me and join my kingdom to yours," she wrote. "Let us unite our countries and rule together."[61]

Al-Zabbā''s letter found Jadhīma in the Iraqi town of al-Baqqa. The queen's words had their intended effect. Before accepting her offer, however, the king sought the counsel of his advisors, all of whom warmly endorsed her proposal—with one notable exception: an intelligent and resolute man named Qaṣīr ("Shorty"), whose father was a certain Sa'd and whose mother was a slave who belonged to Jadhīma.[62] Qaṣīr was thus a member of Jadhīma's household and a loyal and trusted servant who was not afraid to speak truth to power. He warned the king that al-Zabbā' hated him because he had slain her father and that she was laying a dangerous trap. Qaṣīr advised Jadhīma to send the queen a letter suggesting that she travel to him; her agreement would be a sign of her sincerity. As his name suggests, however, Qaṣīr came up on the *short* end. Unwisely, Jadhīma rejected his servant's well-intended advice, and, to make matters worse, he

---

[59] In addition to the onomatopoetic wordplay—al-Zabbā' versus Zabība—the sister's name brings to mind another Arab queen, Zabibi the Queen of Aribi. See note 3.

[60] In Greek, *métis* signifies *cunning intelligence*, i.e., the ability to strategize, cheat, and escape danger, characteristics commonly associated with women. See *Cunning Intelligence in Greek Culture and Society*, ed. M. Detienne et J-P Vernant, trans. by J. Lloyd (Atlantic Highlands, N.J.: Humanities Press, ca. 1978).

[61] al-Ṭabarī, *Ta'rīkh*, 1:618-19; *The History of al-Ṭabarī*, 4:139-40; cf. al-Mas'ūdī, *Murūj al-dhahab*, 2:217; Ibn al-Athīr, *al-Kāmil fī al-Ta'rīkh*, 1:345-6.

[62] His full name is Qaṣīr b. Sa'd b. 'Umar b. Jadhīmah b. Qays b. Rabā [variant: Arbā] b. Numāra b. Lakhm.

now summoned his nephew and surrogate son, ʿAmr b. ʿAdī, and sought his counsel.[63]

Again there was no need to state the obvious: ʿAmr b. ʿAdī had been deprived of the love and nurturing care of his father because of Jadhīma's predilection for wine, irascibility, gullibility, and naiveté. Like the biblical Ishmael, ʿAmr had been raised like a savage in the wilderness. Like the biblical Ishmael, who became the father of a great nation—the Ishmaelites, ʿAmr aspired to succeed Jadhīma as king of Iraq and thus become the leader of a great nation. But ʿAmr apparently sensed that his time had not yet come—hence, his earlier prediction that he would *not* receive the staff of royal authority from his uncle/surrogate father. Surely ʿAmr's motivation to take revenge on Jadhīma was as great as that of al-Zabbāʾ, whose father—another ʿAmr—had been slain in battle by the same man. One way or another Jadhīma was not long for this world.

When ʿAmr b. ʿAdī came face-to-face with the man who was directly responsible for his father's disappearance and indirectly responsible for his death, he dissembled. Knowing full well what the consequences would be, he encouraged his uncle to proceed to Palmyra: "The clan of Numāra are my people," he said. "They are with al-Zabbāʾ but they will join forces with you if given an opportunity to do so." After weighing Qaṣīr's advice against that of ʿAmr, the king rejected (*ʿaṣā*, from the root *ʿ-ṣ-y*) the counsel of the man who was the son of a female slave and accepted that of his nephew. Before setting off, however, Jadhīma made two key decisions: He appointed (*istakhlafa*) ʿAmr b. ʿAdī as his deputy over al-Ḥīra; and he appointed (*jaʿala*) yet another ʿAmr—ʿAmr b. ʿAbd al-Jinn al-Jarmī[64]—as commander of his cavalry. Once again, the storyteller was sending a signal to his audience. The duplication of the name suggests that Jadhīma could not make up his mind about which ʿAmr was best qualified to succeed him as king of Iraq—the ʿAmr who was his beloved nephew/surrogate son or the ʿAmr who was Servant of al-Jinn. Be that as it may, ʿAmr b. ʿAdī remained behind in al-Ḥīra, while ʿAmr b. ʿAbd al-Jinn marched out of al-Baqqa together with

---

[63] al-Ṭabarī, *Taʾrīkh*: 1:619; *The History of al-Ṭabarī*: 4:140-1; cf. al-Masʿūdī, *Murūj al-dhahab*, 2:218; Ibn al-Athīr, *al-Kāmil fī al-Taʾrīkh*, 1:346.

[64] The *nisba* al-Jarmī points to a connection with Sampsiceram (Shamas + Jarm), an Arab chief who ca. 64 CE founded a dynasty at Emesa in northern Syria. The royal house of Emessa was related by marriage to the semi-Arab house of the Herods of Judea. See Abbott, "Pre-Islamic Arab Queens," 8.

Jadhīma, heading west in the direction of Palmyra. As for Qaṣīr, he too accompanied the army—a key narrative detail—despite the fact that his good advice had been rejected.[65]

When the troops alighted at al-Furḍa ("the Gap"), Jadhīma began to have second thoughts about the mission. He asked Qaṣīr, "What is the prudent course?" To which his advisor responded, "You left prudence in al-Baqqa"—an expression that became proverbial. The king ignored the warning. As soon as Jadhīma and his forces had reached the outskirts of Palmyra, al-Zabbā' dispatched messengers who flattered the king and showered him with gifts. Again he asked Qaṣīr, "What do you think?" The advisor replied, "A minor occurrence in a major affair"—another expression that become proverbial. Again the king paid no attention. Qaṣīr now offered Jadhīma one final piece of advice, telling him to pay careful attention to the manner in which the Palmyrene cavalry deployed themselves. "If they march in front of you," he said, "then the woman is sincere. But if they surround you from the sides and behind, then they mean treachery." And, he added, in the event that the king was forced to flee, he should make sure to ride his finest and swiftest horse al-ʿAṣā or "the Staff" (from the root *ʿ-ṣ-w*)—a symbol of royal authority; indeed, Qaṣīr assured the king, he himself would be riding al-ʿAṣā and would bring the horse to the king. When the cavalry and other regiments gathered, however, Jadhīma was separated from the Staff, whereupon Shorty jumped on the horse and galloped off into the sunset. A slave on a royal horse—another inversion of the social order. After covering a long distance, the horse expired and was buried at a place that came to be known as Burj al-ʿAṣā or the Tower of Royal Authority.[66]

The Palmyrene cavalry surrounded Jadhīma—the king ignored Qaṣīr's third and final piece of advice—and brought him to al-Zabbā'. The male and female protagonists came face-to-face. Only now do we learn why the queen was called al-Zabbā' or "the woman with much or long hair." Contrary to our expectations, the epithet does not refer to the hair on her head. The queen brazenly lifted her dress to her waist and exposed herself to Jadhīma: Lo and behold, her genital hair was braided. By means of this erotic gesture, al-Zabbā' signaled her true intentions. The queen taunted Jadhīma, asking, "Do

---

[65] al-Ṭabarī, *Ta'rīkh*, 1:619-20; *The History of al-Ṭabarī*, 4:141; cf. al-Masʿūdī, *Murūj al-dhahab*, 2:220; Ibn al-Athīr, *al-Kāmil fī al-Ta'rīkh*, 1:346-7.

[66] al-Ṭabarī, *Ta'rīkh*, 1:620; *The History of al-*Ṭabarī, 4:141-2; cf. al-Masʿūdī, *Murūj al-dhahab*, 2:218; Ibn al-Athīr, *al-Kāmil fī al-Ta'rīkh*, 1:347.

you think this is the handiwork of a bride?" (*a-da'b 'arūs tarā?*)—this too became proverbial. Only now did the gullible king realize that al-Zabbā' had outwitted him and that he unwittingly had walked into a trap (just as, years earlier, he had been outwitted by Raqāsh and unwittingly authorized his sister's marriage to his slave). There would be no uniting of the kingdoms of Iraq and Syria.[67]

Al-Zabbā' was possessed by jinn and she knew it. She had been informed, however, that royal blood would cure her condition. For the cure to work, it was essential that not one single drop of royal blood spill on the ground. How to secure the royal blood? Al-Zabbā' forced her would-be husband to drink strong wine. In the end—as in the beginning—wine would be the vehicle of Jadhīma's undoing. When the red liquid had done its work, the queen seated her victim on a rug, placed a golden bowl in front of him, and ordered her attendants to take out a razor. Out of respect for Jadhīma's status as a king, the queen did not cut off his head. Instead, she ordered her attendants to slit his wrists. As the blood flowed out of his body, the queen collected it in the bowl. Before Jadhīma lost consciousness, however, his hand fell to his side and a few drops of blood spilled on the ground. Alarmed, the queen screamed, "Do not lose any of the king's blood." In desperation, she grabbed some cotton and attempted to soak up the drops of blood that had spilled on the ground. Within minutes, Jadhīma had expired.[68]

A South Arabian Camel Caravan—or a Trojan Horse?

Jadhīma's death triggered a succession crisis in al-Ḥīra. The inhabitants of the city had split into two factions, one following 'Amr b. 'Adī, the other following 'Amr b. 'Abd al-Jinn al-Jarmī.

The resolution of the crisis would be the achievement of Qaṣīr, last seen in the area where the Staff had expired, having taken refuge with an unidentified tribe. Qaṣīr now emerged from (*kharaja*) Burj al-'Aṣā, the Tower of Royal Authority. In Arabic, the expression *shaqqa al-'aṣā* signifies *to split the staff*, and by extension, *to*

[67] al-Ṭabarī, *Ta'rīkh*, 1:620-1; *The History of al-Ṭabarī*, 4:142; cf. al-Mas'ūdī, *Murūj al-dhahab*, 2:219-20; Ibn al-Athīr, *al-Kāmil fī al-Ta'rīkh*, 1:347.

[68] al-Ṭabarī, *Ta'rīkh*, 1:621; *The History of al-Ṭabarī*, 4:142-3; cf. al-Mas'ūdī, *Murūj al-dhahab*, 2:219-20; Ibn al-Athīr, *al-Kāmil fī al-Ta'rīkh*, 1:347-8.

contravene the collective body of Islam; this expression is applied specifically to the Kharijis, about whom it is said, *qadd shaqqū ʿaṣā al-muslimīn*, i.e., *they have made a schism in the Muslim community*, referring to the split between the supporters of Muʿāwiya, the supporters of ʿAlī and the Kharijis. Just as the Kharijis went out (*kharajū*) from ʿAlī's camp at Ṣiffīn, so too Qaṣīr went out (*kharaja*) from Burj al-ʿAṣā. More wordplay.[69]

Qaṣīr rejoined ʿAmr b. ʿAdī in al-Ḥīra, where—unlike the mediators at Ṣiffīn—the able son of a female slave conducted shuttle diplomacy and succeeded in negotiating a settlement (*ṣulḥ*) between the two factions, as memorialized in poetry recited by the two ʿAmrs.[70] Qaṣīr now advised ʿAmr b. ʿAdī that he must exact vengeance for the murder of his uncle, Jadhīma, whose body had just been emptied of its blood by al-Zabbāʾ. Just as the cautious ʿAmr previously was reluctant to carry out Raqāsh's scheme, so too he was wary about Qaṣīr's scheme. The queen, he said, was "more inaccessible than the eagle of the air"—another proverbial expression.[71]

Back in Palmyra, al-Zabbāʾ—who presumably was still possessed by demons—consulted with a female soothsayer (*kāhina*) who rendered an ominous prediction: "I see that you will die because of a youth who is vile and disloyal—ʿAmr b. ʿAdī. You will not die, however, by his hand but rather by your own, although on his account." In an attempt to defy fate, al-Zabbāʾ ordered the construction of a tunnel that connected her public audience hall with her fortress inside the royal city. If any danger were to present itself while she was in the public space, she could escape unseen to the fortress. But how would she recognize ʿAmr b. ʿAdī, a man whom she had never seen but who, according to the soothsayer, was destined to kill her? More *métis*. The queen summoned Palmyra's most talented portrait artist and ordered him to disguise himself and then infiltrate ʿAmr's camp. Once inside enemy lines, he was to let it be known that he was a portrait artist. As soon as his talents had become common knowledge, he was to befriend ʿAmr and paint color portraits of him in as many poses as possible: seated, standing, riding a horse, wearing

---

[69] Lane, *Arabic-English Lexicon*, s.v. sh-q-q.

[70] al-Ṭabarī, *Taʾrīkh*, 1:621-2; *The History of al-Ṭabarī*, 4:143.

[71] al-Ṭabarī, *Taʾrīkh*, 1:622; *The History of al-Ṭabarī*, 4:143; cf. al-Masʿūdī, *Murūj al-dhahab*, 2:220; Ibn al-Athīr, *al-Kāmil fī al-Taʾrīkh*, 1:348; al-Nuwayrī, *Nihāyat al-arab*, 15:317.

civilian clothes, and fully armed. The artist did as he was told and returned to Palmyra, where he presented the portraits to the queen.[72]

Meanwhile, in al-Ḥīra, Qaṣīr was hard at work on his master plan. He needed a ruse that would make it possible for him to ingratiate himself to the queen. He decided on a drastic measure, instructing ʿAmr to cut off his—that is Qaṣīr's—nose and scourge him with a whip. When the ever-cautious ʿAmr could not bring himself to perform the cruel deed, Qaṣīr took matters into his own hands, cutting off his nose and flaying himself on the back until his body was covered with cuts and welts. About this act the pre-Islamic poet al-Mutalammis (d. ca. 580)[73] declaimed:

> It was for the sake of treachery (*makr*) that Qaṣīr cut off his nose
> —a line that became proverbial.

The Ḥīran kingmaker and poet ʿAdī b. Zayd had a more generous interpretation of Qaṣīr's action:

> Like Qaṣīr when he found nothing else
> Qaṣīr cut off his ears and nose for gratitude (*shukr*).[74]

Qaṣīr pretended to flee from ʿAmr b. ʿAdī, spreading a false rumor that Jadhīma's nephew had disfigured him because he believed that the slave had been complicit in the murder of his maternal uncle. He made his way to al-Zabbāʾ in Palmyra. When he approached the gate of the city, the queen issued an order that he be admitted into her presence. Once again the Queen of Palmyra came face-to-face with a dangerous male adversary. History does repeat itself—or can be made to do so. The woman who had shocked Jadhīma by lifting her dress and exposing her braided pudendum was herself shocked at the sight of Qaṣīr's disfigured face. How was it, she asked, that he had been reduced to this sorry state? Qaṣīr dissembled, telling the queen that ʿAmr b. ʿAdī had cut off his nose because he believed that Shorty had deceived Jadhīma by encouraging the king to make his fatal trip to Palmyra. Qaṣīr told the queen that the reason for his visit was his conviction that she—and no one else—would support him against ʿAmr. The woman who earlier had rejected Jadhīma's offer

---

[72] al-Ṭabarī, *Taʾrīkh*, 1:622; *The History of al-Ṭabarī*, 4:144; Ibn al-Athīr, *al-Kāmil fī al-Taʾrīkh*, 1:348.

[73] *EI*², s.v. "al-Mutalammis" (Ch. Pellat).

[74] al-Ṭabarī, *Taʾrīkh*, 1:623; *The History of al-Ṭabarī*, 4:144-5. Cf. *Dīwān ʿAdī b. Zayd*, 91 (no. 9); al-Masʿūdī, *Murūj al-dhahab*, 2:222; Ibn al-Athīr, *al-Kāmil fī al-Taʾrīkh*, 1:348-9; Nuwayrī, *Nihāyat al-arab*, 15:317.

to unite the kingdoms of Syria and Iraq now accepted ʿAmr's proposal of a strategic alliance. The woman who had outwitted the hapless Jadhīma was about to be outwitted herself. Al-Zabbā' grabbed the bait, and Qaṣīr proved to be the perfect advisor: decisive, intelligent, experienced and knowledgeable in matters of state. The queen did everything she could to help him.[75]

As soon as Qaṣīr had gained the queen's trust, he proposed to travel to Iraq, where he would use his wealth and resources to acquire clothes, perfumes and other precious objects. He promised to make al-Zabbā' rich, as befitting a queen whose name brings to mind *inter alia* the image of the biblical Queen of Sheba. She equipped the expedition and instructed Qaṣīr to purchase rare textiles and other precious commodities on her behalf. Traveling in disguise—outwardly, it will be recalled, he was on bad terms with ʿAmr b. ʿAdī—Qaṣīr made his way to al-Ḥīra, where, after establishing contact with ʿAmr, he explained his scheme and asked ʿAmr to supply him with valuable textiles and precious goods. If ʿAmr cooperated, Qaṣīr said, he would make it possible for him to avenge the death of his uncle/surrogate father by slaying the woman who had murdered the king. ʿAmr complied, and Qaṣīr returned to Palmyra, where he presented the queen with all of the merchandise that he had acquired in Iraq. Duly impressed—and eager for even greater material gain, she sent Qaṣīr on a second expedition to Iraq, providing him with more resources than before. The results were equally impressive, and the queen now sent ʿAmr to Iraq for a third time.[76]

The third trip was different. Upon his arrival in al-Ḥīra, Qaṣīr instructed ʿAmr to collect strong sacks and thick twine and to summon his most trustworthy supporters and fighters. On this occasion, ʿAmr did as he was told, whereupon Qaṣīr ordered him to place two men inside every sack and to load each sack on a camel. Once in position, the men sealed the sacks from the inside with the twine. When the preparations were complete, the caravan set off for Palmyra laden with soldiers—an inversion of the biblical narrative in which the Queen of Sheba made her way to Solomon in Jerusalem at the head of a caravan laden with spices, gold, and precious stones

[75] al-Ṭabarī, *Ta'rīkh*, 1:623; *The History of al-Ṭabarī*, 4:145; cf. al-Masʿūdī, *Murūj al-dhahab*, 2:220-1; Ibn al-Athīr, *al-Kāmil fī al-Ta'rīkh*, 1:349; al-Nuwayrī, *Nihāyat al-arab*, 15:317.

[76] al-Ṭabarī, *Ta'rīkh*, 1:624; *The History of al-Ṭabarī*, 4:145-6; cf. al-Masʿūdī, *Murūj al-dhahab*, 2:221; Ibn al-Athīr, *al-Kāmil fī al-Ta'rīkh*, 1:349; al-Nuwayrī, *Nihāyat al-arab*, 15:317.

(I Kings 10:2). As the caravan approached the city, Qaṣīr rode ahead and invited al-Zabbāʾ to come out and inspect the merchandise. "I brought what shrieks yet keeps silent," he said, alluding to the contents of the sacks. The gullible and unsuspecting queen ignored the warning. When al-Zabbāʾ inspected the caravan, she noticed that the camels were straining under a heavy load. "O Qaṣīr," she asked, "what is the matter with the camels? Are they carrying stone, iron or lead?" No response is recorded, and the queen took no action. The caravan now passed through the gates of the city. As the last camel made its way past the Nabataen gate-keeper, he poked a sack with a stick, hitting one of the men in the stomach and causing him to break wind. Alarmed, the gate-keeper exclaimed in Nabataen, "There is mischief in the sacks"—an expression that became proverbial. As the caravan wended its way through the city, Qaṣīr signaled ʿAmr, letting him know the location of the entrance to the secret tunnel—another key narrative detail. Upon their arrival at the center of Palmyra, the camel-riders hobbled their beasts, whereupon the soldiers emerged from their hiding places, slaughtered the Palmyrenes and pillaged the city—just as in Virgil's *Aeneid* the Greek soldiers emerged from the Trojan horse, slaughtered the inhabitants of Troy and pillaged the city.[77]

When all was lost, al-Zabbāʾ implemented her emergency escape plan, hastening toward the tunnel where, unbeknownst to her, ʿAmr b. ʿAdī was waiting. As the queen was about to enter the tunnel, she caught sight of ʿAmr standing (*abṣarat ʿAmr*[an] *qāʾim*[an]); she recognized him from the color portraits painted by the artist. Rather than allow herself to be slain by the nephew of the man whose blood she had drained from his body, the queen resolved to commit suicide, having prepared herself for this moment by putting poison in her signet ring (*khātam*), another symbol of royal authority. As she sucked on the ring, she announced, "By my own hand, not yours, O ʿAmr!" For a moment it appeared as if the prediction of the soothsayer would come true, but ʿAmr quickly unsheathed his sword and slew al-Zabbāʾ, thus ending the career of the Arab queen of Palmyra.[78]

---

[77] al-Ṭabarī, *Taʾrīkh*, 1:624-5; *The History of al-Ṭabarī*, 4:145-6; cf. al-Masʿūdī, *Murūj al-dhahab*, 2:222; Ibn al-Athīr, *al-Kāmil fī al-Taʾrīkh*, 1:349-50; al-Nuwayrī, *Nihāyat al-arab*, 15:318.

[78] al-Ṭabarī, *Taʾrīkh*, 1:625; *The History of al-Ṭabarī*, 4:147; cf. al-Masʿūdī, *Murūj al-dhahab*, 2:222; Ibn al-Athīr, *al-Kāmil fī al-Taʾrīkh*, 1:350; al-Nuwayrī, *Nihāyat al-arab*, 15:318.

Resumption of The Historical Narrative

After completing the legend of al-Zabbā', Ṭabarī returns to the history of al-Ḥīra, taking care to alert the reader to the fact that his account is based upon written sources composed by the Ḥīrans and preserved in their churches—no doubt the same sources that he used to produce the list of Roman kings (see above).[79]

The irony of 'Amr b. 'Adī's rise to power would have been obvious to Ṭabarī's immediate audience: It was only by avenging the death of his uncle/surrogate father, the man who was himself responsible for the disappearance and premature death of his natural father, that 'Amr realized his political ambition. He did not, however, become the king of Iraq but rather the king of al-Ḥīra. The historian now reminds his audience that 'Amr's full name was 'Amr b. 'Adī b. Naṣr b. Rabī'a b. al-Ḥārith b. Mālik b. 'Amr b. Numāra b. Lakhm. Unlike his maternal uncle, Jadhīma, a proto-Arab descended from Noah, 'Amr was a pure Arab descended from Lakhm. Indeed, Ṭabarī explains, 'Amr b. 'Adī was the first pure Arab to become king of al-Ḥīra and the first Arab king of al-Ḥīra to be memorialized in writing by the inhabitants of that city. His descendants, known as either the Family of Victory (Naṣr) or the Lakhmids, ruled al-Ḥīra without interruption until 602, just prior to the emergence of Islam in northwest Arabia. 'Amr b. 'Adī—like the biblical Moses—is said to have lived to the age of 120, and during his long reign the king conducted numerous raids and seized large quantities of booty. He did not recognize the regional princes of Iraq, nor did they recognize him. Iraq remained politically fragmented until it was unified by the Lakhmid kings of al-Ḥīra who, as Ṭabarī was careful to point out, were direct descendants of 'Amr b. 'Adī. The Lakhmids were employed by the Sassanians to patrol the desert regions (*bādiya*) of Iraq and to prevent the nomads from wreaking havoc on the townsmen. The Lakhmid kingdom lasted until Parvīz b. Hurmuz (Khusraw II) ordered that al-Nu'mān b. al-Mundhir be trampled to death by elephants, after which control of al-Ḥīra was transferred to unnamed "others."[80]

Only now does Ṭabarī tell his audience why the story of 'Amr b. 'Adī was so important to him: "[W]e wanted to connect the fulfill-

---

[79] al-Ṭabarī, *Ta'rīkh*, 1:627-8; *The History of al-Ṭabarī*, 4:149-150; cf. al-Mas'ūdī, *Murūj al-dhahab*, 2:223-5.

[80] al-Ṭabarī, *Ta'rīkh*, 1:627; *The History of al-Ṭabarī*, 4:150. See EI^2, s.v. "Lakhmids" (I. Shahid).

ment of history to the dominion (*mulk*) of the Persian emperors."[81] In this instance, the fulfillment of history was embodied in a connection between the pure Arab king ʿAmr b. ʿAdī and the Lakhmid king al-Nuʿmān b. al-Mundhir. The connection was genealogical. Drawing on information transmitted by Ibn Ḥumayd (d. 248/862),[82] Ṭabarī established that al-Nuʿmān III was not only a direct lineal descendant of Naṣr but also the great-great-grandson of ʿAmr b. ʿAdī. The last king of al-Ḥīra was al-Nuʿmān b. al-Mundhir b. al-Nuʿmān b. al-Mundhir b. ʿAmr b. ʿAdī b. Rabīʾa b. Naṣr. For the historian, this was a perfect fit. By linking a genealogical "fact" to an historical "fact," Ṭabarī showed how it was that the pure Arabs had taken power from the proto-Arabs in Iraq, thereby confirming the inner logic of history, itself a manifestation of divine will. The point of the story was etiological: to show how the present state of affairs had come to be. The function of the Muslim historian is not only to preserve the record of the past but also to re-present it in a way that makes it possible for the discerning and committed reader to identify its uncanny recurring patterns. Only the active and engaged reader who is prepared to pierce the smooth linguistic surface of the narrative has the potential to gain access to its underlying meaning. To facilitate this process, Ṭabarī staged a morality play that highlights the themes of infatuation, social inequality, female cunning, revenge, and gullibility.[83]

---

[81] Text: *fa-dhakarnā mā dhakarnā min amri Jadhīma wa-ʿAmr b. ʿAdī min ajli dhālika: idh kunnā nurīdu an nasūqa tamāma al-taʾrīkh ʿalā mulki mulūki Fāris* (al-Ṭabarī, *Taʾrīkh*, 1:628). Cp. Perlmann, who translates as follows: "Regarding this we discussed the story of Jadhīmah and ʿAmr b. ʿAdī. We did this as we wanted to continue the complete history of the Persian kings, and to confirm what has been told about them, insofar as we are able to do so" (*The History of al-Ṭabarī*, 4:149).

[82] Muḥammad b. Ḥumayd b. Ḥayyān al-Rāzī, a traditionist cited frequently by Ṭabarī, especially in the *isnād*: Ibn Ḥumayd—Salama—Ibn Isḥāq. See Ibn Ḥajar al-ʿAsqalānī, *Tahdhīb al-tahdhīb*, 12 vols. (Hayderabad: Dāʾirat al-Maʿārif al-Niẓāmīya, 1325-1327/1907-1909; reprinted Beirut: Dār Ṣādir, 1968), 9:127-31.

[83] al-Ṭabarī, *Taʾrīkh*, 1:628; *The History of al-Ṭabarī*, 4:150; cf. al-Masʿūdī, *Murūj al-dhahab*, 2:223-4; Ibn al-Athīr, *al-Kāmil fī al-Taʾrīkh*, 1:351; al-Nuwayrī, *Nihāyat al-arab*, 15:318. The historicity of ʿAmr b. ʿAdī is confirmed by an inscription found at Namāra written in the Arabic language but using the Nabataean script. The text mentions Imruʾl-qais the son of ʿAmr b. ʿAdī. The inscription is dated 328 CE, which presumably is the year in which Imruʾl-qais died. See Bowersock, *Roman Arabia*: 134.

The Art of Arab Storytelling

Beginning in the 4th century CE, the Zenobia of history was transformed into a legendary figure by the storytellers of Syria and Iraq. The Syro-Iraqi version of the legend may have been known to the Muslims of Arabia during the lifetime of the Prophet. But even if that was not the case, the legend was picked up in the aftermath of the Arab conquests, at which time Muslim storytellers revised the story and adapted it to a new and rapidly changing religio-historical environment. Although it is difficult to pinpoint the date on which one or another oral version of the legend was first recorded in writing, Ṭabarī's reliance on Ibn al-Kalbī (d. 204 or 206/819 or 821) suggests that a written text existed in the last quarter of the 2nd/8th century, if not before.

The literary cycle just examined is an example of the art of Arab storytelling. The storytellers' fascination with language manifests itself in naming patterns, puns, proverbs and other forms of linguistic ingenuity. By carefully selecting the names of the *dramatis personae*, the storytellers helped their audience to distinguish heroes from villains and positive figures from negative ones. Although the individuals in the legend are recognizable as historical figures, their names are typological. Each name signals the character and function of a figure: Jadhīma is the Luminous Leper and a *decisive man* (*rajul mijdhām*); Raqāsh is Snake; 'Amr is Life; Umm 'Amr is the Mother of Life; Qaṣīr is Shorty; and al-Zabbā' is the Woman with Much or Long Hair.

The fact that several characters in the narrative cycle share the same name is a literary device that supports the plot. For example, the fact that there are two Umm 'Amrs not only raises questions about 'Amr's identity but also facilitates the inverse relationship between Jadhīma's rebuke of Umm 'Amr (= Raqāsh) and 'Amr's rebuke of a figure with the same name who is the antithesis of the nurturing mother. Similarly, the fact that Jadhīma was directly or indirectly responsible for the deaths of two men named 'Amr suggests that the king was a target for an act of revenge. And the fact that Jadhīma appointed one man named 'Amr as his deputy and another man named 'Amr as the commander of his army points to his uncertainty about who should succeed him as king of Iraq.

Another literary device is the invocation of maxims and proverbs. After 'Amr b. 'Adī emerges from the wilderness—wild, haggard, dirty, and hungry, Umm ʿAmr says, "Give a slave a wing and he will take a whole arm." When Jadhīma is reunited with ʿAmr b. ʿAdī, the king does not recognize his beloved nephew until he is shown the necklace that he had given the boy years earlier, whereupon he exclaims, "ʿAmr has outgrown the necklace." Qaṣīr, the outwardly loyal but inwardly rebellious slave, is the source of two maxims—both intended as political advice: "You left prudence in Iraq" and "a minor occurrence in a major affair." Surely the most powerful—indeed, shocking and unforgettable—maxim is the statement uttered by al-Zabbāʾ after lifting her dress and exposing herself to Jadhīma: "Do you think this is the handiwork of a bride?" In addition to being the source of one maxim, al-Zabbāʾ is the object of another. When Qaṣīr advises ʿAmr b. ʿAdī that the time has come to exact vengeance for the murder of his uncle by al-Zabbāʾ, he responds that the queen is "more inaccessible than the eagle of the air." Qaṣīr too is the object of a maxim. His self-mutilation is memorialized in a verse of poetry attributed to al-Mutalammis, "It was for the sake of treachery that Qaṣīr cut off his nose." Finally, when the gate-keeper of Palmyra poked one of the men hidden in the camel sacks, causing him to expel gas, he exclaimed, in Nabatean, "There is mischief in these sacks." The maxims and proverbs point to the origin of the stories in folk literature.[84]

The complex relationship between social (in)equality, domestic politics and political legitimacy is a key theme in the narrative cycle. Is it conceivable that the son of a royal princess and a slave might succeed his maternal uncle as the king of Iraq? It is perhaps no surprise that the storytellers use the verb *ʿaṣā* (from the root *ʿ-ṣ-y*), to signify both *rebellion or disobedience*, on the one hand, and *the refusal of a marriage offer*, on the other. What is surprising is the juxtaposition of words derived from the root *ʿ-ṣ-y* with homonyms derived from the root *ʿ-ṣ-w*. Although ʿAmr aspired to succeed his uncle as king of Iraq, his hopes were dashed when he was captured by jinn and spirited off to the wilderness. When he emerged from the wilderness, he told the two men who discovered him, "You will see me tomorrow, among the clans of Numāra, having been denied the staff of royal authority" (*ghayr muʿaṣṣan*, a passive participle from

---

[84] See G. Ḥasan-Rokem, *Web of Life: Folklore and Midrash in Rabbinic Literature*, trans. from Hebrew by B. Stein (Stanford: University of California Press, 2000); cf. S. Niditch, *A Prelude to Biblical Folklore* (Urbana and Chicago: University of Illinois Press, 1987).

the root ʿ-ṣ-*w*). From the same root is derived the noun *al-ʿaṣā* which signifies *staff*, a symbol of royal authority. Al-ʿAṣā or the Staff was the name of the king's horse that was appropriated by the slave Qaṣīr, who literally rode the Staff to death. Over the spot where the horse died was erected a tower that came to be known as Burj al-ʿAṣā. It was from this very spot that Qaṣīr "went out" (*kharaja*), thereby signaling his rebelliousness. The juxtaposition of words derived from the root ʿ-ṣ-*y*, which signify *rebellion* and *disobedience*, and words derived from the root ʿ-ṣ-*w*, which signify *royal authority*, is another literary device.

A face-to-face encounter between two antagonists who engage in dialogue is another literary device. The resulting verbal exchange highlights the character of one or the other figure. A face-to-face encounter between ʿAdī b. Naṣr and Jadhīma exposes the king's irascibility and willingness to blame others—in this case ʿAdī—for his own deeds and actions; and a follow-up encounter between Raqāsh and Jadhīma exposes the king's gullibility and reluctance to take responsibility for the deeds and actions of others—in this case, Raqāsh. The king's gullibility would prove fatal. After Jadhīma had killed ʿAmr b. Ẓarib in battle, he received a marriage proposal from the dead man's daughter, the new Queen of Palmyra. Ignoring the good advice of his servant Qaṣīr, the king traveled to Palmyra. When Jadhīma came face-to face with al-Zabbāʾ, he naively assumed that she really wanted to unite their two kingdoms. In fact, al-Zabbāʾ was intent upon exacting revenge and exorcising her demons. She may not have accomplished the second objective, but she did accomplish the first. It was not long before the tables were turned. In a face-to-face encounter with Qaṣīr, the once wily queen who only recently had rejected a marriage alliance with Jadhīma now displayed her own gullibility by going to bed—figuratively—with the rebel slave, thereby setting in motion the sequence of events that would result in her murder—or was it suicide—or was it both?

The inversion of a motif is a favorite device of the storytellers. We have already seen how both Jadhīma and ʿAmr b. ʿAdī rebuked a woman named Umm ʿAmr. Another inversion relates to the motif of recognition. When ʿAmr b. ʿAdī was discovered by Mālik and ʿAqīl, the two Syrians recognized him as soon as they heard his name—and this despite the fact that he was naked, undernourished, sick, and dirty. But when the two Syrians brought the youth to Jadhīma, the king did not recognize his beloved nephew—and this despite the fact that he had bathed, shampooed his hair, cut his nails and donned fresh clothes (one might say about Jadhīma—as the rabbis said about his biblical counterpart Ahitophel—that he beheld but did not see). Indeed, Jadhīma still did not recognize the youth even after sending him to spend time with the real Umm ʿAmr. It was only after the Syrians produced the necklace worn by ʿAmr when he disappeared that Jadhīma was persuaded that the person standing before him was his beloved nephew and not an imposter. In another inversion of the same motif, al-Zabbāʾ was slain by ʿAmr b. ʿAdī after she recognized him on the basis of portraits drawn by an artist who had himself infiltrated ʿAmr's camp in disguise. The theme of recognition (*anagnorisis*) is an ancient literary device that was discussed already by Aristotle (d. 322 BCE) in his *Poetics*.[85]

In Arabo-Islamic literature the intoxicating effect of wine serves as a metaphor for human intemperateness and irrationality.[86] In the legend of al-Zabbāʾ two red liquids, blood and wine, serve as the fuel that drives the literary engine. It was the drunkenness of the guardians of the two Dayzans that facilitated Jadhīma's acquisition of ʿAdī b. Naṣr, who immediately was put in charge of the king's liquid refreshments. ʿAdī's position as overseer of the king's wine made it possible for Raqāsh to devise the scheme that resulted in the short-lived marriage between the royal princess and the slave. But the king was incorrigible. When Mālik and ʿAqīl recovered ʿAdī and brought him to Jadhīma, the king rewarded the men by making them his boon companions for life. And when the gullible Jadhīma fell into the trap that had been set for him by al-Zabbāʾ, the queen used one red liquid to pacify him before draining another red liquid from his body. Here, as elsewhere, the literary interface between wine and blood symbolizes the overlapping relationships between politics and violence, reason and anger, egoism and indulgence.[87]

Intertexts

Consciously or unconsciously, the Muslim storytellers who formulated and transmitted the Islamic version of the legend of al-Zabbāʾ

[85] Aristotle, *Poetics*, trans. S. Halliwell (Cambridge, Mass.: Harvard University Press, 1995), 83-7. This point is noted in Ḥasan-Rokem, *Web of Life*: 30.

[86] al-Hibri, *Reinterpreting Islamic Historiography*: 198.

[87] Ibid.: 197-8.

appropriated themes, structures, motifs, and language found in earlier narratives. Drawing upon a substantial corpus of pretexts, the storytellers produced a story that reflects specifically Islamic assumptions about truth, nature, reality, and history. The relationship between the Islamic narratives and their surrounding oral and textual environment resembles a dialogue between two or more persons. The process whereby earlier texts are re-cycled and re-presented is referred to by literary historians as *intertextuality*. I shall now attempt to expose the intertextual nature of the relationship between the legend of al-Zabbāʾ, on the one hand, and the story of ʿAdī b. Zayd and Hind, on the other. After making the case for literary interdependence, I shall analyze the intertextual relationship between both of these stories and yet other Islamic narratives—a process that in theory might continue indefinitely.[88]

1. *From ʿAdī b. Zayd to the Legend of al-Zabbāʾ*

The earliest reference to the legend of Zenobia in Arabic literature may be the *qaṣīda* attributed to ʿAdī b. Zayd, the accomplished Ḥīran diplomat, kingmaker and poet. At the beginning of this essay, I suggested that the narrative account of ʿAdī b. Zayd's marriage to Hind, as preserved by al-Iṣfahānī (d. 356/957), may be relevant to the legend of al-Zabbāʾ. Let us now attend to the parallels between the two narratives, beginning with the Ḥīran poet-diplomat.

One day ʿAdī b. Zayd—who was strikingly handsome, and Hind—who was strikingly beautiful (*min ajmal nisāʾ ahlihā wa-zamānihā*), found themselves in the same church. Unbeknownst to Hind, ʿAdī caught sight of the young beauty (*fa-raʾāhā ʿAdī wa-hiya ghāfilat*[un]) and immediately fell in love with her—even if he kept his true feelings a secret; one year later Hind caught sight of, and immediately fell in love with, ʿAdī. Hind's status as the daughter of the Lakhmid prince al-Nuʿmān III posed an obstacle to marriage, an obstacle that was overcome by means of female cunning—and a few glasses of red wine. One of Hind's servants, a woman named Māriya, was secretly

[88] On intertextuality, see J. Kristeva, *Desire in Language: A Semiotic Approach to Literature and Art* (New York: Columbia University Press, 1980); D. Boyarin, *Intertextuality and the Reading of Midrash* (Bloomington and Indianapolis: Indiana University Press, 1990); *Reading Between Texts: Intertextuality and the Hebrew Bible*, ed. D. Nolan Fewell (Louisville: Westminster/John Knox Press, 1992); M.E. Biddle, "Ancestral Motifs in 1 Samuel 25: Intertextuality and Characterization," *Journal of Biblical Literature*, 121:4 (2002): 617-38.

in love with ʿAdī. After persuading the handsome diplomat to satisfy her sexual desires, Māriya instructed him to invite al-Nuʿmān to a dinner party, ply him with wine, and then ask him for the hand of his daughter in marriage. The scheme worked and within three days the marriage had been consummated. Unwittingly, the prince had given his daughter in marriage to a commoner. Any misgivings that al-Nuʿmān may have had about his son-in-law were allayed when ʿAdī secured his father-in-law's accession to the throne of al-Ḥīra. Alas, one of the king's jealous brothers succeeded in driving a wedge between al-Nuʿmān and ʿAdī, with the result that the king imprisoned his son-in-law and arranged to have him murdered. Ironically, al-Nuʿmān took the dead man's son under his wing and promoted his career. But Zayd b. ʿAdī was determined to take revenge against al-Nuʿmān, even if the king was his maternal grandfather. Zayd bided his time until the opportunity arose and then devised a clever scheme that resulted in the Lakhmid king's falling out of favor with the Persian emperor, who ordered that his vassal be thrown in front of elephants and trampled to death. Mission accomplished.[89]

It was while ʿAdī b. Zayd was in prison that he composed his *qaṣīda* about the Queen of Palmyra, a poem that contributed to what would become the Islamic legend of al-Zabbāʾ. Let us compare the life story of ʿAdī b. Zayd with that of ʿAdī b. Naṣr: Both were handsome men, both served powerful masters, and both attracted the attention of a royal princess. In both cases a royal princess fell in love with a commoner or slave, but the gap in social status posed an obstacle to marriage. In both cases the obstacle was overcome by means of female cunning and the trick or stratagem involved the use of wine; in both cases an intoxicated marriage guardian unwittingly gave away his ward; in both cases the marriage was quickly consummated but lasted only long enough to produce a son; in both cases, the marriage drove a wedge between father-in-law and son-in-law, with fatal consequences for both; in both cases, these consequences gave rise to a desire for revenge; and in both cases the act of revenge resulted in the death of a king or queen. One might say that the two narratives are cut out of the same literary cloth. Both narratives draw upon a shared repertory of themes, motifs, structures, and rhetorical devices. Indeed, the more that one reflects on the two stories, the

[89] al-Iṣfahānī, *Kitāb al-Aghānī*, vol. 2, part 1: 107-9.

harder it becomes to distinguish one from the other. But there is more.

2. *From al-Zabbā' to Bilqīs*

One of the richest and best known stories in Near Eastern literature is the narrative account of a face-to-face encounter between King Solomon and the Queen of Sheba. Like Zenobia, the Queen of Sheba undergoes a radical transformation in the Arabo-Islamic literary tradition: Her name is changed and she morphs into a demonic figure.[90]

In brief, the story is as follows: After completing the construction of the Temple in Jerusalem, Solomon went on pilgrimage to the Sacred Precinct in Mecca, where he announced that Muḥammad was destined to appear as the Lord and Seal of Prophets, as purportedly attested in the Book of Psalms. One member of the king's retinue was a hoopoe bird (*hadhad*) who had a special talent for finding water. While the servants of the Israelite king were setting up camp in the Hijaz, the hoopoe flew to the Yemen, where he learned that the people of Sheba were ruled by a sun-worshipping queen. The excursion caused the hoopoe to be late in returning to Solomon. When the king threatened to kill the hoopoe for its tardiness, the bird saved its life by informing Solomon about the Queen of Sheba, as related in the Quran (27:22-3): "I found a woman ruling over them..."[91] This queen was herself the daughter of a king named al-Bashrakh,[92] who, in his time, controlled all of the chiefs of the Yemen, none of whom, he claimed, was equal to him in status. For this reason, he refused to marry the daughter of any of the Yemeni chiefs. The king's insistence on the principle of social equality between marriage partners posed a potentially fatal threat to dynastic continuity. The threat was averted by arranging for the king to marry a female *jinnī* named Rayḥāna bt. al-Shukr. The king and the *jinnī* had one child, a girl whose name was Bil'amah bt. Sharāḥīl b. Dhī

[90] On this transformation, see J. Lassner, *Demonizing the Queen of Sheba: Boundaries of Gender and Culture in Postbiblical Judaism and Medieval Islam* (Chicago and London: University of Chicago Press, 1993); *EI*², s.v. "Bilḳīs" (E. Ullendorff).

[91] al-Thaʿlabī, *Qiṣaṣ al-anbiyā' al-musammā ʿarā'is al-majālis* (Cairo: ʿĪsā al-Bābī al-Ḥalabī, ca. 1900): 277-8; trans. into English by W.M. Brinner as *Lives of the Prophets* (Leiden: Brill, 2002): 519-20.

[92] The king's nickname, al-Hadhdhād, has the same consonantal form as *hadhad* or hoopoe. More word-play.

Jadan b. al-Bashrakh b. al-Ḥārith b. Qays b. Ṣanʿāʾ b. Sabaʾ b. Yushjib b. Yaʿrib b. Qaḥṭān. Bil'amah's nickname was Bilqīs, perhaps from the Hebrew *pilegesh*, which means *concubine*—surely no compliment. If someone objects that a human being cannot co-habit with a *jinnī*, the reply is to invoke the following statement attributed to the Prophet Muḥammad, "One of Bilqīs' parents was a *jinnī*."[93]

The death of al-Bashrakh was followed by a succession contest that pitted a woman against a man. Bilqīs asked the people of the Yemen to swear the oath of allegiance to her. One group accepted her as queen, but another rejected her (*ʿaṣāhā*). The latter group chose a man and made him their king. As a result, the Yemen was now divided into two realms, with Bilqīs ruling over one region and her unnamed male counterpart over the other. The male king was an evil man who committed serious crimes, the most heinous of which was his engaging in sexual relations with the women of his realm against their will. Although the king's subjects wanted to depose him, they were powerless against him (*lam yaqdirū ʿalayhi*).[94] When his crimes came to the attention of Bilqīs, the horrified queen devised a scheme to eliminate the problem: she sent a message to the king offering herself to him. The gullible king responded that he himself would have initiated a marriage proposal but for his despair that the queen would reject his offer. To this Bilqīs responded, disingenuously, that if the king had initiated the proposal, she would not have refused him, for surely he was her equal (*kafʾ*). Because the queen's father was dead, the notables of the realm served as her marriage guardian. When the king summoned the notables and told them that he wanted to marry their queen, their initial response was negative. "We do not think that she will agree," they said. The king protested that it was the queen herself who had initiated the proposal. For this reason, he insisted, they should inform her of his offer and bear witness to her statement. The notables approached the queen seeking clarification of her true wishes and desires. She told them that she did indeed love "the boy," that she had not responded to him previously because initially she had been averse to the idea, but that she now desired him. So they married her to him (*fa-zawwajūhā minhu*).[95]

---

[93] al-Thaʿlabī, *Qiṣaṣ al-anbiyāʾ*, 278; *Lives of the Prophets*: 523.
[94] al-Thaʿlabī, *Qiṣaṣ al-anbiyāʾ*, 278; *Lives of the Prophets*: 523.
[95] al-Thaʿlabī, *Qiṣaṣ al-anbiyāʾ*, 278; *Lives of the Prophets*: 523-4.

The wedding celebration, a large, costly and spectacular affair, culminated when a vast retinue of servants and attendants carried Bilqīs to the man who thought that he was about to become her husband and co-ruler of a united kingdom. Before the marriage could be consummated, however, the queen pacified the groom by plying him with wine. When the red liquid had done its work, the queen took out a razor and decapitated the king, whose bloody head was discovered the next morning impaled on the gate of the palace. Only now did the notables understand that the proposal of a royal union had been a ruse (*makr wa-khadīʿa*) devised by Bilqīs to eliminate the wicked king. The subjects of the slain king, who were delighted at the outcome, now approached Bilqīs and expressed their readiness to accept her as their queen. Bilqīs, in turn, apologized for her murderous behavior, explaining that the king's abominable acts had compelled her to take drastic action. Thus it was that the divided Yemeni polity was reunited by a female queen. One of the first acts undertaken by Bilqīs upon assuming office was to order the construction of a magnificent palace, at the center of which was a magnificent throne, as attested by the Qur'ān (27:23): "... and she has a throne that is magnificent."[96]

The story of how Bilqīs slew her male counterpart serves as a prelude to a face-to-face encounter between the Queen of Sheba and Solomon. Following an exchange of letters between the sun-worshipping queen and the king who worshipped only one God, Bilqīs traveled to Jerusalem at the head of a caravan that included twelve thousand provincial rulers. Fearing that Solomon might marry Bilqīs and produce a son and heir, the satans at his court circulated a rumor that the queen's ankles were covered with unsightly hair and that her feet resembled the hooves of a mule. In an effort to determine the truth of the matter, the wise king devised a test. He ordered the construction of a floor covered with polished glass that had the appearance of shimmering water. When Bilqīs approached the floor, she mistook the glass for water and lifted her skirt, albeit only high enough to expose her beautiful—but indeed hairy—ankles. After further exchanges between the king and queen, Solomon invited Bilqīs to become a Muslim, and the former sun-worshipper converted to Islam. Some say that Solomon desired to marry Bilqīs but was repulsed by her hairy ankles. When the king's advisors informed him

---

[96] al-Thaʿlabī, *Qiṣaṣ al-anbiyāʾ*, 279; *Lives of the Prophets*: 525.

that the hair could be removed with a razor, Bilqīs protested, saying, "No blade has ever touched me." Solomon now pressed his advisors, who reluctantly acknowledged that it would be possible to concoct a special cream to remove the hair from the queen's legs. It was the invention of the depilatory that made it possible for Solomon to marry the Queen of Sheba. The rest is history. As would have been well-known to an Islamic audience, the Israelite kingdom was later defeated, first by the Babylonians and then by the Romans. Hence, the moral of the story, as confirmed by a prophetic *ḥadīth* that brings this section of the narrative to an end: "No people will be successful that is ruled by a woman."[97]

One might say that the legend of al-Zabbā' and the legend of Bilqīs are cut out of the same literary cloth. Both narratives draw upon a shared repertory of themes, motifs, plots, and rhetorical devices. In both cases, the daughter of a king succeeds her father as queen of the realm; in both cases the new queen builds a fortress or palace; in both cases the queen finds herself in an adversarial relationship with the king of an adjacent realm; in both cases, one adversary approaches the other riding at the head of a long caravan; in both cases, the queen uses cunning intelligence to eliminate her male adversary by making a disingenuous proposal of marriage and flattering her adversary with the assertion that he is her peer and equal; in both cases the gullible king responds favorably to the proposal; in both cases, the queen pacifies her adversary by plying him with wine; and in both cases the queen uses a razor to murder the king, either by draining the blood from his body or decapitating him. In both cases, the queen lifts her skirt and exposes hair on one or another part of her body—although here there is a crucial difference: Whereas al-Zabbā' lifts her skirt to her waist, exposing her long braided pubic hair, Bilqīs lifts her skirt only far enough to expose her hairy ankles and mule-like feet. Finally, in both cases, a kingdom ruled by a woman was eventually destroyed, thereby driving home the lesson that no polity will prosper that is ruled by a woman. Their differences notwithstanding, the two legends belong to a larger cycle of folk narratives. This larger narrative cycle included certain components of the

[97] al-Tha'labī, *Qiṣaṣ al-anbiyā'*, 279; *Lives of the Prophets*: 525; *EI*², s.v. "Bilḳīs" (E. Ullendorff). According to others, Solomon arranged for Bilqīs to marry one of the Tubbas of Hamdan.

biography of the Prophet Muḥammad. We turn now from the domain of legend to that of history.

3. *From al-Zabbā' and Bilqīs to Zaynab—or back to Zenobia?*

One of the Muslims who made the hijra to Medina in the year 1/622 was a beautiful woman named Zaynab, whose name is the Arabic equivalent of Zenobia. Zaynab's father was Jaḥsh (= *a young ass*—surely no compliment) and her mother was Umayma bt. ʿAbd al-Muṭṭalib. Through her mother, Zaynab was Muḥammad's paternal cross-cousin and a direct descendant of Ishmael and Abraham. On her father's side, she was the daughter of a donkey. *Nomen est omen.*

In Medina, Muḥammad arranged for Zaynab to marry his adopted son Zayd. Apart from Muḥammad, Zayd may be the most important—and least appreciated—figure in early Islamic history.[98] This is not the place to correct this oversight, but a few words about Zayd are in order. Islamic historical sources report that Zayd b. Ḥāritha al-Kalbī was born ca. 580 CE somewhere on the steppes between Syria and Iraq. When he was about twenty years old, Zayd was captured by Arab horsemen and taken to the Hijaz, where he was acquired by Khadīja bt. Khuwaylid. When Khadīja married Muḥammad b. ʿAbdallāh al-Qurashī, she gave the slave to her husband as a gift.[99] Meanwhile, back in Syria, Zayd's father was inconsolable. By a stroke of good fortune—or perhaps it was divine providence—Ḥāritha learned that Zayd was a slave living in the household of Muḥammad b. ʿAbdallāh al-Qurashī. Zayd's father traveled to Mecca in order to ransom his son from Muḥammad—who had not yet received his first revelation—and bring him back to Syria. Muḥammad responded to the ransom offer by devising a test: Zayd himself would choose whether to return to Syria with his father or remain in Mecca with his master. Of his own free will, Zayd chose slavery over freedom.

[98] To the best of my knowledge, the only modern scholar who has noted the importance of Zayd is K.Y. Blankinship. See his "Imārah, Khilāfah, and Imāmah: The Origin of the Succession to the Prophet Muhammad," in *Shiʿite Heritage: Essays on Classical and Modern Islam*, ed. L. Clarke (Binghamton, NY: Global Publications, 2001): 19-44.

[99] Ibn Saʿd, *Kitāb al-Ṭabaqāt al-kabīr*, ed. E. Sachau et al. (Leiden: E.J. Brill, 1905-21), III/i: 27; al-Balādhurī, *Ansāb al-ashrāf*, ed. M.Ḥ. Allāh (Cairo: Dār al-maʿārif, 1987), 1:467; *The History of al-Ṭabarī, vol. 39: Biographies of the Prophet's Companions and their Successors*, trans. Ella Landau-Tasseron (Albany: State University of New York Press): 6.

Muḥammad, he said, was both his mother and his father! It was only after Zayd had demonstrated his absolute loyalty to his master that Muḥammad took Zayd to the Kaʿba, where he adopted the youth in a formal ceremony. Mutual rights of inheritance were created between father and son. To mark the new filial relationship, Zayd's name was changed from Zayd b. Ḥāritha to Zayd b. Muḥammad. *Nomen est omen.*[100]

It was shortly after adopting Zayd that Muḥammad received his first revelation and emerged as a Messenger of God. Zayd was one of the first men—arguably the first—to embrace Islam. As a sign of affection, Muḥammad called him Ḥibb Rasūl Allāh or the Beloved of the Messenger of God. In Mecca, Zayd married Umm Ayman, an Abyssinian who had been Muḥammad's wet nurse. Ca. 612-14 Umm Ayman gave birth to a son named Usāma. As a sign of his affection, the Prophet called his grandson Ḥibb b. Ḥibb Rasūl Allāh or the Beloved Son of the Beloved of the Messenger of God. He is also said to have dressed his grandson in fine clothes and adorned him with beautiful jewelry.[101]

In Medina Zayd informed his father that he wanted to marry Zaynab bt. Jaḥsh, who, as noted, was the Prophet's paternal cross-cousin and a strikingly attractive woman. At first Muḥammad rejected the idea on the grounds of the social inequality between his adopted son, who was a former slave, and his cousin, who, on her mother's side, was of noble descent.[102] Undeterred, Zayd asked ʿAlī b. Abī Ṭālib to intercede on his behalf with the Prophet. "Surely," Zayd said, "he will not turn you down" (*lan yaʿṣiyaka*). ʿAlī went to see Muḥammad and, as Zayd had anticipated, the Prophet relented. Muḥammad now designated ʿAlī as his agent and sent him to the House of Jaḥsh to deliver the marriage proposal. Jaḥsh, however, was nowhere to be seen. Presumably he was dead. For this reason, Zaynab's brother ʿAbdallāh served as her marriage guardian. Both ʿAbdallāh and Zaynab objected vehemently to the marriage proposal. ʿAbdallāh refused to give his sister in marriage to a former slave; and

---

[100] Ibn Saʿd, *Kitāb al-Ṭabaqāt al-kabīr*, III/i: 27-9; al-Balādhurī, *Ansāb al-ashrāf*, 1:467-9; *The History of al-Ṭabarī*, 39:6-9.

[101] Ibn Saʿd, *Kitāb al-Ṭabaqāt al-kabīr*, III/i: 30-1; Ibn Saʿd, *al-Ṭabaqāt al-kubrā*, 8 vols. plus index (Beirut: Dār Ṣādir, 1377/1957), 4:61; al-Balādhurī, *Ansāb*, 1:469-71.

[102] On social equality as a prerequisite for marriage in Arabia, see M.M. Bravmann, "Equality of Birth of Husband and Wife (*kafāʾah*), an Early Arab Principle," in idem, *The Spiritual Background of Early Islam: Studies in Ancient Arab Concepts* (Leiden: E.J. Brill, 1972): 301-10.

Zaynab objected on the grounds of her great physical beauty. The stalemate was eliminated by divine intervention. ʿAlī informed ʿAbdallāh that the Prophet had *chosen* Zayd for Zaynab and that he had *ordered* ʿAbdallāh to give his sister in marriage to the Beloved of the Messenger of God. The consequences of such an order are spelled out in the Qur'ān (33:36): "When God and His messenger have decided a matter, it is not for any believing man or woman to have any choice in the affair. Whoever disobeys God and His Messenger has gone astray in manifest error." Faced with the *choice* of obeying or disobeying God and His Apostle, ʿAbdallāh and Zaynab had *no choice* but to obey. Reluctantly, Zaynab became Zayd's wife. Thus it was that Muḥammad's paternal cross-cousin became his daughter-in-law.[103]

Shortly after the marriage was consummated, Zayd began complaining to his father about his wife's behavior. Different versions of the circumstances in which the marriage would come to an end are preserved by the Qur'ān commentators. The first full version of the story is found in the *Tafsīr* of Muqātil b. Sulaymān (d. 150/767). The commentator relates that Muḥammad paid a visit to the couple with the intention of repairing the relationship. As it happened, only Zaynab was at home. Somehow—the details are unclear—the Prophet caught a glimpse of his daughter-in-law in the acting of standing up (*fa-abṣarat Zaynab qā'imat*[an]) and—presumably—with one or more parts of her body exposed. Muqātil waxes eloquent:

> She was beautiful and white of skin, one of the most perfect women of Quraysh (*min atamm nisā' Quraysh*). The Prophet—may God bless him and grant him peace—immediately fell in love with her (*hawiyahā*), and he exclaimed, "Praise be to God who changes the hearts [of men]."[104]

Ṭabarī reports that the entrance to Zayd's dwelling was covered with a curtain made of animal hair. By an act of nature, a sudden wind lifted the curtain and exposed Zaynab in her chamber, uncovered. Immediately, the Prophet's heart was filled with admiration for his daughter-in-law.[105] In a variant preserved by Qurṭubī, an act of nature becomes an act of God: "God sent a wind that lifted up the

---

[103] Muqātil b. Sulaymān, *Tafsīr*, ed. A. Farīd, 3 vols. (Beirut: Dār al-kutub al-ʿilmīya, 1424/2003), 3:46-7.

[104] Muqātil, *Tafsīr*, 3:47, ll: 20-3.

[105] al-Ṭabarī, *Jāmiʿ al-bayān ʿan ta'wīl āy al-qur'ān*, 30 vols. in 12 (2nd ed. Cairo: Muṣṭafā al-Bābī al-Ḥalabī, 1373/1954), 22:13, ll. 9-12. Text: *fa-rafaʿat al-rīḥ al-sitr fa-inkashafa wa-hiya fī ḥujratihā ḥāsirat*[an].

curtain to reveal Zaynab wearing a single apron in her quarters. When the Prophet saw Zaynab, she sank into his heart." Dumbstruck, Muḥammad retreated from this arresting vision; the only words that he could utter were, "Praise be to God who changes the hearts [of men]."[106] Later that day, Zaynab told Zayd about the strange encounter with her father-in-law. Relations between husband and wife went from bad to worse. According to Zaynab, her husband suffered from a sexual dysfunction (*lam yastaṭiʿnī wa-lā yaqdiru ʿalayya*). Be that as it may, the couple ceased having sexual relations—a key narrative detail.[107]

In a curious reversal, the man who had begged his father for permission to marry Zaynab now pleaded with him for permission to divorce her. A highly compressed version of what happened next is found in the Qurʾān. Although Muḥammad was in love with Zaynab, he understood that her status as his daughter-in-law meant that he could not marry her. Fearing public outrage if he did, the Prophet kept his love for the woman a secret and told Zayd to "keep your wife to yourself and fear God." Just as the social obstacle to the earlier marriage was removed by divine intervention (Q. 33:36), so the legal obstacle to the upcoming marriage was removed by divine intervention. As indicated in the Qurʾān (33:37), God first rebuked Muḥammad for placing his fear of men over that of God but then gave the Prophet permission to marry Zaynab—albeit on two conditions: First, it had to be established that Zayd had satisfied his sexual desire for Zaynab (*qaḍā Zayd*^{un} *minhā waṭar*^{an}); second—and more important—Muḥammad had to renounce Zayd as his adopted son.[108] The first condition, as we have seen, had already been satisfied, and Zayd therefore proceeded to divorce Zaynab. As for the second condition, it must have been during the short interval between Zayd's divorcing Zaynab and Muḥammad's marrying her that the Prophet *repudiated* Zayd as his son by uttering the formula, "I am not your father," thereby dissolving the filial relationship that had been created approximately two decades earlier. Zayd accepted the demotion in

[106] al-Qurṭubī, *al-Jāmiʿ li-aḥkām al-qurʾān*, 20 vols. (Cairo: Dār al-kutub al-miṣrīya, 1387/1967), 14:190, ll. 5-6. Text: *Inna allāha baʿatha rīḥ*^{an} *fa-rafaʿat al-sitr wa-Zaynab mutafaḍḍila fī manzilatihā.*

[107] al-Qurṭubī, *al-Jāmiʿ*, 14:189.

[108] As indicated by Q. 33:4-5, which specify, *inter alia*, that God has not "made your adopted sons your [real] sons... [so] call them by the names of their [true] fathers."

status without complaint. "O Messenger of God," he said, "I am Zayd b. Ḥāritha and my genealogy is well known." It was only after Zayd had forfeited the right to call himself Zayd b. Muḥammad and had been stripped of his status as Muḥammad's son and legal heir that God authorized the union between Muḥammad and Zaynab, as indicated in the Qur'ān (33:37): "We gave her to you in marriage" (*zawwajnākahā*). A marriage made in Heaven.[109]

Zayd may have been repudiated, but he retained the confidence of the Prophet, who appointed him as the commander of six military expeditions in the year 6 AH alone. Zayd's credentials as the first male Muslim, the Beloved of the Messenger of God, and a brave military commander suggest that he may have had political ambitions of his own. If he did, those ambitions were dashed by his demotion from adopted son to client (*mawlā*). If that were not sufficient, Zayd predeceased Muḥammad, thereby making his political ambitions a moot point. The circumstances of Zayd's death were as follows: In the year 8/629, a messenger dispatched by the Prophet to the king of Buṣra was captured, incarcerated, and beheaded by a Ghassānid tribesman. Seeking to avenge the brutal murder of his messenger, Muḥammad assembled an army of 3000 Muslims commanded by Zayd. The Muslim forces marched off to southern Jordan, where they learned that between 100,000 and 200,000 Byzantine soldiers were waiting for them. It was a suicide mission, but Zayd pressed forward, riding a horse named Sabḥa—also the name of a horse belonging to Muḥammad and thus a symbol of prophetic authority. The battle was engaged at or near the village of Mu'ta, a word that conjures up notions of *death*, *madness*, *insanity*, and *diabolical obsession*. Zayd was the first to fall. Thus it was that the first man to become a Muslim became the first Muslim to die as a martyr fighting against non-Arabs on foreign soil. A statement attributed to 'Ā'isha suggests that if Zayd had outlived Muḥammad, he would have succeeded him as caliph: "Had [Zayd] outlived [the Prophet], he would have made him his successor" (*wa-law baqiya ba'dahu istakhlafahu*).[110] Be that as it may, the Prophet is said to have grieved for Zayd until the day he died. Indeed, only a few days before he died Muḥammad appointed Usāma b. Zayd as the commander of a

[109] Muqātil, *Tafsīr*, 3:47-9.

[110] Ibn Sa'd, *Kitāb al-Ṭabaqāt al-kabīr*, III/i: 31, ll. 9-13; note the variant in al-Balādhurī, *Ansāb*, 1:472 (bottom): *wa-in baqiya ba'dahu istakhlafahu 'alā al-madīna*.

military expedition sent to southern Syria. Just as the goal of the earlier military mission was to exact revenge for the death of the Prophet's messenger, so too the goal of this military mission was revenge. Muḥammad instructed Usāma that the Muslim forces were *not* to summon the infidels to Islam and that they were to burn and lay waste to whoever and whatever they encountered. Riding Sabḥa—the very horse ridden by Zayd on the day that he was martyred—Usāma set out (*kharaja*) for southern Syria. The Muslims killed many men and seized large amounts of booty. Remarkably—or perhaps it was an act of divine providence—not a single Muslim soldier was killed, and Usāma succeeded in killing the man who had slain Zayd. Mission accomplished.[111]

The cluster of episodes that has just been summarized forms part of the biography of the Prophet. This cluster includes Zayd's capture and adoption, his marriage to Zaynab, the breakdown of relations between husband and wife, the encounter between the Prophet and his daughter-in-law, Zayd's divorce of Zaynab, Muḥammad's repudiation of Zayd, the Prophet's marriage to Zaynab, the martyrdom of Zayd, and Usāma's retaliation against the man who killed his father. Viewed from a literary perspective, these episodes bear a striking resemblance to the narratives examined earlier in this essay. Let us now attend to the parallels. For convenience, I divide the Islamic episode into two parts: (1) Zaynab's marriage to Zayd; and (2) Zaynab's marriage to Muḥammad.

Zayd b. Ḥāritha was a man of common origins who rose to a position of influence with a man who was about to emerge as a prophet (just as ʿAdī b. Zayd and ʿAmr b. ʿAdī b. Naṣr were men of common origins who rose to a position of influence with a powerful king). As a reward for his loyalty, Muḥammad adopted Zayd as his son and heir (just as Jadhīma treated ʿAmr b. ʿAdī as his surrogate son and heir-apparent). In Medina, Zayd determined to marry the Prophet's paternal cross-cousin Zaynab, but the difference in social status posed an obstacle to the marriage. Muḥammad feared that Zaynab and/or her marriage guardian would reject the proposal (just as Hind feared that her father would reject a marriage proposal from ʿAdī b. Zayd; just as Raqāsh feared that her brother would reject a marriage proposal from ʿAdī b. Naṣr; and just as the king of the Yemen feared

[111] al-Wāqidī, *Kitāb al-maghāzī*, ed. M. Jones, 3 vols. (London: Oxford University Press, 1966), 3:1117-27.

that Bilqīs would reject a marriage proposal initiated by him). The Prophet's objection to Zayd's request to marry Zaynab was overcome with the assistance of ʿAlī b. Abī Ṭālib (just as al-Nuʿmān's anticipated objection to ʿAdī b. Zayd's request to marry Hind was overcome with the assistance of Māriya; and just as the Yemeni chiefs' objection to the unnamed Yemeni king's request to marry Bilqīs was overcome by Bilqīs herself). Because Zaynab's father was dead, her brother ʿAbdallāh served as her marriage guardian (just as Jadhīma served as the marriage guardian of his sister Raqāsh; and just as the Yemeni chiefs served as Bilqīs' marriage guardian). When ʿAbdallāh and Zaynab rejected the proposal, their opposition was overcome by a combination of prophetic and divine intervention—in an Islamic context, *métis* and wine would have been inappropriate. After learning that the Prophet had selected Zayd for Zaynab, brother and sister had no choice but to obey (just as Raqāsh protested that she had no choice but to accept her brother's decision that she marry ʿAdī b. Naṣr). The marriage between Zayd and Zaynab (like the marriages between Hind and ʿAdī b. Zayd and between Raqāsh and ʿAmr) was short-lived, but (unlike those two marriages), it produced no offspring. Zayd's marriage to Zaynab was terminated by the intervention of God and the Prophet—who was Zayd's father (just as Hind's marriage to ʿAdī b. Zayd was terminated by her father, the King of al-Ḥīra; and just as Raqāsh's marriage to ʿAdī b. Naṣr was terminated by her brother, the King of Iraq). The divorce was accompanied by Muḥammad's repudiation of Zayd (similar albeit not identical to Jadhīma's passing over ʿAmr as his successor). The repudiation resulted in a name change and loss of inheritance rights. Had it not been for the repudiation, Zayd would have been the prime candidate to succeed Muḥammad as the first caliph (just as ʿAmr aspired to succeed Jadhīma as King of Iraq). The demotion from son to client struck a severe blow to Zayd's political ambitions. If that were not sufficient, the Prophet sent his former son to certain death in southern Jordan. Zayd's death triggered the desire for revenge—but against whom? Had the story been told by a non-Muslim, one might have expected Usāma to retaliate against the man who had sent his father on a suicide mission. In an Islamic context, a different scenario was required. Nothing would have been more inappropriate than for Usāma to retaliate against Muḥammad, even if the Prophet was indirectly responsible for Zayd's death. The Prophet may have sent Zayd to certain death, but it was a Byzantine soldier who killed him. Before he died, the last act undertaken by Muḥammad was to appoint Usāma as the commander of a military expedition whose goal was to exact revenge for Zayd's death. Although the expedition was interrupted by the Prophet's death, following the funeral Usāma led his forces into southern Syria, riding a horse named Sabḥa—a symbol of prophetic authority (just as Qaṣīr rode "the Staff," a symbol of royal authority). Usāma went out (*kharaja*) from Medina (just as Qaṣīr went out from Burj al-ʿAṣā or the Tower of Royal Authority). Usāma's *khurūj* was an act of obedience (whereas Qaṣīr's *khurūj* was an act of rebellion). Usāma succeeded in killing the Byzantine solider who had killed his father (just as Zayd b. ʿAdī succeeded in bringing about the murder of the king who had killed his father; and just as ʿAmr b. ʿAdī succeeded in killing al-Zabbāʾ).

Let us now turn to the marriage between Zaynab and Muḥammad. Zaynab was one of the most beautiful women of Quraysh (just as Hind was one of the most beautiful women of Lakhm). Muḥammad fell in love with Zaynab after he inadvertently caught sight of her in a state of dishabille (just as ʿAdī b. Zayd fell in love with Hind after catching a glimpse of her in a church; and just as Raqāsh fell in love with ʿAdī b. Naṣr after catching a glimpse of him at an unspecified location). The visual encounter that resulted in Muḥammad's falling in love with Zaynab was facilitated by an act of nature or divine intervention: a strong wind lifted a curtain that gave Muḥammad a glimpse of Zaynab wearing only a thin dress. By contrast, al-Zabbāʾ intentionally lifted her dress to her waist; and Bilqīs was tricked into lifting her dress, albeit only high enough to expose her hairy ankles. Unlike al-Zabbāʾ and Bilqīs, who are both portrayed as demons, no agency is attributed to Zaynab who, on balance, is a positive character. In Zaynab's case, the uplifted curtain draws attention to an inadvertent and unintended violation of the norms of female modesty and gender separation; in the other two cases the uplifted skirt is associated with a woman who has inverted the social and political order by occupying an office customarily associated with men. In all three cases the lifting of a curtain or skirt draws attention to long hair and female sexuality: The curtain that covered the entrance to Zaynab's apartment was made of animal hair (surely a sexual metaphor); al-Zabbāʾ had braided her long pubic hairs; and Bilqīs' ankles were hairy (a displacement of the hair from the genital region to the feet). The mere sight of Zaynab caused Muḥammad to fall in love with her. The Prophet was struck dumb by Zaynab's physical beauty (just as Hind was struck dumb by 'Adī b. Zayd's physical beauty). Muḥammad kept his feelings for Zaynab a secret for some time, fearing public reaction (just as 'Adī b. Zayd kept his feelings for Hind a secret for a year). Apparently, Arabian provincial law prohibited a marriage between a man and his daughter-in-law, but the legal obstacle was overcome through divine intervention (rather than *métis* or wine). However, Muḥammad could not marry Zaynab until it had been established that Zayd had satisfied his sexual desire for his wife (just as 'Adī b. Zayd could not marry Hind until he had satisfied Māriya's sexual desire for him). Finally, it was God himself who gave Zaynab to the Prophet in marriage (*zawwajnākahā*)—just as it was the Yemeni chiefs who gave Bilqīs to the unnamed king of Yemen in marriage (*zawwajūhā minhu*).

The number, cumulative weight and density of these parallels point to a shared literary repertoire and, perhaps, literary dependence.[112] The literary devices employed by the Muslim storytellers have a long and distinguished genealogy. As noted earlier, the theme of recognition (*anagnorisis*) can be traced back to the writings of Aristotle in the 4th century BCE; and the men-inside-the-camelsacks ruse can be traced back to the *Aeneid* of Virgil at the beginning of the 1st century CE. Similarly, the motif of the lifted skirt (*anasyrma*) appears in hymns attributed to Orpheus (ca. 6th century BCE) and in the writings of Herodotus (d. ca. 425 BCE), Diodorus Siculus (d. 30 BCE), Hyginus (d. 17 CE), and Plutarch (d. 127 CE).[113] Other themes are biblical. For example, Zaynab, the beautiful wife of Muḥammad, brings to mind Sarah, the beautiful wife of Abraham, Rebecca, the beautiful wife of Isaac, Rachel, the beautiful wife of Jacob, and Bathsheba, the beautiful wife of David. Muḥammad's repudiation of Zayd brings to mind Abraham's expulsion of Ishmael.[114]

---

[112] See again Biddle, "Ancestral Motifs".

[113] H. King, "Agnodike and the profession of medicine," *Proceedings of the Cambridge Philological Society*, no. 212 (n.s. no. 32), 1986: 53-77; M. Marcovich, "Demeter, Baubo, Iacchus, and a Redactor," *Vigiliae Christianae*, 40 (1986): 294-301. The brazen gesture reappears in Machiavelli. See J.L. Hairston, "Skirting the Issue: Machiavelli's Caterina Sforza," *Renaissance Quarterly*, 53:3 (2000): 687-712. I am grateful to my colleague J. Najemy for guiding me to these sources.

[114] So too the story of 'Amr b. 'Adī b. Naṣr. Like Ishmael, 'Amr was the product of a "mixed" marriage between a prominent free man and a slave concubine. Like Ishmael, 'Amr went out into the wilderness, where he had a near-death experience. Like Ishmael, 'Amr was passed over in favor of others. Like Ishmael, 'Amr overcame adversity to become a great tribal leader.

The Prophet's willingness to "sacrifice" the Beloved of the Messenger of God brings to mind Abraham's willingness to sacrifice his favored son Isaac. Viewed from a different vantage point, Muḥammad's decision to appoint Zayd—Zaynab's former husband—as commander of a military expedition sent on a suicide mission to southern Jordan brings to mind David's instruction to place Uriah the Hittite in the front lines of the Israelite forces in southern Jordan: Zayd fell in battle at Mu'ta, only 30 km. or so from the spot where Uriah fell in battle outside the walls of Rabbat Ammon. Still other themes are universal folk motifs: reversal of fortune, testing of the beloved son, tragic love, social inequality between lovers, and love triangles. One such theme that shows up in the stories we have examined is the connection between vision and infatuation. Just as the Prophet fell in love with Zaynab after catching a glimpse of her standing (*fa-abṣarat Zaynab qā'imat*[an]),[115] so too 'Adī b. Zayd fell in love with Hind after catching a glimpse of her while she was unaware of his presence (*fa-ra'āhā 'Adī wa-hiya ghāfilat*[un]). Similarly, King David fell in love with Bathsheba after catching a glimpse of her bathing (*va-yar ishah roḥetset*; II Sam. 11:2).

The cluster of episodes associated with Zaynab's marriage to Zayd, on the one hand, and her marriage to Muḥammad, on the other, are treated as history not only by Muslims but also by many—if not most—western scholars.[116] The earliest written texts in which these episodes are preserved were produced in the middle of the 2nd/8th century. The evidence of the *isnād*s attached to these narratives takes us back to the last quarter of the 1st/7th century. During the approximately fifty that separate the first reported transmission of these events from the events themselves, the narratives circulated as oral

[115] Cp. the language used to describe al-Zabbā''s catching sight of 'Amr b. 'Adī standing in front of the entrance to the secret tunnel: *abṣarat 'Amr*[an] *qā'im*[an]. In this instance, the visual encounter did not lead to infatuation.

[116] See, for example, T. Andrae, *Mohammed: The Man and His Faith*, trans. Th. Menzel (New York: Charles Scribner's Sons, 1936; reprinted Harper and Row, 1955); W.M. Watt, *Muhammad at Medina* (Oxford: at the Clarendon Press, 1956); F. Gabrieli, *Muhammad and the Conquests of Islam*, trans. V. Luling and R. Linell (New York: McGraw-Hill, 1968); M. Rodinson, *Mohammed* (New York: Random House, 1974); M.Ḥ. Haykal, *The Life of Muḥammad*, trans. from 8th ed. by I.R. al Fārūqī (n.p.: North American Trust Publications, 1976); M. Lings, *Muhammad: his life based on the earliest sources* (Cambridge: The Islamic Texts Society, 1983); F.E. Peters, *Muhammad and the Origins of Islam* (Albany: State University of New York Press, 1994); K. Armstrong, *Muhammad: A Biography of the Prophet* (San Francisco: Harper, 1992).

traditions. It is certainly possible that these events are historical and that they unfolded more or less in the manner portrayed in Islamic sources: Zayd was captured and enslaved, and he did choose slavery with his master over freedom with his family; Muḥammad did adopt Zayd as his son; Zaynab was a strikingly beautiful woman; God—or mother nature—did send a strong wind that lifted the curtain covering the entrance to Zaynab's apartment; Muḥammad did catch a glimpse of his daughter-in-law wearing a thin dress and immediately fell in love with her; Zayd did divorce his wife so that his father could marry her; the Prophet did repudiate Zayd and send him to certain death at Mu'ta; and Usāma did exact revenge for his father's death. Alternatively, it is possible—and in my view likely—that these "events" are literary fictions formulated by Muslims over the course of the 1st and 2nd centuries AH. To produce these new Islamic narratives, the Muslims appropriated and modified earlier plots, themes, motifs, *topoi*, language, and rhetorical structures. The particular shape taken by the new Islamic narratives was driven by the demands of theology, first and foremost, the imperative to establish Muḥammad's credentials as *khātam al-nabīyīn* or the Seal of Prophets. To fully support this assertion, it will be necessary to identify and analyze the theological, political, legal, cultural and social factors that lie behind the Islamic narratives.[117]

Bibliography

Primary Sources

Aristotle. *Poetics*, translated by Stephen Halliwell. Cambridge, Mass.: Harvard University Press, 1995.

BT = *Babylonian Talmud*

al-Balādhurī. *Ansāb al-ashrāf*, edited by Muḥammad Ḥamīd Allāh. Cairo: Dār al-maʿārif, 1987.

Dīwān ʿAdī b. Zayd al-ʿIbādī, edited by Muḥammad Ḥabbār al-Muʿība. Baghdad: Shirkat Dār al-Jumhūrīya li'l-nashr wa'l-ṭabʿ, 1965.

Ibn al-Athīr. *al-Kāmil fī al-Ta'rīkh*. 13 vols. Beirut: Dār Bayrūt, 1992.

Ibn Saʿd, *Kitāb al-Ṭabaqāt al-kabīr*, edited by E. Sachau et al. Leiden: E.J. Brill, 1905-21.

——. *al-Ṭabaqāt al-kubrā*, 8 vols. plus index. Beirut: Dār Ṣādir, 1377/1957.

al-Iṣfahānī, Abū al-Faraj. *Kitāb al-Aghānī*. 25 vols. Beirut: Dār al-thaqāfa, 1955.

[117] See now D.S. Powers, *Muḥammad is not the Father of any of your Men: The Making of the Last Prophet* (Philidelphia: University of Pennsylvania Press, 2009).

Jāḥiẓ. *al-Burṣān wa'l-'urjān wa'l-'umyān wa'l-ḥūlān*, edited by Muḥammad Mursī al-Khūlī. Cairo: Dār i'tiṣām li'l-ṭab' wa'l-nashr, 1972.
al-Mas'ūdī. *Murūj al-dhahab wa-ma'ādin al-jawhar*, edited by Charles Pellat. 4 vols. Beirut: Dār al-Andalus, 1965-6.
Muqātil b. Sulaymān. *Tafsīr*, edited by Aḥmad Farīd. 3 vols. Beirut: Dār al-kutub al-'Ilmīya, 1424/2003.
al-Nuwayrī. *Nihāyat al-arab fī funūn al-adab*. 33 vols. Cairo: al-Mu'assasa al-Miṣrīya al-'āmma li'l-ta'līf wa'l-tarjama, 1964.
al-Qurṭubī. *al-Jāmi' li-aḥkām al-qur'ān*. 20 vols. Cairo: Dār al-kutub al-miṣrīya, 1387/1967.
al-Tha'labī. *Qiṣaṣ al-anbiyā' al-musammā 'arā'is al-majālis*. Cairo: 'Īsā al-Bābī al-Ḥalabī, ca. 1900. Translated into English by William M. Brinner as *Lives of the Prophets*. Leiden: E. J. Brill, 2002.
al-Ṭabarī. *Jāmi' al-bayān 'an ta'wīl āy al-qur'ān*. 30 vols. in 12. 2nd ed. Cairo: Muṣṭafā al-Bābī al-Ḥalabī, 1373/1954.
——. *Ta'rīkh al-rusul wa'l-mulūk*, edited by Muḥammad Abū al-Faḍl Ibrāhīm. 11 vols. 4th ed. Cairo: Dār al-ma'ārif, 1960-77.
——. *The History of al-Ṭabarī, vol. iv. The Ancient Kingdoms*. Translated by Moshe Perlmann. Albany: State University of New York Press, 1987.
——. *The History of al-Ṭabarī, vol. xxxix: Biographies of the Prophet's Companions and their Successors*. Translated by Ella Landau-Tasseron. Albany: State University of New York Press.
al-Wāqidī. *Kitāb al-maghāzī*, edited by Marsden Jones. 3 vols. London: Oxford University Press, 1966.

Secondary Sources

Abbott, N. "Pre-Islamic Arab Queens." *The American Journal of Semitic Languages and Literatures*, 58:1 (1941), 1-22.
Andrae, T. *Mohammed: The Man and His Faith*. Translated by Theophil Menzel. New York: Charles Scribner's Sons, 1936; reprinted Harper and Row, 1955.
Armstrong, K. *Muḥammad: A Biography of the Prophet*. San Francisco: Harper, 1992.
Biddle, M.E. "Ancestral Motifs in 1 Samuel 25: Intertextuality and Characterization." *Journal of Biblical Literature*, 121:4 (2002), 617-38.
Blankinship, K.Y. "Imārah, Khilāfah, and Imāmah: The Origin of the Succession to the Prophet Muḥammad." In *Shi'ite Heritage: Essays on Classical and Modern Islam*, edited by L. Clarke, 19-44. Binghamton, NY: Global Publications, 2001.
Bowersock, G. *Roman Arabia*. Cambridge and London: Harvard University Press, 1983.
Boyarin, D. *Intertextuality and the Reading of Midrash*. Bloomington and Indianapolis: Indiana University Press, 1990.
Bravmann, M.M. "Equality of Birth of Husband and Wife (*kafā'ah*), an Early Arab Principle." In idem, *The Spiritual Background of Early Islam: Studies in Ancient Arab Concepts*, 301-10. Leiden: E. J. Brill, 1972.
Detienne, M. and Vernant, J-P. (eds.). *Cunning Intelligence in Greek Culture and Society*, translated by Janet Lloyd. Atlantic Highlands, NJ: Humanities Press, ca. 1978.
Dols, M.W. "The Leper in Medieval Islamic Society." *Speculum*, 58:4 (1983), 891-916.

EI^2 = *Encyclopaedia of Islam*, second edition, I-XII. Leiden: E.J. Brill, 1960-2007. S. vv. "'Adī b. Zayd" (F. Gabrieli); "Bilḳīs" (E. Ullendorff); "Djadhīma al-Abrash or al-Waḍḍāḥ" (I. Kawar); "al-Kalbī" (W. Atallah); "Lakhmids" (Irfan Shahid); "al-Mughīra b. Shu'ba" (H. Lammens); "al-Mundhir IV" (Irfan Shahid); "Musta'riba" (Ilse Lichtenstädter); "Muta'arriba" (Ilse Lichtenstädter); "al-Mutalammis" (Ch. Pellat); "al-Nu'mān (III) b. al-Mundhir" (Irfan Shahid); "Zaynab bt. Jaḥsh" (C.E. Bosworth); "Zaynab bt. Khuzayma" (C.E. Bosworth); "Zaynab bt. Muḥammad" (V. Vacca).

Fewell, D.N. (ed.). *Reading Between Texts: Intertextuality and the Hebrew Bible.* Louisville: Westminster/John Knox Press, 1992.

Gabrieli, F. *Muḥammad and the Conquests of Islam*, translated by Virginia Luling and Rosamund Linell. New York: McGraw-Hill, 1968.

Hairston, J.L. "Skirting the Issue: Machiavelli's Caterina Sforza." *Renaissance Quarterly*, 53:3 (2000), 687-712.

Ḥasan-Rokem, G. *Web of Life: Folklore and Midrash in Rabbinic Literature*, translated from Hebrew by Batya Stein. Stanford: University of California Press, 2000.

Haykal, M.Ḥ. *The Life of Muḥammad.* Translated from 8th edition by Isma'īl Rāgī al Fārūqī. N.p.: North American Trust Publications, 1976.

al-Hibri, T. *Reinterpreting Islamic Historiography.* Cambridge: Cambridge University Press, 1999.

King, H. "Agnodike and the profession of medicine." *Proceedings of the Cambridge Philological Society*, no. 212 (n.s. no. 32), (1986): 53-77.

Kristeva, J. *Desire in Language: A Semiotic Approach to Literature and Art.* New York: Columbia University Press, 1980.

Lane, E.W. *An Arabic-English Lexicon*, 8 parts. London and Edinburgh: Williams and Norgate, 1863-93; reprinted 1984, The Islamic Texts Society.

Lassner, J. *Islamic Revolution and Historical Memory*, AOS 66. New Haven: American Oriental Society, 1986.

——. *Demonizing the Queen of Sheba: Boundaries of Gender and Culture in Postbiblical Judaism and Medieval Islam.* Chicago and London: University of Chicago Press, 1993.

Leder, S. "al-Madā'inī's Version of *Qiṣṣat al-Shūra*: The Paradigmatic Character of Historical Narration." In *Ideas, Images, and Methods of Portrayal: Insights into Classical Arabic Literature and Islam*, edited by Sebastian Günther, 379-98. Leiden: E.J. Brill, 2005.

Lings, M. *Muḥammad: his life based on the earliest sources.* Cambridge: The Islamic Texts Society, 1983.

Marcovich, M. "Demeter, Baubo, Iacchus, and a Redactor." *Vigiliae Christianae*, 40 (1986), 294-301.

Nicholson, R.A. *A Literary History of the Arabs.* Cambridge: Cambridge University Press, 1909.

Niditch, S. *A Prelude to Biblical Folklore.* Urbana and Chicago: University of Illinois Press, 1987.

Noth, A. "Quellenkritische Studien zu Themen, Formen und Tendenzen frühislamischer Geschichtsüberlieferung, I. Themen und Formen." Ph.D. thesis, University of Bonn, 1973. Translated into English by Michael Bonner as *The Early Arabic Historical Tradition: A Source-Critical Study.* 2nd ed., Princeton, NJ: Darwin Press, 1994.

Peters, F.E. *Muḥammad and the Origins of Islam.* Albany, NY: State University of New York Press, 1994.

Powers, D.S. *Muḥammad is not the Father of any of your Men: The Making of the Last Prophet* (Philidelphia: University of Pennsylvania Press, 2009).
Rodinson, M. *Mohammed.* New York: Random House, 1974.
Silverstein, A.J. *Postal Systems in the pre-modern Islamic World*, Cambridge Studies in Islamic Civilization. Cambridge: Cambridge University Press, 2007.
Stoneman, R. *Palmyra and its Empire: Zenobia's Revolt against Rome.* Ann Arbor, MI: The University of Michigan Press, 1992.
Wansbrough, J. *The Sectarian Milieu: Content and Composition of Islamic Salvation History.* Oxford and New York: Oxford University Press, 1978.
Watt, W.M. *Muḥammad at Medina.* Oxford: at the Clarendon Press, 1956.
Westbrook, R. (ed.). *A History of Ancient Near Eastern law*, 2 vols. Leiden and Boston: E. J. Brill, 2003.

THE VIEW FROM THE SOUTH: THE MAPS OF THE *BOOK OF CURIOSITIES* AND THE COMMERCIAL REVOLUTION OF THE ELEVENTH CENTURY

Yossef Rapoport[1]

In January 2000, A. L. Udovitch gave a guest lecture in the Mortimer and Raymond Sackler Institute of Advanced Studies in Tel Aviv University, speaking on "North and South in the Medieval Mediterranean World: The View from the South." The talk was a dialogue of sorts with the central thesis of his own teacher and mentor at Yale, Robert Lopez, who famously coined the term 'commercial revolution' in order to describe the changes taking place in Europe beginning in the mid-tenth century. Unlike Lopez, however, Udovitch argued that the expansion in international commerce along the coasts of the Mediterranean was not an internal European affair, and was driven by thriving production centers and markets in the southern shores. Basing himself on the letters of the Geniza from the pivotal eleventh century, he documented the shipping of large quantities of Egyptian linen and flax to the Maghreb, Spain, Italy, and other parts of Christian Europe.[2]

---

[1] The preparation of this paper has benefited from the collaboration of numerous colleagues over a long period of time. Professor E. Savage-Smith, senior researcher in the Medieval Views of the Cosmos Project and my co-editor in the electronic publication of the *Book of Curiosities*, allowed me to read and use prior to publication her "The *Book of Curiosities*: An Eleventh-Century Egyptian View of the Lands of the Infidels", in *Geography, Ethnography, and Perceptions of the World from Antiquity to the Renaissance*, ed. by K.A. Raaflaub and R. Talbert [The Ancient World: Comparative Histories, 1], (Malden [Mass.] and Oxford: Blackwell Publishers, 2010). I greatly benefited from the comments made at presentations at two Byzantine seminars at Oxford, at the kind invitation of J. Howard-Johnston and E. Jeffreys. R. Unger and Y. Lev have devoted time to discussions of aspects of the material. Finally, I would like to thank A.L. Udovitch, my mentor at Princeton, for much more than guiding me to the history of the medieval Mediterranean.

[2] See A.L. Udovitch, "International Trade and the Medieval Egyptian Countryside," in *Agriculture in Egypt from Pharaonic to Modern Times*, ed. A. Bowman and E. Rogan (Oxford: Oxford University Press, 1999): 267-86, esp. 274. Compare R.S. Lopez, *The Commercial Revolution of the Middle Ages, 950-1350* (Cambridge University Press, 1971): esp. 98-9. See also M. Gil, "The Flax Trade in the Mediterranean in the Eleventh century A.D. as Seen in Merchants' Letters from the Cairo Geniza," *Journal of Near Eastern Studies* 63/2 (2004): 81-96.

On 10 October of 2000, nine months after the talk in Tel Aviv, a unique Arabic manuscript went on auction in London. The previously unknown treatise, entitled *Kitāb gharā'ib al-funūn wa-mulaḥ al-'uyūn* (*The Book of Curiosities of the Sciences and Marvels for the Eyes*), contains a series of maps and cartographic designs, most of which are unparalleled in the tradition of Arab-Islamic cartography. Although the manuscript is a thirteenth century copy, a dedication to the Fatimid caliphs and references to historical events show that the original treatise was composed between 1020 and 1050, most probably in Egypt. The manuscript was acquired by the Bodleian Library in Oxford, where it has been the subject of a major research project. It has been recently published in its entirety on a website hosted by the Bodleian (http://www.bodley.ox.ac.uk/bookofcuriosities).[3]

Six out of the seventeen maps contained in the treatise depict the coasts and islands of the Eastern Mediterranean. The treatise contains a map of the Mediterranean as a whole, and individual maps of Sicily (still under Muslim rule), Cyprus, Mahdiya, the Egyptian textile island-city of Tinnīs and a diagram representing Aegean bays in south-west Anatolia. These maps are incorporated into a framework that uniquely emphasizes categories of waterways, starting with a depiction of the three great seas (Indian Ocean, Mediterranean and Caspian Seas), and following with accounts of individual islands, peninsulas, bays, lakes and rivers. This organization of geographical material by bodies of water is completely different from the description of the Muslim-ruled provinces typical of the tenth-century geographers al-Muqaddasī (d. ca. 1000) and Ibn Ḥawqal (d. ca. 977).[4] The special interest of the author in the affairs of the sea and his focus

[3] Y. Rapoport and E. Savage-Smith, *The Book of Curiosities: A Critical Edition.* Worldwide Web publication of Oxford, Bodleian Library, MS Arab. c. 90. (http://www.bodley.ox.ac.uk/bookofcuriosities) (March 2007). The site is constantly updated, and contains explanatory chapters on the dating of the treatise, the conservation of the manuscript and bibliographical references to related literature. For earlier discussions of the treatise, see J. Johns and E. Savage-Smith, "The *Book of Curiosities*: A Newly Discovered Series of Islamic Maps," *Imago Mundi* 55 (2003): 7–24; Y. Rapoport and E. Savage-Smith, "Medieval Islamic View of the Cosmos: The Newly Discovered *Book of Curiosities*," *The Cartographic Journal* 41 (2004): 253–9.

[4] See P. Heck, *The Construction of Knowledge in Islamic Civilization: Qudāma b. Ja'far and his* Kitāb al-Kharāj wa-ṣinā'at al-kitāba (Leiden: E. J. Brill, 2002): 94-145, for discussion of organization of material in Arab geographical literature.

on the eastern Mediterranean fit in well with the maritime orientation of the Fatimids during the tenth and eleventh centuries.[5]

Three of the maps in the *Book of Curiosities*—the map of the Mediterranean, the map of Cyprus and the diagram of Aegean bays, followed by textual description—offer unprecedented detail on the coasts of Byzantium, which surpasses any other geographical account in contemporary Arabic, Greek or Latin sources. Furthermore, these three maps contain a unique wealth of material on navigation along the coasts, including details on the quality and size of anchorages and harbors, sailing distances, water sources and wind directions. This is the earliest example of such material on navigation in medieval Arabic geographic literature, while still superior to the later maritime itineraries by al-Bakrī (d. 1094) and al-Idrīsī (d. 1165).[6] The focus on the coasts of Byzantium, together with the inclusion of navigational material, is distinct to these three maps, and sets them apart from other maps in the treatise.[7] As will be shown below, it is likely that the author of the *Book of Curiosities* derived all three from a single source.

Taken together, these maps graphically depict the coasts and islands of Byzantium in the eleventh century as viewed by an Arabic-speaking Muslim, most probably Egyptian. They are of major interest for several directions of research, most obviously for historical geography of the Byzantine coasts, and for history of Mediterranean navigation and cartography before the portolan charts of the later Middle

---

[5] On the exceptional interest of the Fatimids in maritime policy, see A.L. Udovitch, "A tale of two cities: commercial relations between Cairo and Alexandria during the second half of the eleventh century," in *The Medieval City*, edited by H. Miskimin, D. Herlihy, and A.L. Udovitch (New Haven, CT: Yale University Press, 1977): 146; *EI*², s.v. "Milāḥa: 1. In the Pre-Islamic and Early Mediaeval Periods" (V. Christides), 7:46; L.I. Conrad, "Islam and the Sea: Paradigms and Problematics," *al-Qanṭara* XXIII, 1 (2002): 123-54.

[6] See al-Bakrī, *Al-Masālik wa-al-mamālik*, ed. A.P. Van Leeuwen and A. Ferre. 2 vols. (Tunis: al-Dār al-ʿArabiya lil-Kitāb, 1992): 754-62 (list of anchorages from Morocco to Syria along the North African coast); al-Idrīsī, *Opus geographicum, sive "Liber ad eorum delectationem qui terras peragrare studeant" (Kitāb nuzhat al-mushtāq)*, ed. A. Bombaci et al. 9 parts (Naples and Rome: Istituto universitario orientale di Napoli and Istituto italiano per il medio ed estremo oriente, 1970–76): 623-5 (list of anchorages and the distances between them along the coasts of Sicily).

[7] The map of Mahdiya in the *Book of Curiosities* contains a textual maritime itinerary from Mahdiya to Palermo in Sicily, with indication of the distance in miles between each stop (Oxford, Bodleian Library, MS Arab. c. 90, fol. 34a). This type of itinerary is typical of al-Idrīsī, and differs from the description of ports and bays in the chapters under discussion.

Ages. These maps are also of primary importance for our understanding of international commerce in the eleventh century Mediterranean. Are these detailed maps a visual reflection of the intensifying maritime trade between Egypt and Byzantium, the necessary accessories facilitating the commercial revolution that swept through the Mediterranean? Were they used by merchants travelling up and down the coasts of the eastern Mediterranean?

I will argue here that this is probably an overly rosy interpretation. First, it should be emphasized that the treatise as a whole, with its lavish illustrations, was a literary artifact for intellectual, urban consumption. The maps as we have them were not intended as functional navigation aides. Moreover, there are solid indicators that the maps were drawn from the records of the Fatimid navy, reflecting persisting military competition between Byzantium and its Muslim neighbors. However, the level of familiarity with the Byzantine coasts demonstrated by the maps of *The Book of Curiosities*, even if derived from military sources, was probably an indirect result of increasing trade and maritime-based contacts, which only came about since the middle of the tenth century.

I

The Mediterranean Map

The map of the Mediterranean Sea in the *Book of Curiosities* [Fig. 1] is an oval whose dark-green sea is crammed with 118 islands, all conveniently round except for two rectangular islands. Around the periphery, 121 anchorages on the mainland are labelled. The red title across the top of the map reads: 'The Tenth Chapter: The Western Sea—that is, the Syrian Sea—and its Harbors, Islands and Anchorages'. This map deviates from earlier Islamic cartographic tradition in several ways. First, in line with almost all other maps in the treatise, there is no attempt to trace any of the actual coast lines. Not even the Iberian Peninsula, which is very prominent on earlier Islamic maps of the Mediterranean, is represented.[8] It differs from earlier

[8] Compare with the maps of the Mediterranean in the works of al-Iṣṭakhrī and Ibn Ḥawqal in G.R. Tibbetts, "The Balkhī School of Geographers," in *History of Cartography, Vol. II, Book 1: Cartography in the Traditional Islamic and South Asian Societies*, edited by J.B. Harley, and D. Woodward (Chicago: University of Chicago Press, 1992): 120. See also M. Pinna, *Il Mediterraneo e la Sardegna nella cartografia*

representations of the Mediterranean also by its toponymic detail, both for the coasts and for the islands; its exclusive focus on the coasts to the exclusion of any inland features; and, most importantly, by the navigation material provided in the labels. While earlier maps of the Mediterranean are arm-chair attempts to give general geographic orientation, this unique map is the first surviving example of a map drawn from the perspective of sea-going mariners.

The map is orientated with the Straits of Gibraltar indicated by a thin red line at the far left of the oval, and with north at the top (roughly speaking). Proceeding clockwise, the next seven ports above the Straits are anchorages on the Atlantic coast of Morocco, such as Tangiers; each of these seven labels begins with the word 'toward', indicating that the localities are not actually on the Mediterranean rim. Thereafter, the mapmaker briefly alludes to the ports of Muslim Spain and Europe, reading clockwise: 'the anchorages of al-Andalus', 'the anchorages of the Galicians', 'the anchorages of the Franks', 'the anchorages of the Slavs', 'the anchorages of the Lombards.' The following label 'The Gulf of Burjān', refers to the Black Sea, which was conceived as a north-south narrow strait flowing from the Encompassing Ocean to the Mediterranean, as is seen on Islamic world maps of the period.[9]

Proceeding clockwise from the Gulf of Burjān, the mapmaker started indicating individual anchorages in Byzantium. The next three are as yet unidentified, but two of them are associated with local churches. The following label, the fourth from the Gulf of Burjān, reads 'The city of Sh.j.n.s, having a large harbor which has been blocked with sand'. This is very probably Sigeion, at the southern entrance to the Hellespont (Dardanelles), on the Asian coast. Sigeion is followed by 'The land of Sāsah', probably Sestos, the port facing Abydos on the European coast of the Dardanelles. The labels on the map continue with four more harbors along the Dardanelles until reaching Constantinople, said on our map to be 'the fortress of Constantinople on which there is a tower [?] and an armoury'. Then the map continues to indicate a few harbors on the western coasts of Anatolia, including Atarneus, Erythrai and Trogilium, each of

---

musulmana: dall'VIII al XVI secolo (Nuoro: Istituto superiore regionale etnografico, [1996?]).

[9] For maps by al-Iṣṭakhrī and Ibn Ḥawqal that show the Black Sea as narrow straits or canal, see Tibbetts, "The Balkhī School of Geographers": 120-3. On the Burjān, see *EI*[2], s.v. "Bulghār" (I. Hrbek), 1:1304–8.

them facing one of the major Micro-Asiatic islands—Lesbos, Chios and Samos respectively.

The area of greatest detail on the map refers to the coasts of south-western and southern Anatolia, Syria, Palestine and Egypt. These coasts are represented with a dense network of harbors and ports. The coasts of southern Anatolia, which were during the eleventh century under Byzantine control, are represented by more than thirty anchorages and ports, including the major Byzantine ports of Strobilos, Attaleia and Tarsos. A few thin red lines between the red dots indicate rivers flowing into the sea. This is the most detailed list of Byzantine anchorages found in any medieval source before the appearance of the Italian portolan charts in the late thirteenth century.

The list continues with ports and harbors under Muslim control, starting with the region around Latakia. This was the frontier between the Byzantines and Fatimids during the first half of the eleventh century, but the mapmaker made no visual or textual attempt to indicate this political boundary. The dense account of anchorages and ports continues, listing thirty-five place-names from Latakia down the Syrian and Palestinian coasts to the port of Alexandria. West of Alexandria, however, the North African coast is represented with far less detail. Few major North African ports are mentioned, such as Barka, Tripoli and Mahdiya (although some more are yet to be identified). Taken as whole, the ports of Latin Europe and Byzantium occupy nearly the entire upper half of the oval, and Islamic anchorages the lower half.

As mentioned above, this map is unique in providing information on capacity of anchorages and ports, defensive installations and protection from prevailing winds. With regard to capacity, many ports are described as large or small. In a few cases, the information is more specific. The ports of Trogilion in the Aegean, 'the anchorage of the Oak' and Syke in southern Anatolia, and the port of Barka on the Libyan coast are said to be able to accommodate one hundred ships each, while two unidentified ports on the North African coast are said to accommodate 200 ships. Four Byzantine ports are said to be able to accommodate an *usṭūl* (from the Greek *stylos*, fleet). These are Sestos in the Dardanelles, Jurjiya (probably Agios Georgios at the head of the Gallipoli peninsula)[10], Erythrai in the Aegean coast of

[10] Georgios Agios is mentioned as a stop on the way to Constantinople by Saewulf in 1102, and then by 14th century portolans. Pryor identified it with the

Anatolia, and an unidentified anchorage north of Patara. The term *usṭūl* sometimes designated an individual heavy galley, and was interpreted as such by Goitein in his discussion of Geniza letters. But here it is certainly used in its original meaning of a fleet or convoy of military ships. Such usage is also attested in the contemporary chronicle of Yaḥyā of Antioch.[11] It is noteworthy that indications of size or capacity are found on the coasts of Aegean, Anatolia and North Africa, but not for the ports of Egypt and Syria, which were under Fatimid control.

The labels also mention defensive aspects of ports, and especially the existence of a fort (*ḥiṣn*), which is mentioned for most Byzantine and Muslim harbors. The port of Mahdiya is said to be protected with a gate and a chain, a system that was common to a number of the major ports of the medieval Mediterranean.[12] Arsenals, used for the construction and storage of military galleys, are mentioned for Byzantine Strobilos, in south-west Anatolia, as well as for Fatimid Alexandria and Tunis. Strobilos, opposite the island of Kos, is known to have been an important naval and military post in the middle Byzantine period.[13] The author was aware of the existence of other

Byzantine town of Ganos (mod. Gaziköy). See J. Pryor, "The Voyages of Saewulf," in *Peregrinationes tres: Saewulf; John of Würzburg; Theodericus*, ed. R.B.C. Huygens (Tuonholti: Brepols, 1994): 55-6. Al-Idrīsī mentions Shanṭ Jirjī in the Dardanelles, south of Gallipoli (al-Idrīsī, *Opus geographicum*, 800).

[11] The definition of *usṭūl* as a military fleet is found in several medieval Arabic sources from the tenth century onwards, such as in al-Mas'ūdī, *Kitâb al-Tanbîh wa'l-ischrâf*, ed. M.J. de Goeje (Leiden: E. J. Brill, 1894; rpr 1967): 141; and Qudāma ibn Ja'far, *al-Kharāj wa-ṣināʿat al-kitāba*, ed. M.Ḥ. al-Zubaydī ([Baghdād]: Wizārat al-Thaqāfa wa-al-I'lām: Dār al-Rashīd, 1981): 188. For the unambiguous use of the term *usṭūl* as a military fleet, and not an individual galley, referring to events in the 990s, see Y. al-Anṭākī (d. 1065 or 6), *Tārīkh al-Anṭākī*, ed. 'Umar 'Abd al-Salām al-Tadmurī (Tripoli [Lebanon]: Jarrūs Press, 1990): 233, 240-2. Some North African writers do use the term in reference to individual galleys, as attested by Ibn Khaldūn and others (see Y. Lev, "The Fāṭimid Navy, Byzantium and the Mediterranean Sea 909-1036 C.E./297-427 A.H.," *Byzantion* 54 [1984]: 247; but compare Ch. Picard, *La mer et les musulmans d'occident au Moyen Âge, VIIIe-XIIIe siècle* [Paris: Presses Universitaires de France, 1997], 117). For Goitein's interpretation of the use of the term in the Geniza, see his *Mediterranean Society. The Jewish Communities of the Arab World as Portrayed in the Documents of the Cairo Geniza*. 6 vols. (Berkeley & Los Angeles: University of California Press, 1967-1993), 1:307-8, where the evidence appears inconclusive.

[12] A chain is also noted for the port of Palermo on the map of Sicily.

[13] On Strobilos, on the northwestern tip of the Ceramic Gulf, 10 km southwest of modern Bodrum, see C. Foss, "Strobilos and Related Sites," *Anatolian Studies* 38 (1988): 147-77; repr. in idem., *History and Archaeology of Byzantine Asia Minor* (Aldershot: Ashgate, Variorum, 1990); E. Malamut, "The Region of Serçe Limani in

arsenals in the eastern Mediterranean, as he indicates their existence on the individual maps of Tinnīs and Sicily.[14] The map of the Mediterranean also mentions an armoury situated at Constantinople and a *manẓara* (watch-tower) at Sousse, probably referring to the well-known *ribāṭ* of the city.

Protection from prevailing winds is mentioned for a large number of ports and anchorages, on both Byzantine and Fatimid coasts. This is in keeping with the accounts of al-Idrīsī and al-Bakrī, who occasionally mention the protection from the wind, or lack thereof, offered by ports on the North African coast.[15] Some of the best anchorages, such as Tyre, Caesarea, and Tinnīs are said to offer protection from all winds. Most, however, offer protection only from certain winds, whose names are drawn from a four-point Greek system of wind navigation. Thus, for example, the mapmaker notes that the anchorages of Iasos and Jaffa offer protection from the *Boreas* (north) wind, while the ports of Tripoli (Syria) and Gaza offer protection from the *Notos* (south) wind. The direction of wind required to enter a harbor, on the other hand, is only noted for the port of Tarsos, which is to be entered 'with a gentle *Boreas* (north) wind' (*wa-dukhūluhu fī al-buryās al-layyinah*). The adoption of the Greek nomenclature for wind navigation by Arab mariners is not otherwise attested in the medieval period.[16]

Byzantine Times," in G. Bass et al. *Serçe Limani: An Eleventh-Century Shipwreck.* [The Nautical Archaeology Series; no. 4]. vol. 1. The Ship and its Anchorage, Crew and Passengers (College Station, TX: Texas A&M University Press, 2004): 23-4.

[14] On the arsenals and other naval structures of the Muslim Mediterranean, see the recent work of P. Jansen, A. Nef, and C. Picard, *La Méditerranée entre pays d'Islam et monde latin: milieu Xe-milieu XIIIe siècle* ([France]: Sedes, c2000): 159, 168-9.

[15] The Arabic text here poses a problem of interpretation. In many cases, the copyist of the manuscript wrote '*tasīru min* X', which means 'you go' or 'you enter with X wind'. According to this reading, the mapmaker indicates winds favorable for entering a harbor. But in some labels the manuscript reads '*yasturu min* X ', meaning '[the harbor] protects from [X wind].' In the edition of the *Book of Curiosities* we have preferred the second reading and consistently amended '*tasīru min*' to '*yasturu min*'. This emendation is chiefly in light of the text of al-Idrīsī, where the form '*yasturu min*' is used to indicate protection from winds offered by North African ports. See al-Idrīsī, *Opus geographicum*: 252 lines 11-13 (Wahrān): 272 line 14 (Waqūr): 280 line 10 (Gabes).

[16] The Greek system of wind navigation dates from at least 900 B.C., with the four cardinal directions used first and then expanded to an eight-winds system. (P. Kemp (ed.), *The Oxford Companion to Ships & the Sea* [London: Oxford University Press, 1976]: 941). A few of these terms found their way into Ottoman Turkish, but almost certainly directly from Greek and not through the intermediary of Arabic.

The labels also indicate other aspects of harbors, such as the existence of sources of fresh water or rivers, especially for the anchorages of southern Anatolia. Several harbors are described as being blocked, such as the harbor of Sigeion at the southern entrance to Dardanelles. The quality of the ports of Tyre and Acre is praised, while Sidon's is said to be poor. Distances between neighboring anchorages, however, are never given. In a few cases, the map indicates distances measured in days and nights of sailing. Mylai, on the southern Anatolian coast, is said to be one day and one night sailing from Cyprus; Barka one's day sailing from Alexandria; and Surt a further half a day's sailing from Barka. The direction of travel along the coasts of the Mediterranean is here conceived as clock-wise, from Anatolia to Cyprus, and from Egypt towards North Africa—a choice that may have been arbitrary.[17]

The wealth of information on the ports and harbors of the coasts, on the rim of the oval, contrasts with the dearth of information regarding the islands in the middle of the map. The islands to the far left (four columns) are each labeled merely 'island' (*jazīra*) and given no names. The remainder—the vast majority of the 118 islands—are mentioned in name only, but not described. Only Sicily and Cyprus, represented as rectangles, have longer descriptive labels, which correspond to some of the material on the individual maps of these two islands in the following folios. The sequence of the islands is confused, and not consistent with regard to each other or in relationship to the mainland rim of the sea. In general, the Aegean islands are clustered to the left of the gutter, while the groups of islands surrounding Sicily are clustered to the right. The major islands of the western Mediterranean, such as Sardinia, Corsica and Mallorca are

---

See H.&R. Kahane and A. Tietze, *The Lingua Franca in the Levant. Turkish Nautical Terms of Italian and Greek Origin* (Urbana, IL: University of Illinois Press, 1958). A 12-point Greek wind system is described elsewhere in the *Book of Curiosities*, in a chapter dealing with winds and earthquakes (Oxford, Bodleian Library, MS Arab. c. 90, fol. 21b). This is a version of the classical 12-point rose, based on astronomy, and used in Latin encyclopedias of the early Middle Ages. See P. Gautier Dalché, *Carte marine et portulan au XIIe siècle: le "Liber de existencia riveriarum et forma maris nostri Mediterranei" (Pise, circa 1200)*. Texte édité et commentée par P. Gautier Dalché (Rome: École française de Rome, 1995): 70.

[17] In fact, prevailing winds and currents made it possible to sail directly from the Aegean to Alexandria. It was travelling from Alexandria to Constantinople that always required hugging the Syrian coasts. See J.H. Pryor, *Geography, Technology and War: Studies in the Maritime History of the Mediterranean, 649-1571* (Cambridge: Cambridge University Press, 1988): 88-9.

not mentioned at all. The lack of precision regarding location is not, however, a sign of ignorance. In fact, the list of islands recorded for the Aegean, at the time under complete Byzantine control, is far superior to all other medieval Arabic geographies, and includes even islands of the northern Aegean such as Samothrace.[18] The difference between the rich description of mainland ports and the terse listing of island names is striking, especially since many of the islands would have had serviceable ports and harbors of their own. It is quite possible that additional material on individual islands was omitted due to limitations of space on the crammed map, since the small circles indicating the numerous islands could not accommodate longer labels.

The Cyprus Map

The separate map of Cyprus [fig. 2] appears to be in close relationship with the general map of the Mediterranean, and is almost certainly drawn from the same source. This diagram of Cyprus is the first detailed Arabic map of the island to be recorded.[19] It opens the fifteenth chapter entitled 'The Islands of the Infidels', in which the author describes Mediterranean and Indian Ocean islands in the hands of non-Muslims, including Cyprus, which fell under full Byzantine control in 965. The island is represented by a square surrounded on all four sides by a strip of green-colored sea. Twenty-five cells along the edges, or 'coasts', are meant to represent harbors, although some have been left empty. Nine additional ports are represented by a strip of nine cells in the middle of the square, the strip entitled 'the names of the remainder of its harbors'. There is little doubt that the mapmaker, or copyist, was forced to place these harbors in the middle of the square as a result of lack of space along the edges. All in all, twenty-five separate harbors are recorded, on par with the account of Cypriot ports in the late Antique *Stadiasmus*.[20]

---

[18] In a different chapter in the treatise the author provides short textual descriptions of Rhodes, Crete, and the small islands of Khalki and Tilos, just north of Rhodes. Matters of navigation and ports are not discussed (Oxford, Bodleian Library, MS Arab. c. 90, fol. 37a).

[19] A. Stylianou and J.A. Stylianou, *The History of the Cartography of Cyprus* (Nicosia: Cyprus Research Centre, 1980): 3.

[20] A.E. Nordenskiöld, *Periplus. An Essay on the Early History of Charts and Sailing-Directions.* Translated from the Swedish original by F.A. Bather (Stockholm: P. A. Norstedt & Söner, 1897): 10-15.

The author also added a few lines of historical information and a brief account of the principal exports from Cyprus. This historical material bears close relationship to the short account of Cyprus by Ibn Ḥawqal.[21]

The harbors are listed in approximate correct sequence, although with no correlation to actual directions. The harbors on the northern coasts of Cyprus are represented on the middle strip, starting from the north-western Acamas Peninsula on the left-hand side of the strip and proceeding eastwards to the anchorage of Akraia, located at Cape Apostolos Andreas in the north-east tip of Cyprus. The list then proceeds in anti-clockwise order along the four edges of the rectangle, representing harbors on the eastern, southern and western harbors of the island. It culminates with Paphos, on the eastern coasts, on the bottom right.

The type of information provided for each of the harbors of Cyprus is very similar to that provided in the map of the Mediterranean, though often more expansive. Protection from prevailing winds is almost always recorded. The winds named are the *Boreas* (north), *Notos* (south) and *Euros* (east or south-east), as well as a wind called 'the Frankish' (*al-ifranjī*). This term clearly refers to westerly winds, but it is not attested in Greek sources.[22] Harbor size is infrequently mentioned. The ports of Paphos and of Jurjis (probably Hagios Georgios, a monastery east of modern Limassol on the southern coasts), are both said to accommodate 950 ships, an incredibly large number that is probably a copyist mistake. As in the Mediterranean map, there are occasional references to water sources (such as the Basileus River on the south-east coast of Cyprus, appearing here as 'river of the King' in Arabic translation), and to prominent churches and fortresses. Sailing distances are given from Akraia (Cape Apostolos Andreas) to Rhodes, said to be one day and one night with the Boreas (north) wind; and between Akraia and Latakia, said to be one night.[23] The port of Soloi on the northern coasts is said to harbor

---

[21] Ibn Ḥawqal, *Opus geographorum auctore Ibn Ḥauḳal (Kitāb Ṣūrat al-arḍ)*, ed. J. H. Kramers [Bibliotheca Geographorum Arabicorum, 2; 2nd ed.], 2 vols. (Leiden: E. J. Brill, 1938–1939): 205.

[22] The standard Greek term for westerly wind is *Zephuros* (Kemp, *The Oxford Companion to Ships*, 941). See also the discussion of variants in Gautier Dalché, *Carte marine*, 70ff.

[23] The reference to a sailing distance of only one night between Latakia and Cyprus is almost certainly a copyist mistake, as it is strange for the author to define the distance solely in terms of nocturnal sailing. Ibn Ḥawqal mentions a sailing

the ships of the merchants of the island. No other port is associated with commercial activity.

The Bays of Byzantium

The information on navigation along the Byzantine coasts is complemented by a unique chapter on the bays and gulfs of the Aegean Sea. The sixteenth chapter, entitled 'On the Depiction of Inlets, that is Bays, and in particular the Bays of Byzantium', describes in detail twenty-eight bays in the Aegean Sea. It opens with a schematic diagram of the first five bays [Fig. 3], starting with two bays facing Rhodes on the south western shores of Anatolia, called here the Smaller and Larger Tracheia Bays. In the next folios, the author opts for merely textual descriptions of the remaining twenty-three Byzantine bays. The omission of diagrams allows for longer accounts. The author follows the Aegean bays and inlets along the west coast of Anatolia up to the mouth of the Dardanelles, and then continues westward to Thessalonica, then down to Corinth, and along the coasts of the Peloponnesus as far as Patras. At the end of the chapter, the author repeats the description of the Peloponnesus' bays in more expanded form, and then concludes the text abruptly.

This account of the Aegean bays provides a surprising amount of detail on areas which lay deep inside the Byzantine domains. The format of the chapter is also unique, and has no parallels in other medieval Arabic sources. The information regarding each bay concerns width and length, direction of entry according to an eight-point rose, major forts, small islets and prominent landmarks. As an example, this is the entry for the eighth bay in the sequence, Smyrna:[24]

> Further to the north is the Bay of Izmirnah [Smyrna]. This bay is 30 miles long, and in its widest place it is 10 miles wide. At the head of the bay is the fortified settlement of Izmirnah [Smyrna], located three miles from the sea. At the entrance to the bay there is a small and uninhabited island called Jurjis. The fortress of Qlazūmnī [Klazomenai] is to the south of the bay and the fortress of Fūqīyah [Phocaea] is to the north. One enters it from the west to the east. It has also an inhabited island.

---

distance of one day and one night between Cyprus and Jabala (near Latakia). See *Kitāb Ṣūrat al-arḍ* (ed. Kramers): 179, 205.

[24] Oxford, Bodleian Library, MS Arab. c. 90, fol. 38b, lines 5-8.

This format is repeated for most of the bays along the coasts of the Aegean. Additional details usually refer also to navigational features. In the account of the Bay of Miletus, for example, the author mentions that the wide Byzantine *shelandia* galleys can enter the river Meander.[25] In the account of the Argolic Gulf of the Peloponnesus, it is mentioned that cape Malāas [mod. Maleas] marks the halfway point along the maritime routes between Constantinople and Sicily.[26] In contrast, inland features are only infrequently alluded to. Of special interest are several references to Slav populations in the northern Aegean and the Peloponnesus.[27]

Like the maps of the Mediterranean and Cyprus, the account of the Aegean bays provides material that is overwhelming concerned with navigation. But while the Mediterranean and Cyprus maps are chiefly concerned with harbors, the account of the Aegean bays rarely makes any reference to mooring facilities.[28] Even the toponyms of the ports are hardly ever repeated.[29] There is also no mention of the large micro-Asiatic islands near the western shores of Anatolia. It seems then that the account of the Aegean bays complements the list of harbors and islands depicted on the map of the Mediterranean, at least with regard to the western coasts of Anatolia.

The maps of the Mediterranean, Cyprus and the bays of the Aegean share common characteristics, and complement each other as in a

[25] The Arabic term *shalandiya* is from the Greek *chelandion*. It was a ship used by the Byzantines for military and commercial purposes in the Mediterranean, and adopted by the Fatimids and the Almohads (see D. Agius, "The Arab Šalandī," in *Egypt and Syria in the Fatimid, Ayyubid, and Mamluk eras. III: Proceedings of the 6th, 7th and 8th International Colloquium Organized at the Katholieke Universiteit Leuven in May 1997, 1998, and 1999*, ed. U. Vermeulen and J. van Steenbergen [Leuven: Uitgeverij Peeters, 2001]: 49-60).

[26] Oxford, Bodleian Library, MS Arab. c. 90, fol. 39b, line 10.

[27] On the Slav migrations and installation in the Peloponnesus in the early medieval period, see A. Avraméa, *Le Péloponnèse du IVe au VIIIe siècle: changements et persistances* (Paris: Publications de la Sorbonne, 1997): 67-86.

[28] Only two examples are cited: A small bay to the north of Ḥamdīs (?), a site to the east of mod. Piraeus, which allows ships to moor protected from all winds; and in the bay of Methone in the Peloponnesus there is an island called al-M.rūd (?), which has a harbor that protects from all winds (Oxford, Bodleian Library, MS Arab. c. 90, fol. 39a, lines 7-11; lines 22-4).

[29] The single exception is the port of Tracheia opposite Rhodes, shown on the map of the Mediterranean. This port also gave its name to two nearby gulfs, which are mentioned in the account of the Aegean bays. On the location of the port, see F. Hild, "Die lykischen Bistümeer Kaunos, Panormos und Markiane," in Λιθοξτρωτον. *Studien zur byzantinischen Kunst und Geschichte. Festschrift für Marcell Restle*, ed. B. Borkopp and Th. Steppan (Stuttgart, 2000): 109.

jigsaw puzzle. It therefore seems likely that they were derived from one single source, which was some sort of manual of navigation. These three maps present an unprecedented wealth of navigational knowledge regarding the coasts of Byzantium. All three offer technical information, with hardly any interest in inland topography or historical details. They also mark a clear break with the rich Arabic geographic literature, which tended to be land-based and increasingly Islamo-centric. The maps of the eastern Mediterranean in the *Book of Curiosities* represent something new and different, which seems to coincide with the eleventh-century expansion in international commerce across the Mediterranean.

II

The author of the *Book of Curiosities* makes an explicit connection between commerce and navigation in a preliminary chapter on cartography, entitled 'The sixth chapter on the depiction of the seas, their islands and havens'. In this chapter, the author explains that his maps of the Indian Ocean, the Mediterranean, the Caspian, and the individual maps of Mediterranean islands, peninsulas and gulfs, are all based on the reports of sailors and merchants, checked against the personal knowledge of the author:

> We have only mentioned here what we have heard from trustworthy[30] sailors (*baḥrīyīn*), from which I selected and made my own judgments; and from what had reached my ears from the wise merchants (*tujjār*) who traverse the seas, and from any ship captain (*rubbān*) who leads his men at sea, I mentioned what I have knowledge of.[31]

Closer examination reveals, however, that not all the following maps were based on the lived experience of the men of sea. The author had occasional recourse to literary sources, some of them dating a century and a half before his lifetime. In the map of the Indian Ocean, for example, the maritime route to India is taken, directly or indirectly, from the ninth century account known as *Akhbār al-Ṣīn wa-al-Hind*.[32] The chapter on Tinnīs is a verbatim quotation of the treatise on the

[30] Arabic: *thiqāh* (?). No diactrical points are indicated. The correct plural form is *thiqāt*.

[31] Oxford, Bodleian Library, MS Arab. c. 90, fol. 29a, lines 3-5.

[32] *Akhbār al-Ṣīn wa-al-Hind. Relation de la Chine et de l'Inde, rédigée en 851*, texte établi, traduit et commenté par J. Sauvaget (Paris: Belles Lettres, 1948).

city composed by its market inspector, Ibn al-Bassām, in the beginning of the eleventh century.[33] The chapter on Sicily is an updated version of the material found in the geography of Ibn Ḥawqal.

That is not to say that the author of the *Book of Curiosities* was a land-lubber who never set foot on a ship, or that his information was only derived from literary accounts. The details concerning the African coasts of the Gulf of Aden in the map of the Indian Ocean are unparalleled, and may well be derived from the growing experience of these seas by Arab sailors since the beginning of the tenth century. The map of Mahdiya, with its realistic depiction of the topography of the peninsula on which the city stands, appears to be based on the perspective of a sailor approaching the city on board a ship. Together with new information on Sicily, it seems more than likely that the author had in fact travelled the eastern Mediterranean, visited in person the cities of Tinnīs, Mahdiya and Palermo, and had access to reports of merchants and sailors from the Mediterranean rim and the Gulf of Aden.

But were the chapters and maps relating to navigation along the coasts of Byzantium derived from the accounts or registers of merchants? The possibility is tempting, but the internal evidence of the material rather suggests that the author used a military, naval source for the compilation of this material. First, there are very few references to topics of interest to merchants, like local products[34] or custom houses. Second, the occasional indications of size, or capacity of ports and harbors, on the maps of the Mediterranean and Cyprus, are suggestive of a military perspective. A merchant has no obvious interest in noting that a certain harbor can fit a hundred or two hundred ships, let alone an *usṭūl*, a naval fleet or squadron. For a military officer in command of a fleet consisting of a large number of galleys, on the other hand, such information would be of utmost importance. As John Pryor and Elisabeth Jeffreys remark in their study of the Byzantine *dromon* galley, fleets "could not simply be parked bumper to bumper." Each vessel needed space to allow it to

[33] Ibn Bassām, *Kitāb Anīs al-Jalīs fī Akhbār Tinnīs*, ed. J.D. al-Shayyāl (Cairo: Maktabat al-Thaqāfa al-Dīnīya, 2000); Y. Lev, "Tinnīs: an Industrial Medieval Town," in *L'Égypte fatimide: son art et son histoire. Actes du colloque organisé à Paris les 28, 29 et 30 mai*, 1998, ed. M. Barrucand (Paris: Presses de l'Université de Paris-Sorbonne, 1999): 83-96.

[34] The only direct reference to Byzantine commercial goods is to products imported through Cyprus listed at the bottom of the Cyprus map. The list appears to be based on Ibn Ḥawqal and is not an integral part of the map of the island.

swing around its anchor a diameter of 80 meters if anchored in shallow waters, more if deeper. Limiting this diameter, for example by adding a second anchor, risks the stability of the galley. Pryor and Jeffreys calculate that a fleet of 100 ships would require at least 3 km of shoreline, and much time to arrange the ships properly. In fact, they point out that there are but few Aegean harbors with such long coastlines.[35] As noted above, the Mediterranean map indicates a large capacity -whether one hundred ships or an *usṭūl*—only for a few Aegean and Anatolian ports, including Trogilion, Sestos, Agios Georgios (?), Erythrai, and Syke.

There are other features of the maps of the Mediterranean and Cyprus that fit in well with the needs of naval warfare at the time. The indications of forts and other defensive structures are obviously useful for an attacking fleet, and so would be information on water sources, important for all vessels but crucial for the oarsmen rowing in the Mediterranean summer. Even protection from gales was more important for a galley than for larger, heavier ships. While commercial ships would often travel long distances without any stopover, as is attested in the records of the Geniza[36], galleys were used only for short distances, their range limited above all by physical limitations of the oarsmen. The maps of Cyprus and the Mediterranean indicate a large number of anchorages and ports in close proximity to each other, as one would expect in naval records.[37] The inclusion of material on Fatimid ports, and not only Byzantine enemy bases, could also be explained by contemporary military tactics, as raiding fleets always coasted their own territory before making short passages to

[35] J.H. Pryor and E.M. Jeffreys, *The Age of the Dromon: The Byzantine Navy ca. 500-1204* (Leiden: E. J. Brill, 2006), 373ff.

[36] S.D. Goitein, *A Mediterranean Society. The Jewish communities of the Arab world as Portrayed in the Documents of the Cairo Genizah*, vol. 1 (Berkeley, CA: University of California Press, 1967-93) 211-13, 318-20; R. Gertwagen, "Geniza letters: Maritime Difficulties along the Alexandria-Palermo Route," in *Communication in the Jewish Diaspora: The Pre-Modern World*, ed. Sophia Menache (Leiden: E. J. Brill, 1996): 73-92.

[37] The maritime itinerary of al-Bakrī shares some of these features, such as close proximity between ports (about ninety anchorages and ports from Tangier to Alexandria), safety from adverse winds (the term used is *ma'mūn*) and the sweet water sources (Bakrī, *Masālik*: 754-62). It is quite possible that al-Bakrī himself used official military records in Cordoba when compiling his geographical treatise. See Bakrī, *Masālik*, 16ff; T. Lewicki, "Les voies maritimes de la Méditerranée dans le haut Moyen Age d'après les sources arabes," in *Navigazione Mediterranea nell'alto Medioevo*, vol. II (Spoleto: APR , 1977): 439-69.

their targets of attack. The limited range and the restrictions of line of sight meant that no navy could completely block off any of the major sea lanes. The lines of demarcation between one's own territory and the enemy's could easily be crossed.[38]

The chapter on the Aegean bays was, most likely, also drawn from the records of the Fatimid navy. At first sight, the account of the bays of the Aegean appears to be a navigation guide, proceeding bay by bay from the south-west tip of Anatolia to the mouth of the Dardanelles and then turning south towards the Peloponnesus. But such a route does not in fact follow any likely maritime itinerary. Commercial vessels travelling to Byzantium from Fatimid lands would almost certainly try and reach the markets of Constantinople, rather than turn west at the mouth of the Dardanelles, while ships en route to the Adriatic or to Sicily would go directly from Rhodes to Modon in the Peloponnesus, sometimes making stops on islands in the southern Aegean.[39] Moreover, while medieval ships travelling along would almost always resort to island-hopping, using anchorages on Chios, Samos and Lesbos, the account of the Aegean fails to mention any of the large micro-Asiatic islands facing the western Anatolian coasts. Even when taking the difficult northward journey against the summer *meltemi*, ships avoided the toothed coastline of the shallow and narrow bays, as this would have made their route significantly longer and riskier. The island route, through Lesbos, Chios, and Samos was indeed taken by Byzantine fleets traveling to Cyprus or to Crete.[40] A ship may sometimes enter one of the bays, but not all of them. In 1102, the English Crusader Saewulf passed through the mainland port of Smyrna on his way from Palestine to Constantinople. But his other Aegean stops—Rhodes, Chios, Lesbos and Tenedos at the mouth of the Dardanelles—were all islands.[41]

[38] J.H. Pryor, "Byzantium and the sea (900—1025)," in *War at Sea in the Middle Ages and Renaissance*, ed. J.B. Hattendorf and R.W. Unger (Woodbridge: Boydell, 2003): 87-8; Pryor and Jeffreys, *Age of the Dromon*: 105, 333-55 and passim.

[39] Pryor, *Geography, technology and war*, 97ff; D. Jacoby, "Byzantine Crete in the Navigation and Trade Networks of Venice and Genoa,"in *Oriente e occidente tra Medioevo ed éta moderna: studi in onore di Geo Pistarino*, ed. L. Balletto (Genova: G. Brigati, 1997): 517-40, repr. in idem., *Byzantium, Latin Romania and the Mediterranean* (Aldershot: Ashgate, 2001); E. Malamut, "The Region of Serçe Limani": 21-9.

[40] See several examples in Pryor and Jeffreys, *The Age of the Dromon*, 333ff.; G. Huxley, "A Porphyrogenitan Portulan," *Greek, Roman and Byzantine Studies* 17:3 (1976): 295-300; Pryor, "Byzantium and the Sea": 92-4; Lewicki, "Les voies maritimes,": 449 and passim.

[41] J. Pryor, "The Voyages of Saewulf": 53-5.

Against this backdrop of island-hopping itineraries, a coast-hugging route along the coasts of each of the bays of the Aegean, without ever reaching Constantinople, does not make sense as an aid to navigation. Unlike the later Italian and Catalan portolans, this chapter is not written for the express use of a navigator. There is no mention of navigational hazards, such as shoals and reefs, and the reader is not addressed in the second person, as in the portolan guides.[42]

If the account of the bays of the Aegean does not follow any likely or standard maritime itinerary, and is not written as an aid for navigation, what was the purpose of recording the Aegean coastline in such precision? Again, as in the Mediterranean and Cyprus maps, the account of bays would be useful when planning a raid on Byzantine coasts. Compiling information on the ports and inlets, especially in enemy territory, was one of the responsibilities of a naval commander. This is expressly stated in appointment decree for a governor of a Mediterranean port town, dating from the Abbasid period and preserved in the administrative work of Qudāma b. Jaʿfar (d. 948 ?). In this appointment decree the commander is told, inter alia, to build new galleys to high standards and maintain the upkeep of existing ones, beaching them during the winter; select carefully his crews of sailors and throwers of Greek fire (*naffāṭūn*); and prevent the enemy from purchasing military equipment from the lands of Islam. The gathering of intelligence regarding the ports and bays of the enemy receives special attention:

> It is the commander's responsibility to see that the reconnaissance forces (*fawātīr*) and spies (*ʿuyūn*) which are sent to gather information about the enemy, are trustworthy, able to give good advice, of good religion, and honest. They must have experience of the sea, its ports (*mawānīhi*), inlets (*dakhalātihi*), and hiding places (*makhābīhi*), so that they bring only correct and reliable reports. In case you are overtaken by enemy ships which you cannot resist, then withdraw to the places which they know well and where they know that you will be safe.[43]

---

[42] See a translation of an excerpt from the earliest preserved portolan guide, dating to the late 13th century, in P. Gautier Dalché, "Portulans and the Byzantine World," in *Travel in the Byzantine World: Papers from the Thirty-Fourth Spring Symposium of Byzantine Studies, Birmingham, April 2000*, edited by Ruth Macrides (Aldershot: Ashgate Variorum, 2002): 62.

[43] Qudāma, *al-kharāj*, 48. Paraphrased in A.M. Fahmy, *Muslim Sea-Power in the Eastern Mediterranean, from the Seventh to the Tenth century A.D: Studies in Naval Organisation* ([London]: Tip. Don Bosco, 1950), 141-2; V. Christides, "Two parallel naval guides of the tenth century: Qudama's document and Leo VI's *Naumachica*. A Study on Byzantine and Moslem Naval Preparedness," *Graeco-Arabica* 1 (1982): 100.

Like its Muslim counterparts, the Byzantine navy was equally interested in the anchorages and inlets of the Muslim lands. The similarity between the appointment decree preserved by Qudāma b. Jaʿfar and the *Naumachica* of Leo VI (reg. 886-912) has been pointed out by V. Christides.[44] In his *Taktika* military manual composed around 1000-1011, the Byzantine governor of Antioch Nikephoros Ouranos lists the categories of information that would be required by a commander of a naval fleet. These are fairly similar to those found in the *Book of Curiosities*:

> It is appropriate for a stratēgos to have with him men who have accurate knowledge and experience of the sea in which he is sailing, which winds cause it to swell and which blow from the land. They should know both the hidden rocks in the sea, and the places which have no depth, and the land along which one sails and the islands adjacent to it, the harbors and the distance such harbors are the one from the other. They should know the countries and the water supplies; for many have perished from lack of experience of the sea and the regions, since winds frequently blow and scatter the ships to one region and another. And it is appropriate that not only the stratēgos should have men with this knowledge we have discussed, but also each and every ship should have someone knowing these things to advise well when appropriate.[45]

III

But if the material in the *Book of Curiosities* was drawn from military records, one still has to address the wealth of detail concerning the coasts of Byzantium. How did the Fatimid navy get hold of such detailed records of coasts and bays lying deep in Byzantine territory? Up until the middle of the tenth century, the continuous naval raids of the Muslim powers meant that military commanders were the ones best informed on the affairs of the Mediterranean. This is reflected in a passage by al-Masʿūdī, who attempts to estimate the size and shape of the major seas. While for the Indian Ocean

[44] Christides, "Naval guides." On intelligence gathering by naval forces, see also Pryor and Jeffreys, *The Age of the Dromon*: 393-4, and the sources cited there.

[45] The citation is from Pryor, "Byzantium and the Sea": 93. The text is a paraphrase of the *Taktika* of Leo VI. See discussion of the author and his career in Pryor and Jeffreys, *The Age of the Dromon*, 181-183; E. McGeer, *Sowing the Dragon's Teeth: Byzantine Warfare in the Tenth Century* (Washington, DC: Dumbarton Oaks Research Library and Collection, 1995): 79-86.

al-Mas'ūdī relied on reports by Omani and Sirafi captains (*nawākhida*) of commercial ships traveling towards India or Africa[46], he attests that for the bays and coastlines of the Mediterranean it is the naval commanders who are most reliable. In particular, al-Mas'ūdī singles out the governor of Jabala:

> 'Abd Allāh b. Wazīr, the governor of the town of Jabala in the coast of Homs in Syria, has remained today—in the year 332 AH (943-44 AD)—the most knowledgeable and experienced person with regard to the Mediterranean. Whenever any of the ship captains (*arbāb al-marākib*), whether military or commercial (*'umāla*) wishes to ride the Mediterranean Sea, they refer to his opinion and attest to his knowledge, wisdom, piety and long experience of Holy War at sea.[47]

But by the time the *Book of Curiosities* was composed, about a century after al-Mas'ūdī wrote this passage, much of the political and economic framework of the eastern Mediterranean has changed. In the 960s the Byzantines seized back areas they have lost in previous centuries, conquering Crete, Cyprus and the south-east Anatolian major port of Tarsos. Even the frontier port of Jabala itself was lost, with the new border passing around Latakia. Coinciding with the Fatimid conquest of Egypt and Syria, Byzantium's relations with its Muslim neighbors was entering a new stage. Military confrontation was, for the first time, overshadowed by a marked increase in commercial relations, fuelled by a shift in the routes of international trade. As Alexandria emerged as the major outlet for Indian spices coming through the Red Sea, the volume of trade between Egypt and Byzantium increased substantially from the late tenth century, as has been demonstrated by D. Jacoby.[48] A series of peace treaties stipulated freedom of trade, and the presence of Byzantine merchants in

---

[46] The reliance of the geographer on the merchants of the Indian Ocean is even more pronounced with al-Muqaddasī later in the tenth century. Al-Muqaddasī asks a certain Abū 'Alī, head of the merchants in Aden, to draw in the sand a detailed map of the Indian Ocean. See al-Muqaddasī, *Aḥsan al-taqāsīm fī ma'rifat al-aqālīm*, ed. M.J. de Goeje [Bibliotheca Geographorum Arabicorum, 3] (Leiden: E. J. Brill, 1877; rpr 1906), 10; al-Muqaddasī, *The Best Divisions for Knowledge of the Regions: A Translation of Ahsan al-Taqasim fi Ma'rifat al-Aqalim*, trns. B.A. Collins (Reading: Garnet Publishing and The Centre for Muslim Contribution to Civilisation, 1994): 10.

[47] Al-Mas'ūdī. *Les prairies d'or* [*Kitāb Murūj al-dhahab wa-ma'ādim al-jawhar*], ed. and trns. by C. Barbier de Meynard and P. de Courteill, rev. ed. by Ch. Pellat, 7 vols. (Beirut: Manshūrāt al-Jāmi'a al-Lubnāniyya, 1965–79), vol. 1, 151 (no. 305).

[48] The argument is presented most comprehensively in Jacoby, "Byzantine trade with Egypt from the Mid-Tenth Century to the Fourth Crusade," *Thesaurismata* 30

Cairo and Alexandria, as well as Muslim merchants in Constantinople, is well attested in literary sources.[49] This picture is amplified by the documentary evidence of the Geniza, where letters refer often to the activities of '*Rūm*' merchants, many of whom were Byzantine (and not necessarily European, as assumed by Goitein), and to the importation of mastic and other medical plants and drugs from Anatolia and the Aegean to Egypt.[50]

Increased trade brought about a revival in the fortunes of the towns of the eastern Mediterranean and the Aegean. In 1047, Nāser-e Khosraw depicts the bustling commerce in Tripoli, visited by ships from all over the Mediterranean, and the demographic and topographic expansion of Sidon and Tyre.[51] The archeological evidence for Anatolia suggests a similar trend of recovery, with sites such as Smyrna and the above-mentioned Strobilos showing considerable demographic expansion.[52] The most impressive and tangible testimony of Byzantine-Fatimid trade in the eleventh century is the unique shipwreck that sank circa 1030 in Serçe Limani, in southwest Anatolia opposite Rhodes. Excavations concluded that the ship carried a cargo of Syrian glass and glazed pottery destined to be sold in Constantinople, whence the ship had originally embarked.[53]

(2000): 102-32; repr. in idem., *Commercial Exchange across the Mediterranean: Byzantium, the Crusader Levant, Egypt and Italy* (Aldershot: Ashgate Variorum, 2005).

[49] S.W. Reinert, "The Muslim Presence in Constantinople, 9th-15th Centuries: Some Preliminary Observations," in *Studies on the Internal Diaspora of the Byzantine Empire*, ed. H. Ahrweiler and A.E. Laiou (Washington, DC: Dumbarton Oaks Research Library and Collection, 1998), 130ff. See also D. Jacoby, "Byzantine Trade with Egypt," 35, 65; and idem., "Diplomacy, Trade, Shipping and Espionage between Byzantium and Egypt in the Twelfth Century," in *Polypleuros nous: Miscellanea für Peter Schreiner zu seinem 60. Geburtstag*, edited by C. Scholz und G. Makris (Munich: Saur, 2000), 96 n73, 97 n75.

[50] Jacoby, "What Do We Learn about Byzantine Asia Minor from the Documents of the Cairo Genizah," in *Hē Vyzantinē Mikra Asia, 6.-12. ai.* [Byzantine Asia Minor, 6th-12th cent.], ed. by S. Lamprakēs (Athens: Ethniko Hidryma Ereunōn, Instituto Vyzantinōn Ereunōn, 1998): 83-95.

[51] Nāser-e Khosraw's *Book of travels (Safarnāma)*, translated from Persian, with introduction and annotation by W.M. Thackston, Jr. (Albany, NY: Bibliotheca Persica, 1986), 15-17; T. Bianquis, *Damas et la Syrie sous la domination fatimide: 359-468/969-1076: essai d'interprétation des chroniques arabes médiévales* (Damas: Institut français de Damas, 1986-1989): 535-9.

[52] J-C. Cheynet, "Basil II and Asia Minor," in *Byzantium in the Year 1000*, ed. P. Magdalino (Leiden: E. J. Brill, 2003): 71-108; H. Ahrweiler, *Byzance et la mer. La marine de guerre, la politique et les institutions maritimes de Byzance aux VIIe-XVe siècles* (Paris, 1966): 163-71.

[53] See G. Bass et al., *Serçe Limani.*

The expansion of trade did not, however, completely overshadow the underlying political and military competition between the two dominant powers. The peace treaties were interrupted by periods of violent conflict, mainly over the control of Aleppo, which Byzantium held as a protectorate. This was especially true in the 990s, when Fatimid naval forces attempted to secure provisions for land armies operating deep in the enemy's territory.[54] The importance of naval dominance was recognized by al-ʿAzīz, who in 996 ordered the construction of a fleet—an *usṭūl*—in the arsenal in Cairo in preparation for a major naval expedition. After a fire in the dockyards destroyed sixteen ships and their armaments, a new fleet of twenty-four galleys was built and sent to Syria. When it arrived in Ṭarṭūs, near Tripoli, it was scattered by strong winds, and the crews, together with some serviceable ships, were taken captive.[55] As far as we know, this ill-fated naval expedition of 996 was the largest of its kind undertaken by the Fatimids. It is tempting to speculate that intelligence gathering on the Byzantine coasts formed part of the preparations for this expedition, and that the data on ports and bays collected in the process was then used by author of the *Book of Curiosities* a few decades later for compiling his maps of the Byzantine coasts.

The construction of a Fatimid fleet in the last decade of the eleventh century shows the Caliph's ambitions with regard to Byzantine territories, and it is likely that such an endeavor would have required an effort at gathering intelligence on enemy coasts. But how would the information have been collected? The degree of detailed knowledge of the Byzantine coasts in the *Book of Curiosities* could not have been gained through the direct experience of Fatimid military commanders. Following Byzantiyum's capture of Cyprus, Crete and

---

[54] For accounts of Byzantine-Fatimid warfare, see Y. Lev, "Fāṭimid Navy": 220-52; idem., "The Fatimids and Byzantium, 10th—12th Centuries," *Graeco-Arabica* 6 (1995): 190–208; W. Farag, "The Aleppo Question: a Byzantine-Fatimid Conflict of Interests in Northern Syria in the Later 10th Century," *Byzantine and Modern Greek Studies* 14 (1990): 44–60; Bianquis, *Damas et la Syrie*, 208, 236-7, 478ff; Pryor and Jeffreys, *The Age of the Dromon*, 75ff.

[55] al-Anṭākī, *Tārīkh* (ed. Tadmurī): 233-5, 240-2; al-Maqrīzī, *al-Mawāʿiẓ wa-al-iʿtibār fī dhikr al-khiṭaṭ wa-al-āthār*, ed. A.F. Sayyid (London: Mu'assasat al-Furqān lil-Turāth al-Islāmī, 2002), 3: 619-21. The incident has received much attention in secondary literature, and the riots of the Cairene mob against the Amalfitan merchants accused of setting fire to the fleet are well known. See Lev, "Fāṭimid Navy"; Jacoby, "Byzantine Trade with Egypt": 103; and al-Tadmurī, *Ta'rīkh Ṭarābulus al-siyāsī wa-al-ḥaḍārī ʿabra al-ʿuṣūr* (Tripoli: Maṭābiʿ Dār al-Bilād, 1978), 1: 295-6.

Tarsos in the 960s, the maritime dominance of the Byzantine navy prevented Fatimid galleys from approaching the southern coasts of Anatolia and the Aegean. Raids of North African pirates continued, the most successful leading to the sack of Myra on the southern coasts of Anatoia in 1035. Geniza letters also attest to the activity of pirates capturing Jewish merchants from Attaleia and Strobilos.[56] But these raiding fleets were not under the control of the Fatimids. Al-Muqaddasī, writing at the end of the tenth century, notes that the men with most experience of the Mediterranean are the Byzantines and their military foes, the Muslims of Sicily and al-Andalus.[57] Unlike al-Masʿūdī in the 940s, who singles out the governor of Jabala as the foremost authority on the Mediterranean, al-Muqaddasī could no longer rely on the maritime knowledge of Syrian naval commanders.

Without direct experience of the Byzantine coasts, Fatimid naval commanders could have employed indirect methods, such as interrogating prisoners of war, relying on the experience of North African corsairs, or even translating Byzantine navigation guides, if such actually existed. It is also possible that the Fatimids could rely on the experience of the surviving commanders of the navy of Muslim Crete, conquered by the Byzantines in 961.[58] Contemporary sources, however, point to the importance of merchants as conduits for the transmission of military intelligence. The Byzantine merchant as a potential spy is the subject of a diatribe by Ibn Ḥawqal in the late 10th century, who reports that Byzantine commerce has largely replaced Byzantine piracy.[59] The Byzantine governors of Attaleia now

---

[56] On Muslim pirate raids in the eleventh century, see W. Felix, *Byzanz und die islamische welt in früheren 11. Jahrhundert: Geschichte der politische Beziehungen von 1101 bis 1055* (Wien: Verlag der Österreichischen Akademie der Wissenschaften, 1981), 202ff; J-C. Cheynet, "Basil II and Asia Minor," 97-8, 102-3; Lev, "Fāṭimid Navy": 251; Pryor and Jeffreys, *The Age of the Dromon*, 87; Ahrweiler, *Byzance et la mer*: 130-4; Jacoby, "Genizah." The Geniza letters dealing with the capture of Jewish merchants from Attaleia and Strobilos are edited and translated by J. Starr, *The Jews in the Byzantine Empire, 641-1204* (Athens, 1939): 186 (no. 128), 190 (no. 132), 191 (no. 133).

[57] al-Muqaddasī, *Aḥsan al-Taqāsīm* (ed. Goeje), 15, lines 5-9; Muqaddasī, *Best Divisions*: 16-17.

[58] On the fate of Cretan navy and its commanders after the fall of Crete, see V. Christides, *The Conquest of Crete by the Arabs (ca. 824): A Turning Point in the Struggle between Byzantium and Islam* (Athens, 1984): 184-5. I owe this suggestion to Y. Lev.

[59] Ibn Ḥawqal, *Kitāb Ṣūrat al-arḍ* (ed. Kramers): 197-8. This interpretation is significantly different from the translation in *Configuration de la terre (Kitāb ṣūrat*

prefer to send merchants, not galleys, to the Muslim ports, but these merchants are also spies in disguise, collecting intelligence in preparation of further attacks:

> They [the Byzantine commanders] send their ships (*marākib*) to trade with the land of Islam. The men of the ships spy, observe and explore it inside out, and when they go back they bring first-hand information to the [Byzantine commanders] with regard to its affairs, and advise them on how to harm it. In this way they reach the interior, the plains and the rugged terrain of the lands of Islam, in the full view and knowledge of the Muslim rulers. Many of these rulers even assist them [the merchants] in what they seek, reinforcing the enemy with a wonderful weapon and an effective tool. They do so out of desire for a few objects of vanity to come from the trade with Byzantium, a trade which gives them only a meager profit.[60]

The merchant-cum-spy was an accusation that had a long history and cut both ways. An anecdote in Byzantine chronicles tells of an Arab Syrian spy who came to Byzantium in the 880s to assess the state of Byzantine naval forces and to evaluate the success of an eventual attack by an Arab fleet.[61] The military treatise of Emperor Nikephoros Phokas (963-969) recommends the dispatch of merchants to Muslim territory in times of tension, so that they will gather information.[62]

At the turn of the eleventh century, the increasing number of merchants traveling along the eastern Mediterranean coasts would have enabled the Fatimid navy to gather information on Byzantine coasts in ways that were not possible previously. Thus, the intimate knowledge of the Byzantine waters in the *Book of Curiosities* could well have been a result of the expansion of trade between the southern and northern shores of the eastern Mediterranean. It evidently surpasses by far any surviving account from preceding centuries of raids and conflict. Although the material has a clear military orientation, it comes at time of relative peace, and it is precisely the increased contacts between the Fatimids and Byzantium that may have allowed for such familiarity with Byzantine coasts. The maps of the Byzantine

---

al-arḍ), trns. J.H. Kramers, ed. G. Wiet, 2 vols. (Paris: G.-P. Maisonneuve & Larose, 1964): 192-3.

[60] Ibn Ḥawqal, *Kitāb Ṣūrat al-arḍ* (ed. Kramers): 198; Ibn Ḥawqal, *Configuration de la terre*: 193. My translation slightly differs from Kramers.

[61] N. Koutrakou, "Diplomacy and Espionage: Their Role in Byzantine Foreign Relations, 8th-10th Centuries," *Graeco-Arabica* 6 (1995): 132.

[62] Jacoby, "Diplomacy, Trade, Shipping and Espionage": 84.

coasts in the *Book of Curiosities* were by-products of the commercial revolution of the eleventh century, even if they were not at its service.

IV

The *Book of Curiosities* as a whole is a literary production, a compilation intended for an audience of wealthy and urban Fatimid patrons. It should be re-emphasized that the richly illustrated treatise was not intended to be used on board ships or galleys. However, the author incorporated into his work a wealth of navigation material on the eastern Mediterranean, including detailed accounts of ports, anchorages, islands and bays lying deep in Byzantine waters. The author appears to have derived this information from the records of the Fatimid navy. The military orientation is particularly evident when the maps note the ability of anchorages and ports to accommodate a fleet of galleys (*usṭūl*). References to commerce, on the other hand, are generally missing. It seems likely that the details on Byzantine ports and bays in the *Book of Curiosities* were the fruit of intelligence gathering on the part of the Fatimid navy, possibly in preparation for a naval expedition. One such major expedition towards Byzantine territories took place in 996, just a few decades before the approximate compilation date of the *Book of Curiosities*.

The wealth of detail concerning the Byzantine coasts in the *Book of Curiosities* is unprecedented, utterly surpassing any earlier account of Byzantine coasts in Arabic geographical literature. This quite sudden level of familiarity is likely to have come about through the increased volume of trade and contact at the turn of the eleventh century. Many commercial vessels, similar to the unique shipwreck of Serçe Limani, were travelling back and forth between Byzantine and Fatimid ports. The commercial revolution of the eleventh century, all across the Mediterranean, brought renewed urban expansion and economic prosperity, as well as better knowledge of the territories of one's enemy. Merchants were often accused of acting as spies, and prescriptive military manuals actually encouraged them to do so.

The *Book of Curiosities* represents a unique moment in the eastern Mediterranean, the peak of a period of shared maritime culture that ended with the arrival of the Crusaders and their Italian associates in the eastern Mediterranean. For all their rivalry, Byzantines and Muslims had built similar galleys and commercial vessels, followed comparable tactics of naval warfare, and influenced each other in the development of maritime law.[63] As the *Book of Curiosities* attests for the first time, Muslims also used the Greek nomenclature of wind navigation. This shared maritime culture, given such striking visual representation in the map of the Mediterranean in the *Book of Curiosities*, was soon superseded by the dominance of the Italian fleets. In terms of cartography, the dominance of the European fleets was expressed through the novel form of the portolan maps, which depicted Mediterranean coastlines and wind-rose directions much more accurately than any previous type of map. By the twelfth century, after the Palestinian coastal towns fell to the hands of the Crusaders, few Muslim or Byzantine ships travelled between the northern and southern shores of the Mediterranean.[64] The decline and subsequent virtual disappearance of Muslim shipping towards the Aegean must have led to a decline in the interest of Muslim navies in the coasts of Byzantium. The detailed maps of Anatolian and Aegean coasts in the *Book of Curiosities* had, by a matter of less than a century, become an archaic relic of a maritime culture that had lost the day.[65]

Bibliography

Agius, D. "The Arab Šalandī." In *Egypt and Syria in the Fatimid, Ayyubid, and Mamluk eras. III: Proceedings of the 6th, 7th and 8th International Colloquium Organized at the Katholieke Universiteit Leuven in May 1997, 1998, and 1999*, edited by U. Vermeulen and J. van Steenbergen, 49-60. Leuven: Uitgeverij Peeters, 2001.

[63] See the articles by A. Baubin, D.G. Letsios, and Ch.G. Makrypoulias in *Aspects of Arab Seafaring: An Attempt to Fill in the Gaps of Maritime History*, edited by Y. al-Hijji and V. Christides (Athens: 2002). On maritime law in particular see H. Khalilieh, *Admiralty and Maritime Laws in the Mediterranean Sea (ca. 800-1050): the* Kitāb Akriyat al-Sufun *vis-á-vis the Nomos Rhodion Nautikos* (Leiden: E. J. Brill, 2006); A.L. Udovitch, "An Eleventh Century Islamic Treatise on the Law of the Sea," *Annales Islamologiques* 27 (1993): 37-54.

[64] Pryor, *Geography, Technology and War*: 147-8, 158-9, 161-4; Jacoby, "Byzantine Trade with Egypt": 69-70.

[65] This may partly explain why these maps and diagrams are not preserved in any other manuscript, unlike some of the astronomical, astrological and *mirabilia* chapters, which were copied in later centuries and are found in parallel manuscripts. On the afterlife of the treatise, see http://cosmos.bodley.ox.ac.uk/content.php/boc?expand=732.

Ahrweiler, H. *Byzance et la mer. La marine de guerre, la politique et les institutions maritimes de Byzance aux VIIe-XVe siècles.* Paris: Presses Universitaires de France, 1966.

Akhbār al-Ṣīn wa'l-Hind. Relation de la Chine et de l'Inde, rédigée en 851. texte établi, traduit et commenté par Jean Sauvaget. Paris: Belles Lettres, 1948.

al-Anṭākī, Y.b. S. (d. 1065 or 6). *Tārīkh al-Anṭākī*, edited by 'Umar 'Abd al-Salām Tadmurī. Tripoli (Lebanon): Jarrūs Press, 1990.

Avraméa, A. *Le Péloponnèse du IVe au VIIIe siècle: changements et persistances.* Paris: Publications de la Sorbonne, 1997.

al-Bakrī, A.U. *Al-Masālik wa-al-mamālik*, edited by A.P. Van Leeuwen and A. Ferre. 2 vols. Tunis: al-Dār al-'Arabiya lil-Kitāb, 1992.

Bianquis, T. *Damas et la Syrie sous la domination fatimide: 359-468/969-1076: essai d'interprétation des chroniques arabes médiévales.* Damas: Institut français de Damas, 1986-89.

Cheynet, J-C. "Basil II and Asia Minor." In *Byzantium in the Year 1000*, edited by Paul Magdalino, 71-108. Leiden: E. J. Brill, 2003.

Christides, V. "Milāḥa. 1. In the Pre-Islamic and Early Mediaeval Periods." *Encyclopaedia of Islam*, 2nd edition, 7: 40-6.

——. *The Conquest of Crete by the Arabs (ca. 824): A Turning Point in the Struggle between Byzantium and Islam.* Athens, 1984.

——. "Two Parallel Naval Guides of the Tenth Century: Qudama's Document and Leo VI's *Naumachica.* A Study on Byzantine and Moslem Naval Preparedness." *Graeco-Arabica* 1 (1982): 51-103.

Conrad, L.I. "Islam and the Sea: Paradigms and Problematics." *al-Qanṭara* XXIII, 1 (2002): 123-54.

Fahmy, A.M. *Muslim Sea-power in the Eastern Mediterranean, from the Seventh to the Tenth century A.D: Studies in Naval Organisation.* [London]: Tip. Don Bosco, 1950.

Farag, W."The Aleppo Question: a Byzantine-Fatimid Conflict of Interests in Northern Syria in the Later 10th Century." *Byzantine and Modern Greek Studies* 14 (1990): 44—60.

Felix, W. *Byzanz und die islamische welt in früheren 11. Jahrhundert: Geschichte der politische Beziehungen von 1101 bis 1055.* Wien: Verlag der Österreichischen Akademie der Wissenschaften, 1981.

Foss, C. "The Lycian Coast in the Byzantine Age." *Dumbarton Oaks Papers* 48 (1994): 1-52, reprinted in idem., *Cities, Fortresses and Villages of Byzantine Asia Minor.* Aldershot: Ashgate, Variorum, 1996.

——. *History and Archaeology of Byzantine Asia Minor.* Alderschot: Ashgate, Variorum, 1990.

Gautier Dalché, P. *Carte marine et portulan au XIIe siècle: le "Liber de existencia riveriarum et forma maris nostri Mediterranei" (Pise, circa 1200).* Texte édité et commentée par Patrick Gautier Dalché. Rome: École française de Rome, 1995.

——. "Portulans and the Byzantine world." In *Travel in the Byzantine World: Papers from the Thirty-Fourth Spring Symposium of Byzantine Studies, Birmingham, April 2000*, edited by Ruth Macrides. Aldershot: Ashgate Variorum, c2002.

Gertwagen, R. "Geniza letters: Maritime Difficulties along the Alexandria-Palermo route." In *Communications in the Jewish diaspora: The Pre-modern World*, edited by Sophia Menache, 73-92. Leiden: E. J. Brill, 1996.

Gil, M. "The Flax Trade in the Mediterranean in the Eleventh Century A.D. as Seen in Merchants' Letters from the Cairo Geniza." *Journal of Near Eastern Studies* 63/2 (2004): 81-96.

Goitein, S.D. *A Mediterranean Society. The Jewish Communities of the Arab world as Portrayed in the Documents of the Cairo Geniza.* 6 vols. Berkeley, CA: University of California Press, 1967-93.

Heck, P. *The Construction of Knowledge in Islamic Civilization: Qudāma b. Ja'far and His* Kitāb al-Kharāj wa-ṣinā'at al-kitāba. Leiden: E. J. Brill, 2002.

al-Hijji, Y. and Christides, V. eds. *Aspects of Arab Seafaring: An Attempt to Fill in the Gaps of Maritime History.* Athens, 2002.

Hild, F. "Die lykischen Bistümeer Kaunos, Panormos und Markiane." In *Λιθοξτρωτον. Studien zur byzantinischen Kunst und Geschichte. Festschrift für Marcell Restle*, edited by Birgitt Borkopp and Thomas Steppan, 107-16. Stuttgart, 2000.

Hrbek, I. "Bulghār." In *The Encyclopaedia of Islam*, second edition, 1:1304–8. Leiden: E.J. Brill, 1960.

Huxley, G. "A Porphyrogenitan Portulan." *Greek, Roman and Byzantine Studies* 17:3 (1976): 295-300.

Ibn Bassām, M. b. A. *Kitāb Anīs al-Jalīs fī Akhbār Tinnīs*, edited by Jamāl al-Dīn al-Shayyāl. Cairo: Maktabat al-Thaqāfa al-Dīnīya, 2000.

Ibn Ḥawqal. *Opus geographorum auctore Ibn Ḥauḳal (Kitāb Ṣūrat al-arḍ)*, edited by J.H. Kramers [Bibliotheca Geographorum Arabicorum, 2; 2nd ed.], 2 vols. Leiden: E. J. Brill, 1938–39.

———. *Configuration de la terre (Kitāb ṣūrat al-arḍ)*, translated by J.H. Kramers, ed. G. Wiet, 2 vols. [Collection UNESCO d'oeuvres représentatives, Série arabe]. Paris: G.-P. Maisonneuve, 1964.

al-Idrīsī. *Opus geographicum, sive "Liber ad eorum delectationem qui terras peragrare studeant" (Kitāb nuzhat al-mushtaq)*, edited by Alessio Bombaci, Umberto Rizzitano, Roberto Rubinacci and Laura Veccia Vaglieri. 9 parts. Naples and Rome: Istituto universitario orientale di Napoli and Istituto italiano per il medio ed estremo oriente, 1970–76.

Jacoby, D. "Byzantine Crete in the Navigation and Trade Networks of Venice and Genoa." In *Oriente e occidente tra Medioevo ed éta moderna: studi in onore di Geo Pistarino*, edited by Laura Balletto, 517-540 (Genova: G. Brigati, 1997); repr. in idem., *Byzantium, Latin Romania and the Mediterranean.* Aldershot: Ashgate, c2001.

———. "Diplomacy, Trade, Shipping and Espionage between Byzantium and Egypt in the Twelfth Century." In *Polypleuros nous: Miscellanea für Peter Schreiner zu seinem 60. Geburtstag, mit einem Geleitwort von Herbert Hunger*, edited by Cordula Scholz und Georgios Makris, 83-102. Munich: Saur, 2000.

———. "What Do We Learn about Byzantine Asia Minor from the Documents of the Cairo Genizah." In *Hē Vyzantinē Mikra Asia, 6.-12. ai.* [Byzantine Asia Minor, 6th-12th cent.], edited by Stelios Lamprakēs, 83-95. Athens: Ethniko Hidryma Ereunōn, Instituto Vyzantinōn Ereunōn, 1998.

———. "Byzantine Trade with Egypt from the Mid-Tenth Century to the Fourth Crusade." *Thesaurismata* 30(2000): 102-32, repr. in idem., *Commercial exchange across the Mediterranean: Byzantium, the Crusader Levant, Egypt and Italy.* Aldershot: Ashgate Variorum, 2005.

Jansen, Ph., Nef, A., and Picard, Ch. *La Méditerranée entre pays d'Islam et monde latin: milieu Xe-milieu XIIIe siècle.* [France]: Sedes, 2000.

Johns, J., and Savage-Smith, E. "The *Book of Curiosities*: a newly discovered series of Islamic maps." *Imago Mundi* 55 (2003): 7–24

Kahane, H. and Tietze, R. *The Lingua Franca in the Levant. Turkish Nautical Terms of Italian and Greek Origin.* Urbana, IL: University of Illinois Press, 1958.

Kemp, P. *The Oxford Companion to Ships & the Sea*. London: Oxford University Press, 1976.

Khalilieh, H.S. *Admiralty and Maritime Laws in the Mediterranean Sea (ca. 800-1050): the* Kitāb Akriyat al-Sufun *vis-á-vis the Nomos Rhodion Nautikos*. Leiden: E. J. Brill, 2006.

Koutrakou, N. "Diplomacy and Espionage: Their Role in Byzantine Foreign Relations, 8th-10th Centuries." *Graeco-Arabica* 6 (1995): 125-44.

Lev, Y. "Tinnīs: an Industrial Medieval Town." In *L'Égypte fatimide: son art et son histoire. Actes du colloque organisé à Paris les 28, 29 et 30 mai*, 1998, edited by Marianne Barrucand, 83-96. Paris: Presses de l'Université de Paris-Sorbonne, 1999.

———. "The Fāṭimid navy, Byzantium and the Mediterranean Sea 909-1036 C.E./297-427 A.H." *Byzantion* 54 (1984): 220-52.

———. "The Fatimids and Byzantium, 10th-12th centuries." *Graeco-Arabica* 6 (1995): 190–208.

Lewicki, T. "Les voies maritimes de la Méditerranée dans le haut Moyen Age d'après les sources arabes." In *Navigazione Mediterranea nell'alto Medioevo*, 2:439-69.

Lopez, R.S. *The Commercial Revolution of the Middle Ages, 950-1350* (Cambridge University Press, 1971): esp. 98-9. Spoleto: APR , 1977.

Malamut, "The Region of Serçe Limani in Byzantine Times." In George Bass et al., *Serçe Limani: An Eleventh-Century Shipwreck*. The Nautical Archaeology Series, no. 4. vol. 1. The Ship and its Anchorage, Crew and Passengers, 21-9. College Station, TX: Texas A&M University Press, 2004.

al-Maqrīzī, A. *Al-Mawāʿiẓ wa-al-iʿtibār fī dhikr al-khiṭaṭ wa-al-āthār*, edited by Ayman Fu'ād Sayyid. London: Mu'assasat al-Furqān lil-Turāth al-Islāmī, 2002.

al-Masʿūdī. *Les prairies d'or* [*Kitāb Murūj al-dhahab wa-maʿādim al-jawhar*], edited and translated by C. Barbier de Meynard and Pavet de Courteill. Rev. ed. Charles Pellat [Qism al-Dirāsāt al-Ta'rīkhīyah, 10]. 7 vols. Beirut: Manshūrāt al-Jāmiʿa al-Lubnānīya, 1965–79.

al-Masʿūdī. *Kitâb al-Tanbîh wa'l-ischrâf*, edited by Michael Jan de Goeje [Bibliotheca Geographorum Arabicorum, 8]. Leiden: E. J. Brill, 1894; reprinted 1967.

McGeer, E. *Sowing the Dragon's Teeth: Byzantine Warfare in the Tenth Century*. Washington, DC: Dumbarton Oaks Research Library and Collection, c1995.

al-Muqaddasī. *Aḥsan al-taqāsīm fī maʿrifat al-aqālīm, Descripto imperii moslemici*, edited by Michael Jan de Goeje [Bibliotheca Geographorum Arabicorum, 3]. Leiden: Brill, 1877; rpr. 1906.

———. *The Best Divisions for Knowledge of the Regions: A Translation of Ahsan al-Taqasim fi Maʿrifat al-Aqalim*, translated by Basil Anthony Collins, reviewed by Muḥammad Hamid al-Tai. Reading: Garnet Publishing and The Centre for Muslim Contribution to Civilisation, 1994.

Nāser-e Khosraw. *Book of Travels (Safarnāma)*, translated from Persian, with introduction and annotation by W. M. Thackston, Jr. Albany, N.Y.: Bibliotheca Persica, c1986.

Nordenskiöld, A.E. *Periplus. An Essay on the Early History of Charts and Sailing-Directions*, translated from the Swedish original by F.A. Bather. Stockholm: P. A. Norstedt & Söner, 1897.

Picard, Ch. *La mer et les musulmans d'occident au Moyen Âge, VIIIe-XIIIe siècle*. Paris: Presses Universitaires de France, 1997.

Pinna, M. *Il Mediterraneo e la Sardegna nella cartografia musulmana: dall'VIII al XVI secolo*. Nuoro: Istituto superiore regionale etnografico, [1996?].

Pryor, J.H. "Byzantium and the Sea (900–1025)." In *War at Sea in the Middle Ages and Renaissance*, edited by by John B. Hattendorf and Richard W. Unger, 83-104. Woodbridge: Boydell, 2003.

——. "The Voyages of Saewulf." In *Peregrinationes tres: Saewulf: John of Würzburg: Theodericus*, edited by R. B. C. Huygens, 35-57. Tuonholti: Brepols, 1994.

——. *Geography, Technology and War: Studies in the Maritime History of the Mediterranean, 649-1571*. Cambridge: Cambridge University Press, 1988.

Pryor, J.H., and Elizabeth M. Jeffreys. *The Age of the Dromon: The Byzantine Navy ca. 500-1204*, with an appendix translated from the Arabic of Muḥammad Ibn Mankali by Ahmad Shboul. Leiden: E. J. Brill, 2006.

Qudāma, b. Jaʿfar. *Al-Kharāj wa-ṣināʿat al-kitābah*. Edited Muḥammad Ḥusayn al-Zubaydī. [Baghdād]: Wizārat al-Thaqāfah wa-al-Iʿlām: Dār al-Rashīd, 1981.

Rapoport, Y., and Savage-Smith, E. *The Book of Curiosities: A Critical Edition*. Worldwide-Web publication of Oxford, Bodleian Library, MS Arab. c. 90. (http://www.bodley.ox.ac.uk/bookofcuriosities). 2007.

——. "Medieval Islamic View of the Cosmos: The Newly Discovered *Book of Curiosities*." *The Cartographic Journal* 41 (2004): 253–9.

Reinert, S.W. "The Muslim Presence in Constantinople, 9th-15th Centuries: Some Preliminary Observations." In *Studies on the Internal Diaspora of the Byzantine Empire*, edited by Hélène Ahrweiler and Angeliki E. Laiou, 125-150. Washington, DC: Dumbarton Oaks Research Library and Collection, c1998.

Savage-Smith, E. "The *Book of Curiosities*: An Eleventh-Century Egyptian View of the Lands of the Infidels." In *Geography, Ethnography, and Perceptions of the World from Antiquity to the Renaissance*, edited by Kurt A. Raaflaub and Richard Talbert. [The Ancient World: Comparative Histories, 1]. Malden (Mass.) and Oxford: Blackwell Publishers, forthcoming.

Starr, J. *The Jews in the Byzantine Empire, 641-1204*. Athens, 1939.

Stylianou, A., Stylianou, J.A. *The History of the Cartography of Cyprus*. Nicosia: Cyprus Research Centre, 1980.

al-Tadmurī, U. A.S. *Ta'rīkh Ṭarābulus al-siyāsī wa-al-ḥaḍārī ʿabra al-ʿuṣūr*. Tripoli: Maṭābiʿ Dār al-Bilād, 1978.

Tibbetts, G.R. "The Balkhī School of Geographers." In *History of Cartography, Vol. II, Book 1: Cartography in the Traditional Islamic and South Asian Societies*, edited J. B. Harley, and David Woodward, 108-36. Chicago, University of Chicago Press, 1992.

Udovitch, A.L. "International trade and the Medieval Egyptian countryside." In *Agriculture in Egypt from Pharaonic to Modern Times*, edited by A. K. Bowman and E. Rogan, 267-86. Oxford: Oxford University Press, 1999.

——. "A Tale of Two Cities: Commercial Relations between Cairo and Alexandria during the Second Half of the Eleventh Century." In *The Medieval City*, edited by Harry A. Miskimin, David Herlihy, and A.L. Udovitch, 143-62. New Haven, CT: Yale University Press, 1977.

——. "An Eleventh Century Islamic Treatise on the Law of the Sea." *Annales Islamologiques* 27 (1993): 37-54.

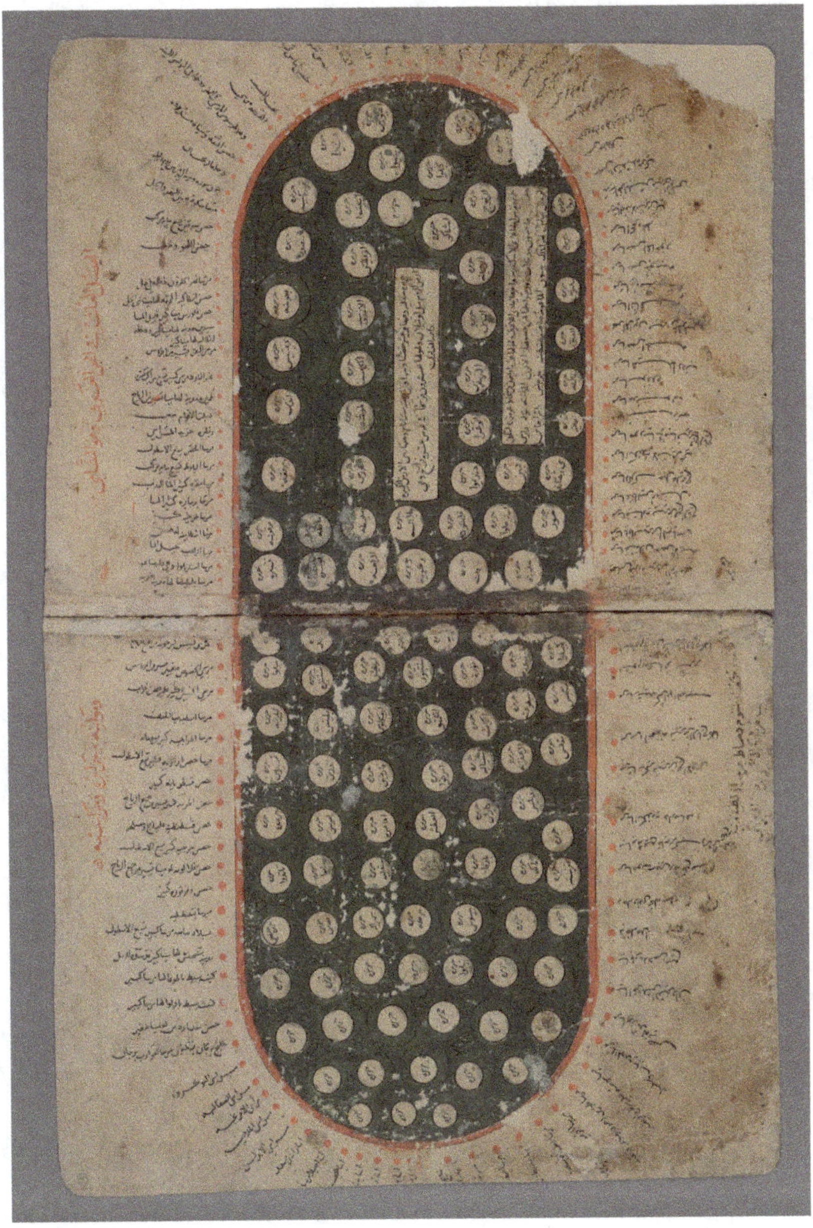

Fig. 1. The map of the Mediterranean from the *Book of Curiosities*. Oxford, Bodleian Library, MS Arab c. 90, fols. 31b-32a (undated, c. 1200). Reproduced with permission of the Bodleian Library.

Fig. 2. The map of the Cyprus from the *Book of Curiosities*. Oxford, Bodleian Library, MS Arab c. 90, fol. 36b (undated, c. 1200). Reproduced with permission of the Bodleian Library.

Fig. 3. Diagram of Aegean Bays from the *Book of Curiosities*. Oxford, Bodleian Library, MS Arab c. 90, fol. 38a (undated, c. 1200). Reproduced with permission of the Bodleian Library.

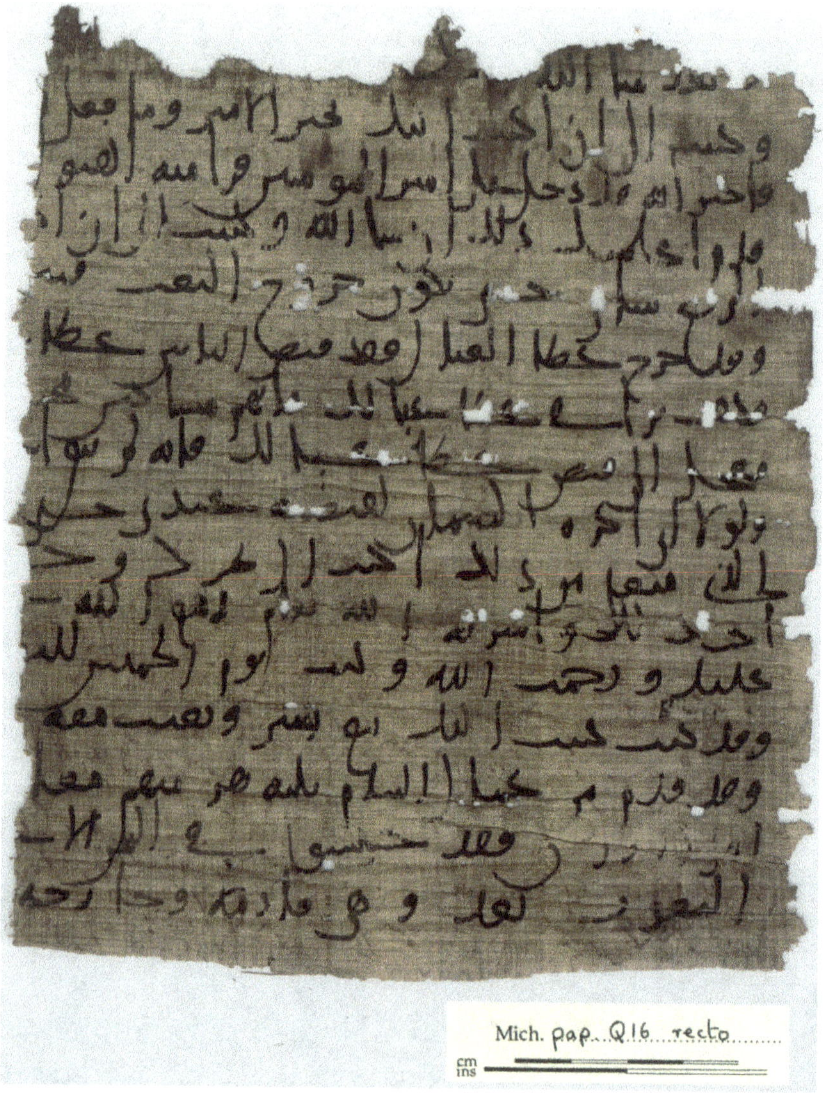

Ill. 1. P. Michaelides Q16.

FROM ARTISAN TO COURTIER: SUFISM AND SOCIAL MOBILITY IN FIFTEENTH-CENTURY EGYPT

Adam Sabra

Social historians of the Medieval Middle East are always searching for new sources. Increasingly, they are making use of chronicles, documents, and archeology to write the social history of the region at a time when archival collections are largely lacking. This article attempts to draw attention to another genre of writing that can be of considerable value to social historians—hagiography. For some time now, historians of medieval Europe have been utilizing the lives of saints to learn about various aspects of medieval society that do not appear in other sources. In addition to learning about the religious beliefs of medieval people, historians also find various kinds of details about everyday life which appear in the lives of saints. Although one must be careful not to lose sight of the original purposes for which these texts were written, and of the rules of the genre which shape these texts, they can offer a window into many aspects of medieval society.

In the case of the medieval Islamic world, the study of the lives of Sufi saints has generally been restricted to religious studies. Although important work has been done in studying and classifying the types of hagiographical literature and of the variety of types of sanctity, social historians have yet to make full use of these texts or to come to grips with the important social roles played by Sufis, especially in the late medieval period when Sufism became increasingly popular and politically important. The reluctance to use hagiographical texts (loosely *kutub al-manāqib*) as sources for social history may be attributed to the nature of the texts themselves. These works frequently focus on miraculous incidents intended to demonstrate the saintly character of their subject. Such miracle stories may appear more useful as evidence of popular beliefs (or superstitions as some would say) than as sources of reliable information about daily life. Nonetheless, some hagiographical works contain a surprising amount of material of interest to the social historian.

This article focuses on one such work, *Kitāb al-sirr al-ṣafī fī manāqib al-Sulṭān al-Ḥanafī* by ʿAlī ibn ʿUmar al-Batanūnī (d. circa 900/1494).[1] The subject of this work, Shams al-Dīn Muḥammad al-Ḥanafī (d. 1443) was the most prominent Shādhilī master of the first half of the fifteenth century in Egypt. As such, he illustrates several important aspects of Egyptian Sufism and its relationship with Egyptian Mamluk society as a whole. Orphaned as a small child, Muḥammad al-Ḥanafī was able to escape poverty and convert a limited education into considerable power, wealth, and influence in fifteenth century Egypt. Sufism thus offered him considerable social mobility as an individual. In addition, the study of Muḥammad al-Ḥanafī's life reveals the ways in which Sufism became a powerful presence in Egyptian society from the Mamluk court to villages of the Egyptian countryside.

Muḥammad al-Ḥanafī was born in approximately 767/1365-6.[2] He lost both his father and his mother as a child and was raised by his maternal aunt. She married a man whom al-Batanūnī contemptuously refers to as "worldly" (*min abnāʾ al-dunyā*), who mistreated and beat his stepson.[3] Muḥammad's stepfather may simply have been practical for when the boy was seven, he tried to find him a trade. He was first apprenticed to a sieve maker but he ran away and took refuge in a Quran school. His stepfather tracked him down and took him to another sieve maker saying, "Take this boy and teach him the trade. Don't be lenient with him; I fear how he may live without a trade."[4] Once again, Muḥammad fled from his master to the Quran school. His step father came again to retrieve him and began to slap him in the face until he fell unconscious. When he awoke, his weeping attracted the attention of a good woman who

---

[1] A. al-Batanūnī, *Kitāb al-sirr al-ṣafī fī manāqib al-Sulṭān al-Ḥanafī* (Cairo: Shaykh Salīm Shirāra al-Qabbānī, 1306/1888). This account is the basis for that in al-Shaʿrānī, *al-Ṭabaqāt al-kubrā* (Beirut: Dār al-Jīl, 1988): 88-101. Unfortunately, we know very little about al-Batanūnī. Even his death date is an approximation. See C. Brockelmann, *Geschichte der arabischen Litteratur* (Leiden: E. J. Brill, 1949), 2:151; Supplementband, 2:152. For works attributed to M. al-Ḥanafī, see Brockelmann, *Geschichte*, 2:148; Supplementband 2:150.

[2] al-Sakhāwī, *al-Tibr al-masbūk fī dhayl al-sulūk* (Cairo: Maktabat al-Kullīyāt al-Azharīya, n. d.): 84; A.R. al-Munāwī, *al-Kawākib al-durrīya fī manāqib al-sūfīya* (Cairo: al-Maktaba al-Azharīya lil-Turāth, 1994), 3:166.

[3] al-Batanūnī, *Sirr*, 1:6.

[4] Ibid.

tried to intervene. A crowd gathered and people insisted that the stepfather allow Muḥammad to pursue his education.[5]

In the end, the stepfather was forced to relent. The education that Muḥammad al-Ḥanafī received in the Quran school was limited, but it gave him an important opportunity to acquire basic literacy and to interact with scholars. The friendships he made with other students lasted a lifetime and were of great significance in introducing him to a circle of wealthier and more learned men. Among these fellow students was Ibn Ḥajar, who later went on to become the greatest *ḥadīth* scholar of his generation and a judge.[6] He also met some of his future disciples, including Sayyidī Abū al-'Abbās, who played an important role in the future saint's life. Apparently, the teacher at the Quran school saw signs of promise in Muḥammad and advised his students to remain close to him. Abū al-'Abbās was the son of a Ḥanafī judge, who was accompanied to the Quran school by a slave who carried his tablet and inkwell while he rode on the back of a donkey.[7] Impressed by the poor boy who walked to school, he began to give him a ride on the donkey, and eventually decided to walk on foot while the young saint rode in his place.

Once Muḥammad al-Ḥanafī graduated from the Quran school, he did not go on to attend a *madrasa*, but rather acquired a basic education in *ḥadīth* and Sufism.[8] He also began to work, using his new skills to earn a living. He taught in the Citadel schools, presumably instructing young mamluks in the Quran. Although this task may have made him familiar with some young mamluks, it is unclear how important these connections were to his later political success. He also sold books in the book market, perhaps copying some of them out himself.[9] An excellent preacher, he sold small pieces of paper on which he had written sermons.[10] These may have been for use as amulets. The money he made from selling these sermons paid for three or four books that would allow him to work in the book market.

This period of modest work did not last. Following a meeting with al-Khiḍr, Muḥammad abandoned his work in the book market,

---

[5] Ibid., 1:7.
[6] Ibid.
[7] Ibid., 1:8.
[8] al-Sakhāwī, *Tibr*: 84.
[9] al-Munāwī, *Kawākib*, 3:167.
[10] al-Batanūnī, *Sirr*, 1:9.

leaving behind his remaining stock in order to seclude himself from society.[11] His school friend Abū al-ʿAbbās led him to a well he owned near a location used by laundrymen to dry clothes. The wealthy young man built a cell for Muḥammad on this site. He also had a *zāwiya* built, but by this time Muḥammad had secluded himself in his cell. The boy was only fourteen years of age, but he spent the next seven years in the cell (with Abū al-ʿAbbās serving him), emerging at age twenty one (circa 788/1386).

Immediately after completing this feat of asceticism, Muḥammad began to teach. He established a weekly session (*mīʿād*) where he would preach and where *samāʿ* would take place.[12] Whether due to the story of seven years in pious seclusion or the quality of his sermons, the *zāwiya* became crowded with people who came to attend his sessions. Originally these sessions took place on Tuesdays, but he changed them to Sundays in order to compete with Christian religious services. The people who attended came from a variety of backgrounds, including rich and poor, amirs, scholars, and state officials.[13] Whenever Muḥammad al-Ḥanafī rode on camel in the city, he would be surrounded by a throng of admirers and would be preceded by a crier.

As is frequently the case in Sufism, prophecies began to circulate validating the status of the young and popular Sufi preacher. In one such prophecy, Abū al-Ḥasan al-Shādhilī is quoted as naming Muḥammad al-Ḥanafī as the one who will "open (or conquer, *fātiḥ*) this household (*bayt*)."[14] Abū al-Ḥasan al-Shādhilī is supposed to have prophesied that Muḥammad al-Ḥanafī would be his fifth *khalīfa*.[15] It is unclear, in fact, how Muḥammad al-Ḥanafī became acknowledged as the leading Shādhilī master of his time, although this seems to be what happened. According to one narrative, Abū al-ʿAbbās suggested that he and Muḥammad approach Nāṣir al-Dīn ibn bint al-Maylaq (d. 797/1395) to receive the Shādhilī way.[16] The

[11] Ibid.

[12] al-Batanūnī, 1:10.

[13] Ibid., 1:11.

[14] Ibid., 1:12.

[15] For the *silsila*s of the Egyptian Shādhilīs, see, É. Geoffroy, *Le Soufisme en Égypte et en Syrie sous les derniers mamelouks et les premiers Ottomans : orientations spirituelles et enjeux culturels* (Damascus : Institut Français de Damas, 1995): 513 ; al-Batanūnī, *Sirr*, 1:23.

[16] al-Batanūnī, *Sirr*, 1:13. On Nāṣir al-Dīn, see Ibn Ḥajar al-ʿAsqalānī, *al-Durar al-kāmina fī aʿyān al-miʾa al-thāmina* (Cairo: Umm al-Qurā lil-Tabāʿa wa al-Nashr, n. d.), 4:114-5.

story is problematic since the decision to seek initiation is supposed to have taken place when Muḥammad was twenty, at the same time that he was in seclusion. Still, some connection with Nāṣir al-Dīn seems to be certain, and later Shādhilī sources accepted Muḥammad al-Ḥanafī's bonafides.

In addition to using Abū al-ʿAbbās's inheritance to build a *zāwiya*, Muḥammad al-Ḥanafī also prevailed upon his friend to spend the remainder of the estate on charitable deeds. The money was distributed to debtors and by symbolically throwing some in the Nile.[17] Although this kind of ritual renunciation of wealth is a common way to begin on the Sufi path, it was not necessarily intended to lead to real poverty. Indeed, the decision to distribute one's wealth among the needy tended to attract the patronage of the wealthy and powerful who made gifts to Sufi shaykhs with the understanding that they would redistribute the funds among the holy and the impoverished on their behalf. Such a public display of charity could be a good career move.

One such donor was Sultan al-Ashraf Barsbāy (reigned 1422-38). On the birthday of the Prophet and on the night of mid-Shaʿbān, he would visit the *zāwiya*, bringing with him cows, sheep, and dirhams to be distributed to those assembled.[18] Such occasions, whether held in the *zāwiya* or on the island of al-Rawḍa drew large crowds, including leading amirs. One year, on the Prophet's birthday, the crowd of women who observed the *mawlid* celebrations from a room overlooking Jāmiʿ al-Raḥma grew so large that the room collapsed and the women fell to the ground killing one.[19] Sultan Barsbāy sent a Baʿlbakkī robe to serve as the woman's shroud. Naturally, the shaykh was expected to feed these enormous crowds. This kind of charity was common in the Mamluk period, and sultans made regular use of the Sufi shaykhs to distribute alms to the poor.[20] The amir Sunqur al-Bashmiqdār donated 1,200 dinars to the shaykh.[21] When word spread of this gift, the poor, needy, and debtors descended on

[17] al-Batanūnī, *Sirr*, 1:14.

[18] Ibid., 1:42.

[19] Ibid., 2:32.

[20] A. Sabra, *Poverty and Charity in Medieval Islam: Mamluk Egypt, 1250-1517* (Cambridge: Cambridge University Press, 2000): 52-5.

[21] al-Batanūnī, *Sirr*, 2:29. The term *bashmiqdār* refers to the sultan's sandals-carrier. See M.Q. al-Baqlī, *al-Taʿrīf bi-muṣtalaḥ Subḥ al-aʿshā* (Cairo: al-Hayʾa al-Miṣrīya al-ʿĀmma lil-Kitāb, 1983): 65.

al-Ḥanafī to receive alms. He sent them to Sunqur, who distributed the money until it ran out.

In addition to his initiation into the Shādhilī order, Muḥammad al-Ḥanafī's authority also derived from his claim to be the renewer (*mujaddid*) of the century and the axial saint (*quṭb*). The assumption of these titles suggests rising ambition and influence within the Sufi community and beyond. In Muḥarram 800/December 1397, al-Ḥanafī asked his followers to take the oath of obedience to him as the renewer of the age.[22] He further claimed to have ascended to the role of axial saint after the death of ʿAlī Wafā (d. 807/1404).[23] The choice of predecessor is interesting. ʿAlī Wafā was heir to a Sufi household that branched off from the Shādhilīya. In addition to being important Sufi thinkers, the Wafās were also extremely wealthy and politically influential.[24] By presenting himself as their successor, Muḥammad al-Ḥanafī may also have intended to follow their model as Sufi notables. Just as the Wafās derived prestige from their descent from ʿAlī ibn Abī Ṭālib, Muḥammad al-Ḥanafī claimed descent from Abū Bakr, which was validated by a dream attributed to a sayyid.[25]

Muḥammad al-Ḥanafī was known in particular for his preaching. This activity was a specialty of the Shādhilīs. On one occasion, he ordered a disciple named Aḥmad ibn Lāshīn al-Abūṣīrī to walk through every major street and market, exhorting people to say their prayers.[26] In general, however, al-Ḥanafī preferred to take a positive approach to his preaching. Rather than threaten his listeners with hellfire, he preferred to speak of the blessings and pleasures of paradise.[27] This more optimistic approach to preaching no doubt contributed to his popularity.

Political Influence

Muḥammad al-Ḥanafī was one of the most influential political figures of his age, one of a long line of politically powerful Sufi shaykhs.

[22] Ibid., 1:22-3.

[23] Ibid., 1:16.

[24] On the Wafās, see R.J.A. McGregor, *Sanctity and Mysticism in Medieval Egypt: The Wafāʾ Sufi Order and the Legacy of Ibn ʿArabī* (Albany: SUNY Press, 2004), especially chapter three.

[25] al-Batanūnī, *Sirr*, 1:17-18.

[26] Ibid., 2:9.

[27] Ibid., 2:24.

Al-Sakhāwī notes, "He was revered by kings and important men, especially al-Ẓāhir [Ṭaṭar (reigned 1421)]."[28] This relationship apparently preceded Ṭaṭar's brief sultanate during which he bestowed a huge *iqṭāʿ* on al-Ḥanafī's *zāwiya*. Ibn Taghrībirdī writes that he "enjoyed fortune with kings," and that he was a companion of his father the Amir Taghrībirdī for many years.[29] He also notes the close relationship between al-Hanafī and al-Ẓāhir Ṭaṭar, but mentions that al-Ḥanafī was a polarizing figure. Some people had great respect for him while others denounced him forcefully. Al-Batanūnī explicitly compares al-Ḥanafī's role as axial saint with that of the sultan. In each case, the man assuming the office took on the almost unbearable burden of bearing the people's cares for them.[30] He describes kings, amirs, and high ranking state officials and scholars sitting passively in front of the shaykh, heads turned downwards out of modesty.[31]

The influence that Muḥammad al-Ḥanafī exercised over Mamluk sultans and other prominent political figures apparently dates to the reign of al-Nāṣir Faraj ibn Barqūq (reigned 1399-1412, with an interruption in 1405). According to Abū al-Ghayth, the son of Shams al-Dīn ibn al-Katīla, a prominent disciple and shaykh in his own right, al-Ḥanafī intervened with the sultan after his Ustādār made forced sales to the population.[32] When al-Ḥanafī implied that the sultan was as much to blame for the policy, the sultan grew angry and expelled the Ustādār from his presence. The sultan then turned to the shaykh and asked, "Does the kingdom belong to you or to me?" To which al-Hanafī replied, "The kingdom does not belong to me or you, it belongs to God, the One, the Overpowering."[33] The sultan was then struck with an illness which could only be cured by al-Ḥanafī who had left Cairo. After various attempts at appeasement, the shaykh sent the sultan a loaf of bread dipped in oil to cure him.[34]

Members of the mamluk elite recognized the special status that Muḥammad al-Ḥanafī had with the sultans and sought his intervention in disputes within the mamluk elite. For example, when one of

---

[28] al-Sakhāwī, *Tibr*: 84.

[29] Ibn Taghrībirdī, *al-Nujūm al-zāhira fī mulūk Miṣr wa al-Qāhira* (Cairo: al-Hay'a al-Miṣrīya al-ʿĀmma li'l-Ta'līf wa al-Nashr, 1971), 15:500.

[30] al-Batanūnī, *Sirr*, 1:30.

[31] Ibid., 2:15.

[32] Ibid., 1:18. On Ibn Katīla, see al-Sakhāwī, *al-Ḍawʾ al-lāmiʿ li-ahl al-qarn al-tāsiʿ* (Beirut: Dār al-Jīl, 1992), 8:248-9.

[33] al-Batanūnī, *Sirr*, 1:19.

[34] Ibid., 1:19-20 for various versions of this story.

Jamāl al-Dīn al-Ustādār's men found himself hopelessly in debt to his boss, his friends advised him to take refuge in al-Ḥanafī's *zāwiya*. He went there and submitted a petition (*qiṣṣa*) stating his problem, just as if he were submitting a petition at a *maẓālim* court.[35] After passing the petition around the group under the prayer beads (*subḥa*), the shaykh granted him sanctuary and he spent a year at the *zāwiya* without anyone knowing where he was. After he left the safety of the *zāwiya*, however, he was quickly arrested and imprisoned. After a miraculous rescue by the shaykh, he was once again arrested and brought before the sultan to face charges of destroying the sultan's property. The sultan, perhaps realizing that there was no way that he could recover his money, ordered him released and he spent the rest of his life at the *zāwiya* reciting the Quran and doing errands in the market for the mendicants.[36]

The shaykh's connections with the wealthy and powerful also allowed him to obtain the freedom of imprisoned men. In one story, his prayers resulted in the release of a man whose brother had appealed to Muḥammad al-Ḥanafī for aid. Muḥammad al-Ḥanafī regarded the privilege of intercession in Cairo as being his monopoly, at least among Sufi shaykhs. Shaykhs who came from elsewhere were expected to consult him before interceding on behalf of others with the sultan. This seems to be the message of an anecdote in which a number of shaykhs from Upper Egypt tried to intercede with Sultan al-Ẓāhir Jaqmaq for the Shaykh al-'Arab Ibn 'Umar.[37] They failed to make the customary visit to Muḥammad al-Ḥanafī before going to see the sultan. As a result, when they returned home Ibn 'Umar was exiled to Kerak instead of being released. On the other hand, when the Jerusalemite Zayn al-Dīn Abū Bakr ibn Abī al-Wafā' came to Cairo to petition the sultan, he stayed in al-Ḥanafī's *zāwiya*.[38] When the time came for him to leave, he reluctantly accepted some traveling money from al-Ḥanafī, saying with embarrassment, "Your gift is larger than the sultan's gift."

---

[35] Ibid., 1:21. On the functioning of the *maẓālim* courts, see J. Nielsen, *Secular Justice in an Islamic State: Maẓālim under the Baḥrī Mamlūks, 662/1264-789/1387* (Leiden: Nederlands Historisch-Archaeologisch Instituut te Istanbul, 1985).

[36] al-Batanūnī, *Sirr*, 1:21-2. For a similar story that ends with the petitioner being restored to his post, see ibid., 1:51. Another incident of this kind took place in the reign of al-Ashraf Barsbāy. See ibid., 2:21.

[37] Ibid., 2:30.

[38] al-Batanūnī, *Sirr*, 2:40.

On one occasion a man whose inheritance had been confiscated by the sultan came to the shaykh for help.[39] The shaykh advised him to attend the *maẓālim* session at the citadel and stand in the back until he was invited to join the meal. Afterwards he had a chance to speak with the sultan when some of his father's soldiers appeared to inform the sultan of an amir's death. The sultan then ordered the father's *iqṭāʿ*, horses, estate and mamluks be turned over to the disinherited son. Obviously, the shaykh was well familiar with the ceremonial of the *maẓālim* court and understood the importance of being in the right place at the right time.

The respect with which the mamluk elite viewed Muḥammad al-Ḥanafī led them to treat him with considerable deference. Like many wealthy and powerful figures of his time, he had a house on the island of al-Rawḍa. On one occasion when he was processing to his house in the company of a group of Turks (i. e. soldiers), judges, merchants, and notables, he met Ibn al-Bārizī, the confidential secretary (Kātib al-Sirr) of Sultan al-Mu'ayyad Shaykh (r. 1412-21), who was traveling with the Nāzir al-Khāṣṣ and their retinues towards Old Cairo.[40] Seeing the huge retinue that accompanied the Shaykh, the Confidential Secretary said to his companion, "Do you see this man—what has he left for the sultan? This is not the way of the mendicants." Against his companion's advice, the Confidential Secretary sent his messenger to the shaykh to tell him, "This is not the way of saints; this is the way of kings." Muḥammad al-Ḥanafī responded by announcing that the Confidential Secretary was fired, demonstrating that he did in fact possess the powers of a king. In another anecdote, al-Batanūnī mentions that al-Hanafī refused a dinner invitation at Ibn al-Bārizī's home, openly accusing him of hypocrisy.[41] It may have been this incident that provoked the confrontation on the road.

In another similar incident, one man challenged al-Hanafī to remove his luxurious clothes and walk with him on foot to visit the Qarāfa.[42] To his surprise, al-Ḥanafī agreed. One the way, they encountered an amir riding with his mamluks and followers. Upon seeing al-Ḥanafī walking on foot in course clothes, the amir hastened to dismount and give his horse to the shaykh and clothed him in

---

[39] Ibid., 2:26.
[40] Ibid., 1:34.
[41] Ibid., 2:16
[42] Ibid., 2:17-18.

robes fit for a king.[43] The amir took the horse's reigns and let him on foot until the shaykh and his companion had completed their visit to the cemetery and returned to the *zāwiya* whereupon al-Ḥanafī returned the amir's possessions. The shaykh then informed the man that what he had seen was God's will and warned him against opposing him again.

When Muḥammad al-Ḥanafī rode in public, he was accompanied by his disciples who performed *dhikr* out loud.[44] This noise would attract attention and the merchants from neighboring markets would come out to pray for the shaykh as he and his followers passed by. The procession sometimes included prominent people such as amirs and judges.[45]

The source of Muḥammad al-Ḥanafī's wealth appears to have been entirely from gifts. He never had to purchase his own clothing or horse because these items were given to him by his admirers and disciples of their own free will.[46] One of his followers was a merchant named ʿAbd al-Qādir, whose son Muḥammad learned to recite the Quran at the Quran school attached to the *zāwiya*.[47] The father was formerly a poor man, but had become wealthy thanks to the shaykh's *baraka*. One suspects that his rise in the world may have been facilitated by the contacts that he made through the shaykh. As al-Batanūnī writes, "God gave him an opening and he bought and sold a lot. People (important people?, *nās*) became acquainted with him and they sought him out to buy and sell."[48] When he became a rich man, he agreed to give one quarter of his *zakāh* to the mendicants of the *zāwiya* on a yearly basis. The shaykh would send the mendicants to him to receive the alms in the form of clothes. On one occasion, he refused to give a mendicant anything but quickly changed him mind for fear of being reduced to his original poverty. Having become wealthy by virtue of the shaykh's blessing, he would not risk losing it. Another disciple of Muḥammad al-Ḥanafī, al-Ḥājj Jamāl al-Dīn ibn Sulayman was responsible for guarding the roads (*mudarrik*) on some land in Gharbīya.[49] He went to visit his shaykh in Cairo and

[43] Ibid., 2:18.
[44] Ibid., 2:19-20.
[45] Ibid., 2:20.
[46] al-Batanūnī, *Sirr*, 2:18
[47] Ibid., 2:18-19.
[48] Ibid., 2:19.
[49] Ibid., 2:23.

stayed in a cell at the *zāwiya*. He loaned some money to his shaykh and profited from the shaykh's *baraka* as a result.

These gifts and loans could also cause the shaykh problems. During his final illness, al-Ashraf Barsbāy agreed to turn over an apartment building that he had constructed to his wife, the daughter of Sultan al-Ẓāhir Ṭaṭar.[50] An admirer of al-Ḥanafī, she then turned over the building to the shaykh, registering the transfer with a Ḥanafī judge. A man later appeared in the *zāwiya* claiming that the building originally belonged to him. He felt obliged to sell it to the sultan for a paltry price because parts of it were run down and he feared what would happen if he refused. This kind of acquisition of property by sultans and powerful amirs was not uncommon in the Mamluk period. Faced with this moral dilemma, the shaykh agreed to turn the building over to its original owner.[51]

Sufi shaykhs frequently competed for the patronage of important persons and the financial gain that went with it. For example, one Turk endowed his house to Muḥammad al-Ḥanafī's *zāwiya*, but this attracted the envy of Abū Bakr al-ʿAjjān, a shaykh of the Sutūḥīya.[52] Al-ʿAjjān went to this Turk's wife who was sympathetic to him. She agreed to conceal the original *waqf* deed and endow the house in favor of al-ʿAjjān upon her husband's death. Unknown to them, however, Muḥammad al-Hanafī had in his possession a second copy of the original endowment deed and he took possession of the house. When al-ʿAjjān complained about this to an amir, they agreed to take the case to the sultan and to have al-Ḥanafī's *zāwiya* demolished. The scheme failed since the sultan, upon realizing that they were complaining against Muḥammad al-Ḥanafī, ordered them exiled to Alexandria.[53] Al-ʿAjjān had managed to rent the house to an amir who came into conflict with the Sufis in al-Ḥanafī's *zāwiya*. When Sultan al-Ashraf Barsbāy heard the case, he consulted with his Dawādār, Sūdūn al-Sūdūnī, who had in his possession a copy of both endowment deeds. Although he attempted to conceal the earlier endowment, he accidentally showed the sultan the wrong deed, thereby validating al-Ḥanafī's claim.[54] Al-Batanūnī claims to have attended this session and indicates that there were a number of Turks

50 Ibid., 2:28.
51 Ibid., 2:28.
52 Ibid., 1:38-9.
53 Ibid., 1:39.
54 Ibid., 1:40.

who were present and took al-Ḥanafī's side against the Dawādār. In the end, the Dawādār was induced to turn over the original deed to al-Ḥanafī.[55] It is not clear whether he did so out of fear of al-Ḥanafī or of the sultan.

Among Muḥammad al-Ḥanafī's followers were a number of Turkish soldiers and their wives. In one anecdote, for example, his group includes the wife of the sultan's *muhtār*.[56] Another disciple was a Turk named Ṭūghān, who regularly attended the *mīʿād* and recited the master's *aḥzāb*.[57] He also met with a group of wives of amirs and members of the *khāṣṣakīya*. A female neighbor who visited the *zāwiya* found him surrounded by this group of beautiful, well-dressed, and perfumed women who were staring at him.[58] The neighbor was reassured when she had a vision in which the women appeared as skeletons, indicating that the shaykh saw them for what they truly were.[59] The judge Nūr al-Dīn ibn Aqbars, who administered the endowments and other financial assets of the sultan in the reign of al-Ẓāhir Jaqmaq came to the shaykh pleading bankruptcy due to the excessive spending of his wife, the daughter of (Sultan ?) Īnāl.[60] The shaykh took up a collection among the members of his family to aid the man.

Although they do not appear as benefactors, a number of prominent religious scholars also attended Muḥammad al-Ḥanafī's *mīʿād*. These included Jalāl al-Dīn al-Bulqīnī, Sirāj al-Dīn al-Bulqīnī, Badr al-Dīn al-ʿAynī, Shams al-Dīn al-Bisāṭī, and ʿAlam al-Dīn al-Akhnāʾī.[61] The respect he received from some of the highest ranking jurists and judges of his time must have increased his reputation, both among scholars and statesmen. It also gave him more access to the Mamluk court, where men like al-ʿAynī, to give one example, were held in considerable esteem. These sessions were also attended by preachers and their students, who would record the shaykh's words. The Sufis resident in Cairo's cemeteries and on Mount Muqaṭṭam also attended.[62] Another consequence of al-Ḥanafī's influence among the

---

[55] al-Batanūnī, *Sirr*, 1:40-1.

[56] Ibid., 1:35. The *muhtār* was responsible for the slaves in various branches of the sultan's household. See al-Baqlī, *Muṣṭalaḥ*: 333-4.

[57] al-Batanūnī, *Sirr*, 1:35.

[58] Ibid., 1:36.

[59] For another version of this story see ibid., 1:45.

[60] Ibid., 2:31.

[61] Ibid., 2:4. See also, ibid., 2:22.

[62] Ibid.

scholars is that his recommendation was sought for the appointment of officials. For example, on one occasion a prominent person asked al-Ḥanafī to intercede with his old friend Ibn Ḥajar to have a student appointed as a *shāhid*. Initially al-Ḥanafī agreed until he had a vision revealing the poor moral character of the student.[63]

As a result of his influence among the scholars and of his many students, Muḥammad al-Ḥanafī had contacts with *zāwiyas* throughout the Mamluk empire, many of which were administered by former students. In Mecca, a disciple known as Abū al-ʿAbbās presided over Ribāṭ Rabīʿ.[64] Al-Ḥanafī's political contacts were so widespread that he employed ʿAbd al-Raḥmān al-Suwayfī to compose official letters on his behalf.[65] In effect, he had his own confidential secretary, as would the sultan or a provincial governor. When one disciple took the oath of allegiance to the shaykh, al-Suwayfī composed the diploma (*manshūr*) granting him the rank of shaykh and making him the administrator of the grave of Khālid ibn al-Walīd in Homs.[66] This document confirmed a decree (*marsūm*) from Sultan al-Ashraf Barsbāy. This incident suggests that Muḥammad al-Ḥanafī worked in a semi-official way to fill posts in Sufi institutions throughout the Mamluk empire.

One consequence of the spread of the shaykh's reputation is that he began to receive gifts from foreign Muslim rulers. He received robes from the "king of India" and a *duwayba* from "Rūm."[67] From the ruler of Tunis Mawlāy Abū al-Fāris al-Khiḍr (=Abū Fāris ʿAbd al-ʿAzīz al-Mutwakkil, reigned 796-837/1394-1434?), he received a comb for his beard that could be folded into the shape of a Quran stand. This item he gave to Sultan al-Ashraf Barsbāy as a gift. When he received plums from Damascus, he sent some to Barsbāy, who distributed them to his amirs and state officials. This practice of exchanging gifts with rulers might be regarded as inappropriate for a Sufi shaykh, but al-Batanūnī defends it saying, "Sayyidī's practice of exchanging gifts with kings was for the benefit of the Muslims for many people needed him and he frequently interceded (*shafāʿa*) with

[63] Ibid., 2:13. It is not clear from the context whether the term *shāhid min ṭalabat al-ʿilm* refers to a notary or to another functionary at a *madrasa* or similar institution.
[64] Ibid.
[65] Ibid., 2:33.
[66] Ibid.
[67] al-Batanūnī, *Sirr*, 2:17.

kings, amirs, and other office holders. All of his intentions were beautiful, may God have mercy on him."[68]

Influence in the Provincial and Rural Areas

Muḥammad al-Hanafī's influence was not limited to his Sufi community in Cairo or to the Mamluk court located there. He also had contacts with and often control over a number of Sufi monasteries located throughout the Nile Delta. One of these institutions was the Zāwiya al-Mukhliṣīya located in town of Ṣandafā.[69] The shaykh who presided there was Nūr al-Dīn al-Shādhilī. On one occasion, he intervened miraculously in a dispute involving one of his disciples in al-Maḥalla.[70] Another disciple, Shaykh Nūr al-Dīn al-Ūrīnī, was active in spreading the way in al-Buḥayra.[71] The shaykh ordered one of his disciples, Shaykh Khalaf al-Mashālī (d. 874/1469) to go to Burullus, where he spent seven years until he called him back to Old Cairo.[72] Later Sultan al-Ẓāhir Jaqmāq appointed Khalaf to teach Ḥanafī law in a *madrasa* in Alexandria.[73] Like his master, he grew up an orphan, although in the village of Mashāl in Gharbīya, rather than in the capital.

The shaykh seems to have made regular visits to the provinces in order to visit his former disciples and perhaps inspect the institutions they ran. One occasion, he made a trip to al-Maḥalla al-Kubrā with a large retinue.[74] He received and invitation to stay with Nūr al-Dīn ibn al-Nawsānī, who was the official (*mutadarrik*) in charge of policing the roads at Ṣandafā.[75] Al-Hanafī stayed two days with al-Nawsānī, during which time he was visited by the local dignitaries, including the chief judge. Al-Nawsānī provided a full menu of meat, other foods, and sweets, but the shaykh abstained from eating. His disciples

---

[68] Ibid.

[69] Ibid., 1:30.

[70] Ibid., 1:36.

[71] Ibid., 2:25-6.

[72] Ibid., 2:4-5. On him, see al-Sakhāwī, *Ḍaw'*, 3:185-6.

[73] It is not entirely clear whether Khalaf was supposed to teach Hanafī law, serve as a judge, or both.

[74] al-Batanūnī, *Sirr*, 1:46.

[75] Variations of the root d-r-k appear in this text. They appear to be equivalent to the *arbāb al-idrāk* who were responsible for guarding public roads in rural areas. See Baḥr Majdī, *al-Qarya al-Miṣrīya fī 'aṣr salāṭīn al-mamālīk, 647-923/1250-1517* (Cairo: al-Hay'a al-Miṣrīya al-'Āmma li'l-Kitāb, 1999): 67.

took full advantage of the occasion. Some of his disciples were from the town of Bulqīnā, and they too awaited the arrival of their shaykh so that they could offer him hospitality.[76] There too, he refused to eat.

In rural areas, as in the capital, Muḥammad al-Hanafī arbitrated disputes and righted wrongs. In one case, narrated by Ṭalḥa al-Mansha'āwī, the shaykh arbitrated a family dispute between Ṭalḥa and his paternal cousins during a stay at their *zāwiya* in al-Mansha al-Kubrā (=al-Manshīya al-Kubrā).[77] Apparently, the dispute was over the income from a number of properties (*ruzayqāt*) that presumably benefited the family *zāwiya*. Since Ṭalḥa's father was dead, he needed someone to demand his share from his uncles and cousins. The shaykh may not have been able to intervene in the dispute directly, but he promised the boy Ṭalḥa (who later married at age fifteen) that his progeny would outlive that of his cousins.[78] In this way, his branch of the family came into their rightful inheritance.

Since his Cairo *zāwiya* benefited from more than one *iqṭā* 'Muḥammad al-Ḥanafī was also involved in rural society as a *muqṭa'*, albeit one with a reputation for unusual kindness. For example, on one occasion he requested twenty *ardabb*s of wheat from the village of Shannīsa in Sharqīya, which was part of the *zāwiya*'s *iqṭā'*.[79] The ship carrying the grain sank in the Nile and the ship's captain took refuge in the *zāwiya* from the Chamberlain's men who blamed him for the loss of grain. The captain fled from the *zāwiya* when the Chamberlain's men arrived, but the shaykh rescued him by paying some dinars in compensation for what had been lost.[80] In another incident, al-Ḥanafī gave up a *ruzayqa* of three or four *faddān*s in Giza to provide an income for a poor but learned scholar from the Maghrib.[81] He wrote a *tawqī'* on which he obtained the *'allāma* of Sultan al-Ashraf Barsbāy. A few days later, he was compensated with a *ruzayqa* of ten *faddān*s in the village of Barājīm.[82] Clearly, the sultan wished to reward him

[76] al-Batanūnī, *Sirr*, 1:46. For another story of the shaykh's abstemiousness, see ibid., 2:3.

[77] al-Batanūnī, *Sirr*, 1:48.

[78] Ibid., 1:49.

[79] Ibid., 2:29. A village by this name is located in al-Daqahlīya, but there may have been another village with a similar name in Sharqīya.

[80] Ibid., 2:30.

[81] Ibid., 2:39.

[82] I have been unable to locate a village by this name, although there are others with very similar names.

for his taking a foreign dignitary under his wing. Perhaps he did so at the sultan's request. The shaykh sent a group of his mendicants to Barājīm to wait until the harvest was gathered and threshed and bring wheat for use in the *zāwiya*. They stayed with the village elder, who respected the Sufis.[83]

Similarly, Muḥammad al-Ḥanafī intervened to help the peasants who resided in the village of Mākūsa in the district of Ibn Khaṣīb. The village was also part of an *iqṭāʿ* which benefited the *zāwiya*.[84] In this case a man was found murdered in a neighboring village and the inhabitants of the village, fearing the wrath of the authorities, threw the body into a field in Mākūsa. When the Kāshif learned of the body, he had many of the village's peasants arrested. Apparently, it was his intention to extract a fine from them. The shaykh sent his messenger, Nāsir al-Dīn al-ʿAzīz, to Sultan al-Ashraf Barsbāy. The Sultan, who held the village in which the murder had actually taken place, sent a decree to the Kāshif, instructing him to release the peasants without a fine.

Muḥammad al-Ḥanafī's political connections and influence in the provinces made him a logical figure for peasants to turn to in order to obtain justice from *muqṭa*ʿs and their administrators. One such incident involved an accountant (*mubāshir*) named Ibn al-Nimār, who had a reputation for being a tyrant. One such oppressed peasant turned to al-Ḥanafī, who sent his messenger to Ibn al-Nimār to plead the peasant's case. Ibn al-Nimār responded with a letter in which he wrote, "If you are a shaykh, sit in your *zāwiya* and don't intervene between accountants and peasants."[85] The shaykh then ordered his messenger to take Ibn al-Nimār by the ear and tell him, "Ibn al-Nimār, we have lifted his hand from you and tied his tongue so that he will not answer you. Muḥammad al-Ḥanafī says to you, 'We have torn you up just as we tore up your letter. Even if you have a thousand Bisṭāmīs by your side.'" Not long afterwards, the sultan sent men to demolish Ibn al-Nimār's home. His property was seized and he was taken off to jail where he died of hunger and poverty.[86] Interestingly, this anecdote can be seen as a part of a competition between different Sufi groups and their patrons. Ibn al-Nimār was

[83] Ibid.
[84] Ibid.
[85] Ibid., 1:31.
[86] Ibid., 1:31

the patron of the Bisṭāmī Sufis while the Shādhilī shaykh Muḥammad al-Ḥanafī enjoyed the support of the sultan.

Although peasants sometimes abandoned their lands to emigrate to the city, they always faced the possibility that they might be located by the *muqṭaʿ* of their village and sent back to farm. One such case is narrated by Shams al-Dīn al-Sakhāwī (not to be confused with the more famous biographer, chronicler, and *ḥadīth* scholar), who eventually went on to be appointed a judge in Medina. "We were obliged to farm a plot of land [*kānat ʿalaynā falāḥa*] and I was resident at the *zāwiya* of Sayyidī, may God have mercy on him. The peasants who resided at Maḥallat al-Qaṣab (al-Sakhāwī's home village) reported us to the amir. They sought after me because of the plot and harassed me until I was in a bad state."[87] Faced with the possibility of arrest and deportation to the village, al-Sakhāwī sought the help of his shaykh. The amir who held the *iqṭāʿ* promptly suffered a riding accident and was replaced with another amir, who was a disciple of the shaykh. At the master's request, the amir wrote a proclamation (*manshūr*) informing the judges (*hukkām*) that al-Sakhāwī had been emancipated (*maʿṭūq*) from his obligations as a peasant and should not be interfered with. He then turned over the proclamation to al-Sakhāwī.

Naturally, the fact that a number of amirs were admirers of Muḥammad al-Ḥanafī allowed him to intervene on behalf of the peasants who lived on lands in their *iqṭāʿ*. In one case, an impressive looking man arrived at the *zāwiya* under arrest in chains in the company of a messenger. He indicated that he was al-Ḥājj Ibrāhīm ibn Sābiq from the village of Damlū, and that he was "a peasant of your admirer al-Timurāzī."[88] He had been imprisoned due to the debt he owed al-Timurāzī, and unnamed persons had advised him to seek the help of the shaykh. The shaykh had the amir brought to the *zāwiya* and addressed him, "This man informs us that he is one of your peasants and that he has spent quite some time in prison. I didn't think that the master (*makhdūm*, here an honorary title) would do this to a Muslim due to what I know of your goodness and love for the poor (*fuqarāʾ*, possibly mendicants)."[89] The amir then promised to treat the man well from now on. When the shaykh

[87] Ibid., 1:38.

[88] Ibid., 1:52-3. Again, this village is unknown, although its name resembles that of several other known villages. A number of amirs shared this name.

[89] Ibid., 1:53.

inquired, the peasant, who was apparently a wealthy man informed him that he owed the amir 160,000. Presumably this refers to dirhams *min al-fulūs*, but it is still a substantial sum. If correct, it suggests that the peasant was an entrepreneur who rented the amir's *iqṭāʿ* and farmed it for a profit. The amir then agreed to forgive half of the debt and accept payment of the remainder in installments. He then released Ibn Sābiq to return to his home and family.

Another story of the same type involved a peasant of the amir Ṭūghān al-Ustādār, who spent four years in prison before convincing his jailers to allow him to visit Muḥammad al-Ḥanafī to seek his intervention.[90] The shaykh spent for Ṭūghān, who appeared. The shaykh complimented the amir's outer garment, which he immediately offered to the shaykh. The shaykh then sold it back to him for 100,000, which he used to settle the man's debt adding a sermon to frighten the amir of the consequences of his deeds on the Day of Judgment.[91]

Muḥammad al-Ḥanafī's influence on his disciples allowed him to restrain their oppression of peasants. One disciple, a man from al-Maḥalla al-Kubrā named al-Ḥājj ʿAlī ibn Qudayḥ, operated an oil press.[92] As he customarily did, he loaned some peasants a few dirhams to pay seeds to plant flax. When the flax season arrived, however, the peasants denied having received the loan. Unable to get his money back, he approached the amir who held the village and purchased the power of policing (*tadrīk*) over the village intending no doubt to punish the dishonest villagers. Before heading home, however, he stopped at Muḥammad al-Ḥanafī's *zāwiya* and told him what he had done. The shaykh demanded that he give up his police powers, which he did at a cost of a one hundred dinars.

In the final years of his life, Muḥammad al-Ḥanafī seems to have returned to where he began. According to al-Batanūnī, his final illness lasted for seven years, the same period he spent in seclusion at the beginning of his Sufi career.[93] During that time he suffered greatly, and he adopted a policy of extreme asceticism, a remarkable change from his life of power, wealth, and influence. He is said to have prayed to God to be tested with lice, to sleep with the dogs, and

[90] Ibid., 1:53. The author mentions that this occurred in the reign of al-Ashraf Barsbāy.
[91] Ibid., 1:54.
[92] Ibid., 2:36.
[93] Ibid., 2:56.

to be left to die in the middle of the road.[94] He then proceeded to fulfill his own prophecy, even having himself placed in a location in his house where people would constantly pass by, as if he were in a public street. In this way, he sought to imitate the example of pious ascetics like ʿAbdallāh ibn Mubārak, who prepared for death by adopting rituals of extreme poverty and asceticism. His death on 5 Rabīʿ II 847/1 August 1443 was accompanied by a debate among family and disciples about where he should be buried. In the end, he was buried in his cell in the *zāwiya*, as he wished. An attempt to bury him in the Qarāfa was prevented by the intervention of Sultan al-Ẓāhir Jaqmaq.[95] Perhaps he had informed the sultan of his wishes before he died, or maybe his family sought the sultan's intervention. Even after death, he is supposed to have briefly opened his eyes and informed his mourners that death would not prevent him from interceding on their behalf.[96] They need only visit his grave and present their complaint to him as before.

Indeed, Muḥammad al-Ḥanafī's ability to provide for his family did not end after his death. His son Maḥmūd tells a story of how the family became destitute.[97] He went to his father's grave to pray for help and shortly after returning home one of his father's admirers (*muḥibb*) sent a messenger with a platter of roast lamb and bread. Similarly, when Maḥmūd had nothing but a torn shirt to wear, a slave girl arrived bearing new clothes.[98] She was sent by Khawand, the daughter of Sultan Ṭaṭar and the wife of Sultan al-Ashraf Barsbāy. Clearly, Muḥammad al-Hanafī's patrons had not forgotten his family.

Muḥammad al-Ḥanafī's life, even in some of its more improbable miraculous events, demonstrates the power which a few select Sufi shaykhs could exercise in Mamluk Egypt. Although from modest origins, al-Ḥanafī's reputation for piety brought him into contact with the wealthy and the powerful. Access to the court provided al-Ḥanafī with substantial economic resources which he could redistribute at his discretion. His power of intercession in worldly as well as supernatural affairs made him a valuable ally and a powerful patron. His disciples spread throughout Egypt and the Mamluk

94 Ibid.
95 Ibid., 2:57-8.
96 Ibid., 2:58.
97 Ibid., 1:49-50; 2:59.
98 Ibid., 1:50.

empire and he was well-known and respected, especially in the Nile Delta region. His life illustrates the power wielded by shaykhs in a society increasingly permeated by Sufism from top to bottom.

Bibliography

Primary Sources

al-Baqlī, M.Q. *al-Ta'rīf bi-muṣtalaḥ Subḥ al-a'shā*. Cairo: al-Hay'a al-Miṣrīya al-'Āmma li'l-Kitāb, 1983.

al-Batanūnī, A.b.U. *Kitāb al-sirr al-ṣafī fī manāqib al-Sulṭān al-Ḥanafī*. Cairo: Shaykh Salīm Shirāra al-Qabbānī, 1306/1888.

Ibn Ḥajar al-'Asqalānī. *al-Durar al-kāmina fī a'yān al-mi'a al-thāmina*. Cairo: Umm al-Qurā li'l-Tabā'a wa al-Nashr, n. d.

Ibn Taghrībirdī. *al-Nujūm al-zāhira fī mulūk Miṣr wa al-Qāhira*. Cairo: al-Hay'a al-Miṣrīya al-'Āmma li'l-Ta'līf wa al-Nashr, 1971.

al-Munāwī, A.R. *al-Kawākib al-durrīya fī manāqib al-sūfīya*. Cairo: al-Maktaba al-Azharīya li'l-Turāth, 1994.

al-Sakhāwī, Sh.D. *al-Ḍaw' al-lāmi' li-ahl al-qarn al-tāsi'*. Beirut: Dār al-Jīl, 1992.

——. *al-Tibr al-masbūk fī dhayl al-sulūk*. Cairo: Maktabat al-Kullīyāt al-Azharīya, n. d.

al-Sha'rānī, 'A.W. *al-Ṭabaqāt al-kubrā*. Beirut: Dār al-Jīl, 1988.

Secondary Sources

Baḥr, M.'A.R. *al-Qarya al-Miṣrīya fī 'aṣr salāṭīn al-mamālīk, 647-923/1250-1517*. Cairo: al-Hay'a al-Miṣrīya al-'Āmma li'l-Kitāb, 1999.

Brockelmann, C. *Geschichte der arabischen Litteratur*. Leiden: E. J. Brill, 1949.

Geoffroy, É. *Le Soufisme en Égypte et en Syrie sous les derniers mamelouks et les premiers Ottomans : orientations spirituelles et enjeux culturels*. Damascus: Institut Français de Damas, 1995.

McGregor, R.J.A. *Sanctity and Mysticism in Medieval Egypt: The Wafā' Sufi Order and the Legacy of Ibn 'Arabī*. Albany: SUNY Press, 2004.

Nielsen, J. *Secular Justice in an Islamic State: Maẓālim under the Baḥrī Mamlūks, 662/1264-789/1387*. Leiden: Nederlands Historisch-Archaeologisch Instituut te Istanbul, 1985.

Sabra, A. *Poverty and Charity in Medieval Islam: Mamluk Egypt, 1250-1517*. Cambridge: Cambridge University Press, 2000.

MINI-DRAMAS BY THE WATER: ON IRRIGATION RIGHTS AND DISPUTES IN FIFTEENTH-CENTURY DAMASCUS

*Boaz Shoshan**

Generating institutional patterns of a local nature, irrigation systems functioned in Mediterranean societies since ancient times. To avoid conflict over scarce water a fair distribution was necessary and such dictated certain arrangements that have been variously elaborated. The existence of some shared principles upon which to establish such arrangements in order for them to succeed must be assumed: distribution proportional to the size of cultivated land and an individual's sense of obligation to the community, for example.[1] That codifying regulations of water supply was a desideratum in the medieval Islamic world may be concluded from the Persian *Kitāb-i Qāni* ("The Book of Qānāt"), written possibly in the eleventh century A.D., which purpose was to protect owners of subterranean aqueducts, that is, subsurface canals that were engineered to collect ground water and direct it through a gently sloping underground conduit to surface canals.[2]

Apart from discussions of matters of irrigation in legal works,[3] medieval sources provide us with little information on the human dynamics and social interaction that are an integral part of irrigation

* I am indebted to Professor Geert Jan van Gelder of the University of Oxford for some suggestions of interpreting the Arabic.

[1] T.F. Glick, *Irrigation and Society in Medieval Valencia* (Cambridge, Mass.: Harvard University Press, 1970): 187; idem, "Conflict in Irrigation Communities: One Decade in Medieval Valencia 1407-1416," in *Irrigation and Hydraulic Society* (Aldershot: Variorum, 1996). In Sunnī Islam, for example, river water can be used for irrigation, provided that it does not harm the community. See D.A. Caponera, "Ownership and Transfer of Water and Land in Islam," in *Water Management in Islam*, ed. N.I. Faruqui, A.K. Biswas and M.J. Bino (Tokyo: United Nations University Press, 2001): 96-7, quoting al-Māwardī.

[2] P.W. English, "The Origin and Spread of Qanats in the Old World," *Proceedings of the American Philosophical Society* 112 (1968): 170-81, reprinted in *Production and the Exploitation of Resources*, ed. M.G. Morony (Burlington, VT.: Ashgate Publishing, 2002): 273-84; D.R. Lightfoot, "Syrian qanat Romani: history, ecology, abandonment," *Journal of Arid Environments* 33 (1996): 321.

[3] H. Bruno, *Contribution à l'étude du régime des eaux en droit musulman* (Paris, 1913). For Mālikī discussion of irrigation in the medieval Maghreb, see N. Hentati,

systems. Their silence hides from us the intricacies involved and energy that must have been spent by all those engaged in matters concerning a frequently scarce resource that water has been. Exceptional in this respect is information that can be found in Shihāb al-Dīn Aḥmad Ibn Ṭawq's *Taʿlīq*, less a conventional chronicle and more a "diary" (*yawmīyāt*)[4] produced by a Damascene notary (*shāhid*) who lived between 834/1430 and 915/1509. The *Taʿlīq* is known to have covered the relatively short time span of 885/1480 to 908/1503 only; furthermore, the single copy (autograph) that is extant at the Ẓāhiriyya Library is incomplete and terminates in reports on 902/1497. Despite these limitations it is unquestionable that, upon comparison with other sources for Damascus of the same period, Ibn Ṭawq's work supersedes all other in terms of the richness of material it offers about the social scene in the largest Syrian city during the last years of the fifteenth century A.D.[5] And although it by and large neglects political affairs, it provides most detailed and variegated information about what is known as *Alltagsgeschichte* namely, the history of daily life.

Of special value is the inclusion in this work of many dozens of notarial documents that Ibn Ṭawq himself produced. They pertain to a whole gamut of social and economic reality and refer to various acts involving the most basic routine of every-day life in a large urban center: transactions and sales, inheritances, agreements with peasants of the neighboring villages, financial disputes and much more. As to matters of irrigation, what Ibn Ṭawq provides is not abundant but is certainly invaluable in the light of the general rarity of this sort of information and, as we shall see below, is certainly superior to what one finds in the chronicle written by his contemporary Ibn Ṭūlūn. And thus, while we know from legal work that Muslim jurists regarded water as a commodity that could be sold and traded in,[6] a

"L'eau dans la ville de l'occident musulman medieval d'apres les sources juridiques malikites," *Revue d'histoire maghrebine* 28 (2001): 163-220.

[4] Thus subtitled by Jaʿfar al-Muhājir, its editor, who in his introduction has some biographical details on Ibn Ṭawq. See also my forthcoming article in a collection edited by R. Amitai and A. Levanoni.

[5] Thus, while in Ibn Ṭūlūn's *Mufākahat al-khillān*, the standard source for fifteenth-century Damascus, the years 886-902 H receive about 40 pages in the printed edition, In the *Taʿlīq* these years receive about 1,000 pages, certainly a staggering difference.

[6] M.T. Kadouri, Y. Djebbar, and M. Nehdi, "Water Rights and Water Trade: An Islamic Perspective," in *Water Management in Islam*: 89; Caponera, "Ownership": 98, quoting Māwardī.

transaction notarized by Ibn Ṭawq himself in 887/1482 attests to the working of this idea in practice. Here, one Aḥmad b. ʿUthmān al-ʿAjlūnī al-Qādirī sold to ʿAbd al-Wahhāb al-Ṭarābulusī, for the sum of one thousand dirhams, due upon demand (*ḥālla*) and payable in the latter's presence (*maqbūḍa bi'l-ḥaḍra*), "the entire lawful share" (*jamīʿ al-farḍ*) of the restored water tower (*al-ṭāliʿ al-mustajadd*) at the barn known as the Black Stone (*al-ḥajar al-aswad*) in the vicinity of the East (Sharqī) Gate of Damascus.[7]

Not all cases involving water were straightforward as this one, however. Water being a scarce commodity, one may assume that it was not infrequently in the focus of conflicts. A laconic statement about a settlement (*ṣulḥ*) that was reached in Muḥarram 886/March 1481, in the presence of the viceroy of Damascus and the chief *qāḍī*s, between one Kamāl al-Dīn and Shihāb al-Dīn al-Muḥawjib concerning water that was coercively (*ẓulman*) diverted from the al-Manshīya river canal, provides us with only a faint echo about such conflict and is an example of a case now lost to the modern reader.[8] Fortunately, on other occasions of water disputes Ibn Ṭawq paints a more detailed picture that allows some idea about their nature. To these I now wish to turn.

* * *

The first incident about which Ibn Ṭawq elaborates occurred in Jumādā II 886/July 1481, when the viceroy of Damascus (*malik al-umarā'*) and three of the leading *qāḍī*s of the city arrived at the Dāʿiya, a branch of the Barada that bifurcates near the north-eastern gate of the city known as Bāb Tūmā (St. Thomas).[9] The reason was an initiative taken by the inhabitants of the village al-Manīḥa, located in the cultivated region outside Damascus and known as the Ghūṭa,[10] who without having a legal right, opened the barrage operating there and drew water to the disadvantage of other cultivators of the area. Now the Mamluk party decided to block the barrage. However, one [Muḥammad] al-Khalīlī "the muezzin" testified to the fact that the rights of irrigation of those in the vicinity of the Dāʿiya were in the fields above the home of one Ḥalbuṣ (Ṭubrus, according to Ibn

---

7 *Taʿlīq*: 134.

8 *Ibid.*: 41. Although the text refers to *nā'ib al-qalʿa* it is more likely, given the information for other cases (see below), that *nā'ib* is the relevant term.

9 It is known now as Daʿiyānī. See editor's note.

10 It is now known as al-Mulayḥa.

Ṭūlūn) al-Iqbāʿī, known as al-Zaynabī, whereas the people of al-Manīḥa were operating the barrage by Birkat al-Ḥaydar. Subsequently, the Viceroy (*nāʾib*) reversed his decision and ordered to reopen the barrage. Then the Ḥanbalī chief *qāḍī* presented a report (*kitāb*), according to which, already as early as Umayyad time, the local cultivators (*ahl al-bilād*) had complained about the scarcity of water. The decision was then changed once again, the Mamluk dignitary now ordering that the inhabitants living by the Yazīd River, north of Damascus,[11] would be entitled to a share in the water, as would those residing by other rivers or canals, the Dāʿiya included. Here Ibn Ṭawq notes that this was an unprecedented decision (*lā ʿibra bihi fi'l-sharʿ*). But this was not the end of the case, for after the session had been adjourned people petitioned to the *nāʾib* to review his decision. Then the *qāḍī*s discussed the matter and, subsequently, the *nāʾib* decided once again to block the river and that the disputing parties produce their relevant documents (*bayyina*). Despite objections raised by the inhabitants of Manīḥa and its neighboring Bilāṭ and the support they received from some highly-positioned Mamluks, it was decided that the right to the water was after all with the Dāʿiya people.[12]

Another dispute occurred about half a year later, in the winter of 887/1481-2, normally a time of high water in the "large river" Barada,[13] but in that particular year the low level of the water was a reason for concern. [14] Villagers drawing their water of the Thawra (Tūra) river, north of Damascus,[15] came before Taqī al-Dīn Ibn Qāḍī ʿAjlūn, the prominent Shāfiʿī scholar of the city.[16] The reason was what they

---

[11] For its early history in the Umayyad period, see N. Elisséeff, *La déscription de Damas d'Ibn ʿAsākir* (Damascus: Institut Français de Damas, 1959): 253-5.

[12] *Taʿlīq*: 71. Ibn Ṭūlūn, *Mufākahat al-khillān fi hawādith al-zamān*, ed. M. Mustafā (Cairo: Dār Iḥyāʾ al-Kutub, 1962), 1:445, quotes Ibn Ṭawq almost verbatim without acknowledging his source.

[13] A-M. Bianquis, "Le problème de l'eau à Damas et dans sa Ghouta," *Revue de Géographie de Lyon* 1 (1977): 37.

[14] For the importance of this river in irrigating the Ghūṭa, see e.g., ibid.: 36-7.

[15] For the Barada and the Thawra rivers and their role in the supply of water to Damascus, see D. Sack, "Die Wasserversorgung und das Entwasserungssystem der Altstadt von Damaskus," in *Damaskus—Allepo: 5000 Jahre Stadtentwicklung in Syrien*, ed. Beate Bollmann (Mainz: Philipp von Zabern, 2000): 335-40

[16] Ibn Qāḍī ʿAjlūn (841/1438-928/1522), first studied in Damascus, his hometown, then, about the age of twenty traveled to Cairo. At a later stage he was entitled *shaykh al-mashāʾikh*, taught in Damascus at the Umayyad Mosque and the Barrānīya Madrasa, and also served as a *muftī*. See entry on him in al-Sakhāwī, *al-Ḍawʾ al-lāmiʿ fi aʿyān al-qarn al-tāsiʿ* (Cairo: Maktabat al-Qudsī, 1934-36), 6:38. Ibn Ṭawq admired

learned about an advice given (*ḥassanū lahu*) to the viceroy (*kāfil*), to make use of their rights to the water during the time of irrigation and to divert water (*yasūquhā*) to the village of ʿAdhrā. In return, so it was planned, they would receive water on the days that the ruler himself drew water of the river. The assembling villagers feared the damage this change may cause and that such procedure would become permanent. Then the preacher (*khaṭīb*) of the Ghūṭa village of ʿArbīl went to see one Jalāl al-Dīn Yūsuf al-Rūmī, of the ruler's circle, and conveyed to him what had been said (*ʿalā lisān*) by Ibn Qāḍī ʿAjlūn, although without the latter's knowledge: that the ruler's plan was unjust (*ẓulm*). When it came to the ruler's knowledge, he tried to be complacent (*yatalaṭṭaf*) and promised to issue a special report (*maḥḍar*) in which it would be stated that the suggested operation did not apply permanently (*istaʿartuhu ḥattā lā taṣīra ʿāda*). However, the villagers were not content with the reply and retained their assembly. Subsequently, it was suggested that the ruler's operation of "advanced water" (?) (*muʿajjala*) would last three days only. For some reason the meeting was adjourned without any real agreement. On the next day, possibly as an outcome of the apparent deadlock, some leading villagers involved in this case went to meet Ibn Qāḍī ʿAjlūn and discuss the issue of land survey (*rawk*) in villages such as Dūma and Ḥarasta, north-east of Damascus.[17]

Another dispute, in Rabīʿ II/May-June of that year, resulted in no less than a declaration of the apostasy (*kufr*) of one ʿAbd al-Karīm al-Qārī. This was a punishment for his criticism of the blockage (*sadd*) of water of the al-Manshīya river canal, which had been in effect for about a year, and worked to the benefit of those whose right to irrigation had been established and their prior suffering of aggression (*ẓulm wa-ʿudwān*) with respect to the use of water had been recognized by Shaykh Muḥibb al-Dīn[18] and Shaykh Taqī al-Dīn [Ibn Qāḍī ʿAjlūn]. At the time, there had been no dispute concerning the blockage but now, when ʿAbd al-Karīm passed by the Damascus neighborhood of al-Qarāwāna[19] and saw the two villagers Ibn Abī Rāfiʿ and Abū Bakr b. ʿĪsā, he castigated them (*ghawwasha*) and

---

him and refers to him as "sīdī al-shaykh." The *Taʿlīq* contains much data on the activities of Ibn Qāḍī ʿAjlūn.

[17] *Taʿlīq*: 129-30.

[18] Possibly cousin of Ibn Qāḍī ʿAjlūn. See al-Buṣrawī, *Taʾrīkh al-Buṣrawī* (Damascus: Dār al-Maʾmūn, 1988): 99; Ibn Ṭūlūn, *Mufākahat,* 1:25.

[19] A neighborhood south of al-Shāghūr. See editor's note 2: 160.

declared: "God's curse on these men [meaning the peasants] and their ancestors, and on those who blocked the water and on those ordering it and their ancestors, were they even Alid *sharifs.*" His statement was notified and, a few days later, he was attacked and threatened, most likely by men whose right he challenged. It appears that an apostasy too was decided, for the aforementioned Muḥibb al-Dīn, most likely offended by the reaction, sent a message to the Shāfiʿī *qāḍī*, instructing him that his deputies should not accept ʿAbd al-Karīm's "return to Islam" (*istislām*).[20]

The next day, ʿAbd al-Karīm al-Qārī and ʿĪsā al-Qārī, the latter of a commanding position among the merchants (*kabīr al-tujjār*),[21] together with Shams al-Dīn al-Khaṭīb and ʿAlā al-Dīn, the latter being head of the Alid Syndicate (*naqīb al-ashrāf*), went to the residence of Ibn Qāḍī ʿAjlūn. In the long session that took place ʿAbd al-Karīm was the object of resentment. Although the meeting was concluded seemingly well (*ʿalā khayr*), "the hearts were filled with [adverse] feelings" (*lākin fi'l-qulūb shay'*). The following day, it was revealed that "conversion" from his imposed state of apostasy was offered clandestinely to ʿAbd al-Karīm by Zayn al-Dīn al-Ḥisbānī, the Ḥanafī *qāḍī*.[22] Then Muḥammad b. Muḥibb al-Dīn al-Ḥiṣnī (d. 889/1484),[23] accompanied by a large group of Sufis (*fuqarā'*) and other men, came to Ibn Qāḍī ʿAjlūn to review the situation. A rumor spread that the man orchestrating the compromise was the Mālikī *qāḍī* Shihāb al-Dīn al-Ḥamrāwī.[24] As a result, a great deal of agitation took place. ʿAbd al-Karīm, on his part, went into hiding and was thrice summoned by Ibn Qāḍī ʿAjlūn to repent as a means to achieving reconciliation.

In the meantime, Shaykh Burhān al-Dīn [Ibrāhīm] al-Sūbaynī, one of the leading notaries in Damascus,[25] told the aforementioned Muḥammad al-Ḥiṣnī that, were ʿAbd al-Karīm to show up, something of consequences ought to occur (?) (*yakūnu al-maqām qawl*

---

[20] See editor's note 3: 160.

[21] He died in 895/1490; see biography in al-Buṣrawī, Ta'rīkh: 142.

[22] See further on him in al-Buṣrawī, Ta'rīkh: 116.

[23] He was nephew of Taqī al-Dīn al-Ḥiṣnī, founder of a Sufi lodge (*zāwiya*) known as al-Turābīya at the Shāghūr quarter, and himself was mentor of Sufis. See al-Buṣrawī, *Ta'rīkh*: 99-100; É. Geoffroy, Le soufisme en Égypte et en Syrie sous les derniers Mamelouks et les premiers Ottomanes (Damascus: Institut Français de Damas, 1995): 216-17

[24] See on him Ibn Ṭūlūn, *Mufākahat*, e.g., 1:32.

[25] See editor's note 2: 161.

aw fiʿl). Al-Ḥiṣnī flew into rage and shouted loudly (? *Nafara*, perhaps should be read *na'ara*), then he went in a fury to have an audience with the Shāfiʿī *qāḍī*. There also came ʿAbd al-Karīm, our protagonist, who explained that fear was the reason for his refusal to surface. In the course of the session also ʿAbd al-Karīm al-Kurdī, the sufi (*al-mutasawwif*),[26] showed up. His intervention aroused some uproar since it was interpreted as siding with ʿAbd al-Karīm. He talked facetiously (*amthāl fashrīya*), displaying his animosity toward Muḥammad al-Ḥiṣnī. The latter pointed at his headgear (*imāma*) and it rolled down, then al-Kurdī left. Subsequently, some men, each in his turn, tried to reach a resolution and approached al-Ḥiṣnī, with no success, however. It was only after ʿAbd al-Karīm was pleaded to repent and uncovered his head in the presence of al-Ḥiṣnī, apparently in token of humiliation, that a resolution was reached. Finally, ʿAbd al-Karīm appeared in a session where Muḥyī al-Dīn al-Ikhnāʾī, the Shāfiʿī *qāḍī*,[27] and Shihāb al-Dīn b. ʿAjlān, the *naqīb al-ashrāf*, were present.[28]

It is of some interest that a couple of years later, in Rabīʿ I 889/ April 1484, two men who played a role in this affair, the merchants ʿĪsā al-Qārī and the *qāḍī* Shihāb al-Dīn al-Ḥamrāwī,[29] now standing on the two sides of the barrier, disputed the question of water at the neighborhood of Raʾs al-Daqqāqīn, by al-Bayṭār.[30] They came before the Shāfiʿī *qāḍī* and discussed the matter for a few hours. Also present were, among other, the viceroy's secretary (*kātib al-sirr*). All united against al-Ḥamrāwī and the latter, submissively, uncovered his head and stepped towards ʿĪsā. The session was then concluded in apparent reconciliation but actually in ill feeling (*ʿalā ṣulḥ ʿalā fasād*).[31] In the following year, in Ṣafar 890/ February-March 1485, al-Ḥamrāwī, once again, together with one [Shihāb al-Dīn] al-Raqāwī, the *kātib al-sirr*, and a Jew named Faraj, was involved in another unspecified water dispute concerning canals in Damascus.[32]

* * *

[26] Geoffroy, *Soufisme*: 111, 311 n. 17, 313, 357 has some material about ʿAlī al-Kurdī, known as the "Pole of Syria," who died in 925/1519.

[27] See al-Buṣrawī, *Taʾrīkh*: 152

[28] *Taʿlīq*: 160-1.

[29] See n. 24 above.

[30] Possibly a name of a mosque. See Elisséeff, *Déscription*: 85.

[31] *Taʿlīq*: 351.

[32] Ibid.: 451.

Ibn Ṭawq's most detailed description is of a water dispute that began on 25 Sha'bān 887/ 9 October 1482. On that day, Ibn Qāḍī 'Ajlūn and the aforementioned Shaykh Muḥibb al-Dīn, who had played a role in 'Abd al-Karīm's "apostasy" affair, arrived at the point of bifurcation (*maqāsim*) of the rivers Barada and Thawra at Rubwa, a few miles west of the Citadel.[33] Also present were, among others, the four chief *qāḍīs*, as well as the Shāfi'ī *qāḍī* Burhān al-Dīn Ibn al-Mu'tamid, the Ḥanafī *qāḍī* Ibn al-Ḥamawī, the *qāḍī* Ṣalāḥ al-Dīn [Muḥammad b. 'Abdāllāh] al-'Adawī,[34] a group of Sufis (*fuqarā'*), those having a right to the water of the Banyas (Bānās) and those having a right to the canals (*qanāwāt*). The purpose of this meeting was discussing the problem of a fracture in the barrage of the river that made water spill to the canals and thus cause a shortage in the river itself. Prior to that, we are told, the Viceroy had been requested several times to investigate the problem but excused himself, explaining that poor health prevented him from arriving at the site. In fact, more than a month earlier, upon his order, the river had been blocked. Later, however, one Ibn al-Khayḍarī, possibly of his administrative circle,[35] was able to convince the ruler that the blockage was illegal and consequently it was undone. As our source notes, Ibn al-Khayḍarī, and possibly others as well, injected a great deal of intrigue into this case.

Somewhat later, in a session in the presence of the Viceroy, which dealt with the spilling of water off the Ḥurjulla village, accusations were exchanged between Ibn al-Khayḍarī and emir Sūdūn (known as "The Tall") al-Aynālī, at that time one of the high-ranking officers (*muqaddamūn*) in Damascus. Soon the confrontation turned to the Banyas case and it reached the point whereby Sūdūn cursed his disputant and almost attacked him physically. An attempt at reconciliation was not much successful and Ibn al- Khayḍarī's gesture to kiss the emir "on his shoulder or head" was rejected, with the result of Ibn al- Khayḍarī leaving in a hurry, "as if in a plight," to the town of Ba'albek. When he returned, and as the quarrel about the Banyas water was being dragged, a man named al-Buṣrawī, possibly no other than the Shāfi'ī *qāḍī* and author of a chronicle about the city during

[33] See Elisseéff, Déscription: 177 n. 5; Yāqūt, *Mu'jam al-buldān*, s.v.

[34] He occupied various administrative positions. According to al-Buṣrawī, *Ta'rīkh*: 191, he was replaced in Muḥarram 902/September 1496 as *wakīl al-sulṭān*. See also Ibn Ṭūlūn, *Mufākahat*, Index, s.v.

[35] Ibn Ṭūlūn has several persons with this name. See *Mufākahat*, Index, s.v..

his own lifetime,[36] stood up to speak against Ibn al-Khayḍarī. It was decided that arguments would now be presented before someone who did not have a right to the water, as it appears, in order to reach an objective decision. However, in what appears to be an inconsistency, the man chosen for that, one Ibn al-Rajīhī, was of the neighboring al-Mizza and served as supervisor (*nāẓir*) of a *madrasa* that drew its water from the Banyas or its canals. At any rate, the *qāḍī* Shihāb al-Dīn al-Ḥamrāwī argued against Ibn al- Khayḍarī. The session established a proof (*bayyina*) in favor of the people of Damascus and their right to the water was proclaimed (*zukkū*). Subsequently, reconstruction work was begun, but even that did not prevent some *qāḍī*s from engaging in further intrigues. When the Viceroy heard of the situation he was enraged (*mutanammir*) and then visited the site with his troops and the entire party involved (*al-jamāʿa kulluhum*). Subsequently, he initiated a meeting with Ibn Qāḍī ʿAjlūn, as a result of which he declared that what had been constructed should be demolished, and so it was done. However, "wicked things" by "wretched men" (*manāḥīs*) were still being spread around and the issue was still lingering.

The next day, another session took place at the ruler's palace (*dār al-niyāba*), in which also the *qāḍī*s and his secretary (*kātib al-sirr*) were present. The aforementioned Buṣrawī cursed and bawled out (*tarraba wa-ghawwasha*), he "filled the ruler with illusions" (*khayyala ʿalā*). Then the Viceroy summoned Ibn Qāḍī ʿAjlūn, yet the Shāfiʿī scholar declined. The *nāʾib* requested that he should at least send the document (*waraqa*) which had been signed in the session the day before by Ibn Qāḍī ʿAjlūn himself, as well as the *qāḍī*s and al-Buṣrawī, and was now missing. Ibn Qāḍī ʿAjlūn replied that he had no information about the whereabouts of the document, yet the ruler sent messengers to him once again, insisting his arrival or else "we shall rather come to him," and that he should supply the document in question. Again, the scholar's answer was that he knew nothing about the document, that it was not his policy to be present in sessions of this sort, and that the arrival of the *nāʾib* himself was unnecessary since ʿAjlūn's opinion has not changed. Apparently, the ruler was not convinced, as his envoy arrived at ʿAjlūn's library (?) (*kutubīya*)

---

[36] See Bibliography below and a few details on him in the editor's introduction: 18-19.

at his residence at the Qaymarīya Madrasa, located in the vicinity of Bab Tūmā.

In the meantime, those present at the *dār al-niyāba* arranged for some witnesses to testify about the exact size of the hole in the barrage, but even about that there was disagreement and the session came to naught. Then the *mihmindār*[37] came to Ibn Qāḍī ʿAjlūn, followed by the *nāʾib* and Qāḍī Shihāb al-Dīn al-Ḥamrāwī and others. An agreement was now reached that what had been demolished should be rebuilt. The next day, the ruler and the market inspector (*muḥtasib*) came to speak to Ibn Qāḍī ʿAjlūn. It appears that the ruler had regrets ("he probably wept during the night") about his (mis) managing the case and about the reconstruction work. However, now he was content with the decision of rebuilt.

A few days later, on the 1st of Ramaḍān/14 October, the aforementioned al-Buṣrawī, apparently dissatisfied with the outcome, began to mobilize men for the cause of the canals. He announced that whoever had a right to the water of the canals should not venture into inappropriate conduct (?) (*lam yushill wa-yutarrib*) or else his water would be cut off. Then a mob (*ghawghāʾ*, *awbāsh*) led by al-Fāriḍī, the preacher (*khaṭīb*) of the Thābitīya Madrasa[38] and some other men, and carrying Qurans (*rabʿāt*) and banners (*aʿlām*), marched towards the Thābitīya Madrasa. More riff-raff joined them and all arrived at the *nāʾib*'s palace. It was rumored that "all this", probably meaning the latest decision, had been pre-arranged the day before, with the ruler's consent and in the presence of some leading men (*kubār*). Then al-Buṣrawī showed up. Thrice the *nāʾib* requested the appearance of the Shāfiʿī *qāḍī* but to no avail. Then he sent Jānī Bek al-Tanamī, the *amīr al-ḥājj*, as well as other officials, to the *qāḍī* with the same request until he was forced to appear against his will. At this point al-Buṣrawī stood up and, so it appears, revealed the nature of his tactics to counter the opinion of Ibn Qāḍī ʿAjlūn and his associate, Shaykh Muḥibb al-Dīn. Then the Shāfiʿī *qāḍī*, single-handedly, delved into (*shadda fī*) the problem. The *nāʾib*, apparently furious at al-Buṣrawī, talked to him rudely (*kalām khashin*). Then a decision was reached and it was against Al-Buṣrawī, who now uncovered his head and kissed the Quran copies (*rabʿāt sharīfāt*). Ibn

---

[37] The mihmindār was the Mamluk administrator in charge of receiving Bedouin delegates. See EI^2 s.v., "Mihmindār" (A.H. Saleh), 7:2.

[38] al-Buṣrawī, *Taʾrīkh*: 152, has Shams al-Dīn Khaṭīb al-Thābitīya.

Ṭawq, who appears to be critical of al-Buṣrawī's performance, elaborates on the absurdities he said (*halasa wal-tagharrub*) and his "false claims". Finally, with respect to the Banyas water, the ruler and the *qāḍīs* now rode again to the rivers' crossing and their deliberation (*ijtihād*) resulted in a decision to rebuild the barrage for the fourth time now to its earlier size minus the measure of 5 *qirāṭ*.[39]

In Ibn Ṭawq's coverage of less than twenty years of almost daily events and his own notarial activity in Mamluk Damascus, the two years 886-7/1481-2 loom large with respect to water disputes. The intensity could well be exceptional, but it is suggested by the available information that water, to one extent or another, was a source of contention throughout. What appears to have been a common feature of the disputes, as related by Ibn Ṭawq, is the tension aroused by conflicting claims to rights of irrigation and by unilateral acts that caused changes in water distribution. A great deal of personal animosity was on occasion part and parcel of the formal disagreement and directed the opposing parties or their representatives. The dynamics of the disputes and the attempts to reach a solution reveal the major role played by the Viceroy, various *qāḍīs* and some local power brokers. Above all, it was the Shāfiʿī *muftī* Ibn Qāḍī ʿAjlūn who was instrumental in reaching solutions. This renowned scholar was highly regarded by all. Given the Viceroy's tendency to act spontaneously and, apparently, without sufficient basis or at least indecisively, and the need to couch decisions legally, Ibn Qāḍī ʿAjlūn's involvement became crucial.

Bibliography

al-Buṣrawī, A. *Ta'rīkh al-Buṣrawī*, edited by Akram Ḥasan al-ʿUlabī. Damascus: Dār al-Ma'mūn, 1988.

Bianquis, A-M. "Le problème de l'eau à Damas et dans sa Ghouta," *Revue de Géographie de Lyon* 1(1977): 35-53.

Bruno, H. *Contribution à l'étude du régime des eaux en droit musulman.* Paris: Arthur Rousseau, 1913.

Caponera, D.A. "Ownership and Transfer of Water and Land in Islam," in *Water Management in Islam*, edited by Naser I. Faruqui, Asit K. Biswas and Murad J. Bino. Tokyo: United Nations University Press, 2001.

[39] *Taʿlīq*: 182-7. Ibn Ṭūlūn, *Mufākahat*, 1:57 summarizes this incident in five lines only.

Elisséeff, N. *La Déscription de Damas d'Ibn ʿAsākir* Damascus: Institut Français de Damas, 1959.
English, P.W. "The Origin and Spread of Qanats in the Old World." *Proceedings of the American Philosophical Society* 112 (1968): 170-81, reprinted in *Production and the Exploitation of Resources*, edited by Michael G. Morony. Burlington, VT.: Ashgate Publishing, 2002.
Geoffroy, É. *Le soufisme en Égypte et en Syrie sous les derniers Mamelouks et les premiers Ottomanes.* Damascus: Institut Français de Damas, 1995.
Glick, T.F. *Irrigation and Society in Medieval Valencia.* Cambridge, Mass.: Harvard University Press, 1970.
Hentati, N. "L'eau dans la ville de l'occident musulman medieval d'apres les sources juridiques malikites," *Revue d'histoire maghrebine* 28(2001): 163-220.
Ibn Ṭūlūn, *Mufākahat al-khillān fī ḥawādith al-zamān*, ed. Muḥammad Muṣṭafā. Cairo: Dār Iḥyā' al-Kutub, 1962.
Kadouri, M.T., Djebbar, Y., and Nehdi, M. "Water Rights and Water Trade: An Islamic Perspective." In *Water Management in Islam*, edited by Naser I. Faruqui, Asit K. Biswas and Murad J. Bino. Tokyo: United Nations University Press, 2001.
Lightfoot, D.R. "Syrian qanat Romani: history, ecology, abandonment." *Journal of Arid Environments* 33 (1996): 321-36.
Sack, D. "Die Wasserversorgung und das Entwasserungssystem der Altstadt von Damaskus," in *Damaskus—Allepo: 5000 Jahre Stadtentwicklung in Syrien*, edited by Beate Bollmann. Mainz: Zabern, 2000.
al-Sakhāwī, S.D.M. *al-Ḍaw' al-lāmiʿ fī aʿyān al-qarn al-tāsiʿ.* 12 vols. Cairo, 1934-36.
Saleh, A.H., "Mihmindār," *Encyclopaedia of Islam*, new ed., Volume 7. Leiden: Brill, 1993.
Yāqūt, *Muʿjam al-buldān*, ed. Ferdinand Wüstenfeld. 6 vols. Leipzig: F. A. Brockhaus, 1866-70.

ARMY ECONOMICS: AN EARLY PAPYRUS LETTER RELATED TO *'AṬĀ'* PAYMENTS[1]

Petra M. Sijpesteijn

Introduction

Armies are complex social and economic machines, serving ends far beyond the limited goals of winning wars. Soldiers march on their stomachs, as Napoleon famously observed; they rarely fight for idealism or ideology alone, and this was clearly true also in the early Muslim armies. The papyrus letter presented in this paper allows us a rare first-hand glimpse of this in practice. Despite its fragmentary state and the lack of context, this letter contains unique information about the running of the early Muslim army and state in Egypt,

[1] I presented this papyrus at seminars at the School of Oriental and African Studies, London, and the Institute of Advanced Study, Princeton. I would like to thank the participants in these seminars for their comments. I also greatly benefited from discussions with S. Bouderbala, P. Crone and L. Sundelin. Any remaining mistakes are, of course, my own. In this article the following abbreviations are used: *CPR* XVI = *Corpus Papyrorum Raineri, Arabische Briefe aus dem 7.-10. Jahrhundert*, ed. W. Diem (Vienna: Verlag Brüder Hollinek, 1993); *EI*[2] = *Encyclopaedia of Islam*, new edition, eds. H.A.R. Gibb *et al.* (Leiden: E.J. Brill, 1954-2004); *P. Berl.Arab.* II = *Arabische Briefe des 7. bis 13. Jahrhunderts aus den Staatlichen Museen zu Berlin*, ed. W. Diem (*Documenta Arabica Antiqua* 4) (Wiesbaden: Harrasowitz, 1997); *P.Cair. Arab.* I = *Arabic Papyri in the Egyptian Library*, ed. A. Grohmann (Cairo: Egyptian Library Press, 1934); *P.Heid.Arab.* I= *Papyri Schott-Reinhardt* I, ed. C.H. Becker (*Veröffentlichungen aus der Heidelberger Papyrussammlung* 3) (Heidelberg: Carl Winter's Universitätsbuchhandlung, 1906); *P.Khalili* I = ed. G. Khan, *Arabic Papyri: Selected Material from the Khalili Collection* (*Studies in the Khalili Collection* 1) (London: Nour Foundation in association with Azimuth Editions and Oxford University Press, 1992); *P.Lond.* IV = *Greek Papyri in the British Museum. The Aphrodito Papyri*, ed. H.I. Bell, with appendix of Coptic papyri ed. W.E. Crum (London: British Museum, 1910); *P.Mil.Vogl.* = Papiri della Università degli Studi di Milano, ed. A. Vogliano (Milan: U. Hoepli, 1961); *P.Mird.* = *Arabic Papyri from Khirbet el-Mird*, ed. A. Grohmann (Leuven: Institut Orientaliste, 1963); *P.Ness.* III = *Non-Literary Papyri*, ed. C.J. Kraemer, Jr. (Princeton: Princeton University Press, 1958); *P.Philad. Arab.*= *Arabic Papyri in the University Museum in Philadelphia (Pennsylvania)*, ed. G. Levi della Vida (Rome: Accademia nazionale dei Lincei, 1981); *P.Ryl.Arab.* I = *Catalogue of Arabic Papyri in the John Rylands Library Manchester*, ed. D.S. Margoliouth (Manchester: The Manchester University Press, 1933).

showing us those behind the generals and how their stomachs were filled in war and in peace.

The Muslim army has left us a surprisingly meager paper trail, at least in the papyri that have come to light so far. This is not merely in comparison to the extensive papyrus records related to the Roman army in Egypt,[2] but in comparison to what we would expect, based on the voluminous quantities of command notes, requisition orders, payment notices, salary stubs, supply receipts, and all the other documentation the army must have generated, and not least the significant amounts of paperwork that must have come from the administration of the annual stipend, whose extensive central registers and payment processes we know from narrative sources.[3] The dearth of documents is doubtlessly partially because the Muslim garrisons in Egypt were located and organized in other places (Fusṭāṭ, Alexandria, Aswān) than the main finding places of most papyri from the Islamic period (Fayyūm, limited number of places in Upper Egypt). The papyri we do have, moreover (less than a dozen in total),[4] all originate from the governors and their retinues, showing us very little of the experience of the rank-and-file soldiery, their maintenance, the organization of their camps, and conditions of service. It is because this papyrus does, in fact, give us such a rare and privileged glimpse into the milieu that produced it that it is so valuable.

P.Michaelides Q16[5]

Summary

The sender of our letter, replying to a request for news, begins by telling the addressee that the *amīr* has been to see the caliph, the

[2] For which, see, for example, R. Alston, *Soldier and Society in Roman Egypt: A Social History* (London/New York: Routledge, 1995) and R.O. Fink, *Roman Military Records on Papyrus* (Philological Monographs of the American Philological Association 26) (Cleveland: Press of Case Western Reserve University, 1971).

[3] There are equally very few personal letters written by and to soldiers published.

[4] For the few texts that do exist, see for example the Greek papyri *SB* VII/VIII 9748-60, and K. Morimoto, "The Diwans as Registers of the Arab Stipendiaries in Early Islamic Egypt," in *Itinéraires d'Orient hommages à Claude Cahen, Res Orientalis* 6 [1994], eds. R. Curiel and R. Gyselen: 353-66.

[5] I would like to thank the Syndics of Cambridge University Library permitting me to publish this text and the staff of the Near and Middle Eastern Department of the Library for their friendly help in accessing the document. I would also like to

amīr al-mu'minīn. Turning then to the topic of *'aṭā'*, the military stipend, the sender writes that the payment of family *'aṭā'*s has already begun and that those who are eligible have received their stipends. The sender urges the addressee to collect not only his own *'aṭā'* but also that of his dependents, because—as he writes—they are "poor and needy," and to make haste because, apparently, the stipends are running out. The sender cannot receive the *'aṭā'* on the addressee's behalf as he would have to give a guarantee, a *ḍamān*, which he is not prepared to do. In a postscript the sender adds that he has already sent the addressee a letter as well as some object—the description of which is now lost—with a certain Baṣīr, and that three officials or administrators from Syria have arrived, while some (other) individuals are being "kept at the high sea," presumably on boats lying at anchor in the Mediterranean. Side B contains a line with two words and traces of another on a lower line written in a hand different from that of side A. The two words can be read as صغيرة وكبيرة, "small and large," and, it would seem, have nothing to do with the text on side A.

17 (H) x 14.5 (W) 1st-2nd/7th-8th century
See illustration 1

Middle brown papyrus written in black ink with a medial pen, perpendicular to the fibers on side A, parallel to the fibers on side B. The writing on side B is written in a larger, different hand. The papyrus is broken off at the top and left sides with an unknown number of lines and words missing. There are several small holes in the papyrus due to worm eating. There are eight horizontal and two vertical folding lines discernable. There are some diacritical dots written. The provenance is unknown.

Text

Side A:

1. فلا يعد منا الله حياتك [17
2. وكتبت الى ان اكتب اليك بخبر الا مير وما فعل [. . .
3. فاخبرانه قد دخل على امير المومنين فرامنه القبول[. . .
4. قد ما اعلمتك ذلك ان شا الله وكتبت الى ان اك[ـتب اليك . . . فلا . . .
5. الربع شاى حتى يكون خروج البعث فسـ[. . .
6. وقد خرج عطا العيال فقد قبض الناس عطا[هم . . .

---

acknowledge the generous help of late Sarah Clackson, who very kindly obtained a scan of the papyrus for me.

7. فكيف ترافى عطا عيالك فانهم مساكين محـ[ـتاجون . . .
8. فعجل الى قبض عطا عيالك فانه لم تبق اعـ[ـطية . . .
9. ولولا انى اكره الضمان لقبضته عندى حتى [. . .
10. الذى منعنى من ذلك اكتب الى بخبرك وحـ[ـالك . . . فانى
11. احب ذلك واسر به الله يعلم دفع الله عـ[ـنك وعنا السو . . . والسلم
12. عليك ورحمت الله وكتب يوم الخميس ليلـ[ـة خلوت\مضيت من . . .
13. وقد كنت كتبت اليك مع بصير وبعثت معه [. . .
14. وقد قدم من عمال الشام ثلثة نفر منهم معا[. . .
15. اهل الورن فقد حبسوا فى البحر الا عـ[ـلى . . .
16. البعوث بعد وهى قادمة وخارجة [. . .

Diacritical dots:

2) ان, فعل 4) ان, ان 6) العيال 7) عيالك 12) بصر 15) حبسوا, في

Translation

1. may God not deprive us of your life [. . .
2. You wrote to me (asking) that I write to you with the news of the *amīr* and what he has done [. . .
3. He reported that he has gone to the *amīr al-mu'minīn* and that he received an audience [. . . and if so-and-so/something
4. arrives, I will let you know, God willing. And you wrote to me (asking) that I in[form you . . . Do not . . .
5. the quarter (*rubʿ*) anything until the dispatch of the army. And . . [. . .
6. and the *ʿaṭāʾ* for the families has already been given out and the people have already received their *ʿaṭāʾ* [. . .
7. Don't you think you should do something about[6] the *ʿaṭāʾ* of your families since they are poor and nee[dy . . .
8. and hurry to receive the *ʿaṭāʾ* for your families for there are (almost) none left [. . .
9. If I did not dislike the *ḍamān* (so much), I would have collected it myself[7] until [. . .
10. which prevents me from that. Write me with your news and your [condition for
11. I like that and it pleases me, God knows. May God ward off from y[ou and from us evil . . . And peace be
12. upon you and God's mercy. It was written on Thursday with one ni[ght remaining/having passed of the month of . . .

---

[6] Lit. "So what do you think about."
[7] Lit. "received it here."

13. I have sent you already a letter with Baṣīr and I sent with him [. . .
14. And from among the tax officials of Syria (*'ummāl al-Shām*) three persons have arrived amongst whom . . [. . .
15. The people of the . . . and they have been kept at the high sea (Mediterranean) [. . .
16. the expeditionary forces afterwards and they are coming and going (moving back and forth) [. . .

Commentary

1. The beginning of the letter with the *basmala* and opening greetings is missing. The beginning of line 1, however, seems to continue the opening greetings and the contents of the letter suggest that not more than two lines are missing at the top. For the expression *lā yu'dimnā Allāh ḥayataka*, see *CPR* XVI 18.9, first-second/seventh-eighth centuries, provenance not mentioned, with further examples in the commentary.
2. In this period, in Greek and Coptic texts, the word *amīr* is used for army leader and for pagarch, the official who stood at the head of an administrative district in Egypt. In Arabic texts the word refers to the governor or financial director of Egypt (P. M. Sijpesteijn, *Shaping a Muslim State: Papyri Related to an Eighth-Century Egyptian Official*, PhD diss. [Princeton University, 2004]).
3. *Akhbara* can also be read as *ukhbiru*, "I inform." The *amīr al-mu'minīn*, commander of the believers, refers to the caliph. For the use of *amīr al-mu'minīn* and other terms referring to the caliph in the papyri, see P. M. Sijpesteijn, "An Early Umayyad Papyrus Invitation for the Ḥajj," *Journal of Near Eastern Studies* (forthcoming). *Mu'minīn* is written without *hamza* (cf. S. Hopkins, *Studies in the Grammar of Early Arabic* [Oxford: Oxford University Press, 1984], §19). *Fa-ra'ā minhu al-qubūl. Ra'ā* is written without *hamza* and with one long vowel (cf. Hopkins, *Grammar*, §25.a). For the expression *ra'ā minhu kadhā*, see E. W. Lane, *An Arabic-English Lexicon* (London: Williams and Norgate, 1968), 1:998.b. The final *lām* of *qubūl* is only partially visible before the lacuna.
4. One expects a subject to have preceded *qadima*, such as a person (proper name) or a product. "When so-and-so/this-or-that] has

arrived, I inform you (about) it." *Shā'a* in *in shā'a Allāh* is written without final *hamza* (cf. Hopkins, *Grammar,* § 20.c). *Katabta ilayya an aktuba ilayka* is reconstructed on the basis of the same construction that appears in line 1. The *kāf* of *aktuba* is only partially visible before the lacuna.

5. *Al-rub'* refers to one of the military and administrative units used in Umayyad *amṣār,* for which see below, the section "Umayyad *'aṭā'*." Cf. R. Dozy, *Supplement aux dictionnaires arabes* (Leiden: E. J. Brill, 1881), 1:502. We expect a negation in the lacuna at the end of line 4. "And there is no/and do not . . .] at all [from/to] the quarter until the army has gone out." The spelling of شاى is very common in the papyri (cf. Hopkins, *Grammar* § 15.d). *Khurūj al-ba'th* refers to a the setting off of military expedition by land or by sea.
6. *Qad kharaja al-'aṭā'* is the expression used to refer to the yearly payment of pensions. See for example, al-Balādhurī (d. 279/892), *Futūḥ al-buldān*, ed. M. J. de Goeje (Leiden : E.J. Brill, 1866; repr. 1992). *'Aṭā' al-'iyāl* appears also in *P.Heid.Arab.* I 1.8, dated 91/709, provenance Ishqāw. For the question of whether family members of those registered on the *dīwān* were entitled to *'aṭā'*, see below, the section "Umayyad *'aṭā'*." *'Aṭā'* is written without final *hamza* (cf. Hopkins, *Grammar*, § 20.c). This word is written in the same way in lines 7 and 8. *'Aṭā'ahum*. The pronominal suffix is expected because of the absence of the article on the second part of the *iḍāfa* structure. For the spelling with *alif mamdūda* with elision of the glottal stop, see Hopkins, *Grammar*, § 21.a.
7. *Tar'a* is written with *alif mamdūda* instead of *yā'* (cf. Hopkins, *Grammar*, § 12.c). *Fa-innahum masākīn muḥtājūn*. This combination of synonyms for the poor appears in other papyri and literary texts, sometimes together with the word *fuqarā'*. See below, the section "Poor and needy."
8. *A'ṭiya* or *a'ṭiyāt* might be restored at the end of the line. For the plural use, see for example, said of the governor al-Ḥajjāj (d. 95/714), *zāda a'ṭiyātahum* (al-Ṭabarī [d. 310/923], *Ta'rīkh al-rusul wa-'l-muluk*, ed. M. J. de Goeje [Leiden: E. J. Brill, 1879-1901, repr. 1964-1965], 2:1033), and of 'Umar II, *zāda ahl al-shām fī a'ṭiyātihim* (al-Ya'qūbī [d. 284/897], *Ta'rīkh*, ed. M. Th. Houtsma [Leiden: E. J. Brill, 1883], 3:50) and *kataba 'Umar ilā Ḥudayfa an a'ṭi al-nās a'ṭiyātahum* (Ibn Sa'd (d. 230/845), *al-Ṭabaqāt al-*

kubrā [Beirut, 1377/1957], 3:299). In Egypt Maslama b. Mukhlid (in office 47-62/667-682) "*aʿṭā ahl al-dīwān aʿṭiyātahum wa-aʿṭiyāt ʿiyālihim wa-arzaqahum*" (al-Maqrīzī [d. 845/1442], *al-Mawāʾiz wa-ʾl-iʿtibār fī dhikr al-khiṭaṭ wa-ʾl-athār*, ed. A. F. Sayyid [London: al-Furqān Islamic Heritage Foundation, 2002-2003], 1:252).

9. *Al-ḍamān*. For the Islamic legal conditions of the *ḍamān*, see P. M. Sijpesteijn, "Profit Following Responsibility: A Leaf from the Records of a Third-Century Tax-Collecting Agent," *Journal of Juristic Papyrology* 31 (2001).

10. *Uktub ilayya bi-khabarika wa-ḥālika* is reconstructed on the basis of the many attestations of this very common expression. See for example *wa-ktu{t}b ilayya bi-khabarika wa-ḥālika* (*P.Philad. Arab.* 74.18, third/ninth century, provenance not mentioned).

10./11. *Fa-ʾinnī*] *uḥibbu dhālika wa-ʿusarru bihi* is attested in another first-second/seventh-eighth-century papyrus (*CPR* XVI 4.7, provenance not mentioned, but probably Ihnās). Diem knew of only one parallel, our letter provides thus a third example. The expression, *Allāh yaʿlamu*, usually appears in parenthesis as an oath to confirm a statement by the sender. See, for example, *wa-anā wa-llāh yaʿlamu ʿalā ʾl-taʿāddul* (*P. Berl.Arab.* II 41.10, third/ninth century, provenance not mentioned). Here it refers to the preceding statement about the sender rejoicing over news from the addressee. *Dafaʿa Allāh ʿa[nka wa-ʿannā al-sūʾ* is reconstructed on the basis of parallels. See the examples given in the commentary to *P.Berl.Arab.* II 49.4 (second/eighth century, provenance not mentioned) where the phrase appears without direct object indicating which unpleasantness God should keep away from the sender and addressee. Other possible reconstructions are: *dafaʿa Allāh ʿa[nka wa-ʿannā al-makrūh*; *dafaʿa Allāh ʿa[nka al-makrūh fī ʾl-dunyā wa-ʾl-ākhira* as given in the commentary to *P.Berl.Arab.* II 49.4.

11./12. *Al-salām*] *ʿalayka wa-raḥmat Allāh* is reconstructed on the basis of countless parallels. *Raḥmat* is written with a *tāʾ tawīla* instead of *tāʾ marbūṭa* in the status constructus (cf. Hopkins, *Grammar*, § 47).

12. *Wa-kutiba yawm al-khamīs layl[a khalawat/maḍayat*. The three letters before the lacuna are read as *lām*-tooth-*lām* allowing for the reading *layla* or *laylatayn* indicating the date. For this man-

ner of dating papyri, see A. Grohmann, I *Arabische Chronologie*. II *Arabische Papyruskunde*, Handbuch der Orientalistik. Erste Abteilung. Der Nahe und Mittlere Osten. Ergänzungsband II (Leiden: E.J. Brill 1966): 224-5. For the dating of private letters, see P.M. Sijpesteijn, "Travel and Trade on the River," in *Papyrology and the History of Early Islamic Egypt*, ed. P.M. Sijpesteijn and L. Sundelin (Leiden: E.J. Brill, 2004).

13. *Wa-qad qadima min ʿummāl al-Shām thalātha nafar minhum. Thalātha* is written with a defective long ā (cf. Hopkins, *Grammar*, § 10.a). *ʿUmmāl* (s. *ʿāmil*) is used in the papyri to refer to all sorts of officials, but especially those involved in the tax-collection (Sijpesteijn, *Official*). Al-Shām in this context refers to the Syrian capital(s) of the Umayyad caliphate in the area coinciding with modern-day Palestine, Jordan, Syria and Lebanon. For the relations between Syria and Fusṭāṭ, see below, the section "Syria and Egypt." The qualification of the three officials starting with *minhum* is lost in the lacuna.
14. I was not able to find a satisfactory reading for the third word on this line which seems to be a noun or a geographical name qualifying *ahl*. The final letter is quite clearly a *nūn*. Preceding it seems to be written a *rāʾ* or *zayn*. *Qad ḥubisū fī ʾl-baḥr. Baḥr* is written with a very small medial *ḥāʾ* and with a large final *rāʾ*, not to be confused with final *nūn* which is written with more curvature. See for example l. 7 *masākīn*, l. 9 *ḍamān*, l. 10 *min*. *Al-baḥr al-aʿalā* refers to the Mediterranean, but can perhaps also be taken literally to mean a high sea.
15. *Wa-hiya qādima wa-khārija* refers to the *buʿūth*, armies or expeditions.

Umayyad ʿaṭāʾ

The papyrus is missing its beginning, as well as an unknown number of words where the left part has been torn off. It has no exact date, address or any indication of who wrote or received the letter, nor is the person mentioned in the text identifiable. The papyrus was found in Egypt where it was bought on the antiquities market by the collector George Michaelides (1900-1973). It was purchased by the University Library of the University of Cambridge along with the rest of the Michaelides collection in 1977 and it has been kept there since.[8] Certain internal evidence, however, gives us some clues as to its time and place of origin.

The script of the papyrus points us to a date in the first two Muslim centuries.[9] We can be perhaps even more precise. The writing of the final *qāf* in the word *tabqa* in line 8, with a long dipping tail extending into or even beyond the next line, is a feature that is attested in papyri from the first/seventh century.[10] There is only one second/eighth-century attestation of such a *qāf* in the famous letter to the Nubians dated 141/758, but that text is in general written in a very archaic script.[11] Some of the terminology (*rubʿ*, *ʿaṭāʾ al-ʿiyāl* for both of which, see below) also points to the Umayyad period.

Both the sender and the addressee are clearly very familiar with the Arab army, judging from the many references to the setting off of military expeditions (ll. 5, 15) and other technical military terms (l. 2 *amīr*; ll. 6, 7, 8 *ʿaṭāʾ*). The sender of the letter wrote from a military encampment in Egypt, probably the capital Fusṭāṭ *miṣr*, from which the Muslim stipends, *ʿaṭāʾ*, were distributed, and from where the army set off on its expeditions. One more indication that the sender was located in an Egyptian military settlement such as Fusṭāṭ or Alexandria, is his reference to the *rubʿ* (l. 4). *Arbāʿ* (and *akhmās*) were the military and administrative divisions used in Umayyad *amṣār*.[12] *Arbāʿ* are known to have existed in Kūfa, Khurāsān, where they were introduced by Ziyād b. Abīhi (in office 45-60/665-680),[13] and Syria.[14] One reference suggests that the troops in Egypt were also divided into *arbāʿ* and there is little doubt that the sender of our letter is referring to these kinds of units.[15] The addressee was located elsewhere, probably somewhere in the Egyptian countryside, where

---

[8] S. Clackson, "The Papyrus Collections of Cambridge," in *Papyrus Collections World Wide*, ed. W. Clarysse and H. Verreth (Brussels: Universa Press, 2000): 25.

[9] *P.Khalili* I: 27-39.

[10] *P.Khalili* I: 30.

[11] M. Hinds and H. Sakkout, "A Letter from the Governor of Egypt to the King of Nubia and Muqurra Concerning Egyptian-Nubian Relations in 141/758," in *Studia Arabica and Islamica: Festschrift for Ihsan Abbās*, ed. W. al-Qadi (Beirut: American University, 2001).

[12] P. Crone, *Slaves on Horses* (Cambridge: Cambridge University Press, 1980): 30-1. Baṣra's *ʿashrāʾ* were joined into *akhmās* in Muʿāwiya's reign.

[13] For Khurāsān, see al-Ṭabarī, *Taʾrīkh*, 2:79. In other places Khurāsān is said to have been divided in *akhmās* (al-Ṭabarī, *Taʾrīkh*, 2:1245, 1290f., 1490, 1690). For Kūfa, see e.g. Ṭabarī, *Taʾrīkh*, 2:326, 644, 709, 720.

[14] Ibn ʿAsākir, *Taʾrīkh Dimashq*, quoted in Crone, *Slaves*: 225 n. 210.

[15] A certain Thābit b. Muthawib al-Qabaḍī (d. ca. 670) is said to have been the *ʿarīf rubʿ Ruʿayn wa-ʾl-Maʿāfir* (head of the quarter assigned to the tribes of Ruʿayn

most papyri are found, in a different place than the sender and probably also away from the addressee's own place of residence. Putting all this information together, we can thus assume that our letter was sent from the Egyptian capital, Fusṭāṭ, to some place in the Egyptian countryside in the Umayyad period, that is to say, the first or the beginning of the second Muslim century.

Now let us turn to the main subject of the letter and the one about which it gives us most new information: the payment of *ʿaṭāʾ* or stipends to Egypt's conquerors. During the earliest conquests the invading troops were supplied by the native population with wheat, food stuffs, fodder for their animals, horses, clothes, saddle bags, and other supplies, as is mentioned in the narrative sources and the papyri from Egypt.[16] In these early days the soldiers' reward or payment presumably consisted of booty which was divided on the spot. When the conquest led to the permanent appropriation of large provinces inhabited by non-Arab non-Muslims, this system of *ad hoc* divisions of booty, of which a fixed part was sent to the caliph in Medina, had of necessity to be revised.

The new solution is ascribed to the caliph ʿUmar I (r. 13-23/634-644), who in the year 20/640 allegedly determined that the conquered lands were not to be divided among the conquerors to live off, but rather to be left in the hands of the indigenous populations while the fruits of their labor were used to provide for the troops both in cash and in kind.[17] While the origins and detailed workings of the payment of stipends or *ʿaṭāʾ* regulated through it remain poorly understood, the basic system is clear: military pensions were distributed to the *muḥājirūn*, who had emigrated to fight in the wars of conquest abroad, as well as their dependents (wives, children, slaves and clients); pension rates were determined by the Islamic *sābiqa*, seniority of membership of the *umma*.[18] Those entitled to a pension and the

---

and Maʿāfir) (Ibn Yūnus, *Taʾrīkh al-Maṣriyīn*, 1:78). I am grateful to Sobhi Bouderbala for this reference.

[16] P.M. Sijpesteijn, "The Arab Conquest of Egypt and the Beginning of Muslim Rule," in *Byzantine Egypt*, ed. R. S. Bagnall (Cambridge: Cambridge University Press, 2007): 440 n. 16.

[17] All references to the ancient sources related to this subject are collected in: L. Caetani, *Annali dell'Islam* (Milan: Ulrico Hoepli, 1911), 4:368-417.

[18] P. Crone, "The First Century Concept of Higra," *Arabica* 41 (1994); G.-R. Puin, *Der Dīwān von ʿUmar ibn al-Khaṭṭāb: ein Beitrag zur frühislamischen Verwaltungageschichte* (Bonn: Rheinische Friedrich-Wilhelms-Universität, 1977): 92-100, but see for the determination of payment rates: M. Hinds, "Review of G.-R. Puin, *Der Dīwān von ʿUmar ibn al-Khaṭṭāb: ein Beitrag zur frühislamischen*

rates at which they were paid were recorded in a register called the *dīwān al-jund.* [19]

It is well-known that the Arabs had no problem continuing the administrative practices of the areas they conquered. The origins of the *dīwān*, however, whether it was a distinctly Islamic institution or continued a pre-Islamic practice remains debated. Both trajectories are claimed in the Arabic sources.[20] While similar organizations did exist in the Sassanid and Byzantine empires, which may have influenced the practical execution of the payment of military stipends and sustenance through a selective register, the fact that, as the sources indicate, the *dīwān al-jund* was kept from the beginning in Arabic suggests that this was conceived of as a specifically Muslim practice.[21]

The *dīwān*s were centrally organized per province. According to the tenth-century Egyptian historian al-Kindī (d. 350/961), the first *dīwān* in Egypt was set up by ʿAmr b. al-ʿĀṣ (in office 21-25/642-645; 38-42/658-663), the general who had headed the army that conquered Egypt.[22] The Egyptian *dīwān* was updated at least four times under the subsequent governors ʿAbd al-ʿAzīz b. Marwān (in office 65-86/685-705), Qurra b. Sharīk (in office 90-96/709-714), and Bishr b. Safwān (in office 101-102/720-721). The last reference we have to it from the early period comes from 109/727, when the names of a group of Muslims from Syria who had been settled in the eastern Delta were added.[23]

"*Verwaltungageschichte*," *Bulletin of the School of Oriental and African Studies* 34 (1971): 145.

[19] *EI²*, s.vv., "ʿAṭāʾ," (Cl. Cahen) 1:729-30; "Dīwān. The Caliphate" (A.A. Duri) 2:323; "Dīwān. Egypt," (H.L. Gottschalk) *2*:327-28.

[20] For Byzantine and Sasanian precedents, see al-Maqrīzī, *Khiṭaṭ*, I: 246-7, Ibn Saʿd, *Ṭabaqāt*, 3:295, 300. See also above n. 17. Cf. Puin, *Dīwān*: 34, 93. See also H. Kennedy, *The Armies of the Caliphs* (London/New York: Routledge, 2001): 60-1.

[21] The word used in the papyri for payments in kind to Muslim soldiers is *rizq* (transcribed in the Greek texts as ρουζικον [*rouzikon*]) (e.g. *P.Apoll.* 49.r5; 94.6; 95FrB2, provenance of all is Edfu, dating to Muʿāwiya's reign, based on J. Gascou and K.A. Worp, "Problèmes de documentation apollinopolite," *Zeitschrift für Papyrologie und Epigraphik* 49 [1982]: 83-95), from the Middle Persian *rozik* (see Kennedy, *Armies*: 73).

[22] The tenth-century *History of the Patriarchs* places a different governor at the foundation of the *dīwān*, namely the governor ʿAbd Allāh b. Saʿd (in office 24-35/644-656) (*History of the Patriarchs of the Coptic church of Alexandria [Agathon to Michael I]*, tr. B. Evetts. *Patrologia Orientalis* V [1910]: 50).

[23] al-Kindī (d. 350/961), *Kitāb al-wulāt*, ed. R. Guest, *The Governors and Judges of Egypt* (E.J. W. Gibb Memorial Series XIX) (Leiden: E. J. Brill, 1912): 92; Maqrīzī, *Khiṭaṭ*, 1:94.

Narrative and papyrological sources from Egypt indicate that Arab soldiers received monthly rations of food and fodder, but that their salary, the *ʿaṭāʾ*, was paid once a year before the summer campaigns took place,[24] after the troops had been assigned their spring grazing grounds in the Egyptian countryside.[25] In a letter from the governor Qurra b. Sharīk to the pagarch or provincial governor Basileios dated Rabīʿ I 91 (January-February 710), Qurra demands a quick payment of the taxes (*jizya*) because "the time has come to pay the *ʿaṭāʾ* of the troops and of their dependents and the going-out of the army."[26] In our letter too, the *ʿaṭāʾ* payment seems related to an army campaign, the *khurūj al-baʿth* mentioned in line 5.

There are, however, very few documents like the one we have here that refer to or originate with those entitled to the *ʿaṭāʾ*. One first/seventh-century Arabic papyrus mini codex, consisting of two folios, might be part of a *dīwān*, listing the names of individuals in groups against those under whose responsibility they seemingly fell, all carrying Arabic names and perhaps referring to army or tribal units.[27] Another first-second/seventh-eighth-century papyrus from Palestine is a list of names seemingly related to the *dīwān*.[28] Two other papyrus documents are first/seventh- or second/eighth-century Arabic lists of houses citing the Arabic-named individuals living there.[29] Whether or not these documents were related to the procedure under the caliph Muʿāwiya (r. 41-60/661-680), reported by the ninth-century

[24] For the monthly payments, see for example *P.Ness.* 3:60-3; *P.Heid.Arab.* I 1, l. 8. Al-Ḥajjāj also paid his troops before they went on the summer campaign (al-Ṭabarī, *Taʾrīkh*, 2:1043-1044). Kennedy discusses other moments of pay in the sources (*Armies*: 72-3).

[25] Ibn ʿAbd al-Ḥakam, *Futūḥ Miṣr*, ed. Ch. Torrey, *The History of the Conquests of Egypt, North Africa and Spain*. New Haven: Yale University Press, 1922: 141-3.

[26] *Wa-ḥaḍara ʿaṭāʾ al-jund |wa-ʿaṭāʾ ʿiyālihim wa-khurūj al-juyūsh* (*P.Heid.Arab.* I 1.8-9).

[27] *P.Mil.Arab.* 6. The Greek list of expenses made for the governor ʿAbd al-ʿAzīzʾ court that K. Morimoto has connected with the *dīwān* seems to me to be rather a list of regular tax payments of the kind of which we have many parallel examples ("Registers"). H. Kennedy identified a Greek papyrus as a *dīwān* ("The Financing of the Military," in *Studies in Late Antiquity and Early Islam*, vol. 2 *States, Armies and Resources*, ed. A. Cameron and L. Conrad [Princeton: Darwin Press,]: 376-7), a claim he seems to have abandoned since (Kennedy, *Armies*: 66-7).

[28] *P.Mird* mentioned by Puin, *Dīwān*: 124.

[29] One is published (*P.Ryl.Arab.* p. 31, mentioned by Puin, *Dīwān*: 123). The other, which also indicates the neighbourhoods in Fusṭāṭ where the individuals resided, has been published (P.M. Sijpesteijn, "A Seventh-Century Arabic Census List? Papyrus OI 17656," in *Festschrift Klaas Worp*, eds. C. Hogendijk and B. Muchs: 369-77 [Leiden: E.J. Brill, 2008]).

Egyptian historian Ibn ʿAbd al-Ḥakam (d. 257/871), of the central authorities sending someone around the tribes stationed in the encampment at Fusṭāṭ to record newcomers, births, and deaths,[30] they do seem to reflect some kind of systematic attempt to record Muslim numbers at this early period.

Our papyrus offers some precious information about the procedure of dispensing the *ʿaṭāʾ* to the soldiers. The remark in line 9 that a *ḍamān* has to be given to obtain the addressee's dependents' *ʿaṭāʾ* is especially valuable. Apparently those collecting stipends in someone else's name had to provide a guarantee to the authorities that the payments would be delivered to their true and intended recipients. Perhaps the practice is related to the contemporary situation in Iraq, where the governor Ziyād b. Abīhi reportedly recommended that those entitled to the *ʿaṭāʾ* collect it in person rather than send their servants for fear they might spend part of it on the way.[31] Our papyrus also contains some references to the procedure of collecting the stipends. First of all, it seems it could be done only by the male head of the household—not his dependents.[32] And even though the sender of this letter can, if necessary, get access to the stipends of the addressee's dependents, he can only do so by providing some kind of guarantee—whatever this exactly means.

In line 8 we read: "and hurry to receive the *ʿaṭāʾ* for your dependents for there are (almost) none left." The urgency with which the sender tells the addressee to collect the *ʿaṭāʾ* for his family, and his remark that the stipends—perhaps the time to collect them or sufficient cash—will be lacking if he does not get to the distribution center promptly, suggests that the stipends were not set aside by name, but rather were disbursed on something like a "first come, first served" basis, or at least that there was a limited time in which the stipends could be claimed.

The Egyptian land taxes did not get spent in their entirety, of course, on the Muslim stipends. Costs for local infrastructure, the upkeep of the irrigation system, the maintenance of churches, baths, and other buildings and public works were all deducted, as were

[30] *Futūḥ*: 102. Repeated in al-Maqrīzī, *Khiṭaṭ*, 1:252.

[31] al-Balādhurī, *Ansāb al-ashrāf*, quoted by Kennedy, *Armies*: 73.

[32] Similarly, it is said that the *ʿurafāʾ, nuqabāʾ and umanāʾ* received the *ʿaṭāʾ* which they in their turn divided among their people (*ahl*), including the soldiers and their dependents (al-Maqrīzī, *Khiṭaṭ*, 1:250).

remittances to the caliphal capital.[33] The question of what should be done with the surplus remaining after local costs and stipends were paid—whether it should be transferred to the caliph or divided among the provincial Muslim élite—was a hotly debated one.[34] The pressure applied by the increasing numbers of those making a claim on the stipends must have intensified it further.[35] Muslim immigrants poured in from the Arabian peninsula, crowding the lots assigned to the tribes and, in the words of Ibn ʿAbd al-Ḥakam, "filling up any free space."[36] Egyptian converts and those moving in from the countryside in search of better living conditions moved to the new center of power as well. In 53/673 the ʿAmr b. al-ʿĀṣ mosque built to serve the new community of believers needed to be expanded.[37] While we cannot take the numbers given by our Arab literary sources at face value, a reported increase from the *ca.* 15,000 names on the first *dīwān* of Egypt under ʿAmr b. al-ʿĀṣ to 40,000 at the time of Muʿāwiya does reflect the enormous increase in those making a claim on Egypt's income.[38]

The *dīwān* and *ʿaṭāʾ* system, adapted to the conditions operative at the time of ʿUmar I, obviously could not continue unchanged. Pressure came from a variety of directions: the natural proliferation of eligible families, conversion, the slowing-down of the rate of the conquests and the concomitant drying-up of booty, the increasing complexity and specialization of military techniques, and the increasing professionalism and progressive "de-arabization" of the army, eventually leading to a distinction between, on the one hand, civil pensions, reserved for the descendants of the Prophet's family, and on the other, military pay for a professional standing army.[39] This process was completed under the ʿAbbasids, but attempts to grapple with the problems inherent in the system are also seen in the Umayyad period.

---

[33] Ibn ʿAbd al-Ḥakam, *Futūḥ*: 151, 153; al-Maqrīzī, *Khiṭaṭ*, 1:252.

[34] See for example M. Hinds, "The Murder of the Caliph ʿUthman," *International Journal of Middle Eastern Studies*, 3 (1972): 450-69.

[35] Abū ʿUbayd (d. 224/838), *Kitāb al-amwāl*, ed. M. Kh. Harrās (Cairo, 1389/1969): 213-15, no. 525.

[36] Ibn ʿAbd al-Ḥakam, *Futūḥ*: 102, 116, 123, 128.

[37] Under the governor Maslama b. Mukhlid (in office 47-62/667-681) (al-Maqrīzī, *Khiṭaṭ*, 4/1:11-12).

[38] Ibn ʿAbd al-Ḥakam, *Futūḥ*: 102, 316.

[39] Non-existent in the earlier period (Puin, *Dīwān*: 97).

Wives, children and other dependents initially also received a pension.[40] When Abū Mūsā al-ʿAshʿarī (d. 42/662) was removed as governor of Baṣra in 29/649-650, it is said that he only took with him 600 *dirhams* as *ʿaṭāʾ* for his dependents (*ʿaṭāʾ ʿiyālihi*).[41] The caliph ʿAbd al-Malik (r. 65-86/685-705) is supposed to have stopped the payment of stipends to soldiers' dependents.[42] It is indeed in the second half of the second/eighth century that we start to encounter for the first time Muslim merchants and Muslims occupied in agriculture in the papyri from Egypt.[43] At the same time, military raids followed by campaigns on land and attacks with the newly built navy continued to be launched from Egypt, suggesting a demilitarization of the Muslim society as a whole and the coming into existence of a specialized, professionalized army. In general, scholars agree that the Marwānid army was a professional force replacing the earlier civilian army and that after the second *fitna* only soldiers received actual *ʿaṭāʾ*.[44] ʿUmar II is said to have reinstituted the payment of *ʿaṭāʾ* to wives and children of soldiers, albeit not systematically.[45] The papyrus quoted above from Qurra b. Sharīk's reign mentions soldiers and their *ʿiyāl*, their dependents, households or families receiving the *ʿaṭāʾ*.[46] The reference to *ʿaṭāʾ* payments to the sender's *ʿiyāl* in our papyrus can therefore not be used to date it. But do the addressee's *ʿiyāl* receive their *ʿaṭāʾ* on the basis of their relation to the addressee and his function in the army?

---

[40] al-Balādhurī, *Futūḥ*: 561-2, Abū ʿUbayd, *Kitāb al-Amwāl*, no. 596; Ibn Saʿd, *Ṭabaqāt*, 3:297. The different legal opinions are collected by Ibn Qudāma (d. 620/1223), *al-Mughnī*, eds. ʿA.A. al-Turkī and ʿA.F. al-Ḥulw (Cairo: Ḥajr, 1987), 13: 92-7.

[41] Ibn Saʿd, *Ṭabaqāt*, 4:111.

[42] al-Balādhurī, *Futūḥ*: 562.

[43] Sijpesteijn, "Arab Conquest": 443.

[44] Kennedy, *Armies*: 77.

[45] "ʿUmar b. ʿAbd al-ʿAzīz included the wives and children of the soldiers who received stipends (in the *Dīwān*). Lots were cast among them, and those on whom the lot fell were assigned one hundred (dirhams), while those on whom the lot did not fall were assigned forty" (al-Ṭabarī, *Taʾrīkh*, 2:1367; tr. D. S. Powers, *The Empire in Transition* [Albany, NY: The State University of New York Press, 1989]: 97).

[46] See above, note 26.

The Poor and Needy

The addressee's *ʿiyāl* are described in our letter as *masākīn muḥtājūn*, poor and needy (l. 7). These are technical terms used in relation to *ṣadaqa* and *zakāt*, alms payments. A first/seventh or second/eighth-century unedited papyrus from Princeton University contains a list of payments made to Muslim-named women and men described as orphans, old women (*ʿajūza*), poor or needy, or a combination of these categories. The terms used for poor and needy are the same as in our text: *maskīn*/*maskīna* and *muḥtāj* or *muḥtāja*.[47] The categories of *masākīn muḥtājūn* were also discussed in Arabic legal sources which aimed at defining the different terms.

We seem thus to have here two conflicting technical expressions: the *ʿaṭāʾ al-ʿiyāl* and the *masākīn muḥtājūn*—one pointing to a military interpretation of the *dīwān*, the other to a civilian one. The latter description seems especially incompatible with and unexpected for the family of our addressee, who appears to have had quite important connections in the army. How are we to connect the words in our papyrus referring to categories of people entitled payment of *ʿaṭāʾ* with that of those entitled to alms payments, namely the poor and needy?

The exact definitions of *faqīr*, *muḥtāj* and *maskīn* differed between the various Islamic law schools and we do not know to what extent those definitions were common at this early stage in Egypt. However, the fact that the same technical terms are used in all three papyri related to payments to the poor suggests that they had a well-defined meaning.

The first indication that a special category for especially needy people entitled to *ʿaṭāʾ* payments existed in the *dīwān* goes back to caliph ʿUmar I, who allegedly founded the institution. ʿUmar used to give *ʿaṭāʾ* and *rizq* to foundlings,[48] and to people in need.[49] He and ʿAlī are also said to have divided the *khums* following the Quranic

---

[47] Princeton Papyri Collections Acc. No. 2002-143. The Qur'ān (IX:60; II:177) uses on the other hand *faqīr* and *maskīn* (*Muḥtāj* does not appear in the Qur'ān.). These are also the terms used in another published early second-century papyrus which contains a list of villages with the money reserved for the *fuqarāʾ wa-masākīn*, the poor and needy (*P.Khalili* I 1).

[48] al-Yaʿqūbī, *Taʾrīkh*, 2:171; Ibn Saʿd, *Ṭabaqat*, 3:298. ʿAlī (r. 35-40/656-61) is reported to have done the same (al-Balādhurī, *Futūḥ*: 563).

[49] *Ahl al-balāʾ* (al-Maqrīzī, *Khiṭaṭ*, 1:247-8).

list of recipients of the *ṣadaqa*.[50] But it is his namesake, the caliph ʿUmar II, to whom we have to turn for the practice of giving stipends to the poor. Of him it is said that he used to give *ʿaṭāʾ* to the poor and the crippled of the city of Basra.[51] Much later, the Abbasid caliph al-Mahdī (r. 169/785) is said to have assigned "for the first time" regular payments (*faraḍa li-*) to lepers and foundlings while also giving donations (*ʿaṭāyā*) to the *ashrāf* and pious inhabitants of the garrison cities as well as to the needy.[52] The literary sources give us thus examples of *ʿaṭāʾ* payments to categories of civilians in special need from the period before *and* after the recipients were supposed to have been limited to professional soldiers (as opposed to the militarised civilians of the first hour).[53] Moreover, in historical and legal sources, the Quranic categories of recipients of the *ṣadaqa* are mentioned in the discussion about the division of the *ʿaṭāʾ*.[54] While the attribution of pensions to poor and needy persons in the narrative sources could be explained as a pious topos, our papyrus shows that *ʿaṭāʾ* and need were sometimes related.

It is difficult to explain, nevertheless, why our addressee's dependents are defined as "poor and needy," a status seemingly incompatible with the addressee's position. Most likely one should interpret these words as technical terms invoked to qualify the addressee's dependents to a stipend at a time when *ʿaṭāʾ al-ʿiyāl* was no longer distributed, i.e. in the period between ʿAbd al-Malik and ʿUmar II or after ʿUmar II's reign. The sender of our letter received the *ʿaṭāʾ* for his dependents after the *ʿaṭāʾ al-ʿiyāl* was abolished by qualifying under a different heading, namely that of *masakīn wa-muḥtajūn*.

Syria and Egypt

We turn now to the first and the last topic of our letter and what it tells us about the relation between the caliphal center and the peri-

---

[50] Q 59:7; al-Ṭabari, *Taʾrīkh*, 1:2417; al-Maqrīzī, *Khiṭaṭ*, 1:248. Walīd I and Walīd II are also said to have done so (P. Crone, *Medieval Islamic Thought* [Edingburgh: Edingburgh University Press, 2004]: 307-8).

[51] al-Ṭabarī, *Taʾrīkh*, 2:1367; al-Balādhurī, *Futūḥ*, 3:562.

[52] Muʾarrij, *Ḥadf*, cited by Puin, *Dīwān*: 117.

[53] Other examples of privileged *ʿaṭāʾ* categories are for example Quran readers (Puin, *Dīwān*: 156).

[54] Puin, *Dīwān*: 157-8; "*Bāb qismat al-fayʾ wa-ʾl-ʿanīma wa-ʾl-ṣadaqa*" (Ibn Qudāma, *al-Mughnī*, 9:281).

phery. The letter starts with the news that the *amīr* has visited the *amīr al-mu'minīn*. The title *amīr al-mu'minīn* appears (transcribed) in Arabic, Greek and Coptic papyri and refers always to the caliph.[55] Both the governor of Egypt and the financial governor responsible for the taxes are called *amīr* in Arabic narrative and documentary administrative texts dealing with the Umayyad period.[56] In the earliest Greek and bilingual papyri dating from the Muslim conquest of Egypt, Muslim army leaders have the title *amīr* transcribed in the Greek (αμιρας).[57] An interesting feature of the contemporary Arabic papyri and the Arabic of the bilingual papyri is that they entirely lack similar titles both for Greek and Arab officials. While Arabic narrative sources dealing with the Umayyad period refer to army leaders as *amīr*s, there are no Arabic papyri from the first two centuries in which *amīr* is used to refer to an army commander.[58]

Towards the end of his letter in line 14, the sender turns to the arrival of three tax officials, *'ummāl* (singular *'āmil*),[59] from *al-Shām*, the area of greater Syria, or the Umayyad capital(s) there. He mentions something specific related to one or more amongst them, but this information is lost. The remark on the next line might refer to these three officials as well, although their relation to the people mentioned at the beginning of line 15 remains unclear. Neither of these partial readings, moreover, sheds much light on what the Syrian officials were doing in Egypt.

Whatever the exact meaning of those lines, their real value lies in the evidence they give us of personal exchanges and contact between officials in Egypt and their Syrian counterparts. It needs to be emphasized: references to places or events taking place outside of Egypt, are *extremely* unusual in the papyri, especially these early ones from

---

[55] P.M. Sijpesteijn, "An Early Umayyad Papyrus Invitation for the Ḥajj," *Journal of Near Eastern Studies* (forthcoming).

[56] For the distinction between the governor and the financial director in our sources, see P.M. Sijpesteijn, *Shaping a Muslim State: Papyri Related to an Eight-Century Egyptian Official* (Phd. dissertation, Princeton University 2004).

[57] E.g.: A. Grohmann, *From the World of Arabic Papyri* (Cairo: al-Maaref Press, 1952): 112-14.

[58] Sa'īd, *amīr al-Iskandarīya* who is the arbiter in a dispute according to a first-second/seventh-eighth-century Arabic papyrus, refers most probably to the city's governor (J. David-Weill, Cl. Cahen *et al.*, "Papyrus arabes du Louvre III," *Journal of the Economic and Social History of the Orient* 21 (1978), no. 25 ll. 2-3). The earliest reference is in an Arabic protocol, dated 298-300/910-912, mentioning an *amīr al-jaysh* (*P.Cair.Arab.* I).

[59] For the definition of *'āmil*, see above the commentary on line 13.

the first two centuries of Muslim rule. That an *amīr* from Egypt personally traveled to see the caliph and that Syrian administrators came to Egypt to transact business activities is important information, because it suggests, among other things, a significant level of control exercised by the caliphal center over the province of Egypt.

Traveling between the countries was no simple matter, and a well-functioning mail system dealing with day-to-day and urgent matters alike would have obviated the need in most cases.[60] Papyri indicate that Egyptian workers and soldiers at this time traveled to serve on military campaigns or work on large building projects in Jerusalem and Damascus.[61] But these calls for workers originated from the caliph's administration not from the caliph personally.[62] The caliph's authority over Egypt was limited to the appointing and recalling of governors. The caliph's name appeared on Egyptian coins, glass weights and papyrus protocols, the earliest from Egypt dates to the caliphate of ʿAbd al-Malik (r. 65-86/705-715), but these represent his symbolic or nominal power rather than a physical hands-on presence in Egypt of the kind to which this papyrus seems to refer.[63]

There is, however, perhaps another explanation for these at first sight somewhat unexpected references to the caliph and his officials in a letter written and found in Egypt. The question is which one of the caliph's courts was close and important enough for an Egyptian *amīr* to travel to at a time when Syrian administrators were in Egypt performing some more or less regular business. The answer must be that the papyrus was written when the caliph was not seated in *Damascus*, but when he and his administrative entourage were in Egypt. One Umayyad caliph to whom this could apply was Marwān (r. 64/684), who in 64/684, after taking control of the province from Zubayrid sympathizers, stayed for a short while in Egypt.[64] Undoubtedly he wanted to secure the province against future rebellion and to make sure that his son ʿAbd al-ʿAzīz, whom he had appointed as governor of Egypt, would have no trouble keeping it

---

[60] A. Silverstein, *Postal Systems in the Pre-Modern Islamic World* (Cambridge: Cambridge University Press, 2007).

[61] *P.Lond.* IV and Sijpesteijn, "Arab Conquest": 448.

[62] K. Morimoto, *The Fiscal Administration of Egypt in the Early Islamic Period* (Kyoto: Dohosha, 1981).

[63] For another example of indirect caliphal control, see the late first-early second/seventh-eighth-century letter in which the *amīr al-mu'minīn* is said to have made the announcement for the yearly *ḥajj* (Sijpesteijn, "Pilgrimage.").

[64] al-Ṭabarī, *Ta'rīkh*, 2:482.

under control. The other candidate for such a scenario is Marwān II (r. 127-132/744-750) who in 132/750 fled to Egypt where he was killed by Abbasid troops. Syrian troops were present in Egypt at other times as well, such as in 125/743,[65] but there is little to connect them to the armies mentioned in our letter.

We can thus speculate that the *amīr* of line 2 was indeed an army commander who had been summoned or requested to talk to the caliph about some other matter involving the military. The sender and addressee's familiarity with the *amīr*'s activities support the interpretation of the *amīr* as an army commander rather than the governor. The other references in the papyrus to armies going out and moving back and forth through the country fit a situation in which military unrest and uprisings required constant vigilance from the army stationed in Egypt. The imprisonment of those "kept at sea" also suits a situation of problems of control, of course, very well.

Conclusion

Many things, alas, remain uncertain in the decipherment and interpretation of this papyrus. It might in fact even have complicated, rather than nicely clarified, our view of the Umayyad *ʿaṭāʾ* system on some points. The *dīwān*, designed to redistribute the wealth from the conquests among all members of the *umma*, and to institutionalize a system of reciprocal exchange and dependence between rulers and subjects, functioned at a high ideological and economic level. This papyrus, however, shows how individual Muslims experienced this institution: their humdrum but entirely comprehensible concern to get to the distribution center before stipends ran out; how they discovered the time of payment and the requirements for providing guarantees and documentation to obtain the *ʿaṭāʾ* on another's behalf.

Finally, it places an intriguing question mark over the issue of entitlement to the pensions, which included apparently a category for poor and needy Muslims. The question arises who these poor Muslims were who needed financial support. Could they have been Arab-Muslim immigrants who had arrived with or after the conquering armies or Egyptian converts? Was this an extra provision that the poorest members of the *umma* received on top of their regular

[65] al-Kindī, *Wulāt*: 83. I am grateful to Patricia Crone for this reference.

stipend? Another possibility, perhaps, is that this was a provision in the revised *dīwān* system for the poor who were no longer generally entitled to a pension but needed extra care.

The family members who made a claim to receive *'aṭā'* in our letter do not seem, however, to have fallen into either category. The sender of our letter has managed to secure the *'aṭā'* for his dependents after the *'aṭā' al-'iyāl* has been abolished by having them qualify as "poor and needy." He still uses both terms, *'aṭā' al-'iyāl* and *masakīn wa-muḥtajūn* when referring to their right to the *'aṭā'* as if he is (still) thinking in two systems. Whether this letter shows us the maze in the military administrative net or a provision built into the system with a political function, remains a question unanswered.

This document has increased our understanding of the working of the Umayyad *'aṭā'*, but most of all it has humanized it, Udovitch-style.

Bibliography

Abū 'Ubayd (d. 224/838). *Kitāb al-amwāl*, edited by M. Kh. Harrās (Cairo, 1389/1969).

Alston, R. *Soldier and Society in Roman Egypt: A Social History*. London/New York: Routledge, 1995.

al-Balādhurī (d. 279/892). *Futūḥ al-buldān*, edited by M. J. de Goeje. Leiden: E.J. Brill, 1866; repr. 1992.

Caetani, L. *Annali dell'Islam*. Milan: Ulrico Hoepli, 1911.

Cahen, Cl. " 'Aṭā'." *Encyclopaedia of Islam*, second edition (*EI*[2]), 1:729-730. Leiden: E.J. Brill, 1960.

Clackson, S. "The Papyrus Collections of Cambridge." In *Papyrus Collections World Wide*, edited by W. Clarysse and H. Verreth: 25-35. Brussels: Universa Press, 2000.

Crone, P. "Khiṭṭa." In *EI*[2], 5:23, Leiden: E. J. Brill, 1986.

——. *Slaves on Horses*. Cambridge: Cambridge University Press, 1980.

——. "The First Century Concept of Higra." *Arabica* 41 (1994): 352-87.

——. *Medieval Islamic Thought*. Edingburgh: Edingburgh University Press, 2004.

David-Weill, J. Cahen, Cl., *et al.* "Papyrus arabes du Louvre III." *Journal of the Economic and Social History of the Orient* 21 (1978): 146-64.

Dozy, R. *Supplément aux dictionnaires arabes*. Leiden: E. J. Brill, 1881.

Duri, A. A. "Dīwān. The Caliphate." *EI*[2], 2:323-37. Leiden: E.J. Brill, 1956.

Fink, R.O. *Roman Military Records on Papyrus* (Philological Monographs of the American Philological Association 26). Cleveland: Press of Case Western Reserve University, 1971.

Gascou J. and K.A. Worp. "Problèmes de documentation apollinopolite." *Zeitschrift für Papyrologie und Epigraphik* 49 (1982): 83-95.

Gottschalk, H.L. "Dīwān. Egypt." In *EI*[2], 2:327-8. Leiden: E.J. Brill, 1956.

Grohmann, A. I *Arabische Chronologie*. II *Arabische Papyruskunde*. (Handbuch der Orientalistik. Erste Abteilung. Der Nahe und Mittlere Osten. Ergänzungsband II). Leiden: E. J. Brill, 1966.

——. *From the World of Arabic Papyri*. Cairo: al-Maaref Press, 1952.

Hinds, M. "Mu'āwiya I." In *EI*², 8:263-8. Leiden: E.J. Brill, 1993.

——. "The Murder of the Caliph 'Uthman." *International Journal of Middle Eastern Studies* 3 (1972): 450-69.

——. "Review of G.-R. Puin, *Der Dīwān von 'Umar ibn al-Khaṭṭāb: ein Beitrag zur frühislamischen Verwaltungageschichte*." *Bulletin of the School of Oriental and African Studies* 34 (1971):144-6.

Hinds, M. and H. Sakkout. "A Letter from the Governor of Egypt to the King of Nubia and Muqurra Concerning Egyptian-Nubian Relations in 141/758." In *Studia Arabica and Islamica*, edited by W. al-Qadi: 209-29. Beirut: American University of Beirut, 2001.

History of the Patriarchs of the Coptic Church of Alexandria (Agathon to Michael I), tr. B. Evetts. *Patrologia Orientalis* V (1910): 1-215.

Hopkins, S. *Studies in the Grammar of Early Arabic*. Oxford: Oxford University Press, 1984.

Ibn 'Abd al-Ḥakam (d. 871). *Futūḥ Miṣr*, edited by Ch. Torrey, *The History of the Conquests of Egypt, North Africa and Spain*. New Haven: Yale University Press, 1922.

Ibn Qudāma (d. 620/1223). *al-Mughnī*, edited by 'A.A. al-Turkī and 'A.F. al-Ḥulw. Cairo: Ḥajr, 1987.

Ibn Sa'd (d. 230/845). *al-Ṭabaqāt al-kubrā*. Beirut, 1377/1957.

Ibn Yūnus (d. 347/958), *Ta'rikh al-Maṣriyīn*, edited by 'A.F. Beirut 1921/2000.

Kennedy, H. *The Armies of the Caliphs*. London/New York: Routledge, 2001.

——. "The Financing of the Military." in *Studies in Late Antiquity and Early Islam*, vol. 2 *States, Armies and Resources*, edited by A. Cameron and L. Conrad. Princeton: Darwin Press. 376-7.

al-Kindī (d. 350/961). *Kitāb al-Wulāt*, edited by R. Guest, *The Governors and Judges of Egypt*, (E. J. W. Gibb Memorial Series XIX). Leiden: E. J. Brill, 1912.

Lane, E.W. *An Arabic-English Lexicon*. London: Williams and Norgate, 1863.

al-Maqrīzī (d. 845/1442) *al-Mawā'iz wa-'l-i'tibār fī dhikr al-khiṭaṭ wa-'l-athār*, ed. A. F. Sayyid. London: al-Furqān Islamic Heritage Foundation, 2002-2003.

Morimoto, K. "The Dīwāns as Registers of the Arab Stipendiaries in Early Islamic Egypt." In *Itinéraires d'Orient hommages à Claude Cahen*, Res Orientalis 6 edited by R. Curiel and R. Gyselen 353-66. Bures-sur-Yvette: Groupe pour l'Étude de la Civilisation du Moyen-Orient, 1994.

——. *The Fiscal Administration of Egypt in the Early Islamic Period*. Kyoto: Dohosha, 1981.

Puin, G.-R. *Der Dīwān von 'Umar ibn al-Khaṭṭāb: ein Beitrag zur frühislamischen Verwaltungageschichte*. Bonn: Rheinische Friedrich Wilhelms Universität, 1977.

Sijpesteijn, P.M. "An Early Umayyad Papyrus Invitation for the Ḥajj," *Journal of Near Eastern Studies* (forthcoming).

——. "The Arab Conquest of Egypt and the Beginning of Muslim Rule." In *Byzantine Egypt*, edited by R. S. Bagnall, 437-59. Cambridge: Cambridge University Press, 2007.

——. *Shaping a Muslim State: Papyri Related to an Eighth-Century Egyptian Official*, PhD diss., Princeton University 2004.

——. "Profit Following Responsibility: A Leaf from the Records of a Third-Century Tax-Collecting Agent. With an Appended Checklist of Editions of Arabic Papyri." *Journal of Juristic Papyrology* 31 (2001): 91-132.

———. "Travel and Trade on the River," in *Papyrology and the History of Early Islamic Egypt*, edited by P.M. Sijpesteijn and L. Sundelin. 115-52. Leiden: E.J. Brill, 2004.

———. "A Seventh-Century Arabic Census List? Papyrus OI 17656." in *Festschrift Klaas Worp*, edited by C. Hogendijk and B. Muchs. 369-77. Leiden: E.J. Brill, 2008.

Silverstein, A. *Postal Systems in the Pre-Modern Islamic World*, Cambridge: Cambridge University Press, 2007.

al-Ṭabarī (d. 310/923). *Ta"rīkh al-rusul wa'l-muluk*, ed. M. J. de Goeje. Leiden: E. J. Brill, 1879-1901, repr. 1964-65. Tr. D. S. Powers *The Empire in Transition*. Vol. XXIV. Albany, NY: The State University of New York Press, 1989.

al-Yaʿqūbī (d. 284/897). *Ta'rīkh*. Edited by M. Th. Houtsma. Leiden: E. J. Brill, 1883.

INDEX

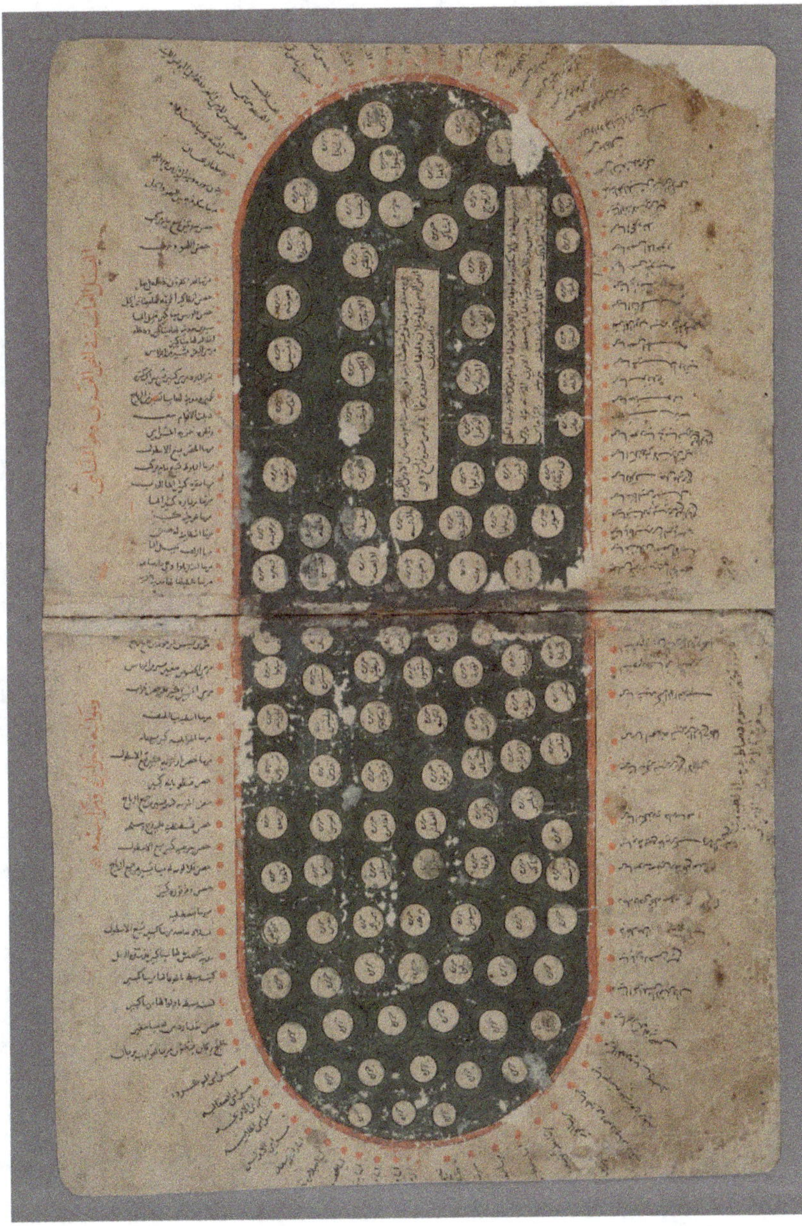

Fig. 1. The map of the Mediterranean from the *Book of Curiosities*. Oxford, Bodleian Library, MS Arab c. 90, fols. 31b-32a (undated, c. 1200). Reproduced with permission of the Bodleian Library.

Fig. 2. The map of the Cyprus from the *Book of Curiosities*. Oxford, Bodleian Library, MS Arab c. 90, fol. 36b (undated, c. 1200). Reproduced with permission of the Bodleian Library.

Fig. 3. Diagram of Aegean Bays from the *Book of Curiosities*. Oxford, Bodleian Library, MS Arab c. 90, fol. 38a (undated, c. 1200). Reproduced with permission of the Bodleian Library.

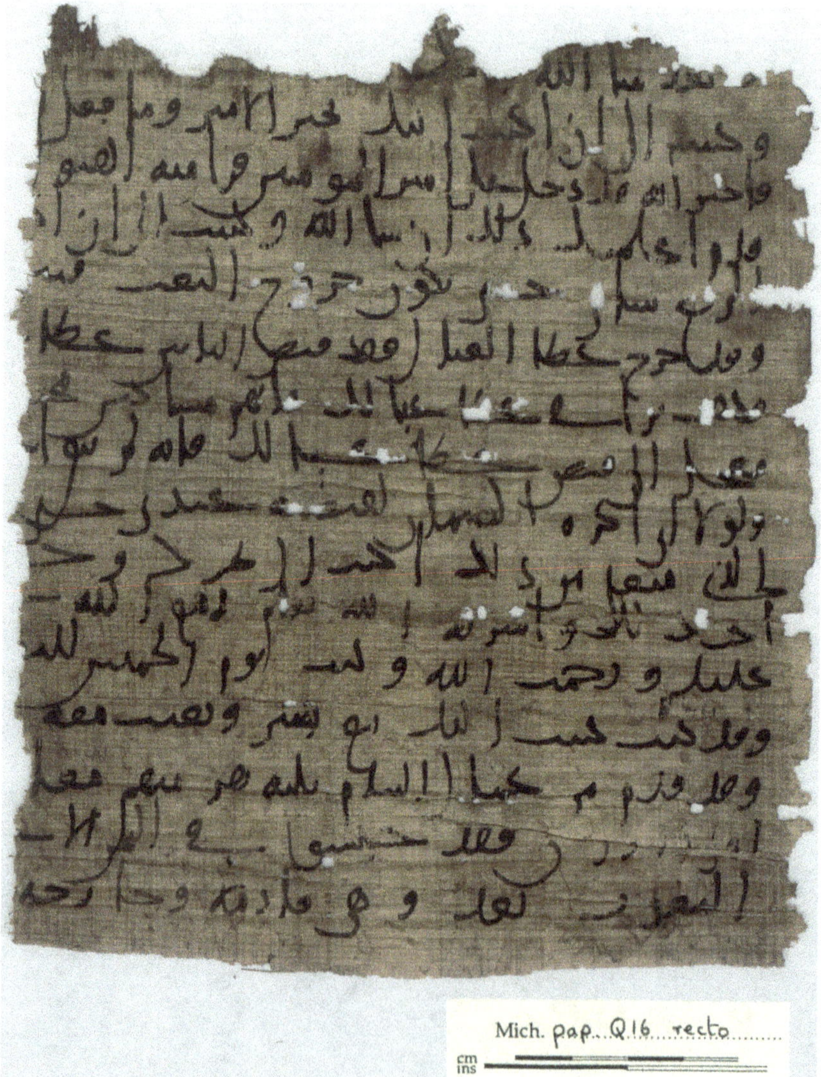

Ill. 1. P. Michaelides Q16.

www.ingramcontent.com/pod-product-compliance
Lightning Source LLC
LaVergne TN
LVHW060616300926
849162LV00008B/1631